More praise for
Becoming Abolitionists

"*Becoming Abolitionists* is a wise and passionate argument for the urgency of first responders without guns. Purnell takes on the hardest questions with analytical rigor and common sense. This is abolition for the people."
—**Paul Butler**, MSNBC legal analyst and author of *Chokehold*

"In this moving and mind-expanding meditation on the nature and possibility of justice, Derecka Purnell traces her personal journey from her hometown of Saint Louis, Missouri, to the frontlines of a global movement against racism and police brutality. A true philosopher, Purnell gleans wisdom at every opportunity, studying and struggling whether she's in a law school seminar or protesting in the street, in a courtroom defending a client or visiting a nail salon. Being radical, this wonderful book reminds us, doesn't mean having all the answers—it means constantly questioning, listening, learning, and being willing to reassess and grow. *Becoming Abolitionists* brilliantly lays out the connections between policing and other forms of oppression and shows why even well-meaning "reforms" won't get us where we need to go. This profound, urgent, beautiful, and necessary book is an invitation to imagine and organize for a less violent and more liberatory world. Everyone should read it."
—**Astra Taylor**, author of *Democracy May Not Exist but We'll Miss It When It's Gone*

"Derecka Purnell's writing is freeing and draws you in. *Becoming Abolitionists* is a beautiful invitation to understand what is possible if we commit to unlearning our dependence on police and address the underlying injustices that cause harm in our communities. This is the book we have been waiting for and knew we needed to advance abolitionist efforts. Purnell is the abolitionist writer of her generation."
—**Bettina Love**, author of *We Want to Do More Than Survive*

"An extraordinary, wonderful, insightful, and immensely generative book that makes the case for abolitionist thinking, amplifying the self-activity of the masses already in motion, and at the same time providing a thoroughly absorbing and captivating description of the author's own journey. Rather than encouraging each of us to brand ourselves as radical, Purnell points us toward the collaborative acts of co-creation and accompaniment that can make revolutionary change possible. She incorporates decoloniality, feminism, Indigeneity, environmental justice, and disability activism organically into her critiques and solutions. One of the most exciting, inspiring, and enlightening books I have read in a long time."

—**George Lipsitz**, author of *The Possessive Investment in Whiteness*

"Purnell is undoubtedly one of the most important writers and activists of our generation, offering us a vivid, moving and compelling book for anyone interested in one of the most urgent issues of our times. Purnell weaves experiences of racism and resistance to articulate a blistering critique of racial capitalism, state power and imperialism, taking readers on a journey towards the radical alternatives to police and prisons which have shaped Black political movements in the 21st century."

—**Adam Elliott-Cooper**, author of *Black Resistance to British Policing*

"*Becoming Abolitionists* provides a front row seat to how a generation of young people have been radicalized by a series of contradictions living within the heart of global empire: the United States. She explains, with powerful stories and brilliant analysis, how she has committed herself to abolition in the context of ongoing collective study and struggle. The abolition she discusses is anti-capitalist and anti-colonialist, committed to racial, economic, and gender justice. A call to not simply tear down prisons and police, but to build a society where our collective needs prevail over profit and punishment. This book is more than a front row seat, it is an invitation to join the most important movement of our time."

—**Amna Akbar**, professor of law, Ohio State University

BECOMING ABOLITIONISTS

POLICE, PROTESTS,

AND THE PURSUIT

OF FREEDOM

BY DERECKA PURNELL

ASTRA HOUSE · NEW YORK

For information about permission to reproduce selections from this book,
please contact permissions@astrahouse.com.

Names and identifying characteristics of some individuals have been changed.

Astra House
A Division of Astra Publishing House
astrahouse.com
Printed in the United States of America

Publisher's Cataloging-in-Publication Data

Names: Purnell, Derecka, author.
Title: Becoming abolitionists : police, power, and the pursuit of freedom/
Derecka Purnell.
Description: Includes bibliographical references. | New York, NY: Astra House, 2021.
Identifiers: LCCN: 2021909564 | ISBN: 9781662600517 (hardcover) |
9781662600524 (ebook)
Subjects: LCSH Police—United States. | Police misconduct—United States. | Police
administration—United States. | Police brutality—United States. | Police-community
relations—United States. | Police and mass media—United States. | Police—
United States—Public opinion. | Racism—United States—History—21st century. |
African Americans—Social conditions—21st century. | Discrimination in law
enforcement—United States. | African Americans—Crimes against. | United States—Race
relations—History—21st century. | Criminal justice, Administration of—United States. |
BISAC SOCIAL SCIENCE / Race & Ethnic Relations | POLITICAL SCIENCE /
Law Enforcement | LAW / Criminal Law / General
Classification: LCC HV8139 .P87 2021 | DDC 363.2/30973—dc23

First edition
10 9 8 7 6 5 4 3 2 1

Design by Richard Oriolo
The text is set in Bulmer MT Std.
The titles are set in ITC Franklin Gothic Std.

To Geuce, Garvey, Ma'Vis, Dereck III, and Demi Elyse, and those to come

To Virginia

And to the maroons, artists, misfits, and political prisoners whose
sacrifices propelled us closer to freedom

CONTENTS

INTRODUCTION:
HOW I BECAME A POLICE ABOLITIONIST
1

1: WHAT JUSTICE?
12

2: FIRST WE WERE FREE
46

3: RESISTANCE AND REFORM
67

4: LOVE AND ABOLITION
98

5: JUSTICE FOR THE LIVING
129

6: SEX, LOVE, AND VIOLENCE
169

7: DEHUMANIZATION, DISABILITY, AND RESISTANCE
202

8: "WE ONLY WANT THE EARTH"
237

CONCLUSION
266

ENDNOTES
285

ACKNOWLEDGMENTS
309

INTRODUCTION

HOW I BECAME A POLICE ABOLITIONIST

WE CALLED 911 for almost everything—except snitching. Nosebleeds, gun-shot wounds, asthma attacks, allergic reactions. Police accompanied the paramedics.

Our neighborhood was making us sick. From 1990 until 2006, my family moved among four apartments in a modest complex called Hickory Square. It was located at the edge of the Gate District between Jefferson and Ohio in St. Louis. A Praxair industrial gas–storage facility was at one end of my block. I had no idea what it was until one year, gas tanks exploded one by one. Grown-ups panicked that the explosions were another 9/11. Scorching asphalt burned our feet as we fled because there wasn't enough time to put on shoes. Buildings and cars immediately caught fire and shrapnel pierced the trees and the houses. Nine thousand pounds of propane exploded and burned that day. Minnie Cooper died from an asthma attack related to the noxious fumes. The Black mother of three was only thirty-two.[1]

At the other end of my block, there was a junkyard with military airplane parts in full view. The owner of the lot collected the parts as a hobby, and had at least twenty-six US and Russian war craft machines. Each one ranged in value between ten thousand dollars and seventy-five thousand dollars, and shipping costs could be as high as thirty thousand dollars. One man's treasure came at the cost of exposing poisonous particles to children in the neighborhood every day. His lot still sits directly across the street from my middle school's playground.

The fish-seasoning plant in our backyard did not smell. The yeast from the nearby Anheuser-Busch factory did. Car honks and fumes from Interstate 64 filtered through my childhood bedroom window, from where, if I stood on my toes, I could see the St. Louis Gateway Arch.

All these environmental toxins that degraded our health often conspired with other forms of violence that pervaded our neighborhood. Employment opportunities were rare, and my friends and I turned to making money under the table. I was scared of selling drugs, so I gambled. Brown-skinned boys I liked aged out of recreational activities, and, without work, into blue bandannas. Their territorial disputes led to violence and more 911 calls. Grown-ups fought too, stressed from working hard yet never having enough bill money or gas money or food money or day-care money. Call 911.

When people come across police abolition for the first time, they tend to dismiss abolitionists for not caring about neighborhood safety or the victims of violence. They tend to forget that often we are those victims, those survivors of violence, too.

THE FIRST SHOOTING I witnessed was by a uniformed security guard. I was thirteen years old. He was employed by Global Security Services, a company founded by a former Missouri police chief who was later convicted of homicide. The former chief managed to secure multi-million-dollar contracts in an embezzlement scheme to provide armed private officers at almost all of St. Louis's city-owned properties—including my public neighborhood recreation center. The armed guards replaced the city police. I was teaching my sister, Courtnie, who was nine, how to shoot free throws at the rec center when the guard stormed in alongside the court, drew his weapon, and shot his cousin in the arm. Courtnie and I hid in the locker room for hours afterward. I thought the guard was angry that his cousin skipped a sign-in sheet, but the victim only told the police the shooting had started as an argument over "something stupid."[2]

Like the boy at the rec center who was shot by the private guard, most victims of law enforcement violence survive. No hashtags or protests or fires for the wounded, assaulted, and intimidated.

In 2020, Minneapolis Police officer Derek Chauvin pinned George Floyd to the concrete as he hollered that he could not breathe. Floyd screamed. He screamed for his mother. He screamed for his breath. For his life. Until he died nine minutes later. Calls for "justice" quickly ensued. I often wonder, *What if the cop who killed George Floyd had kneeled on Floyd's neck for eight minutes and forty-six seconds instead of nine minutes?* Floyd would have lived to be arrested, prosecuted, and imprisoned for allegedly attempting to use a counterfeit twenty-dollar bill. Is that justice? I did not think so. Too often, the public calls for justice when Black people are killed by the police and ignore the daily injustice if the victims would have lived.

I was surprised by what followed next. Unlike the "Black Lives Matter" calls six years prior, protesters were shouting "Defund the police!" Abolition was entering into the mainstream.

Initially, the notion of "police abolition" repulsed me. The idea seemed like it was created by white activists who did not know the violence that I knew, that I have felt. At the time, I considered abolition to be, pejoratively, "utopic." I'd seen too much sexual violence and had buried too many friends to consider getting rid of the police in St. Louis, let alone across the nation. I still lose people to violence. Sapphire. John. Greg. Brieana. Monti. Korie. Christopher. Jarrell. Sometimes, I reread our text messages to laugh again. And cry.

But over time, I came to realize that, in reality, the police were a placebo. Calling them felt like *something*, as the legal scholar Michelle Alexander explains, and something feels like everything when your other option is nothing. Police couldn't do what we really needed. They could not heal relationships or provide jobs. They did not interrupt violence; they escalated it. We were usually afraid when we called. When the cops arrived, I was silenced, threatened with detention, or removed from my home. Today, more than fifteen years later, St. Louis has more police per capita than most cities in the US. My old neighborhood still lacks quality food, employment, schools, health care, and air—all of which increases the risk of violence and our reliance on police. And instead of improving the quality of the neighborhood, St. Louis, which has the highest rate of killings by police among the largest cities in the US, spends more money on police.[3]

Yet I feared letting go; I thought we needed them. I thought they just needed to be reformed. Until August 9, 2014, when police officer Darren Wilson killed Michael Brown in Ferguson, Missouri. Brown had a funeral. Wilson had a wedding. Most police officers just continue to live their lives after filling the streets with blood and bone.[4]

On that day in August, I threw a conference for high school girls in Kansas City, where I had been organizing, attending college, and teaching middle school. This was a part of my farewell tour of the place I had called home for six years. Harvard Law School was on my horizon; I planned to become an education lawyer, and, one day, superintendent of a school district or, possibly, Secretary of Education. After the conference, my hometown, St. Louis, was next. In high school, I had rented a room in my aunt's basement down the street from West Florissant and Chambers. She, like everyone in my family except my mother, lived in "the county." St. Louis City, where I grew up, is independent of St. Louis County, and Black people migrated to north county fleeing the violence and school districts in the city. My furniture was being held in the bright orange Public Storage in the county, on West Florissant—the street where the Ferguson Uprising exploded.

For weeks I protested in Ferguson. We chanted, "Indict! Convict! Send those killer cops to jail! The whole damn system is guilty as hell!" Tanks rolled in, regardless of the crowd size and hype. I was a new mom, breastfeeding my six-month-old, and I learned on the streets that tear gas was not only noxious, but could possibly cause miscarriages. Somehow, I escaped tear gas for a year; I was terrified the chemicals would pass through my breast milk to my child.[5]

I drove from Ferguson to law school after Brown's death. I met, studied with, and struggled alongside students and movement lawyers who explained the power and the purpose of the prison industrial complex through an abolitionist framework. Mass incarceration, I learned, was a manifestation of a much larger, interwoven set of structures of oppression that we had to dismantle.

In Ferguson, I started to understand why we need police abolition rather than reform. Police manage inequality by keeping the dispossessed from the owners, the Black from the white, the homeless from the housed, the beggars from the employed. Reforms only make police polite managers of inequality. Abolition makes police and inequality obsolete.

My journey toward abolition is not mine alone. I'm an elder in what Elizabeth Alexander describes as the "Trayvon generation," the young people who have watched the deaths of Black people go viral, the youth who were born again in the streets under clouds that rained smoke, tear gas, and rubber bullets. Alexander writes that when her sons were young, her love was an armor that sufficiently protected them, but as they aged, she grew to fear for their lives. I'm older than her children, as are many of my peers who organized in the wake of Trayvon's killing. I witnessed activists of this generation organize to send Trayon's killer to prison, like I did, evolve into critical thinkers and budding revolutionaries who organized to close prisons and end policing altogether. The evolution was not linear and remains messy—as birthing ideas and relationships can be. This aligns with what it means to be a "generation." Fear, love, and possibility provide the armor for our generation. Most importantly, this generation, our generation, has been in deep love, study, and struggle with all generations to forge abolitionist futures.[6]

IN THIS BOOK, I share how the lessons from these generations have pushed me toward understanding police abolition, which is just one part of abolishing the prison industrial complex and key to a more just world. This journey has been made possible through radical Black and multiracial social movements, here in the US and abroad. By radical, I mean the people, plans, and practices within democratic traditions of activism that examine how power is arranged in society, and committing to eradicating exploitation where we find it. The commitment is key. James Baldwin wrote that "People can cry much easier than they can change." We need people to commit to changing, and the traditions that inspire these changes are vast. Consequently, *Becoming Abolitionists* is full of time travel and world travel, from the 1500s to the 2020s, from St. Louis to Soweto.[7]

Policing is among the vestiges of slavery, colonialism, and genocide, tailored in America to suppress slave revolts, catch runaways, and repress labor organizing. After slavery, police imprisoned Black people, immigrants, and poor white people under a convict-leasing system for plantation and business owners.

During the Jim Crow era, cops enforced segregation and joined lynch mobs that grew strange fruit from southern trees. During the civil rights movement, police beat the hell out of Black preachers, activists, and students who marched for equality wearing their Sunday best. Cops were the foot soldiers for Richard Nixon's War on Drugs and Joe Biden's 1994 crime bill. Police departments pepper-sprayed Occupy Wall Street protesters without provocation and indiscriminately tear-gassed Black Lives Matter activists for years—including me, twice. Most Black people I know trust the police—they trust them to be exactly what they have always been: violent.[8]

Black people, including Black slavery abolitionists, have tried different routes to stop police violence. They have resisted the role of prisons and police for centuries by physical force, flight, hiding, and the courts. They even tried becoming police officers to protect Black communities from racist mobs and white police officers. Believing that they were entitled to equal protection under the law, they tried, usually to no avail, to reform the patrol and the police.

In recent decades, Black prison industrial complex abolitionists have developed alternatives to 911, created support systems for victims of domestic violence, prevented the construction of new jails, called for the reduction of police budgets, and shielded undocumented immigrants from deportation. They have imagined and built responses to harm rooted in community and accountability. Abolition, I have learned, is a bigger idea than firing cops and closing prisons; it includes eliminating the reasons people think they need cops and prisons in the first place.

After each video of a police killing goes viral, popular reforms go on tour: banning chokeholds, investing in community policing, diversifying departments—none of which would have saved Floyd or most other police victims. Princeton professor Naomi Murakawa wrote to me in an email:

At best, these reforms discourage certain techniques of killing, but they don't condemn the fact of police killing. "Ban the chokehold!" But allow murder with guns and tasers and police vans? The analogy here is to death-penalty reformers who improved the noose with the electric chair, and then improved the electric chair with chemical cocktails.

But the technique of murder doesn't comfort the dead. It comforts the executioners—and all their supportive onlookers. Like so much reform to address racism, all this legal fine print is meant to salve the conscience of moderates who want salvation on the cheap, without any real change to the material life-and-death realities for Black people.[9]

When Donald Trump was elected president, many liberals feared the end of consent decrees (legal agreements between the Department of Justice and police departments) intended to spur real change. After law school, I worked for the Advancement Project, which supported community organizers in Ferguson on the decree that was negotiated in the aftermath of Brown's death. Millions of dollars went toward an investigation, publicity, and a lawsuit to rid the Ferguson Police Department of "bad apples" and transform its culture.

After decades of police terror, widespread unconstitutional policing, and a year of militaristic ambush on the community, the consent decree provided members of the police department with mental health services to cope with the unrest, but no treatment or restitution for the residents who were tear-gassed, shot with rubber bullets, and traumatized by the tanks at the edge of their driveways. The Obama administration's DOJ objected to dismissing thousands of old cases that were the result of unconstitutional policing, and protected the police department from criticisms that community organizers shared with the judge in court.

Constitutional policing is a problem too. As the legal scholar Paul Butler explains, the overwhelming majority of police violence is constitutional. Stops, frisks, and most of the police killings that turn our stomachs are protected by Congress and the Supreme Court. I believe that people began chanting "defund the police" precisely for these reasons. Reforms cannot fix a policing system that is not broken.

Still, many Americans believe that most police officers do the right thing. Perhaps there are a few bad apples. But even the very best apples surveil, arrest, and detain millions of people every year whose primary "crime" is that they are immigrants, Black, poor, and unhoused. Cops escalate violence disproportionately against people with disabilities and in mental health crises, even the ones who call 911 for help. The police officers who are doing the "right thing" maintain the systems of inequality and ableism in Black communities. The right thing is wrong.

Policing cannot even fix what many of us might fear most. People often ask me, "What will we do with murderers and rapists?" Which ones? The police kill about a thousand people every year, and potentially assault, threaten, and harm hundreds of thousands more. After excessive force, sexual misconduct is the second-most-common complaint against cops. Many people are afraid to call the police when they suffer these harms, because they fear that the police will hurt them, too. Thousands of rape survivors refuse to call the police, worried about not being believed or about being reassaulted, or concerned that their rape kit would sit unexamined for years. In three major cities, less than 4 percent of calls to the police are for "violent crimes." Currently, the arrest rate for homicides has declined from 80 percent to 60 percent, and cops frequently arrest and force confessions out of the wrong people.[10]

SO IF WE abolish the police, what's the alternative? Who do we call? As someone who grew up calling 911, I also shared this concern. As *Becoming Abolitionists* explores: Just because I did not know an answer didn't mean that one did not exist. Infinite questions, answers, and possibilities were on the road ahead, and many of them were already in play. Along with others asking similar questions, I had to study and join and create organizations, and find my place in the larger freedom movement. Rather than thinking of abolition as simply getting rid of police overnight, so many of us who were becoming abolitionists started to think about it as an invitation to create and support a range of answers to the problem of harm in society, and, most exciting perhaps, as an opportunity to reduce and eliminate harm in the first place.

That is where you, the reader, come in. This is not a "how-to" book on becoming an abolitionist. This is an invitation to share what I have been pushed to learn in developing the politics of abolition; this is an invitation to love, study, struggle, search, and imagine what we have around us to make this possible, today. This book's purpose is to share the freedom dreams and real contradictions of a movement that I, that many abolitionists, hold dear, and to share how those dreams and contradictions and opportunities inspire me.

Before we begin, I make two requests of you.

First, I write about prison and police abolition as one paradigm, as one way to think about and experiment with problems and solutions. Abolition is important to me, but not abolition alone. I try my best to study abolition alongside other paradigms, such as feminism, decolonization, and internationalism, and hope that you will consider doing this, too. For me, understanding abolition's relationship to capitalism is also essential to our liberation. I think about capitalism as a political and economic system that categorizes groups of people for the purposes of exploiting, excluding, and extracting their labor toward the profit of another group. Those categories can consist of race, gender, disability, sexuality, immigration status, and much more.

The slave trade is an example. By creating a category of enslaved Black people, white people could exploit their labor by benefitting from what slaves produced that they could not benefit from themselves. Additionally, by confining Black people to slave status, white people did not have to compete with it for other jobs on the labor market because Black people were excluded from them. Ironically, slavery became a tense debate among capitalists because slaves performed work that white people could have been paid to perform. But instead, poor white people were paid to manage enslaved Black people, as overseers, slave patrols, police, wardens, sheriffs, and prison guards. Today, the criminal legal system continues to manage people who are excluded from labor markets, education, health care, and quality housing—all of the things we need to reduce harm, and all of the things that cities and the feds choose not to fund when we can.

Extraction is harder for me to explain, but I know it when I feel it. It's the immeasurable and forced removal of our body parts, ideas, and emotions that accompanies capitalism. It's forcing someone to work fifteen-hour days picking cotton so that you can spend your time doing what you wish. It's the two-hour public bus rides that Amazon factory workers take so that the owner, Jeff Bezos, can travel between cities in an hour by a private jet. What's sad is that people claim that poor, Black communities need the police the most to protect them, but this is not quite true. Capitalists need policing the most—to protect their property, billions, businesses, and borders by arresting the people whom they've exploited, excluded, and extracted from the most.

Second, let go. Well, maybe not *let go*, but, notice why you may want to know what "the alternative" is to police or prison. As someone who called 911 regularly as a child, I immediately wanted to know what the alternative would be if and when I was in a situation and needed help. A short answer is this: What if the solution is not one alternative, but many? By solely focusing on a single alternative, we fail to examine and eradicate the harm that gives rise to what we fear. And, we deserve options. "Option" stems from the Latin *optare*, meaning to "choose." Police and prisons—the default responses today—are woefully insufficient because they don't solve harm, they simply react to it. We must choose something better.

Who chose to have police? Originally, kings, colonizers, and capitalists. They chose police to protect their power to rule over people who had less. We must never forget that.

Certainly not the masses of Black people, whom police captured, brutalized, and returned to the plantation. Immigrants did not choose cops either, especially the immigrants who the police threatened to remain in their enclaves. Before the Irish were considered "white" in the US, they experienced policing as colonial subjects under Britain. Then, when they migrated to the United States, police targeted and arrested them so much that police vans are still called "paddy wagons," a derogatory use of the popular Irish name "Padraig." Women, even white women, had relatively little power in "choosing" to have police; during slavery, they were policed for prostitution and faced death for having sex outside of their marriages. And Indigenous people did not choose the police, either, or choose to be subject to the governance of those who displaced and dispossessed them of their lands and relegated them to "reservations."[11] Rather, police and rangers participated in mass genocide and war against Indigenous people in creating artificial borders called "states."

The people who chose the police were the same people who drafted the Constitution, who started the wars, who owned slaves, who possessed property, who had the most to lose if oppressed people ever decided to revolt: wealthy white men. And rather than unifying and organizing against the concentrated wealth of this class, the rest of us have been tricked into demanding that the police protect us, too. They cannot.

Thus, there is no singular alternative to police that does not risk replicating the forms of oppression that we currently face. Police developed through slave patrols, colonialism, and labor suppression. The institution continues to support broader social, economic, and racialized systems that took millions of decisions to create. Together, we will undo them all. Somebody had to hammer "Colored" and "Whites Only" signs at schools, subways, businesses, and parks. Somebody had to remove them, too.

Slavery abolition required resistance, risk, and experimentation. Black people plotted, rebelled, ran away. Built an underground railroad. Marooned. Abolitionists wrote and orated against the "peculiar institution." Allies funded campaigns, passed legislation, and changed the Constitution. Of course, people at the time felt a range of anxieties about abolition. Slave owners worried about their plantations and the profits that the labor camps wrought. White overseers feared joblessness. Both feared the loss of superiority. Some Black people had reservations about how they'd sustain themselves without the steady, yet violent, income from their owners. Police abolition triggers similar anxieties today—moral, economic, and otherwise.[12]

But if abolitionists had waited to convince every single person that freedom was worth the pursuit, Black people might still be on plantations. Slavery's violence and repression was riskier than Black people's plans, imagination, and will to be free. So they held the uncertainty in their bellies and started planning. Some started running. Rather than waiting for comforting answers to every potential harm ahead of us, let's plan. Run. Dream. Experiment. And continue to organize, imagine, and transform this society toward freedom and justice without police and violence.

ONE

WHAT JUSTICE?

S INCE I WAS about three, living in South St. Louis, my mother gave me two
career choices: a lawyer or a doctor. She was neither, only encountering
stethoscopes when she was sick and courts when there was trouble. Yet she
believed that Black people needed Black lawyers to fight racism and poverty in
the courts. She reminded me often that the US government did not care about
the plight of poor people, especially poor Black women like her. Lawyers
could alleviate some of the plight in court by winning trials. We called the court
outcome "justice" when it was favorable. And if there wasn't any justice, then
there wasn't supposed to be any peace. The popular chant demanded protests
and disruptions to make the injustice uncomfortable. But growing up, I saw
Black people lose so much in court—homes, marriages, children, freedom—
and still there was so much peace.

Messages about my mother's lawsuit filled our mailbox and our voicemail.
She was suing the factory where my father, Dereck, had been killed at the age of
twenty-five, leaving her alone with me and pregnant with my brother, Dereck Jr.
He was a machinist at Continco International, a plastics molding manufacturing
company. St. Louis had been a site for many headquarters and industrial jobs,
and Continco was one of the few that remained. In 1991, Daddy was crushed to
death while trying to remove material stuck inside of a machine. I couldn't quite

comprehend the story. For the first few years of my life, I would confuse strangers by saying that my dad died in a washing machine. I also tried to bring him back. My cousins, brother, and I would kneel and hold hands in the dark, near my mom's red leather couch in the basement, mimicking seances from movies to raise the dead. We called out. Nobody ever said anything back.

My mother and grandmother were neighbors. During the day, my mother would knock on the living-room wall that split our apartment from my grandmother's home. My grandmother babysat me and Dereck when my mom worked at a wholesale floral distributor on Lasalle. After work, she'd teach us how to read, spell, identify musical samples, and breakdance. Late nights, she'd tour the nightclub comedy circuit. I loved sitting in the kitchen listening to her practice standup. Especially the dirty jokes. "God gave me one titty and told me to split it." My grandmother would roll her eyes at our bubbling laughter.

With my mother, grandmother, and uncle living between two apartments, I felt immense love and protection in my early years. They set high expectations for me academically, especially as the oldest. The twins, Courtnie and Corey, came along in 1994. Later that year, our apartment caught on fire. I ran next door to warn my grandmother as my mom ran the three other children down the concrete steps to the patchy grass. She didn't know I had gone for help first, so she ran back into the fire searching for me. When she emerged minutes later, frantic that she couldn't find me, my grandmother and I had to grab her wrists to show that I was there. She hated apartments already and the fire made it worse. She had grown up in substandard housing where the pipes always broke and once the ceiling caved. A fresh new home, she figured, would eliminate landlords and slumlords. She resolved that I would become a lawyer in part so that I could protect her from them, and also so that I could make enough money to buy her a house. This was my goal entering kindergarten, where I was the first experiment of my own advocacy.

One day, a cafeteria lunch lady stopped me from grabbing a chocolate milk, but did not stop the kid in front of me. He had handed her quarters so I assumed it was for sale. I had no money. The following day, I came prepared. I quickly grabbed the milk, opened my palm to flash a few coins, and disrupted the food chain. She was shocked. My teacher was standing nearby and she asked what happened. When I explained to her that the cafeteria worker had stopped me the day before, my teacher assured me that I did not have to pay for anything. I was elated and puzzled. The lunch lady couldn't deny me, or anyone else, the sinful beverage. My mom explained to me on the walk home from school that the worker was withholding treats from children whose families belonged to the free lunch and breakfast program. We could not afford to pay for school meals, and to her, that made us unworthy of chocolate milk.

For me and many other students, confronting mistreatment at school was our introduction to self-improvement, punishment, and activism. I wanted to avoid mistreatment by proving that I could be the best student that I could be. School discipline and punishment is rather arbitrary. At schools I attended, "good students" did not talk back to adults and quickly complied with their orders. This environment was not conducive for disabled students and kids who dared to resist unfair treatment. I was *good*, my brother was *bad*. My brother knew that the teachers and school cops treated us differently because of our oversized clothes and natural hair. He defended himself and defied them. They responded with repeated punishment through suspensions. I decided that I would prove the teachers wrong by earning good grades and becoming a lawyer one day. After I scored high on gifted and talented tests, everything changed. Our home filled with my laminated citizenship certificates, academic awards, sports trophies, and medals. The celebration of my obedience increased my brother's justifiable defiance and the school's punishment. I wish we had both known then how to organize. Maybe I would have resisted the urge to be so respectable.

I did not meet student activists who learned to organize against their mistreatment until later. They made the connections that schools were microcosms of neighborhoods we lived in. At school, it was terrible food, school cops, and economic incentives tied to high stakes testing. Our teachers were stressed, too, and not necessarily the enemy. The bell rang each day and most of us went home to street police, segregated blocks, and government divestment from our neighborhoods. My brother and I certainly did. Our apartment complex was nestled in the poorest corner of the Gate District in St. Louis. Elders sat on their porches in the summer and spring. Kids shared portable basketball hoops in the alleys, where we also tumbled on mattresses for fun.

About half of my neighbors were African Americans who worked menial jobs at nearby stadiums, gas stations, and grocery stores. The other half were

Ethiopian and Somali refugees who had fled wars in East Africa for the dream of America. Men drove colorful cabs and kept their apartment doors open when they prayed in Arabic. The kids, all of us, played soccer and did push-ups when the other team scored. Several kids had scars from the war; a few still had pieces of metal inside them. Half of my friend's body experienced the crushing weight of his collapsing house as his dad tried to cover him from a bomb explosion. We would tease that the immobility of his right side made his left hook stronger. He reminded us with a blow every time he'd get into a fight. The women wore colorful hijabs and were reluctant to let me come over. Maybe it was because I wasn't Muslim, or because I was a tomboy, or because they had heard my mother's dirty jokes, too. Still, they were generous to my family with food and supplies when we were in need. My closest friends also wore hijabs—until high school, when they would quickly tuck them into their backpacks once we hopped off the school bus.

Black people in St. Louis have a long history of using education as a site of resistance. After Missouri required the police to suppress educational and religious gatherings for enslaved *and* free Black people in the 1840s, Black Baptist minister John Berry Meachum moved his freedom school to a steamboat on the Mississippi River where the police lacked jurisdiction to enforce state law. After the Civil War, Black people renamed colored schools after abolitionists and revolutionaries. In 1890, my middle school was renamed after Toussaint L'Ouverture, a leader in the largest slave rebellion on the island of Santo Domingo, modern-day Haiti. I grew up around streets named after French colonizers, including Pierre Laclède and Auguste Chouteau. In 1764, the pair had named St. Louis after one of their kings, Louis IX. It's remarkable that fresh off of the heels of the Civil War, Black St. Louisans named a school after a Black insurrectionist.

I started L'Ouverture days late after 9/11. I can't recall why. When I entered the building, I assumed that the school police holding the scanners on the other side of the metal detector were a consequence of the freshly fallen towers. But they were there every day. School districts have had relationships with law enforcement for decades; the Los Angeles school district has its own police department that emerged in 1948. As street police increased for Black people who rebelled over police violence, substandard housing conditions, and unemployment, school police expanded to patrol Black students. Students, parents, and teachers resisted the proliferation; school districts employed them anyway. By the time of my first day of school at L'Ouverture, the federal government used the Columbine High School shooting and 9/11 to increase funding for "school resource officer" positions for cops to perform multiple roles "as law enforcement officer, counselor, teacher, and liaison between law enforcement, schools, families, and the community." The Department of Justice issued more than $750 million to police agencies which paid for almost seven thousand additional school cops between 1999 and 2005.[13]

I couldn't sort out why an all-Black middle school in south St. Louis needed police after 9/11. Since we lived with the Arch in view, my mom's neighborhood friend, Michael Jackson (we always had to say his full name) spread conspiracies that our city was next for an attack. When the Praxair tanks exploded, he incorrectly warned us that it finally happened. However, the only people I saw school police apprehend were my friends and crushes. When the metal detectors, wands, and school cops were there again the first day of seventh grade, I realized that they were there for us. Schools like mine—majority Black and economically divested—had the highest percentages of school cops, and it remains so.

For high school, I spent several miserable weeks at a construction-themed charter school where kids had to wear tan hardware boots. During the welcome orientation, a school administrator did a call and response exercise to help Black families remember which infractions led to detention, suspensions, and expulsions. She'd say, "No belt with your uniform?" We'd say, "You're going home." Without giving the school (or my mom) notice, I stopped attending and enrolled myself in Vashon High. My grandmother had gone to "the V," along with Donny Hathaway, Congresswoman Maxine Waters, and Lloyd Gaines, the student responsible for the Supreme Court decision that required all white law schools to admit Black students if the state did not have a Black law school. He disappeared before he enjoyed the fruits of his suit. Whether he was murdered or fled the country due to threats is still unknown.

The V was named after George Vashon and his son, John. The elder Vashon was the first Black graduate of Oberlin College, an abolitionist, and the first African American to practice law in New York. But I only lasted a few weeks there, too; the school guards there were more aggressive than the ones at my middle school.

Every day, I had to unzip my jacket, open my bookbag, flip through my binders, and raise my pants to show my legs. They never told us what they were looking for and nor asked permission to search our bodies and belongings.[14]

A magnet school accepted me late in the year, so I transferred. Under a court-ordered inter-district desegregation program, several Black schools became "magnets": forceful attempts to attract suburban white families who had been repulsed by the inner city. Over time, the program became voluntary, coinciding with the attempts of the state to remove accreditation from majority Black school districts in St. Louis. My junior year, an education organizer asked if I was interested in planning protests and sit-ins against the state's takeover. I was humbled at the request and scared because we had to prepare to be arrested at any moment. She explained that our education was a civil rights issue, and that we needed to be on the side of justice. We organized demonstrations and chanted, "Don't Slay Our Future!" against Mayor Francis Slay. A handful of us invaded City Hall wearing matching bright yellow T-shirts and occupied his office overnight. Even though we lost our accreditation, the student protests and walkouts all over the city felt like a win. Our student movement planted seeds within the organizers in our group who would eventually bloom into educators— or activists for education civil rights, including me.[15]

My new school was much more diverse than Vashon and still had school cops. I maintained cordial relationships with them; because I had figured out the calculation for "good behavior," I had more privileges and less trouble. Until we had hall sweeps. Hall sweeps were in-school raids to clear the hallways between classes. Students had three minutes to transition between classes at the sound of a bell. At random, our principal or disciplinarian would make this announcement: "Teachers, three minutes have passed. Lock your doors. Security, bring any students caught in the halls to detention. This is a hall sweep." The threat created chaos. Students screamed and ran into each other trying to catch doors from closing. Teachers were hurt by thrusting their weight against the locks. Many of them hated it and would let students in anyway. School guards would then raid each floor and bathroom to round up students who had been locked out. We would spend the remainder of the period in in-school detention. I envied the students who did not run. They called the sweeps silly and defied the commanding voice from the speaker with their slow pace.

After the adrenaline rush from fleeing school cops, the principal expected us to sit quietly and learn geometry. At home, my friends already ran from the police and their families experienced raids on their houses. If cops were supposed to keep kids safe at school, using cops to cause additional chaos and violence through the sweeps opposed that goal. Instead of reducing police violence, local and federal governments funded "school resource officer" programs to improve Black kids' relationships with law enforcement. Maybe it did foster some relationships because many of us had our favorites inside the school. Yet the relationships did not stop the violence, punishment, or discipline at home or school. Relationship building had a perverse effect. School cops could punish us more subtly—because if we liked them, we would accept the punishment along with a hug or fist bump. After hall sweeps, students could cry and complain to their favorite school cop as they headed for in-school suspension anyway.

The federal government's decision to brand school cops as "school resource officers" had initially clouded my understanding of their purpose. My freshman year, rumors had spread about school resource officer who had impregnated a student. We knew that he was flirtatious with students, like the others, but his disappearance confirmed our speculations. Later, I saw one of my favorite school resource officers break up a fight outside the school. The boy he grabbed fell back hard as a result of the momentum, hitting the officer. The school resource officer waited a few seconds in angry disbelief. Then, he punched the student so hard in the ear and head that the boy caved in pain. The blow was worse than the silly back and forth pushing that he was trying to stop. I knew the violence was wrong, I just wasn't sure what to do about it. Before I learned about the "school to prison pipeline" in college, I had already known that it was impossible for the school cops to be resource officers because they were also a constant source or threat of violence. The only "resource" that the school resource officer program provided were jobs to Black people who worked in the district. They could have been trained to be the counselors, coaches, and teachers that we actually needed. Students needed resources, not "officers."

Most of the significant resources from my childhood were tied to law enforcement or the military. Air Force Junior Reserve Officer Training Corps (JROTC) was—by far—the program with the most resources at school. As of 2018, the Pentagon spends $370 million a year on the program that is disproportionately located in diverse, economically disadvantaged schools like the ones I attended. During hall sweeps, sometimes I'd run to JROTC to avoid detention. David, my freshman year sweetheart, jokingly called it my "underground railroad." Our instructors cared deeply about us and saw the program and the military as an opportunity for us to travel, pay for college, and see the world. Like most of my peers living under racism and class exploitation, I certainly did not have these opportunities, so JROTC was responsible for nearly every flight I took in high school. My family could barely afford bus fare to the airport, but once I was there, JROTC covered my travel to the military bases in Illinois and Arizona for elite summer camps. After meeting other Black students from around the country, I realized that we desired the resources that the military provided, not necessarily the military. We should not have had to risk our lives, and the lives of others, to attend college, travel, have income, and avoid the grave or prison.

At my award ceremonies, my mother always bragged about the awards I'd won and how sharp I looked in the pressed light blue shirts and heavily starched navy slacks. On the ride home, she firmly reminded me that I did not need the military to go to college because I would secure a full-ride scholarship. I thought she envied my relationship with one of my Black instructors, but she was afraid that my adoration for the program's teacher would inspire me to enlist. She would say that she did not believe that Black people should enter the military to fight wars for people who don't care about Black people in the US or anywhere else in the world. My mother was right about the military, and more. I received several full-ride scholarships to college. And I watched my less fortunate peers enter jobs that were always hiring: the military and the police.

JROTC is also where I began to read and write about the news. Students could report the news as a current-events exercise at the start of each lesson. The local evening news overwhelmingly covered murders and assaults, so that is what several students reported. One day, an instructor hovered anxiously behind the podium and pleaded with the class to stop reporting shootings. Names could fill the hour, and trying to have a normal class on aerospace science afterward was an impossible challenge. Korie Hodges, my classmate who had prompted his plea, was later murdered following the Ferguson Uprising.[16]

I mostly read news online because I wanted to know what was happening in other parts of the country. I came across tragedies that captured national headlines, including Hurricane Katrina, the police shooting of Sean Bell, and the Jena Six. I reported each of these stories during the current events section of our JROTC class, jumping down rabbit holes of links and clips and pictures of suffering. I also found the protests surrounding these events interesting. Many of the interviews I read and watched demanded "justice," a concept that I was still trying to understand. I shared information about the protests to the class because I found them inspiring, like pieces of history reliving itself in the present.

HURRICANE KATRINA CAME first, in 2005. I thought that I was just reporting on a brewing storm heading directly for Louisiana and Mississippi, but one story quickly became a set of reports about the country's racial climate. Kanye West was my favorite rapper when the storm landed that August. On a nationally televised broadcast to raise money for survivors, West trembled as he uttered, "I hate the way they portray us in the media. If you see a black family, it says they're looting. If you see a white family, it says they're searching for food . . . George Bush doesn't care about black people." West's video was the first viral video I remember. YouTube had only launched months earlier. President Bush did not fly to New Orleans, but rather over the devastation, safe in the stratosphere, peering down from Air Force One. On earth, armed militias stopped and shot Black people trying to enter the suburbs that surrounded the swiftly submerging city. Homeowners placed "We Shoot Looters" signs in their yards. But looting— not the shooting—was the big story, and portraits of Black people as criminal characters. Football stadiums became domestic refugee camps for the disabled, elderly, dark, and dispossessed, while there was public outcry about pet homelessness. Black adults in one parish had a mortality rate up to four times higher than white adults, and still, sixteen years later, there is no official death count for that catastrophe.[17]

A year later, in class, I reported on Sean Bell, the first police killing that I ever wrote about. Each word I read from the thick, black Dell in ROTC's main office twisted my stomach. I wrote a Facebook note about what happened. Five undercover New York Police Department (NYPD) officers surrounded Bell's car after he left his bachelor party at a strip club. Police claimed that they heard one of Bell's friends say that he was going to retrieve a gun from his car following an argument with the club owner. Other witnesses dispute this account, saying that the undercover police officers were not in close enough range to hear anything. Nevertheless, the cops shot fifty rounds of bullets, one of them emptying a magazine and reloading. Sean, who was just twenty-three years old, died. His friends were critically injured. Three cops were charged because of protests that followed the tragedy, but eventually they all were acquitted. Sean never wedded his bride.

I also reported about the Jena Six for class. Black lawyers, I understood at the time, defended Black people from injustice. But I did not really understand the role of prosecutors then, let alone that they could be unjust actors. I knew the metonyms, *they, the man, the system, the law, the court.* Six Black boys in Jena, Louisiana needed protection from their peers, their school district, police, *and* prosecutors.

I told my class about a Black freshman who had asked his high school principal permission to sit under "the white tree" in the school's yard. The principal said yes, assuring that anyone at the school could sit in the shade. The morning after the boy and his friends sat under the tree, three nooses appeared on its branches, hung there by white students. Federal prosecutors refused to prosecute the white teens for a hate crime. For punishment, a local cop scolded that the white boys "should be ashamed of themselves." The school district overruled the principal's recommendation to expel the white boys, who received supervised suspensions. Brian Purvis, one of the Jena Six, explained that Black students and families protested and held demonstrations every day after the noose incident for weeks. This angered and agitated white students and fights ensued. Purvis wrote in *My Story as a Jena 6*: "It was so bad, there were at least two cops and a dog in every hallway throughout the school. Our school was now like a prison."[18]

Racial violence continued in the town of three thousand souls. Black boys were invited to a party that had a "No Niggers Allowed" sign on the door. A white man punched one of them in the face, and later tried to shoot the boy during a confrontation. The boy and his friends took the man's gun from him. Some of the same Black boys who survived the racial violence from the party and gun incident were then accused of beating up a white boy at school. Police cuffed them and put them in jail. The "Jena Six" were charged with attempted murder because one of the boys used what the prosecutor argued was a deadly weapon: a sneaker.

District attorneys have the power to charge widely and harshly, though the same prosecutor had said, months earlier, that he could not find any hate crime charges to prosecute the white kids for the nooses. He additionally charged the Black boy for defending himself against the white man whose gun he took. Purvis was not there during the school fight, but he was prosecuted anyway.

The boys' parents raised awareness about the charges and the death threats that they received. In 2007, more than twenty thousand people packed Jena, creating the largest civil rights protests in a decade. Prosecutors relented and dropped or reduced the charges.[19]

Stories around the Jena Six focus on the nooses, charges, and marches. However, the local resistance to police and white supremacy strikes me as the most important. Black kids conducted sit-ins in their segregated school. They physically defended themselves and took a white man's shotgun. Purvis's family sent him out of state for his safety. He writes that the Black Panthers provided protection during the court hearings. Their parents could not afford bail so Black people created a legal defense fund. From the activism surrounding Jena 6, Hurricane Katrina, and Sean Bell, I began to understand why my mother condemned the government's contempt for poor, Black people. And I hoped that we would continue to fight for each other.

EXTRACURRICULAR ACTIVITIES TOOK up most of my time but I wanted to start learning more about racial justice—especially if I was going to become a civil rights lawyer. I started going to community meetings where I met organizers who increased my participation in local activism. My plate was also full at home. My grandmother's lung collapsed after consecutive strokes; nobody could afford to take her in with the level of care she needed, and she entered an elderly facility. The company that owned the apartment complex where we lived fired the white manager because he was overcharging rent and taking cash instead of money orders from the tenants, including my mom. The new manager, a Black woman, was sent to "clean things up." She evicted my mom for several reasons, including the fact that my mom couldn't make up the rent that she had given the previous manager. Against the terms of the lease, my mom had also opened up a small candy stand on our porch to make money. She paid kids in the neighborhood to bring grocery carts of snacks from the store because we never had a car. It was very little money, but the only chance that some kids had to earn twenty dollars here and there.

Jarrell, my first real crush, would run these errands for my mom. He had round, bright eyes and wore braids. We walked to L'Ouverture together on some mornings when I was in sixth grade and he was in eighth. I tested for gifted and talented early in elementary school, so I was put into his eighth-grade algebra class as a learning accommodation. After school, I would check to see if he was playing basketball at Buder because he would always encourage me to get on the court with the boys. Without me saying a word, he knew that I liked him. Much to my vexation, he mostly treated me like a sister and a friend. By the time he started coming to my house for my mom, I would simply freak out at the thought of him being downstairs in *my* living room. But my mom's business plan and benevolence did not matter to the landlord. Neither did my secret obsession with Jarrell. We were kicked out.

We were evicted again after my mom complained to a new landlord about the conditions of our apartment. My family had grown, with my two youngest sisters, Kayla and Vickie, and asking someone to take in a family of seven was an enormous ask. So we had to split up. I began renting a room in my aunt's basement and catching several buses in Ferguson to get to school in the city. A county school district originally sent taxis to pick me up and drop me off at school through their homelessness services program. I stopped requesting rides after several of the drivers made advances toward me.

I was also working at an after-school and youth empowerment program at the Kingdom House. There, I was a peer counselor to keep students in our communities out of violence and in school. We ran programming, homework support, and a host of social services that gave families in the neighborhood food, gifts, and clothes during the holidays. Ironically enough, through Kingdom House, I was also a local ambassador for Youth Crime Watch of America, a nonprofit dedicated to training middle and high school students to identify teenage and student criminals to report to law enforcement. YCWA receives grants from the Office of Juvenile Justice and Delinquency Prevention. The other ambassador and I traveled to national conferences together to meet a handful of other students who took their positions very seriously, and the rest of the attendees, like us, who wanted to take advantage of free trips to Miami. Fortunately,

I did not have to interact with any law enforcement when I was at work or school. The funding was a way for Kingdom House to pay the bills. However, the other ambassador temporarily became a police officer; she resigned after the protests against police violence began in 2014.

Like the funding for JROTC and school resource officers, the government decided to tie funding for youth to law enforcement. Kingdom House could have done the exact same work in that community if the grants had come from another federal agency, such as the Department of Health or the Department of Education. But, since the grants came through law enforcement agencies, the Office of Juvenile Justice and Delinquency Prevention encouraged young people to snitch on other young people in the name of justice and public safety. Like schools, nonprofits needed the resources to provide services in the community, not stronger relationships to the police. And the families in that neighborhood only needed the Kingdom House because their jobs did not pay them enough to take care of their families; they, too, needed to live under an economic system that ensured the equitable distribution of resources.

When I entered the University of Missouri-Kansas City in fall 2008, I joined and created racial justice organizations to continue my activism. Outside of class, I spent most of my day tutoring and mentoring Black and Latinx students in middle and high school across Kansas City, many of whom were undocumented. These students introduced me to the problems of immigration enforcement and border patrol. One year, I organized a regional college fair with schools from all over the country. A group of about fifteen Latinx students sat on the stairs in the arena. I assumed that they were either shy or acting like they were too cool to participate. "Hey, come on, why are you all sitting here? You can apply to all of these schools today and even get scholarships on the spot!" Not budging, they explained that some schools were requesting social security numbers that many of the students did not have. In solidarity, they all sat down to protect and support each other from being outed. These teenagers had to be vigilant against anything that could signal to law enforcement that they did not have citizenship.

Back on campus, I also realized that the racial violence and discrimination I'd reported about in high school was not just relegated to the south. White student organizations received funding allocations sometimes thirty times higher than diverse affinity groups' allocations for programming. A white student journalist used horribly racist stereotypes to mock a Black fast-food worker in the school paper. Ku Klux Klan members successfully sued to have their rally near the flagship campus. I had studied political science, Black studies, and sociology. After years of student and community activism, the university finally made Black Studies into an official department. They soon undermined its development by refusing to enter an agreement to hire core faculty and rescinded the contract offer for the director who'd grown it. The Black Studies House would become the target of hate acts and vandalized with racial epithets. Each event gave rise to more protests, more student demands, more temporary resolutions by the university.

Beyond school, organizing, and work, I was navigating exciting and troubled waters in my own life. An ex-boyfriend had begun stalking me my freshman year. One day, I'd switched routes and found him there, behind me. I rushed toward the entrance of the cafeteria so that I could confront him in a public setting. I begged him to stop and to please move on. He grabbed my wrists. When I pulled away, he grabbed my backpack to pull me back toward him, a common move he'd done when we were dating. I removed my bookbag to escape and fled to my dorm room. I called my mom, aunt, and boyfriend for help. My mom and aunt told me to come up with a plan so that I would always be with someone else on campus until I could figure out how to handle the situation. Grandon, my boyfriend at the time, did not consider my ex to be a real threat, but still called him to warn him about trying anything else. The stalking stopped.

I'd also started blaming violence I'd experience, like the stalking, and unhealthy friendships on myself. After a series of heartbreaking fights and losing friends, I'd turn to the church to seek spiritual guidance. Grandon was living in St. Louis, and when he told his parents that he might move to Kansas City to be closer to me, they said that we had to get married. Some traditions of Christianity forbid living together before marriage and belong to the set of biblical teachings that condemn premarital sex, adultery, and divorce. I trusted and adored his parents, who were small business owners, ministers, and active in prison ministries for several decades. Grandon's life had also appeared so much more stable than my own, and I largely attributed it to their parenting, not fully understanding the role of our class differences. Not that they were rich, but my family was especially poor. Grandon proposed after a few months and we glee-fully wedded in August 2009. He was twenty-one. I was nineteen.

THROUGH ALL OF the violence and activism, local and national, I was hopeful that the United States was truly becoming an amazing country. Unlike any other generation of Black students ever, my freshman year of college coincided with the election of the first Black president. Barack Obama was my kite. Kites are beautiful. Watching the colorful threads soar made me feel like I was having a conversation with a butterfly, like I could hold one for a while. With wind, kites rise. We are supposed to let them fly, then pull in on the line to manage the climb. Kites reward us when we allow them to work with wind, space, and control. Otherwise, they disappoint, become tangled. Crash. Obama was supposed to be proof that the United States could let people of color soar, with the right space, control, and wind beneath their wings. I voted for him twice. Filled with hope, I set up voter registration sites, organized "get out the vote" rallies, and, the second time he was elected, I saved money to fly to Washington, DC, to attend his inauguration. I stood several hours on a corner in DC for inauguration tickets in January 2013. Not because there was a line stretching around the capitol, but because my best friend was lost in the pre-inauguration traffic and forgot where she had dropped me off. Anyway, I wanted to be like Obama—a Black lawyer who spoke truth about freedom and justice for everyone.

Flags are not as beautiful to me as kites. We honor flags as symbols of pride and freedom, but rarely interrogate what we are proud of or what freedoms we have. Because of JROTC, I have recited the pledge of allegiance hundreds of times. In school, at events, and at military camps. Standing at attention, with the backs of my shiny black oxfords pressed firmly together, I noticed that unlike kites, flags are attached to immovable poles, only waving in response to the wind, unable to roam in search of something more free. We'd pledge allegiance to the republic, "for which it stands, one nation, under God, indivisible, with liberty and justice for all." Reciting the pledge became increasingly difficult because I knew there was not liberty and justice for Sean Bell, for the Jena Six, for the families flooded by Katrina, or for those immigrant students on the steps. *Why would I continue to pledge allegiance to the republic "for which it stands," when it stood for violence against Black and brown people?*

If Obama was a kite, Kris Kobach was a flag. He was proud of nothing worth preserving in this country and the liberty he desired was the freedom to control others. When Obama was running for president, Kobach was a law professor at my college. He was authoring anti-immigration bills all over the country. Dubbed the "Nativist Son," Kobach was the father of Arizona's Senate Bill 1070, or as activists called it, the "Do I look illegal?" bill. Bill 1070 was the most restrictive state immigration law in the United States, mandating that cops racially profile drivers during traffic stops to determine their immigration status. Mexico borders Arizona. Cops used brown hues to make investigatory stops against people they suspected had crossed over. The federal government primarily holds jurisdiction over immigration and cannot force states or municipalities to assist. Here, Arizona was volunteering.[20]

Cities and the federal government have long used law enforcement and the military for border control. During the 1800s, Indigenous peoples and Mexicans fought militiamen, the Army, vigilantes, and rangers who helped colonize the same land where, a century later, Kris Kobach planned to expand police for immigration control. A primary reason that Mexicans were "immigrants" in the first place is because the United States transitioned from a settler colony under Britain to a nation state with borders. Until then, the land had been Mexico, and before that, inhabited by various Native peoples who roamed the land without notions of "legal" or "illegal." The roaming continued after the US was officially formed—except for Indigenous people fighting for their land and enslaved people fleeing the plantation.

But Mexicans were not the initial impetus for "illegal immigration," it was Chinese immigrants. In *Amnesty or Abolition,* historian Kelly Lytle Hernandez explains that white slave owners tried to preserve their economic power by importing Chinese contract laborers to replace enslaved Black people near the end of the Civil War. Congress banned the Chinese immigrants to prevent the emergence of new forms of slavery. Abolitionist Frederick Douglass called the importation the start of a "Asiatic-slave trade" and opposed Congress' actions because it criminalized the Chinese immigrants instead of the exploitative white

Americans. The ban was foundational to the expansion of later immigration bans, law enforcement, border patrol, prisons, and detention centers for other immigrants. Hernandez argues that the white men who worked in Border Patrol specifically "Mexicanized" enforcement to maintain a system of racial control. They used their policing jobs to target and cage undocumented Mexican workers in the local agricultural labor force. Anti-immigrant law enforcement had been an ongoing project to displace people, control land, and protect the economic interests of the colonizers. Kris Kobach was only a fresh face in the long and ugly history of colonization and policing. He made this clear to the committee who drafted the 2012 Republican platform: "If you really want to create a job tomorrow, you can remove an illegal alien today."

I joined students in Movimiento Estudiantil Chicano de Aztlán (MeChA) to raise awareness and organize against the expansion of police power in immigration. In July 2010, MeChA counterprotested a rally celebrating Arizona sheriff Joe Arpaio, the staunch xenophobe and racist who created illegal armed mobs to "round up illegal immigrants" in the state. The rally took place in Overland Park, Kansas. Kobach and Arpaio were championing a similar anti-immigration bill for Kansas. Initially, our group stood across the street with hundreds of people holding signs and chanting. At the Kobach-Arpaio rally entrance, I spotted a table sponsored by Bott Radio. I listened to the Christian station daily on my way to class. Grandon had also spotted a Black student from his bible college there. I figured it might be safe enough to discover what the police were doing in Arizona. We entered the packed arena.

In the sea of nearly two thousand white faces, our Black and brown shells stood out. Veronica, a friend and student from Spain, wore a "Do I look illegal?" shirt that day. My heart raced. *How could this many people cheer on racial profiling by the police? How could Bott Radio support this?* A speaker announced the pledge of allegiance. Without hesitation, almost everyone faced the flag. I did not move. If supporting racial profiling and the police required us to be one nation under God, then there was no way that I would keep pledging. A tall, blond, white woman grabbed and pushed me from behind.[21]

"Put your hand over your heart!" she demanded.

"Don't touch me, don't ever put your hands on me again," I retorted, partially angry, partially afraid.

"Aren't you an American?" After more back-and-forth, she walked away. I was relieved, until she returned with a cop.

"Ma'am." He looked at her. "I can't force her to pledge."

Her disgust was audible. She moaned and groaned until she disappeared again. The speaker on the stage indicated that there were unexpected people in the audience. At a public rally, everyone should be "unexpected." He just meant our group. He escalated the announcement when he added that there was a bomb threat, too. I was terrified because I didn't want to die in an explosion. What followed made little sense. Kobach and Arpaio said they understood if people wanted to leave. The crowd stayed and cheered. I started to realize exactly what they were doing: creating a sense of victimhood in the crowd to make them feel as if their beliefs and bodies were under attack. Who was going to plant a bomb that day and kill two thousand white people? The NAACP counterprotesters? Us? I was standing in the middle of a racial hoax, and the crowd started looking at us, angrily. We hurried out and went back across the street. It was late and most of the counterprotesters had left. As rally attendees exited the parking lot, they shouted at us from their pickup trucks and minivans. "Terrorists!" "Go back to Africa!" "We know you planted the bomb!"

Flags soared high that day in Overland Park, Kansas. I was learning that policing was much larger than how individual cops treated Black people. Policing was, and is, deeply connected to the control of land, labor, and people who threatened white supremacy. Many white people used the police to punish Black and Latinx people who dared to move freely in the US. Even the white woman *who broke the law and assaulted me* went directly to a cop afterward to further punish me. Others, like her, who screamed at us lived in Kansas; they worked in corporate offices and police departments and day cares and community colleges and hospitals. The rally's attendees listened to Bott Radio, like I did, and worshipped in Christian churches, like me. They probably took mission trips and vacations to Mexico, and yet deeply feared "Mexican invaders" who would steal their jobs. And obviously, they hated the kite, and the possibility of losing *their* country to people who were not white.

ALONGSIDE STUDENT ACTIVISTS, administrators and assistants in the chancellor's and diversity offices had become my dear mentors. They pushed me to read widely outside of class to cultivate my budding activism and political analysis around race, class, immigration, disability, and sexuality. So in 2010 the diversity office tapped me to introduce Dr. Angela Davis's Martin Luther King keynote lecture. What an honor—she was a legend, *the* legend, my mom's focal point. My mother associated Davis with the Black Panther Party and told me stories about the Black Power movement each time my hair was being braided down from an Afro. Davis represented an era that I had first understood aesthetically more than politically. I knew the black berets, fros, and fists. I had to learn that the free breakfast and lunch program from my elementary school cafeteria days was co-opted from Black organizers who fed thousands of poor children every day as a moral duty and political practice of their socialist beliefs. Nevertheless, I was largely unfamiliar with Davis's written work and activism on abolishing the prison industrial complex. Abolishing the death penalty made sense to me, especially since my aunt worked on a campaign to free a man from death row. I had also read Sister Helen Prejean's *The Death of Innocents*. But I only believed that prisons, particularly death row, were bad because prosecutors and police caught and executed the wrong people. Or, if they caught the right person, the state disproportionately killed Black people or people who could not understand their crime. However, the problem was not that the system got it wrong sometimes; Davis's work emphasized that the *system* was wrong all the time. I completed her introduction and discussed how activists like her influenced me to become a civil rights lawyer.

After Dr. Davis's speech, I wanted to know everything she had done, she had written, she had believed in. When I headed to the private reception with her at the Black Studies house, a university employee whom I deeply admired stopped me in the hallway. I thought that she was going to congratulate me. She did not. Instead, she asked if I knew that Dr. Davis was in a relationship with a woman. I did not know and the question confused me. She said that I should "be careful" about whom I admire because as a Christian, I was called to rebuke particular lifestyles. It felt like a rug was snatched from beneath my feet. At nineteen, I was trying my best to be a new Christian. I was heavily involved in the church, anti-abortion, and I had even cut off any friends who I suspected were queer or having premarital sex. Including people I loved and danced on teams with in St. Louis. I had thought that I was supposed to hate the sin, love the sinner. All sins equally. My best friend, Porcia, and I would go to nightclubs to try to *save* the souls of young women in the parking lot.

A lot of my justice work had also been influenced by my faith, so I was challenged by the homophobic nudge. I was supposed to love people as I believed that Christ loved me. The hallway conversation did not feel like love. It felt like control and jealousy. The drive to the Black Studies House afterward felt much longer than the three minutes it usually took. And once I went inside, I couldn't bring myself to ask any substantive questions of the funny, charming, and brilliant revolutionary I had just hugged hours earlier. This is how homophobia can create spectacular and mundane forms of violence against queer people. Shouting slurs reveals the hatred and fear. Silence can conceal it. And akin to racism, homophobia and capitalism exploits, excludes, and extracts from people who are marginalized because of who they might be attracted to. For the person in the hallway, homophobia categorically excluded gay people from admiration; it could have been exclusion from housing, employment, health care, and the opportunity to speak at my university.

I think I'm patient with people I organize with who have conflicting ideas about justice because my own ideas about oppression and freedom formed dynamically alongside my ideas about sex and sin. I had been active about racial and economic justice and simultaneously had unexamined commitments to harmful beliefs. Ironically, many people I loved at church and in community organizations thought they were protecting Black people from single mother homes, abortions, and queerness. Fear of additional stigma made us cling to what we perceived as righteousness and purity. To save others, we lost ourselves—because homophobia is bad for the people who carry it, too. Here, it foreclosed a relationship with another human being. It made me cower instead of chasing her ideas that were necessary for my own liberation, too. At least temporarily. Eventually, I emailed Davis, expressing gratitude for our encounter and asked to remain in touch.

AFTER THE KEYNOTE, I sought organizations, movements, and employment that focused on the criminal justice system. In 2011, The Kansas City's Human Relations Department posted an investigations internship position for its Civil Rights Division. They recruited law students, but after I did some pleading, they gave me an interview, then an offer. On day one, I had an hours-long conversation with my new supervisor, Mickey Dean. He had an enormous red, green, and black flag that covered the wall above his desk. He explained that civil rights enforcement was his day job, but he'd spent more than thirty years organizing through the National Black United Front. In Kansas City, members opened an African-centered school and community center. He taught math every Saturday. They were pan-Africanist, greeting each other with "Hotep!" They traveled extensively throughout Africa and launched campaigns to bring the chairman of the Kansas City chapter of the Black Panther Party, Pete O'Neal, home.

Kansas City was a major hub of Black organizing during the Black Power Era. Kansas City's Black Panther Party protested police violence, launched local free breakfast programs, and offered educational programs for students of all races. O'Neal previously spent time in prison, and upon release, the State of California was supposed to expunge the felony from his criminal record. State officials failed to do so, keeping O'Neal in housing, economic, and employment precarity. Not to mention the additional targeting by police who exploited his vulnerable status to threaten imprisonment. O'Neal fled Kansas City in 1969; he was facing a federal charge for transporting a gun across state lines during the height of his political leadership. As Mickey put it, "Pete is in exile due to some bogus charges that he picked up thanks to the government's attack on the Panther Party through its COINTELPRO operations. He can't return to the country without going to prison." Like Angela Davis, police and federal agents imprisoned several Black radicals for their beliefs in socialism and communism. Police killed activists. Others went into exile. O'Neal ultimately landed in Tanzania, where he and his wife, Charlotte, continue their activism and run a school. When Mama Charlotte would visit Kansas City, I'd attend the NBUF events to spend time around her.[22]

When President Obama was leaving office in 2017, I asked Mickey if I should begin organizing a commutation campaign for Pete. Obama commuted sentences for whistleblower Chelsea Manning and Puerto Rican liberation leader Oscar López Rivera, and there was hope among activists that the first Black president might also commute the most famous political prisoner in the world, former Black Panther Mumia Abu-Jamal. Through Mickey, Pete offered his gratitude for my offer, but gracefully bowed out. He believed if there was any chance for Mumia's freedom, then all of the energy should be directed toward that cause.

Under Mickey, I investigated how companies and landlords used criminal records to deny jobs and housing to applicants, particularly people of color. This is precisely what had happened to Pete O'Neal when he left prison and looked for work. The Civil Rights Act of 1964 prohibits companies from denying employment to people on the basis of their race, but if a Black person has a felony, then businesses can deny employment on the basis of the criminal record, which can also serve as a proxy for racial discrimination. At the time of my employment, one report estimated that one-third of Black men had a felony conviction compared to 13 percent of all adult men. Organizations and landlords make millions of people ineligible for housing and jobs due to criminal records, including arrest records that do not result in convictions. Complete bans on criminal records bypass the civil rights laws that were meant to protect people of color who already experienced discrimination and exploitation in the job market, and increased availability for white people seeking employment and homes. Many Kansas City area employers and landlords, I found, had blanket bans on hiring or leasing to people with records. Since police primarily patrol, arrest, and imprison economically exploited Black people, Indigenous peoples, and people of color; these groups were routinely denied housing and jobs. It was not solely about public safety: white men with criminal records were more likely to interview for jobs than Black men without criminal record. Federal government policies exacerbated the discrimination by additionally barring people with records from public housing, welfare, voting, and financial aid for school.[23]

I conducted phone interviews with administrators of local businesses and apartment complexes. They defended the background checks and bans. One woman even bragged that the application and background check did not even matter. If someone even "looked bad," they could be denied. Mickey and I offered a training to an apartment complex association about the impact of their blanket bans and how they might be in violation of the law. The training emphasized how to navigate maintaining a safe environment while limiting racial discrimination against people with records. When we arrived at the location, Mickey stopped suddenly when he opened the door. The apartment complex association had come with the police, who took up half of the medium-sized conference room. I really did not understand why landlords and apartment managers would bring so many cops to this meeting, but I felt so alarmed. Mickey did not waste any time on assumptions. He just asked. Everyone was white except us and the manager who answered Mickey. The manager said that the cops were there to protect the rights of the proprietors. This didn't make any sense. Mickey was a government lawyer who enforced the civil rights code in Kansas City against businesses who were breaking the law by discriminating against people on the basis of race, sex, gender, disability, and family status. He *was* law enforcement. Cops are not lawyers and it was absurd that they would use their publicly funded positions to protect private property owners from the government. Companies defend themselves from law enforcement with lawyers, not cops, at least I had thought. Without flinching at the ridiculous nature of the man's response, Mickey started the presentation.

On the drive back to the office, I asked why the police were there. He explained two reasons. First, police protect private property, and people who control the property can control the police. Second, they thought that they were going to intimidate us with police presence, and they failed. Regardless of our positions in law enforcement, we were Black people trying to tell white people how to use their property. He turned up *Democracy Now!* with Amy Goodman on the radio for the rest of the drive.

Mickey's explanation about who controls the police provided further context to the anti-immigration rally that I had counterprotested the year before; the white kids who "owned" the tree in Jena; and the armed white militias who threatened and shot Black Hurricane Katrina survivors. Police targeted people because of their race and certainly more. Race and ethnicity are inseparable from who hoards wealth and who fills out endless job applications for low wage jobs; who owns apartment complexes and who rents rooms; who celebrates Independence Day and who is deported; and who languishes in prisons and who is free. Cops are the armed force that maintain these divisions.

Changing the race of the people in power did not necessarily end the hierarchies that maintained racism, classism, and xenophobia. The spokesperson for the apartment association was a Black man and he legitimized the police presence at the meeting and property owners who wanted to keep tenants out. Black and Latinx activists were criticizing President Obama's immigration policies for the same reason. The president was clear: "No matter how decent they are, no matter their reasons, the eleven million who broke these [immigration] laws should be held accountable." Activists were critical of his crackdown against the undocumented and labeled him "deporter-in-chief." Immigrants and advocates demanded comprehensive immigration reform rather than detention and expulsion. They started campaigns around the most sympathetic groups, children they called "Dreamers," who were brought here by their parents to flee violence or seek opportunity. While Obama did not spew the kind of xenophobic speech that I had heard at the rally, I realized that his message led to the same outcomes. Border patrol and detention increased and he surpassed his Republican predecessor's record on deportations. My kite was attached to police, private property, prisons, and borders over people. The colors that once made me marvel were a distraction.[24]

Activists continued to pressure President Obama to reform immigration and criminal justice systems that we called "broken." In 2011, I joined thousands of people who were signing, circulating, and making calls around petitions to stop the State of Georgia from executing Troy Davis. Davis was on death row because he had been convicted of killing a cop. Davis's case was obviously flawed. The evidence against him was largely absent and what evidence was present was weak. No weapon tied him to the shooting, and seven witnesses recanted testimonies that cops forced them to make years before. One million people signed petitions for his release. I felt that this was our opportunity to stop the death of an innocent. I found it profoundly unfair that when cops kill Black people, nobody had to be punished, but when a Black civilian kills a white cop, any Black person can be punished.[25]

Black students protested and marched for Davis's freedom. Howard University students went to the White House with signs in their hands and tears in their eyes, imploring the Black president that many of us helped get elected to do something. *Anything.* He did nothing. Thirty minutes before the execution, the White House press secretary issued a statement explaining that while President Barack Obama "has worked to ensure accuracy and fairness in the criminal justice system," it was inappropriate for him to "weigh in on specific cases like this one, which is a state prosecution."[26]

President Obama could have done something. He could have personally condemned the execution, just as he personally condemned states' bans on gay marriage. Per the Death Penalty Information Center, Obama could have possibly investigated any federal issues in the case which would have suspended Davis's execution. Writer Sherry Wolf explained that US presidents have authorized themselves to do catastrophic violence in the world, and the president could have found a way to prevent violence if he had had the will and courage. Calling Obama's silence "bullshit," she wrote: "Presidents have declared multiple wars without Congressional approval, they have defied international law through special renditions torture program, they have run a gulag at Guantánamo Bay, they have ripped up civil liberties to read our e-mails and rifle through our trash. Obama himself has just waged a months-long extra-legal war on Libya." Even William S. Sessions, Ronald Reagan's former FBI director, called for a stay of execution. Politicians on both sides of the aisle called for the death penalty team to strike.[27]

I had known that someone's innocence was not enough to protect them from state violence. Well before I learned about Sean Bell and the Jena Six, I knew the histories of Black bodies swinging from trees in this country. Death penalty abolition would at least stop one form of state executions one day, but we just needed something right then and there. Just as activists had demanded justice for Davis, the slain cop's family demanded justice for their loved one. On September 21, 2011, the State of Georgia answered. An executioner killed Troy Davis. It was a sobering lesson that when Black people are on death row, and activists are fighting for their freedom, the people opposing us say that they want their "justice" too. As I would later learn while awaiting convictions for cops: The same systems responsible for our oppression cannot be the same systems responsible for our justice.

Black and multiracial student activism around Troy Davis catalyzed subsequent organizing around social justice issues. We were always organizing on and off campus in response to racism from our peers, professors, and police, but our activism was evolving. The petitions that I used to carry on brown clipboards shifted to online shareable links. Criminal justice was taking over the mainstream as a popular site of political struggle. I was especially moved by the protests to the extent that, at the end of my civil rights internship with Mickey, I changed my senior thesis topic from education desegregation to "disparate impact discrimination on ex-offenders of color." Lucky for me, Michelle Alexander's *The New Jim Crow* was still fresh on the bookshelves. Alexander's book was a crash course on the criminal legal system and history of racialized control in the United States. Not only did the prison population explode, she explained, but mass criminalization and policing kept Black men trapped in a carceral cycle after they exited prison. Like Angela Davis a couple of years before, Alexander was booked as my college's MLK keynote speaker. But because I was the student speaker then, I couldn't do it again. My mentors in the diversity office, Kristi and Dr. Dace, knew about my research interests and still invited me to the private dinner afterward. Mickey was the first civil rights lawyer I'd met, but Alexander was the first Black woman I met who was a civil rights lawyer, so this was my chance to ask questions about what justice really meant to her. As we were leaving a famed Kansas City BBQ restaurant in a ritzy midtown area called the "Country Club Plaza," I thanked her and asked if I could be her research assistant. She agreed, but I never followed up. The following month, I found myself organizing in another movement for racial justice.

THE SPRING AFTER Davis's execution, when I was finishing my thesis, I learned about the white self-appointed neighborhood watchman who followed, fought, and killed a seventeen-year-old Black boy in Florida. In February 2012, Trayvon Martin was walking home from a 7-Eleven with Skittles and an AriZona iced tea. His hood was over his head. George Zimmerman started following Martin and called the police to report a suspicious character. Zimmerman told the 911 dispatcher, "These assholes . . . always get away." The dispatcher told Zimmerman that he did not need to follow Martin, but he ignored the request and ultimately killed the teen. Following the news story, a shock wave of grief and disbelief washed across the public. *How could a white man follow a Black boy, start a fight, kill him, then go home—in 2012?* I did not have to be a lawyer to know that killing someone after stalking them was illegal. Wasn't it?[28]

Protesters then didn't know what we learned soon after. Police did not originally arrest Zimmerman because of Florida's "Stand Your Ground" law. It did not matter that he initiated the fight; he could claim immunity for using fatal force during the encounter and avoid arrest if the police believed he was justified. Then, in states where the law requires someone to flee a potentially violent encounter, rather than "stand your ground," white people are 250 percent more likely to be deemed justified in the "self-defense" killing of a Black person than a white person. In "stand your ground" states, like Florida, that number jumps to 354 percent. To the contrary, predictably, Black people are almost never found legally justified in the self-defense killing of a white person. The Black boy from the Jena Six was prosecuted for taking the white man's gun in self-defense. If Martin had survived, rather than Zimmerman, he would likely be in prison.[29]

Young Black and brown activists in the Sunshine State started singing freedom songs and demanding justice for Trayvon Martin. This group, some of whom would become the Dream Defenders, blocked the entrance to the Sanford Police Department to put pressure on cops to arrest Zimmerman. They also occupied the governor's office to repeal the Stand Your Ground law. Black organizers from across the country went down to Florida to support them.[30]

Thousands of people were also cheering for George Zimmerman. I thought about all the white people I had seen in Kansas, cheering on the empowering of police to racially profile people. George Zimmerman was not a cop, but the state certainly protected his behavior to racially profile, target, and even kill a Black kid. The media and activists called him a vigilante. A vigilante is someone who takes the law into their own hands to threaten or punish someone without legal authority. But Zimmerman *did* have legal authority to undertake law enforcement under Stand Your Ground—he had the power to strike even when he had no reason to do so.[31]

Hundreds of thousands of people were inspired by the Dream Defenders' activism, including me. Rallies popped up all over the country to seek justice for Trayvon. I didn't go to Florida as I had dreamed in 2012. I remained in Kansas City to organize and plan protests in solidarity to get Zimmerman arrested. I pulled a group of students and clergy together to plan a rally in Kansas City, Missouri. We chose to hold the rally at the J. C. Nichols fountain at the Country Club Plaza because police racially profiled Black teens who visited the scenic, high-end retail and restaurants there. Additionally, J. C. Nichols had been a real-estate developer who had made his wealth by building the Plaza and surrounding homes using racially restrictive covenants, agreements that kept Blacks and Jews out of white neighborhoods. His covenants cemented a racial dividing line in Kansas City that kept Black families in neighborhoods east of the Plaza for the next century. We believed that a racial justice rally near a physical relic of white supremacy would condemn the legacies of racial violence in the US.

"Bring your hoodies and your AriZona tea!" "Meet us at the Plaza!" We circulated flyers in neighborhoods and on Facebook. The media picked it up. Soon, a conciliation specialist from the Department of Justice called me, warning me that white supremacists were threatening to counterprotest our rally. Conciliation specialists mediate disputes in local communities. *White supremacy isn't something to mediate, but eradicate,* I thought. She had called me to put me on notice that we could expect violence, and to think through options for safety. I did not expect the police to protect us from the counterprotesters. Usually, when I counterprotested white supremacist rallies in Kansas City, the police faced us. Besides, our organizing team did not expect a large rally. We thought that the threat would die down as we moved closer to the date so we pressed on. We created a calendar of community events where we made announcements and attended so many meetings that people started mentioning the rally before we could. Alvin Brooks, a Black former police officer and the person who created and directed the department where Mickey eventually worked, announced the rally on his radio show. Brooks's show was a part of his project, AdHoc Group Against Crime, a nonprofit dedicated to responding to violent crimes in Black communities using tips and rewards for information. He commanded the respect of Black Kansas Citians, so when I heard the announcement on my ride home, I started shouting with joy.

The most painful moment happened at my church. I dearly and deeply loved my pastor, who was a critical thinker and fiery preacher, and a warm and inviting spirit. He talked about social issues and encouraged people to go vote, probably as much as any other pastor in a traditional Black church in the Midwest. On the Sunday morning before the rally, he condemned the racism in this country, and described how Black men were so dehumanized and walked around with targets on their backs. Then, he invited all of the Black men in the church to come to the altar. He directed the congregation to stretch our hands toward them in preparation for prayer. He pleaded with God, begging to help us save the souls of Black men, so that when they are hunted and killed, they will go to heaven. I snatched my arm back, raised my head in horror, and promptly exited the church at "Amen."

The prayer hurt me. I felt sad for my pastor who was trying his best and mad that his best only saved Black men in the afterlife. *How could I worship a God who did not have the decency to permit victims of white supremacy and police violence into heaven?* I vehemently rejected the idea that premature death disproportionately sent Black people to hell. *Why weren't we praying to stop the violence? Or at least praying to learn how to fight back?*

I called my friend JP, who was a student at Yale Divinity School. We had met on Alex Haley Farm during our Children's Defense Fund Freedom School training. CDF was modeled after the Mississippi Freedom Summer of 1964 and trained thousands of mostly Black college students to teach in social justice summer programs at schools and churches across the country. JP and I became friends after an argument. I believed in organizing and protests to stop racial violence. JP criticized marching because Black people could enter policy positions. He had been influenced by Warren Kimbro, a former Black Panther in New Haven who ran a program for men exiting prison. "Warren told a group of Black men, 'The time for Molotov cocktails is over. We did that so y'all could be judges and politicians," JP said. Between Kimbro and shadowing leaders at Rev. Al Sharpton's National Action Network, JP was disillusioned with protests. He later told me that Freedom School and Black theologians like Emilie Townes revived his energy for resistance. So I knew that he was the right person to call.

"JP," I said, on the verge of tears "how can you be Black and Christian?" I told him what had happened at church that morning and how I felt about seeing the Christian radio station support the police at the anti-immigration rally. I reminded him that a minister had encouraged me to change majors after I shared that poverty derives from slavery, Jim Crow, and capitalism, not whether we paid tithes. JP explained that there were different traditions of Christianity, and the one he belonged to believed that God was on the side of the oppressed. He recommended Howard Thurman's *Jesus and the Disinherited*, and sermons from Trinity United Church of Christ in Chicago. Trinity, he believed, would help me through my faith and activism. The church's slogan was literally, "Unapologetically Black, Unashamedly Christian." There, I didn't have to choose.

Days before the rally, I received a call from Charlene Carruthers. Carruthers was organizing with Color of Change at the time and wanted to list our rally on a national website featuring Justice for Trayvon Martin events. I sent the logistical details, and Carruthers helped me create a program. She told me that organizers could create space for people to grieve, heal, and act as a community.

That's exactly what we did. We designated times for an open mic, to let different people in the community sing, perform poetry, and express anger. Street violence interrupter groups challenged the crowd to keep our neighborhoods peaceful. Activists helped hundreds of people sign petitions for Zimmerman's arrest. Elders kept saying that it was one of the largest civil rights rallies they'd seen in decades.

Our organizing team tried to prevent police and vigilante shootings locally, so we organized next steps meetings at Believers' Temple who gave us resources and space to gather. We drafted scripts and made hundreds of calls to follow up with anyone who signed up at the rally or online. Our group reached out to law enforcement and neighborhood watch groups to attend. We called ourselves Warriors Actively Transforming & Creating Hope for Kansas City (Watch4KC). It was our attempt to shift neighborhoods from relying on punitive neighborhood watches to building community relationship formations.

Nearly one hundred people showed up. Organizers facilitated small group dialogues around three commitments. The first was community ownership. We believed that violence declined with increased levels of community involvement and care. The small group had brainstormed activities on how to interrupt violence, including deescalating fights that occurred among Black teens on the Plaza. The second commitment involved teaching people how to file complaints at police departments. We wanted to ensure that the police arrested people for crimes, so that they wouldn't remain free like George Zimmerman. At the time, I believed that's what justice required. And finally, the third breakout group helped individuals draft pacts toward peace and relationship building in their community. We asked questions like, do *you know every neighbor on your block? What are good ways to meet them?* At the end of the meeting, we decided that Watch4KC would prioritize deescalating fights among the teens at the Plaza and intervene if law enforcement tried to arrest them. An elder Black man condemned this decision. He didn't like that a racial justice movement was becoming about fixing Black-on-Black crime. His plea prompted pushback and did not change the decision, though it had a lasting impact on me. So for that summer, that's what we did. Deescalated fights; monitored the movie theaters to keep crowds cool; even talked police out of arresting Black boys out past curfew.

I think about that elder's comments when I hear critics of abolition suggest that Black activists just want to hate cops or that we do not care about community-based violence. It's ironic because most of the Black abolitionists I know now came together in 2012 to plead with the police to do what we thought their job was: arrest George Zimmerman for killing Trayvon. That's how I met Charlene Carruthers, who one year later became a founding member of queer, feminist grassroots organization Black Youth Project 100. Carruthers went to Florida to support the Dream Defenders capitol takeover; there she reunited with DD leader Phil Agnew, her elementary schoolmate from Chicago. We were all trying to get the police and prosecutors to do what their job was: secure justice for victims. Watch4KC literally brainstormed ways to make sure that police made arrests, especially for murders in Black communities. We also practiced trying to keep our neighborhoods calm through community-based intervention. But the elder was right. We were mixing up solutions to very different problems.

I EXPECTED THE protests to send Zimmerman to prison, and more importantly, send a warning to white men that would save Black kids' lives. Police eventually arrested George Zimmerman. We felt like we had won. We wept. By fall 2012, it had happened again. Michael Dunn, a white man, reached into his glove compartment and shot indiscriminately into a car that carried Jordan Davis and his friends. Dunn was upset because the Black boys were playing what he called "rap crap." Davis died that day in Florida. Dunn went to his hotel and ordered a pizza.

My belief that Black kids had to be good to survive mistreatment and violence still lingered. Davis's murder erased what remained. Jordan had two present parents and lived a comfortable middle-class life. His grandparents worked in the medical field and owned an African American newspaper. His mom is college educated, a member of Delta Sigma Theta, and had careers in politics and airlines. Jordan's dad had turned down a job with the FBI and had become a regional manager of operations for Delta Airlines, where he worked for decades. He was retired and enjoyed playing video games with Jordan and doing important dad duties, like taking the door to Jordan's room off the hinges after catching a girl in there. This was the kind of Black boy whom I least expected to be gunned down. Not because his life was more valuable than the boys in the Jena Six. But because I assumed that upward social mobility kept us relatively safe. It did not, no more than a having a Black man ascend to the highest office in the country had protected us from police violence, deportations, and dying on the execution table.[32]

I was teaching math at a middle school at the time and became conflicted when telling my students that they could break a cycle of violence and poverty solely by going to college.

This was a major Teach for America mantra—to give every kid in poverty an excellent education. Like with every other educational program I encountered, kids did not just need an excellent education. They needed resources and the elimination of poverty. Overcoming barriers could provide individual social mobility, but it did not keep them safe from violence nor eliminate poverty. I wasn't sure whether my well-meaning teacher colleagues understood this, and I started to feel even lonelier than I already did. I had much more in common with my students than my peers. At any moment, the police, racists, or community members could kill me, my students, and our loved ones. My colleagues felt like witnesses; we felt like targets. During the summer of 2013, I decided to start studying to take the entrance exams for law school, just in case the law could provide more protection for us than education.

That summer, Michael Dunn was in jail and George Zimmerman's trial started. Unlike during the execution proceedings for Troy Davis, President Obama did address Trayvon Martin's death. The mainstream media coverage centered on his comments that Trayvon could have been his son, and that if the boy had been a white teenager, then the outcome and aftermath might have been different. Though what he said next alarmed me: "I think it's understandable that there have been demonstrations and vigils and protests, and some of that stuff is just going to have to work its way through, as long as it remains nonviolent. If I see any violence, then I will remind folks that that dishonors what happened to Trayvon Martin and his family. But beyond protests or vigils, the question is, are there some concrete things that we might be able to do."[33]

Obama's comments were audacious. The US government repeatedly used the deaths of Americans as an excuse to act violently toward people, organizations, and entire nations. Why didn't he honor the dead by telling police and military to not act violently? I found it contradictory that Obama was not practicing what he had been preaching. Here we were as activists, passing around petitions and organizing rallies and sitting-in and praying because a Black boy was killed. Our activism was belittled as "stuff" that needed to "work its way through." Additionally, Obama did not remind white people to not racially pro-file, nor kill, but quite paternalistically, he warned Black people, us, the targets, to remain nonviolent in the face of our demise. Per his own account, the protests were already nonviolent, but still, he felt compelled to scold us for the *potential* of being disruptive. And once again, we listened.

During Zimmerman's trial, I protested and watched and read and sweated and missed meals and cried and journaled and prayed for justice for Trayvon. Back then, justice meant that George Zimmerman had to be convicted and imprisoned. In July 2013, my two friends Luisa and LaShay came from New York to visit me in Boston while I was completing a fellowship at Harvard. We had just left the movie theaters and were still laughing at Kevin Hart's jokes from his latest film. Now, outside, we heard people screaming in the Boston Common. I pulled out my phone.

George Zimmerman had been found "not guilty."

My mother's face and number replaced the news alert on the small screen in my hand. Before I could force a hello through my tears, she asked, "What you gon' do? You gon' cry or you gon' fight?" I wanted to do both. She had witnessed all that I went through to plan the rally, to get petitions signed and people acti-vated, all in the name of "justice" for Trayvon. Jurors denied it, and President Obama encouraged the mournful onlookers to accept the jury's decision in silence. My mother already knew that her six Black children were vulnerable in the United States, and she had little expectation of the courts to do the right thing. What she did not know on the day of the verdict was that I was pregnant.

Luisa and LaShay did not know either.

"Derecka, you okay, sis?" Luisa asked. I was desperately trying to fake it through our dinner at Legal Sea Foods. I'm an Aries' Aries. Big personality, care-taker, a natural host to company. I can be really funny and spontaneous because I was raised by a comedian. I sat eerily silent during our meal. "I'm sorry. We found out that we were expecting a little one last week." I should not have said it. There's an unwritten rule that people are supposed to make it through the first trimester before telling anyone. But I was in Boston, terrified, alone, and angry. Would we be able to protect our children? Would we be able to protect ourselves?

IN THE FALL of 2013, after the verdict, I decided to apply to law school. Dreams from my high school years were simultaneously shattering and actualizing. Shattering because racial tragedy forced me to reckon with the limits of education as a salvific force in the face of white supremacy. Actualizing because maybe, through the law, I could learn how to protect people from their peers, police, prosecutors, and white supremacists. By then, the public was preparing for Michael Dunn's trial. Activists challenged the coverage because pundits kept calling them the "Trayvon Martin case" and "Jordan Davis case," when neither boy was on trial. Media eventually resorted to using the "loud music case" for Dunn.

On February 15, 2014, a week after I was admitted to Harvard Law School, a jury found Dunn guilty on three counts of attempted murder, one for each of Jordan's friends in the car. Jurors could not reach an agreement on whether he was guilty of first-degree murder when he killed Jordan. The judge declared a mistrial on that count. I wrote a letter to my unborn child:[34]

> Dear Son,
> You are literally moments from being with us, so I want to let you know this before you arrive:
> Since we've been expecting you, two men have been on popular trials for murdering Black boys. One found not guilty; the other found "kinda guilty and kinda not." Countless other trials have occurred for your other brothers and sisters, but they have not received the same deserved attention.
> However, I want you to know this: people are fighting so that you will have the luxury of being a child. You will be able to wear hoodies in any neighborhood. You will not have to turn your music down because you are afraid of being killed. You will do more than "survive." You will live.
> You will play. Make mistakes. Grow. Advocate.
> Most of all, you will learn to love—even learn to love the men on trial for taking life. It won't be easy, but it will be worth it.
> Can't wait to meet you.

Three days later, I delivered Geuce.

TWO

FIRST WE WERE FREE

IN THE SUMMER of 2014, after I gave birth, we lived in a modest dorm at Sophia's Heart on a mostly empty wing. Sophia's Heart provides transitional living for homeless families in Nashville. Tennessee has the highest share of vacant houses in the country. Due to racism, segregation, and exploitation, Sophia's Heart residents could not afford one. Grandon and I could not afford a place to stay for the summer, so we gave the organization most of our savings, five hundred dollars, to stay and offered to volunteer. During the day, I was conducting research for the Tennessee Department of Education (TDOE) to revise the state's funding allocation for rural and urban schools. In the evenings and on weekends, I took on random volunteering tasks and met with families who shared their stories of abuse and neglect, tragedy and hope. Sophia's Heart specifically catered to families because they had a hard time finding shelters that could accept them all. Individuals and small families sometimes floated among bedrooms, couches, basements, shelters, to train stations, and tents. I knew personally how easily this rotation could happen because my family had gone through it after we were forced out of our home on Hickory.[35]

Nashville was a familiar place. My brother and I took road trips with our Uncle Phil nearly every year because my maternal grandfather was from there and most of his family remained. Many of them were middle to upper middle class Black people who owned funeral homes or sold real estate or had retired from the military. I always felt especially Midwestern during holiday visits there because the southern scenes were magical. In St. Louis, we'd hang out on our porches and sing songs by Earth, Wind & Fire, trash talking Black people who thought they were better than us because they moved from the city to less poor suburbs like Jennings, Normandy, and Ferguson. But in Nashville, my family would gather around the piano, almost in the general tenor of a show tune, and recount over evening desserts which white planter owned which Black family in which Tennessee county.

My grandfather, William, was a brilliant and complicated person who brought my family laughter and pain. At sixteen, he had learned to fly small planes. Black people marveled at his flight, white people wanted to shoot him down. Like my brother, he knew that the system was rigged against poor, Black people and he rebelled against his stern, religious father. I never knew how my grandfather landed in St. Louis until one trip down, I decided to interview my family about our history. They sat around my Uncle Andrew's dining room and told me that William, a veteran, took a pair of crooked dice to a military base in Washington and hustled some soldiers out of two thousand and eight hundred dollars. The soldiers realized they'd been swindled and called the police. Cops did not put him in jail, but they pocketed the cash and made him walk home from the cold northwest back south. He worked on sheep ranches along the way in exchange for food and a place to sleep.

He was terribly sick and frostbitten when he finally stumbled into Nashville. Freemasons checked him into a hospital for recovery until he healed. Freemasons were highly esteemed members of a secretive mutual aid society. When my grandfather's health improved, they handed him to the police. Cops had been searching for him over outstanding child support payments. My aunt said during the interview, "Back then, they didn't just put you in jail, they put you on the County Road and you worked the road." She was describing a "workhouse," jails where people were forced to labor as punishment. The guard who supervised William happened to live behind my grandfather's family house. Labor on the county road was so savagely violent that the guard begged my great-grandfather to get William out of jail. My great-grandfather was a Freemason and spoke with the judge, who was presumably in the society, too. With the additional advocacy of William's first wife, the judge freed him. William fled to St. Louis to avoid rearrest. There, he met my grandmother, Virginia. My aunt did not see him for forty-three years. Had he stayed home, he might have not lived, and I might not be alive.

The crooked dice and the missed child support payments were related. When my grandfather was in the military, his first wife birthed my aunt, and he briefly went AWOL because he wanted to stay home to help her with the baby. Soldiers raided my family's home looking for him, and he eventually went back and was honorably discharged (I once got in trouble for unfolding the American flag that draped his casket). Yet the need for resources remained. By the time he was gambling and hustling, and then turned in over child support payments, he still did not have much. Yet he could have died in a workhouse because the state criminalized his survival. Slavery as punishment for a crime is permissible under the US Constitution, and the county government profited from my grandfather's slave labor on the county roads. His family, however, did not receive a dime from the punishment or from the government to help with the child support payments. My grandfather's incarceration additionally prevented him from earning money elsewhere *and* inhibited his ability to work later because of a criminal record. This probably exacerbated his gambling, which he did heavily by the time he moved into my mother's basement in 1996, decades after he left Nashville. Racism, exploitation, and the law constrains freedom, and forces people to escape its reach. Who knows what kind of parent or pilot he could have been without the violence of the Jim Crow south. When he took his first commercial flight as an older man, he said in awe to the passenger next to him, "This plane is a big son'a'bitch, ain't it?"

AT THE COMPLETION of my research fellowship in Nashville, I traveled back to Kansas City full from the time with my family and wondering what the rest of the summer would bring. I was organizing an educational empowerment conference for Black and brown middle and high school girls called "No Boys Allowed." This convening was supposed to be the culmination of my education organizing in the Midwest. I was excited to start my mini farewell tour before leaving for Harvard Law School in the fall of 2014. St. Louis is where I grew up, but Kansas City was where I became a wife, mother, and educator. I had plans to meet up with all of my friends before I left, but by the time I made it to one of their homes, the news was on. A cop had killed a Black teenage boy in St. Louis, around the corner from my aunt's house. And people were protesting.

Friends were texting me if I was coming home and I was eager to go back and help. Grandon and I were supposed to drive to St. Louis at some point anyway because we needed to move our furniture to Cambridge; our furniture was occupying a bright orange Public Storage container on West Florissant Avenue in Ferguson. We did not know the street would be the primary site of the uprising and mostly occupied by the police. We cut our trip to Kansas City short and drove back home to protest.

Darren Wilson shot and killed Michael Brown on August 9, 2014, on Canfield Drive. The Ferguson Police Department left his body on the pavement for more than four hours in the scorching heat.[36]

Out of all of the places in the United States where I thought a white cop would kill a Black kid at the time, I would not have guessed Ferguson. Maybe I was naive to assume that murderous racial violence in my era was relegated to the South, especially Florida. Or that police killings were coastal, Sean Bell to the east, Oscar Grant to the west. Videos of Black death weren't going viral on a regular basis on the internet. Before 2014, I didn't feel anxious about a cop killing me. I had other anxieties like facing arrests, tickets, fines, and warrants. These regular acts were also violent and extractive because local police departments funded themselves through an elaborate ticketing scheme. Bullets can kill fast; however, the power of police chips away at poor people's time, finances, and health. We hated driving through the county because their police cars stalked us. Friends would argue about whether the back roads or the highways would be safer from the police, rather than taking the normal routes to drive home. *County Brown bad out there!* Avoiding police sometimes determined what kinds of cars some of us would buy, who could ride with us, who couldn't. One Christmas, my aunt asked her daughters whether they had visited their brother in jail. They had not. My cousins said they did not want to risk getting pulled over by the county police and spend the holidays locked up, too.

Michael Brown was not driving that day. Wilson says he stopped Brown because he was jaywalking. Many streets in Ferguson lack sidewalks altogether and we have to walk on the road. The streets are more comfortable for walking and using a wheelchair because some sidewalks are extremely skinny. Tree roots and grass grow between the cracks as the Earth frees itself from the uneven concrete. A witness said Wilson cursed at Brown and his friend Dorian to get out of the street; Wilson testified that he asked politely. Politeness or not, everything about the encounter was wrong, from the poorly designed sidewalks in a Black neighborhood, to the criminalization of jaywalking. Black residents poured into the streets because they had used those same streets and anyone of us could have been arrested, ticketed, or killed. We chanted, "Whose streets? Our streets!"

There were constant crowds on Canfield Drive—everyone wanted to see the memorial. We all greeted one another. Residents from the apartment complex stood tense on their porches and balconies. The tanks arrived, too. St. Louis summers are humid, and uprising thickened the air. The billowing tear gas clouds that the police fired each night lingered in the next morning's dew. I worried about neighborhood residents breathing in the fumes and felt compelled to act.

First, I started interviewing residents who lived near the uprising sites to ask them what they needed. I approached a woman as she exited her SUV. She lived in a house a few blocks away from the memorial site. I could see the fatigue plague her eyes and body; she said her children couldn't sleep—scared from the shouting, the sirens, the canister explosions. "It's the right thing," she said, "but people just keep coming."

She and her neighbors wanted justice for Michael Brown, and they also wanted the noise to stop, to be able to drive home at predictable hours, and for their kids to go to school. Surrounding school districts delayed opening due to the protests and parents were left with few options to school their kids. Around the same time, a group of Black educators, politicians, students, and activists started meeting to respond to the community's immediate needs. I joined them, and we called ourselves the Young Citizens Council of St. Louis (YCC). Our membership included rapper and activist Tef Poe, educator Brittany Packnett, human rights lawyer Justin Hansford, St. Louis politician Tishaura Jones, educator Charlie Cooksey, and several students from Harris-Stowe State University. I'd gone to church with Brittany when I was in high school and reconnected later when I found out she also did Teach for America. The day Michael was killed, she was keynoting my conference in Kansas City. Together with YCC, we spent weeks planning rallies, recruiting volunteers to teach kids in the libraries, and issuing demands, including calling for the police to stop tear-gassing and assaulting protesters.

A shadow of guilt grew stronger over me each night of protest. I was supposed to drive to Cambridge at some point for law school orientation. I was planning to feel celebratory in the face of the obstacles I had tackled to arrive at this place in my life. Instead, I felt very small. Black people were under attack and law school felt more like another obstacle than an accomplishment. Standing underneath a repurposed pump at the reclaimed QuikTrip, I looked around and started to feel empowered. QuikTrip became a hub for protesters, local residents, clergy, step teams, burgeoning activists, and elders working the cooling stations. Activists brought food, water, and campaign literature to pass out. My aunt who lived nearby did not come out to the protests, but she attended the church meetings and picked up trash the mornings after. Major news networks set up large white tents on the grass and parked their vans just a few yards away. There I met Jelani Cobb, a writer for *The New Yorker*, who told me that in New York City, there was a protest every week. He scanned the crowd, uttering, "These are some regular ass Black folk rising up." He talked about Ferguson in a special way, the way I felt about Jena, Louisiana.

How could I leave all of this, right now?

I waited until the very last minute to leave because I was deciding whether or not I should go law school. Brittany Packnett told me that I must. Nobody in our group knew that I was going to law school until Brittany spoke up, and then Justin, a law professor, agreed with her. All of this organizing, he reassured me, was not going to die down overnight because, unfortunately, the police will continue to kill our people until we have deep systemic change. He explained that we needed lawyers committed to fighting police violence for the long haul. He was right. Before we left, the police had already killed another person in St. Louis—Kajieme Powell.

HOUSES IN CAMBRIDGE were colorfully paneled and tall. The big blue house on Sacramento Street had fooled me. With the seismic loans I needed to pay for living, I thought that the entire home would be ours with room for the baby and dog in tow. But when I walked through the front door, I saw three more doors. I used to tease my friend Luisa that Brooklyn landlords would chop up normal-sized houses into five closets and advertise them as "cute and cozy" studios. Now I was unpacking boxes in a bite-sized apartment renting for almost two thousand dollars a month. Our living quarters shrank and the rent quadrupled.

Tennessee introduced me to white-concentrated poverty, Cambridge introduced me to white-concentrated wealth. On my way to white rural communities to learn about the resources they needed for their students, I rode by trailer parks outside Nashville that I had only seen before on television shows like *Cops*. Months later, I was entering a law school where a student placed her gently used Chanel bag in our buy, trade, sell social media page for five thousand dollars—a steal at that price. I could not say confidently whether anyone in my immediate family ever had that much money in their bank account at one time. Certainly not me. This is partially why I was in disbelief when President Obama lectured Black boys about their spending habits at a 2019 summit. He told them, "If you are really confident about your financial situation, you are probably not going to be wearing an eight-pound chain around your neck." When I was attending the president's alma mater, nobody wore thick gold chains to show off their wealth. They wore thin ones to match their David Yurman bracelets. I had originally thought the Canada Goose down coats were uniforms for people in a service corps because the signature patches were displayed everywhere. Harvard was the first place where I saw a Rolex. I wonder if it was the same model as the fifteen-thousand-dollar Rolex that Mr. Obama wears in the striking Kehinde Wiley painting of him in the National Portrait Gallery.[37]

At Harvard, wealth was displayed through coats, cuffs, Chanel bags, number of homes, and investments. But the students' and professors' bodies conveyed wealth, too. It bought insurance, nannies, access to clean air, and more time to live. My grandmother was in a fetid elderly facility; my wealthy white professors her age still lectured. Afterward, they would become emeriti, live second and third lives in the classroom, on committees, and travel. And in death, be immortalized through buildings and portraits of their own.

At orientation, the dean welcomed the class by saying that Harvard was not simply a law school, but a "justice school." I immediately filled with hope because that's exactly what I came to law school seeking: justice. But I did not find any justice in the hundreds of pages I read each night for class. Nor was it in any of the lectures I attended. My professor taught property without discussing the ownership of Black bodies under capitalist bondage or fully accounting for Indigenous land theft. Rather, he emphasized that white people weren't the only ones starting the fights between them and Native Americans. None of my core classes accounted for the creation of the slave patrols and police to control property, enforce labor and break up worker strikes, and increase protection for the US border. A movement against police violence was pounding at the doors and professors overwhelmingly stuck religiously to the script of the syllabus.

I didn't find Harvard Justice School, but I did find people looking for justice, too. Activists on and off campus were organizing against police violence and I quickly found myself disrupting traffic to do die-ins on the cold concrete roads in Harvard Square. We organized rallies, marches, and protests. I belonged to a multi-racial social justice collective that organized under "Harvard Ferguson Action Committee." We organized direct actions and served as legal observers at protests in different cities. For "Ferguson October," students arranged bus rides to Ferguson. Some were jailed. Others bailed people out. Back on campus, we taped the last words of police victims on the portraits of professors that lined the hall—all while still reading for class, representing clients in court, and taking care of our families back home. The movement against police violence happening outside of the halls of Harvard brought us together in the halls where Harvard University Police Department stopped some of us because we were Black on campus. They patrolled our loud protests and our silent candlelight vigils. Once, I was studying late during finals in Wasserstein Hall and an obviously bored Black guard approached me for some action. I was wearing my University of California, Berkeley sweatshirt and surrounded by piles of books from my trial advocacy class. He demanded to see my student identification card. When I handed the plastic rectangle card to him and asked why, he said that he needed to make sure that I was not homeless.

Campus police and street police are different strands of the same supremacy that plague our resistance. Black men shared anecdotes in class and school meetings about being stopped and carded by the police in Harvard, Cambridge, Somerville, and the worst—Boston. My classmate Jon Wall jokingly called Boston "Atlanta for White People." When I told my mother I was moving nearby for law school, she asked, "Is it bad there, too?" I automatically knew she was talking about racism. I should have wondered, *"Is what bad? The weather? Traffic?"*

In other cities, police stops were reportedly more widespread. For example, in New York City, Black and Latinx men were stopped nine times more than white men. In 2011, the New York Police Department stopped and frisked more Black men aged fourteen to twenty-four in New York City than the total number of Black men between those ages who lived in the city. Between 2009 and 2012, NYPD made more than 2.4 million stops in the name of public safety. The state attorney general found that 0.3% of stops led to jail sentences longer than thirty days and "0.1% led to convictions for violent crime." James Baldwin writes about NYPD stops decades earlier in his 1962 *Letter From A Region in My Mind:*[38]

> I was thirteen and was crossing Fifth Avenue on my way to the Forty-second Street library, and the cop in the middle of the street muttered as I passed him, "Why don't you niggers stay uptown where you belong?" When I was ten, and didn't look, certainly, any older, two policemen amused themselves with me by frisking me, making comic (and terrifying) speculations concerning my ancestry and probable sexual prowess, and, for good measure, leaving me flat on my back in one of Harlem's empty lots.[39]

The gripping violence against the younger Baldwin happened to others like him for centuries before his birth and for decades after. Phrases like "stop and frisk" and "racial profiling" obscure the details and reduce the violence to police *practices*, rather than a function integral to policing itself. A stop and frisk is not simply either. It's the spreading of the legs and the groping of the thighs and genitals, without consent. Because cops overwhelmingly grope poor Black and Brown men, I didn't think about it as gender-based violence or sexual violence, but it is both. If we choose to defend ourselves and protect our bodies, then cops have the power to escalate the violence to an arrest. The number of stops and how often police profile are likely underreported, yet they cannot account for the constant threat of either's occurrence. And therein lies the function of policing. It's not just the number of times we're pulled over or the number of bodily violations or how many shootings occur each year, but that at any moment, any number of unpredictable forms of violence will attempt to control our freedom.

BEFORE I UNDERSTOOD police abolition, racial profiling was the predominate mainstream critique that I had learned about police. I'd been condemning racial profiling at least since the anti-immigrant law in Arizona and organizing against it under Watch4KC. In the early days of Dream Defenders, before the membership started learning and organizing around abolition and socialism, the group heavily advocated for Trayvon's Law, a set of laws to end racial profiling, repeal Stand Your Ground, create police oversight boards and additional training, and mandate that police collect homicide data. Before the Ferguson Uprising, the Black Youth Project 100 (BYP100) launched a #CriminalizedLives campaign to highlight the criminalization and racial profiling of Black youth after a cop at Princeton University pulled over a group of their members and falsely explained that they had a taillight that was out. BYP100 released a statement that read, "There are certainly many police officers that carry out their duties with honor and integrity. Sadly, there are numerous law enforcement officials who continue to criminalize and abuse Black youth through racial profiling, abuse and unlawful arrest." The NAACP expressed a similar sentiment about the *practice* of racial profiling: "[T]he most effective tool for law enforcement has always been to focus on suspicious behavior and credible information about specific crimes and specific suspects—not the way that someone looks." It was as if law enforcement was a neutral institution to stop crime, and cops who used racial profiling were deviating from their crime-stopping duties too often to harass Black kids.[40]

So many of us once shared similar beliefs as young, Black activists earnestly trying to find justice in a horrible system. Before we began studying abolition, many of us tried to improve the system, too. Yet our understanding of police was inaccurate for various reasons, including our unexamined ideas about the histories of policing, capitalism, and colonization. And if people who care about ending police violence aren't careful, we could miss the forest for the trees. Racial profiling, stop and frisk, implicit bias are all timber. The terrain upon which policing exists is treacherous.

I wanted to understand the forest. For almost every class where I had a paper, I read, researched, and wrote about the police. Activists informally shared progressive historical articles and critiques of police with each other and I attended events where academics kept discussing the "Black Radical Tradition." What I gathered from these readings and events was that just because Black people were using language that invoked "freedom" and "justice" to talk about police, it didn't mean that we all wanted the same outcomes. There were traditions where Black people who had wealth and status wanted to increase the legitimacy of police because they marginally benefited from police protection. Other kinds of Black people wanted police to improve because they believed that we deserved equal protection under the law as citizens. And then I found that lots of people in Black radical tradition who refused both. They argued that cops were *created* in a history of oppression to maintain inequality. Viral videos of police shootings were not a deviation of that history; it was the most recent iteration of it.

The history of policing that I became most interested in did not start with cops, but with freedom. The people who suffer the most from police violence descend from peoples who were once free from it. Border creation and patrol in response to Indigenous and Mexicans are just one example. It is similarly true for people of African descent. To make the slave trade possible, capitalists, the owners of the companies that profited from slave labor, paid people to catch, kidnap, purchase, and kill people who were free. The various free peoples of Africa did not willingly skip to the ships to be transported across the Atlantic, so the Portuguese, Dutch, Spanish, French, and English developed and refined many tools, tactics, and practices of subordination to create and maintain slavery, including policing. Because Africans were free, they had to be trapped. Because Africans ran away, new cuffs had to be designed to hold their hands, shackle their necks, and link their ankles. Because Africans fought with weapons, Europeans had to use more powerful ones. Because Africans hid, Europeans had to develop bands to search for them. And because Africans constantly planned rebellions and revolts on the way over, Europeans at the top of the ship had to develop systems of patrols, surveillance, caging, and even African informants to hold the Black bodies at the bottom of the ships. In his comprehensive study of ship revolts, Eric Robert Taylor found that nearly a quarter of ship insurrections resulted in the freedom of at least some of the bondspeople. But success is relative. There were more than thirty-six thousand slave trading voyages between Africa and the new Americas, and thousands more between the ports in the Americas. Scholars explain that without the ship rebellions, Europeans would have transported even more Africans than the millions that they did.[41]

Slave resistance was integral to protect one's freedom, and these revolts informed the earliest forms of policing among ship crewmembers, overseers, the general white population, and slave patrols. In many cases, as soon as the ships landed in the Caribbean, Africans continued plotting their resistance and escapes. Professors Tyler Wall and David Correia explain that the etymology of "cop" likely comes from Middle French *caper*, meaning to capture, or Latin, *capere*, "to seize, to grasp." As early as the 1530s, bands of Spanish catchers in modern day Cuba formed to pillage the Indigenous inhabitants and seize Africans who ran away from enslavement. A similar phenomenon happened in North America, too. Most schoolchildren learn that the Jamestown Colony was the first permanent settlement in the land that became the United States. More accurately, it was the first English permanent colony. Political scientist and Black studies professor Cedric Robinson writes in *Black Movements in America* that more than eighty years before Jamestown, Spaniards brought one hundred enslaved Africans with them to the Carolinas. The slaves rebelled and fled to safety in Indigenous tribes, and the Spaniards who failed to quell them and left for the Caribbean. These African maroons who freed themselves remained with the Indigenous tribes and became the first permanent settlement of non-Native people in North America.[42]

As freedom dreams and uprisings spread throughout the newly forming colonies, so did repression. Capitalists, people who were profiting from slavery on cotton, sugar, and tobacco crops, were sponsoring the invention of new rules, tools, practices, and institutions to discipline, catch, and punish the African and Indigenous rebels. Crewmembers and overseers usually implemented and enforced the rules—and added their own violent tricks to compel the person at the tip of the whip to obey. Although these overseers and patrols were not technically "police officers," they were their predecessors and inform the culture of policing. As long as European settlers have been in contact with Indigenous and African people in the Americas, the former have policed the latter, keeping them at the bottom of the newly forming racial order.

Caribbean revolts were bloody and riotous, and reverberated fear or inspiration throughout the colonies depending on which end of the whip someone was on. More than a hundred years after the slave trade began, a Carolinian congressman noted that one hundred West Indian negroes were scarier than ten thousand Africans. English slavers in Barbados and other parts of the Caribbean learned how to repress resistance from the Spanish, who had been patrolling and catching runaways for decades before them. Maroons and runaways waged attacks on the English, French, and Spanish who enslaved, beat, raped, sold, and killed Africans. Determined to be free and stop the violence against them, they'd burn houses and slaughtered the owners to prevent re-enslavement. Other slaves resisted oppression through slowing down their labor production, helping others flee, and poisonings their owners. The aftermath of the Caribbean slave resistance forced Europeans to escape.[43]

When I think about refugees who flee violence, I think about my childhood friends in St. Louis from Somalia and Ethiopia who left everything they had behind for protection, or the Central American migrants attempting to cross the border in Mexico to flee violence. But following slave revolts, white people in North America often treated the English slavers fleeing slave revolts in the Caribbean like refugees. Different cities had different laws about whether "persecuted" slave owners could bring their slaves with them. They did not want word and stories about resistance spreading among the plantations in the South, so sometimes local governments banned refugees from bringing slaves with them.

South Carolina was a primary destination for slave traders, owners, and white people who resettled from the Caribbean during the sixteenth century. Historians explain that this is why some of the earliest forms of policing in the United States originate there. Half of all Europeans living in South Carolina came from Barbados. They brought knowledge of the slave patrol systems that were instituted on the islands during the 1600s. Their property and workers, the Africans, brought knowledge of the revolts and resistance. South Carolina, which boasted a booming slave economy, followed Barbados and consequently codified a policing system that included slave patrols, a militia, and new sets of laws called "slave codes" that controlled when, where, why, and how Black people could move.[44]

Historian Sally Hadden explains that sometimes, English landowners were so desperate to stop slave revolts, prevent Indigenous resistance, and ward off attacks from the Spanish in Florida that they made the whites who managed plantations in the colonies start arming slaves. White people in the colonies expressed widespread opposition to putting Black people and Indigenous peoples in the militia; they wanted to enslave both groups. The English proprietors made the colonies put slaves in the militias anyway, until a slave rebellion in 1720. Many of the earliest gun control laws in the colonies and United States were a result of armed Black resistance.[45]

Nevertheless, Black people continued to rebel in the quest for their freedom. White people feared rebellion and the threat of it so much because it destroyed their lives, property, and money. Policing in South Carolina consequently required a united front to stop Black people. In the late 1600s, officials there legally mandated that every white man between sixteen and sixty to join the militia, and legally empowered every white person to arrest, punish, and return runaways. White civilians were not only encouraged to monitor and control Black people, but were *required* to do so—sometimes under the threat of being fined. The government criminalized people for *not* policing. As slavery spread, resistance spread, and these policing duties transcended geography and, ultimately, time. Policing was not just found in the formal duties of the patrol and the militias, but also in the lives of everyday white people to control subordinate populations whose freedom threatened their lives, property, and ego. I was learning that white people had been historically conditioned to control the behaviors of others, from the white woman who grabbed me at the Kris Kobach rally in Kansas to George Zimmerman when he stalked Trayvon Martin and Michael Dunn when he killed Jordan Davis; from the white people who held their guns to Black Hurricane Katrina survivors to the armed militias who patrol the Arizona border.

But—the best feature of social conditioning is that the power and impulses to control others are not natural or innate. There are traditions where white people refused this power and practice and instead sided with rebellious Black and Indigenous peoples to end slavery, capitalism, and colonialism. John Brown conspired with free and enslaved Black people to overthrow the institution of slavery. When England brought their colonized subjects, the Irish, to the islands as enslaved and indentured servants, many Irish joined enslaved Blacks in planning rebellions. Black people exploited colonial wars to get free, siding when they could with the side that offered emancipation. Enslaved Africans joined forces with France and Spain, colonial enemies of England, to plot and rebel for their freedom. On the mainland, Spanish settlers and Native Americans helped Black runaways escape to Florida. Black people ran away from northern cities like New York to French territory in Canada. Later, during the Revolutionary War, Black people joined the British to destroy America because the former promised emancipation. The various European nations did not always necessarily side with Black people for moral reasons. Most of them were still actively enslaving Black people and colonizing in other parts of the Americas. Just like there are different traditions of Black resistance, there are different traditions of how white people actively or indifferently perpetuated oppression, and different traditions of how white people tried to destroy it.[46]

For this reason, I decided to try to remember the fact that people were free, and that slavery and colonization were choices. Not chosen by the enslaved and the colonized as Kanye West unfortunately suggested in 2018, but chosen by the enslavers, capitalists, and the colonizers. The length and scope of slavery and colonization were not inevitable. Yet, instead of ending these practices after facing so much resistance and rebellion, the colonizers doubled down on slavery and land theft, and invested in more patrols, police, imprisonment, and surveillance to protect capitalism over human life. For example, European-based business owners created North Carolina by incentivizing white settlers to move there; they encouraged "the bringing in of slaves by offering grants of land, not in excess of fifty acres, to bona fide settlers for each imported able-bodied slave above the age of fourteen." Adding more white people to the area, they believed, would offset threats of Black and Indigenous raids and rebellions. Larger planters received more, and this required a greater system of policing and patrols to monitor the growing potential for revolt. In his classic text, *Black Reconstruction in America*, W. E. B. Du Bois describes the labor of bondspeople and the exploitation of the white worker as an economic rivalry that the latter overcame through jobs as police:[47]

It would have seemed natural that the poor white would have refused to police the slaves. But two considerations led him in the opposite direction. First of all, it gave him work and some authority as an overseer, slave driver, and member of the patrol system. But above and beyond this, it fed his vanity because it associated him with the masters . . . Gradually, the whole white South became an armed commissioned camp to keep Negroes in slavery and to kill the black rebel.[48]

The freedom of the enslaved meant losing a subjugated class of laborers that capitalists exploited for wealth. Freedom also meant the loss of jobs for the thousands of white overseers who received a small wage to control the slaves. These sets of economic arrangements and exploitations built the foundation of the United States, England, the Netherlands, France, Spain, and Portugal, and additionally, as historian Walter Rodney teaches, undermined the development of Africa's land, resources, and people. Police, overseers, militias, and free whites were not solely patrolling Black people because of race. They had to prevent losing a valuable labor source. There was so much invested in slavery—profits, industries, jobs, status—that its abolition seemed unlikely, impossible, and not worthwhile for many people who wanted to preserve it.[49]

The people who policed the slaves, as Du Bois explained, were not slave owners and often quite poor. White planters with means or luck could pay to opt out of their patrol duties, and the patrol gradually shifted to a more systematic policing system, mostly employing poor white workers. During arrests, patrols used weapons and canines to chase down runaways, like today. Lawmakers even tried to reform them by passing regulations to control and limit slave patrols' use of force to forty or fifty lashes instead of significantly more. In North Carolina, officials divided patrols into districts, permitting them to raid slave quarters to search for weapons and report their findings to the court. Raids and search warrants were not simply modern police practices. This was policing.[50]

All of this history started to shape my uninterrogated assumptions that we needed police "to stop the bad guys." Because South Carolina and soon the country made resistance, rebellion, and running away illegal, Black people *were* the bad guys. The difference between what's legal and illegal is not the behavior of the lawbreaker; it is the interests of the powerful people who create the law *and* have control of the police to enforce it. Under slavery, lawmakers sent a message and patrols enforced it: if you run, or try, you will be returned, punished, put to work, or put to death. Thus, flight from the plantations was forbidden and illegal, and yet, many Black people ran away, stole from their slavers, fought off catchers, created fraudulent identities, and for the ones who made it to free territories, lived as fugitives. Modern police, as it turned out, were not simply deviating from their jobs. They had centuries of influence that built habits of surveilling, monitoring, and capturing people, especially Black and Indigenous peoples, who disproportionately suffer police arrests, killings, and imprisonment now.

THE CIVIL WAR provided more opportunities for many enslaved Black people to escape and find refuge in Union Army camps. The Confederate Army drafted patrols, overseers, and slave owners, decreasing the available labor supply for slave repression. With overseers and patrols in the military, new sources of patrol had to learn a balancing act: use violence to keep unfree Blacks in their place, but don't damage their bodies too much to devalue them. And, harrowingly, when some slave owners went off to fight to preserve slavery, they expected their slaves to protect their white families on the plantation.[51]

Hadden explains that slave patrols were supposed to cease at the close of the Civil War, but some remained, and others morphed into or merged with police departments for southern cities. However, she suggests that the "violent aspects were taken up by vigilante groups like the Ku Klux Klan." This is partially true. The Reconstruction Era was a progressive time period entangled in democratic and anti-democratic practices to stop racial terror. In 1871, a Black Union loyalty club converted to a militia of free Black veterans who protected themselves from white violence and killed KKK members who had threatened them and burned a Black church. White mobs and the KKK were pro-power, not necessarily pro-police, and contested the power of Black people who were elected to run local police departments and jails. Black cops who resisted were punished. But these vigilante groups also often shared membership with white police departments. During and following Reconstruction, police joined, supported, or refused to intervene in violence from the Klan and other racist vigilante mobs. *Our Enemies in Blue* author Kristian Williams explains that while there were some cops who genuinely tried to stop racist vigilante violence, "arrests were unusual, prosecutions rare, and convictions almost unknown." Citing historian Melinda Hennessey, Williams offers accounts of police-led violence:

> In only three riots, including Mobile in 1867, Vicksburg in 1875, and Charleston in 1867, did the police or sheriff try to quell the disturbance, and in a third of the riots, the police or sheriff's posse led the violence.[52]

Thus, police racial violence did not stop when racist vigilantism began, but rather, new systems of control and criminalization emerged. Black law enforcement officials had limited to no power to control white people. Conversely, white cops did not need reasons to detain Black people, but if they did, they had so many criminal ordinances at their disposal that they maintained the power to put Black people in jail or back on plantations for punishment. Before the Civil War, Du Bois writes that prisons in the south were primarily filled with poor white men and white immigrants. But after, police—not the KKK—arrested so many Black people that it completely changed the makeup of the prisons.[53]

MORE THAN A century later, protests would arise against law enforcement for still punishing Black people for running away from them. In April 2015, during my first year in law school, white police officer Michael Slager stopped Walter Scott in North Charleston, South Carolina, due to a bad brake light. After exiting his car, Walter started to run. Nobody will ever know why he ran. Perhaps he was afraid of dying. He was pulled over at the height of the Black Lives Matter movement when seemingly each week, a new police killing went viral and sparked protests. His family speculates Walter fled because despite having wonderful relationships with his children, he reportedly owed about eighteen thousand dollars in child support and a family court had issued a warrant for his arrest. The family believes that he feared this traffic stop would lead to an arrest and that the cop would take him to jail due to this debt.[54]

At some point before Slager's stop, a judge had sent Walter to jail for two weeks for the outstanding child support payments. Walter had pleaded with the judge, and argued that the court had already taken money from his check and sent it to the wrong person. The judge sent him to jail anyway. While he was locked up, he lost a job that he loved at a film company, and his thirty-five thousand dollars salary. Additionally, the judge added to his arrest and incarceration record, further damaging Walter's ability to seek employment to provide for his children. (This is why Mickey and I tried to stop employers from using blanket bans against people with criminal records in Kansas City.) Walter was angry that the court made him lose, in his words, "the best job I ever had." He withdrew from his family, turned to alcohol to cope with the suffering, and, according to a news feature about his life, stopped caring about whether he lived another day.

Hoping to change his circumstances, Walter had enrolled in a parenting program called "Father to Father" and created a plan to pay back the outstanding child support balance—presumably including the debt that the court paid to the wrong person. To my shock when I read the story, Walter believed enough in his repayment plan and tried to do the *right thing* by turning himself in to the court in response to an arrest warrant for his debt. My grandfather was lucky that his wife and father got him out of jail over his outstanding child support payments, but he had to skip town for decades as a price. Here, Walter took himself to jail for a fresh start. The judge showed no mercy and sentenced him to five months. "This whole time in jail," Walter explained, "my child support is still going up." His good-faith effort did not matter. The law did. First he had spent two weeks in jail, then five months in jail, and the entire time that his debt was still accruing, he was unable to earn a salary and provide for his children.[55]

South Carolina's history of policing is intimately tied to the state's denial of reparations to Black and Indigenous people for generations of unpaid labor, kidnapping, and land theft. Not to mention the decades of Jim Crow treatment, incarceration, and divestment in Black communities. Half of the people who the state sterilized were Black people in mental institutions and prisons, usually women, to stop them from reproducing "inadequate offspring." Yet still, the state that permitted the sale and slavery of Black children was charging poor Black fathers for their freedom from jail. Police do not have to use racial profiling to accomplish this; cops could choose from thousands of criminal laws that empower them to make arrests, including non-payment of child support. More than 10 percent of people sitting in cages in South Carolina's county facilities are there for child support back payments; most are economically exploited Black men who cannot afford a lawyer for their freedom and don't have their freedom long enough for steady employment. Like wardens who caught runaways under slavery, South Carolina's Department of Social Services usually collects a yearly fee from custodial parents to fund child support law enforcement costs for each case. And for punishment, Walter Scott had been sent to the jail in Charleston County, the offspring facility of the "Workhouse" where runaway slaves were held generations before.

South Carolina's longest family-owned plantation is in North Charleston and was once held by slave owners who had immigrated from Barbados to the state in the 1680s. One owner, Richard Bohun Baker, kept track of his payments for the Black people who ran away from his plantation. In some cases, Baker paid the local warden for the capture and correction of runaways. The warden obliged, and sometimes incarcerated runaways at the Workhouse. Like the men who escaped Baker's plantation, Walter, according to his family, ran to avoid going to jail.

This time however, in April 2015, Officer Slager did not make an arrest or take anyone to jail. He shot Walter several times in the back. A witness nearby recorded Slager walking toward Walter's body and dropping a Taser. In the police report, Slager lied, writing that Walter had stolen his Taser and run. He did not know that a witness would release the footage, hurling the cop into a firestorm of media frenzy. Walter, the victim, who had gone to jail over child support debt, was killed and his children would never see him again. Slager, the police officer, was an expectant father at the time. North Charleston Police Department fired him while he was in jail, but continued to cover the health insurance for his pregnant wife until she delivered the baby. The mayor of North Charleston said that it was "the humane thing to do." When Walter had been in jail, the state permitted his debt to accrue and benefited from his back payments. When Slager was arrested and put in jail, the city paid for the financial care and medical benefits of his family. More accurately, the city's taxpayers paid. North Charleston is 45 percent Black.[56]

The police could not fix Walter's child support back payments, no more than they could have fixed my grandfather's outstanding debts. If South Carolina, Tennessee or any other state that benefited from slave labor actually paid reparations to the descendants of the people they exploited, perhaps "child support" would not exist. Walter needed resources, not jail. North Charleston could have provided resources, but instead they created a jobs program through police departments and prisons to manage the inequality, just as slavery provided jobs for overseers and patrols. The financial cost to police, prosecute, and imprison Walter several times likely exceeded the amount of his debt. The cost of his life is incalculable.

Tragically, Walter's mother, Judy, was on the phone with him when he was murdered. "They tasing me," were the last words she heard him say. She answered, "Just, just do whatever he say. You know North Charleston policemen, so just do whatever they say." Judy's fear for her fifty-year-old son filled my heart with sadness and familiar agony. Her final talk with her son had been *the talk*—the one Black parents rehearse with their children to try to keep them alive during a stop by a cop. She knew, and expressed that Walter *knew*, "North Charleston policemen." She wasn't suggesting that Walter knew individual cops in the department, or knew that he might encounter a bad one. To know police is to know piranhas. Whether or not you bear the bite, you *know* the species could possess violent command over your body, and if you wish or resolve to be safe, stay away from the trouble they cause.[57]

When the news of Walter's murder broke, members of Harvard's Black Law Students Association (BLSA) met in Wasserstein Hall on campus. We decided to wear all black with white name tags that read his name. One by one, we sat on the stairs in silence during the class transitions. The National Black Law Students Association asked all of the chapters to stand in solidarity with the Charleston School of Law and the University of South Carolina for three moments of remembrance, eight minutes each, to represent how many shots Michael Slager fired at Walter Scott.[58]

The activists who had been mobilizing to save a life or raise awareness to increase the calls for justice were fighting back contemporary police violence. And they were also providing me with a portal into our past, where policing has always been used to control Black, Indigenous, and immigrant labor, movement, and freedom. And through that portal into the history of policing, I was so grateful to find that there was first a history of freedom and resistance.

THREE

RESISTANCE AND REFORM

POLICE REFORMS ARE such tyrannical prizes. Winning them feels relieving, never satisfying. Poet Nayyirah Waheed writes that "desire is the kind of thing that eats you and leaves you starving." Each indictment that a cop faced increased my craving for justice, and each non-indictment made me feel that due season would come one day.[59]

Many activists who demanded "Justice for Trayvon Martin" carried the same demand into the movement against police violence. In 2013, the #BlackLivesMatter website listed several demands to "end injustice in our community": federal charges against George Zimmerman, no new jails, prisons, or immigration detention centers, and the re-opening of the cases of all people whose lives had been stolen by law enforcement, security guards, and vigilantes. The following year, the website's creators, Patrisse Cullors, Opal Tometi, and Alicia Garza, were adding to the calls to arrest Darren Wilson as "justice for Michael Brown," and petitioning Attorney General Eric Holder to "release all names of all officers involved in killing black people within the last five years so they can be brought to justice." Though its meaning had been elusive in high school, I was coming around to the idea that justice—for Michael Brown, Rekia Boyd, and Walter Scott among others—clearly meant what we were chanting in the streets: "Indict! Convict! Send that killer cop to jail! The whole damn system is guilty as hell!"[60]

We wanted to win. Cops expected to win, too, and the odds were in their favor. Many wore "I Am Darren Wilson" bracelets around St. Louis. In November 2014, I sat on my gray carpet in the big blue house and cried when a grand jury returned a bill of no-indictment for the killing of Michael Brown. A grand jury also chose not to indict two cops who killed John Crawford, a Black man who was holding an unloaded air rifle while on the phone inside a Walmart; nor Daniel Pantaleo, the cop who placed Eric Garner in a fatal chokehold for selling loose, untaxed cigarettes on Staten Island. Bystander Ramsey Orta captured the encounter and released the footage showing Garner buckling and repeating "I can't breathe!" NYPD officers wore black t-shirts with white writing that read "I Can Breathe." Mayors, governors, and the president asked us to remain calm and trust the system, the same system whose cops mocked the people they gunned down.[61]

Massive protests swept the country for each person, first for their death, then for the deaths of their cases. I hoped that all of our hard work, from the streets to the campuses, would pay off. I thought it had, briefly, in the first half of 2015. New York Police Department officer Peter Liang was indicted for killing Akai Gurley. On February 10, 2015, Liang had killed Gurley, a Black man, in the dark hallway of the Brooklyn projects. Liang opened a door and fired his weapon. A bullet ricocheted and hit Gurley who was coming up the stairs with his girlfriend. Liang's indictment was the first of many high-profile killings since the Ferguson Uprising began. But, unlike the white cops who evaded charges, Liang is Chinese American. Many Chinese Americans and immigrants varied in their reactions to the indictment. Some demanded his prosecution and joined multi-racial protests that had signs with "Black Lives Matter" written in Chinese. Others conveyed that the indictment was racist and that he was a scapegoat for all of the other cops who walked free. In a double-plot twist, Judge Danny Chun convicted Liang and sentenced him to probation and community service. Akai was killed, and there would be no jail time. I think about this when people ask me of abolition, "What about the killers?"

Liang's case demonstrated the limits of calling for cop convictions and the limits of diversity. Having more people of color in a corrupt system did not mean that they would be interested in changing it. Liang is Asian. He was prosecuted by Ken Thompson, the first Black District Attorney in Brooklyn. Liang was sentenced by Judge Chun, the first Korean American prosecutor and first

Korean American judge in New York City. In 2019, Judge Chun did not sentence two NYPD cops, including one Black one, who had "sex" in a police van with a teenager in custody. Rather, the judge defended his decision by saying that the victim *and* the cops were involved in criminal activity, and that the victim could also be charged and found guilty for offering a bribe. Later that year, the judge sentenced a Black former NYPD cop to probation for shooting a man in the face and then planting a knife next to the body. If the criminal legal system only had white judges, prosecutors, and cops, then we could more easily assume the presence of racism or white supremacy. But with diversity, people of color can make the legal system appear more neutral or just by the virtue of them being "firsts." We need "firsts" to do more than break the barriers to get into the system; we need them to break the system itself.

I had not fully come to these conclusions about diversity by the time of the news of Freddie Gray's death. Two weeks after Walter Scott's death, Baltimore cops made eye contact with Freddie Gray. Gray, like Walter, ran. Nobody knows why. The official police report stated that Gray "fled unprovoked," as if police do not regularly cause harm to poor Black men like him, and as if recent viral videos of police shooting and strangling Black men to death did not provide enough provocation for them to flee. Cops chased and caught him, patted him down, and discovered a small switchblade. They dragged his folded body to a cage inside of a van. For forty-five minutes, they drove through the city on a "rough ride," a law enforcement tactic of driving harshly to physically punish arrestees who run. In the process, those cops severed Gray's spine. He died days later on April 19, 2015.[62]

Kevin Moore recorded the police dragging Gray and once he released the footage, Black people poured into the streets. Policymakers tout body cameras as a major reform in the wake of police violence, but civilian cop watch is much more powerful and democratic. When we stop to record police encounters, our presence can sometimes discourage further violence from cops. If we record cops who continue to escalate violence and get it on camera, then we are in control of the footage; this differs from body and dashboard camera footage because cops can turn them off or misconstrue the angle. Cities also withhold footage of cop shootings until a family, journalist, or lawyer sues or protests for access. At risk to themselves, the brave civilians who record cops informally on the streets or formally in community Copwatch programs could literally save lives and expose additional police terror. I would learn more about the short-comings of body cameras after the protests.

Many activists and lawyers went to Baltimore to support the protesters who faced police in riot gear, just as they descended upon Ferguson. Justin Hansford, my friend from St. Louis, was there providing legal support, too. After a few con-versations with him about the need for more legal observers, I decided to go. Harvard's BLSA paid for me and three of my closest friends from law school, Mmiri Mbah, Christina Joseph, and Titilayo Rasaki, to drive from Cambridge to Baltimore to protest and provide legal support to activists.

I woke up the next morning ready to go and quickly learned horrible news. My former classmate, Korie Hodges, had been killed in cold blood and possi-bly in front of her children. Her friend, Keerica Bolden, was also discovered dead right beside her. Korie's father found them. The headline was so horrible that I called the news station and fought with them to change it: "Accused Fer-guson Looter Found Dead Two Days After Being Charged." They kept it. Despite the fact that her death had nothing to do with the charges that she was facing, the news was eager to rely on the sensationalism of Ferguson and looting to attract readers to their site. Friends from my high school wanted justice for Korie. I did, too. They wanted to know why people protested police violence but didn't protest violence in our own Black neighborhoods. I thought about the elder from the community meeting in Kansas City years before. I think he was warning us that many of the underlying causes of community-based vio-lence and police violence were rooted in the same oppressive systems but required different kinds of solutions if we were going to stop the violence. These facts do not bring anyone's baby back from the dead. But we can use them to create better solutions in our communities to save more lives. I wished Korie's father could have found her oversleeping because her alarm failed to ring, instead of finding her lifeless.[63]

Between Korie and Freddie Gray, the drive down was deeply emotional for me. I found solace in being with my friends, reuniting with Justin, and meeting new activists in the streets. During the day, cops mounted horses, drove cars, and raided buildings in response to the protests. In Ferguson, the bulk of the protests happened on two major streets, West Florissant and North Florissant.

But Baltimore's occupation was significantly larger and spread throughout the city. Titilayo, Christina, Mmiri, and I joined lawyers, law students, and legal workers in the National Lawyers Guild and and a formation that became the Black Movement Law Project to monitor police. Several organizations trained us for cop watch, legal observation, bail, and jail support. We connected with other law students from Howard University and Catholic University of America, and lawyers who attended the National Lawyers Guild legal observer training at the University of Maryland. I was shocked by the power and command of Black law students who organized the support networks behind the scenes, especially Marques Banks. Marques became part of the Black Movement Law Project. He was a bubbly, detail-oriented strategist and trainer during the uprising in Baltimore. When we worked together later in Ferguson, activists would run away from the police when they escalated violence. Marques was one of the few people who would run toward the fires to help others. Because of courageous people like Marques, I stopped praying to be fearless and started praying to be relentless, so that even when I am afraid, I try to move to closer to freedom.

During times of protests, I came to realize that government leaders invoke remarkably similar scripts. President Obama's script for the Baltimore Uprising was as almost as formulaic as his remarks surrounding the racial justice protests for Trayvon Martin. *Send empathy to the family, affirm peaceful protest, spend more time criticizing protesters who react to police escalation of violence than the police, remain neutral on the underlying violence, encourage people to trust the system for justice.* Noticeably to me, he did not say that Freddie Gray could have been his son. Gray was a young adult who fled the cops in the projects; the darker and presumably poorer Gray was not the soft, caramel-faced suburban teenager hunted down by a racist.

Addressing the nation, the president listed six points. First, he offered condolences to Freddie Gray's family. Second, he offered sympathy solely to the police who were injured after kids threw rocks at them, even though Baltimore police had also thrown rocks at the kids. Third, he condemned the protesters who set fire to buildings and called them criminals and thugs, but never condemned the actual police officers who killed Freddie. Fourth, he affirmed peaceful protesters and condemned the ones who burned down a CVS. Fifth, he touted his task force on police, which was sought to "build trust" between police and

Black people. Politicians popularized the idea that police shootings led to a breakdown in trust between cops and Black communities. Trust is not neutral; Freddie Gray probably ran because he trusted the police to be exactly what they have been for the entirety of their existence as an institution: violent.[64]

And finally, President Obama announced that the DOJ would give grants to local police departments to purchase body cameras. Yet the public already had video of Gray being dragged by cops and several uprisings were in direct response to footage of police killings. We did not need to see police kill people from the cop's point of view. We needed the killings to stop.

OBAMA'S SPEECH WAS powerful motivation to reexamine my desire for popular police reforms that gave cops more power, money, and legitimacy. I should have known better from my time organizing against immigrant deportations: by the end of his presidency, he expanded the immigration law enforcement budget by 300 percent, and expanded one federal program to deport undocumented immigrants from state and local custody by 3,600 percent. Immigration activists criticized Obama's widening of the deportation regime, and many activists against police violence started criticizing his increasing of resources for cops. And in the wake of the movements against police shootings, he proposed a $263 million investment over three years to help purchase fifty thousand body-worn cameras to build trust between communities and local police departments. Since 2015, the Department of Justice distributed at least $70 million in grants to help cover the cost of the cameras. On top of funding police budgets more than any other department, city councils paid hundreds of thousands every year for equipment and data storage. Akin to the capitalists who were committed to developing destructive tools to protect profits from slavery, body and dashboard cameras were a gift to technology companies profiting from the police killings of Black people. In 2012, executive leadership for Taser, the stun gun company, expressed that this was a win-win because it was a $1 billion opportunity for the company and saved the police from paying out billions to civilians in misconduct lawsuits: "People plead out when there is video." Taser rebranded the company's name to Axon and became the largest seller of police cameras. When the police kill a Black person, the company's investment shares have surged as high as 25 percent.[65]

Beyond the profit incentives for companies, the public has very limited power to access the footage. The day after Baltimore police arrested Freddie Gray, the federal district attorneys had announced that they were investigating the Chicago police shooting of LaQuan McDonald who had been killed in October 2014. Thirty seconds after arriving on the scene, police officer Jason Van Dyke shot McDonald sixteen times as he was walking away with a three-inch blade, folded pocketknife. Eighty-six minutes were missing from the footage from a nearby Burger King, and the city was withholding the footage from the dashboard until a freelance journalist won a lawsuit demanding its release. The city agreed to pay McDonald's family $5 million in a settlement that prohibited the public release of the footage. BYP100 and other coalitions in Chicago pinned the alleged yearlong cover-up on the Chicago Police Department, local prosecutor Anita Alvarez, and Mayor Rahm Emanuel, President Obama's former chief of staff. Activists successfully organized against Alvarez's reelection bid through a #ByeAnita campaign. Van Dyke resigned and was charged with murder and sentenced to six years and nine months in prison. The Chicago Police Department did not fire the three other cops who were on the scene until five years later. The Fraternal Order of the Police's vice president condemned Van Dyke's sentence and suggested that the more recent firing board had succumbed to the pressure of "radical police haters."[66]

What good are body cam videos if the footage can be erased by the cops, covered up by the city, and denied to the public? They create another round of reforms for activists to demand and technology companies to create: accessibility. Some police departments now offer livestreaming. The loops of investments in the reform start repetitive cycles and the same number of people get killed.

Even when body cameras could have theoretically served their purpose, I noticed that cops still get away with murder. Three months after Freddie Gray fled BPD, I felt some relief when University of Cincinnati police officer Ray Tensing was indicted for killing Sam DuBose. Tensing was wearing a body camera when he stopped DuBose for failing to display a front license plate. After asking for a driver's license, Tensing attempts to open DuBose's door and shoots him in the face when DuBose refuses and tries to close the door. The body camera captured the shooting at such close range that the city arranged barricades in the streets and blanketed windows with boards to prepare for the footage release. In a police report, Tensing claims to have been dragged, but his body camera showed that he was not, and that the shot was fired before the car moved. My relief from the indictment did not last long. His first murder trial ended in a mistrial. The second trial ended in a mistrial, too.[67]

DuBose's family received a settlement near $5 million and the University of Cincinnati agreed to pay for the education of twelve of his children. Ray Tensing successfully sued the university for more than $350,000.[68]

BACK IN BALTIMORE, Mmiri, Christina, Titilayo and I were in the hotel room preparing for legal observation and jail support that day. They rushed me out of the bathroom and toward the couch. Marilyn Mosby, the state district attorney, was on television making an announcement—she was going to charge the cops responsible for Freddie Gray's death. Another prize for the movement. Six exactly. The four of us began weeping and hugging each other. Mosby, a Black woman, instantly became a hero for those exhausted by traditional white male prosecutors who were usually explicitly complicit or lacked courage to do what she had done. Baltimore also had Black city council members and a Black woman mayor, so we also thought that might have made a difference. We thanked God for our punishment prizes and entered Baltimore's streets full of pride. Protests scheduled for that day turned into celebratory parades, and after making several rounds for the festivities, we drove joyously back to law school to finish our final exams.

We did not know that three Baltimore cops would be eventually be acquitted and another case would end in mistrial before Mosby dropped the remaining charges. They would be back at work few months after that. The only people Mosby would ultimately send to jail were Black protesters. In fact, all over the country, more Black people went to jail for protesting police killings than police officers who killed Black people.[69]

Putting all of our hope in the criminal legal system for convictions continued to let budding Black lawyers like me down. Prosecutors rarely charge cops, and judges and juries rarely convict them. Many jurors are sold on the mainstream belief that cops put their lives on the line every day for our safety, when actually, according to the Bureau of Labor Statistics, the jobs with the highest fatal work injuries include fishers and hunters, grounds maintenance workers, construction workers, roofers, and tradespeople like my father. Sometimes, as the prosecutors explained in Tensing's case, some jurors will never vote to convict a cop.

Thousands of cops have killed more than ten thousand people between 2005 and 2017; only eighty-two cops have been charged with murder or manslaughter. According to criminologist Phil Stinson, only nineteen cops were convicted and mostly on lesser charges. When the police do go to prison, judges sentence them less harshly than the rest of us. Liang didn't get any prison time at all.[70]

Even when activists and lawyers know that a conviction is unlikely, these facts cannot comfort a grieving family who wants something, *anything* to atone for their involuntary sacrifice. I understand and completely sympathize with people who still want killer cops to go prison. In a society where the options for killer cops seem like prison or nothing, prison and punishment feel like justice. But punishment is not justice, and I do not believe that we can secure justice for anyone killed by the police. Justice is a process where people decide and create the conditions that help us thrive and it involves the people who are most impacted by those conditions. The dead cannot participate in this process. We can demand lots of outcomes for their deaths—punishment, revenge, relief—but not justice. When convictions do lead to cops entering prison, some people are excited because prisons are where we send poor, Black, and disabled people to suffer. This "justice" is built upon maintaining this suffering for everyone else.

Other angry mourners believe, as I once did, that prisons can deter cops from violence—that if we send cops who kill people like Freddie Gray and Michael Brown to prison, then it sends a message to other cops to think before they pull the trigger. However, there's one fatal flaw with this belief: the law protects the police's right *not* to think before they shoot. The Supreme Court opined in *Graham v. Connor* that cops "are often forced to make split-second judgments—in circumstances that are tense, uncertain, and rapidly evolving—about the amount of force that is necessary in a particular situation." This means that police currently have the constitutional authority to quickly decide when to use force. If cops often make split-second decisions about whether to pull the trigger, I doubt that much of that split-second will be used to for them to think, "I probably should not pull this trigger. The last cop who did in this situation went to prison." According to the courts, cops don't have enough time to make that consideration and will be protected when they shoot first, consider later.[71]

Additionally, as I watched each trial and waited intently for prosecutors to deliver "justice," I had never wondered whether the convictions would save more lives. With all of the indictments that activists encouraged, the data shows that the police still kill around a thousand people each year. If cops were not getting the message by now, then how many more people would have to die before they do? And for activists, I had to ask myself, do we want to have more convictions? Or do we want to save lives?

After all of the trials ended for the Baltimore PD cops who killed Freddie Gray, I often wondered what should happen after cops kill someone. I believe that different communities could lead intentional and informed conversations about the possibilities because there is no singular answer. People can (and should) use their anger to rebel. Police officers must know that we will always resist the spectacular or mundane forms of violence that they inflict on our communities. Protests threaten the idea that police violence is reducible to a few bad apples. In response, cops work with lawmakers to pass state laws that criminalize protests, such as limiting how people can demonstrate and increasing the number of crimes that protesters can be charged with. One lawmaker proposed a bill that would bar activists from receiving student grants and loans if they are convicted of a crime related to a protest, rally, march, or other demonstration. The same bill also bars other forms of state aid, like food stamps and unemployment benefits. These measures attack students who are primary drivers of resistance movements, and also poor people who are forced to rely on assistance in the first place. Lawyers, activists, and anyone who cares about civil liberties must vehemently protect the right to protest.

Organizers and people who care about justice must reject calls for "peace" and task forces, and the other ways that people in power waste our time and energy until they announce some future reform that won't get us free, like more body cameras or community relations boards. Instead, activists can call for cops to be fired and never allowed to work in public or private law enforcement. We need an expansion of CopWatch programs as police departments shrink. There must be radical and beautiful trauma and healing responses for those neighborhoods and families who experienced the killing. People organizing in that community should work to come up with a range of responses to all violence, which are more than prison or nothing. Most importantly, we need democratic, multi-racial movements against the carceral state, but more broadly, against a society that uses police and prisons to manage black rebellion, oppressed people, and social inequality.

ONCE I FINISHED with my final exams that spring, I returned to studying books about slavery. Frederick Douglass's autobiography quickly became one of my favorite texts ever. Throughout my life, teachers always presented him as an incredible orator and abolitionist. They never once taught me that he fought a slave owner. And won. Before he escaped, his owner sent him to a slaver breaker, Edward Covey, a poor white Methodist minister who could not afford his own plantation but gained a reputation for beating slaves to set them straight. For a year, he beat and whipped Douglass nearly every day. Once, while he was feeding the horses, Covey entered the stables with a whip. Douglass decided to fight back, resisting bondage by grabbing Covey's throat and kicking him and another man who tried to intervene in the ribs. The brawl lasted for almost two hours, until Covey, bleeding, withdrew. He never hit Douglass again. In fact, Douglass wrote that nobody ever whipped him again, though he had many fights with white men who tried:

> This battle with Mr. Covey was the turning-point in my career as a slave . . . [A slave] only can understand the deep satisfaction which I experienced, who has himself repelled by force the bloody arm of slavery. I felt as I never felt before. It was a glorious resurrection, from the tomb of slavery, to the heaven of freedom. My long-crushed spirit rose, cowardice departed, bold defiance took its place; and I now resolved that, however long I might remain a slave in form, the day had passed forever when I could be a slave in fact. I did not hesitate to let it be known of me, that the white man who expected to succeed in whipping, must also succeed in killing me.[72]

Douglass's resistance was illegal and even violent, but that's what it took for his survival and freedom. While beatings on to plantation were normal, routine, and regular, his writing demonstrated that slavery's violence was possible because of the *fact of the plantation*, not because Black people were misbehaving. To stop the legal whippings, beatings, kidnappings, sale, and sexual violence committed by slave owners, slavery, the root cause, had to be abolished. Douglass explained, "It was slavery, not its mere incidents, that I hated." Slavery as a system was wrong; not just the harms that it created. He further challenged my ideas on police reform. Was it mere incidents of policing that I hated? The shootings, chokeholds, and arrests? Or was it the institution and what it was designed to do?[73]

Full of ideas and new knowledge, I anxiously flew back to St. Louis in summer 2015 for my job at the Advancement Project. AP is a social justice organization that uses movement lawyering, organizing, and media communications for social change. I worked with an AP lawyer in two formations. One was the "Don't Shoot" coalition to organize the one-year anniversary events for Michael Brown, VonDerrit Myers, Jr., and the Ferguson Uprising; the second was another group for legal and policy research around police violence and accountability. Jason Flanery, an off-duty cop working a second job as an armed security guard, had shot Myers. Witnesses report that Flanery did not announce himself as a cop as he chased Myers down a dark alley and allegedly shot him at least eight times, including six times from behind. Contrary to police accounts that the teen shot first, Myers's family says he only had a sandwich in his hand. His lawyer believed that cops planted a gun near the scene. Protesters rebelled and burned American flags in response to the non-indictment that summer and the police continued to respond with militaristic force.[74]

The protests, marches, rallies, and festivals that the Don't Shoot Coalition planned were incredible. Thousands of people participated in dancing, artistic actions, block parties, and theater performances between St. Louis City and North St. Louis County. Several activists who protested in the Ferguson Uprising in 2014 returned to support the celebration and ongoing resistance efforts. By late summer 2015, activists were still occupying parts of Ferguson to protest police violence, making St. Louis a site for one of the longest continually held demonstrations in the history of the United States, rivaling the 381-day-long Montgomery Bus Boycott that started in 1955. A group of protesters called the Lost Voices took over a section of a parking lot in Ferguson and lived in tents for several months demanding prison for Darren Wilson and justice for Michael Brown. Before Wilson's non-indictment several months earlier, one member, Dasha Jones, explained, "He's on suspended leave with pay. He's getting paid right now. They could not even fire him. So do you really think we're gonna get an indictment? No." In 2015, Lost Voices and organizations like HandsUp United were providing youth programming and mutual aid in St. Louis County. HandsUp launched an after-school technology class and a books and breakfast program, inspiring several organizers to start their own, too.[75]

Lawyers, activists, and clergy spent weeks preparing for new rounds of police terror that we expected to take place during the anniversary events. The national spotlight was on the Ferguson Police Department, but everyone locally knew that police were problematic in the entire area. The Department of Justice investigated the Ferguson Police Department in 2014, but police officers from more than fifty law enforcement agencies descended upon protesters in Ferguson during the demonstrations, including the St. Louis Metropolitan Police Department, the St. Louis County Police Department, and the Missouri Highway Patrol. Missouri governor Jay Nixon issued an executive order to unify their command during subsequent states of emergency, specifically granting the St. Louis County Police Department command and control over Ferguson for protests and acts of civil disobedience. By the time I returned for the anniversary in 2015, local police condemned the DOJ investigations report that found widespread practices of racism and classism just three months earlier. The report largely attributed the police practices to a lack of relationships and touted community policing as a cure.[76]

Much like indictments, community policing and increasing diversity are popular responses to police violence that do not reduce police violence. Mere community knowledge and diversity cannot prevent violence in a system that is inherently violent. Plantations were diverse and overseers *knew* the Black people they policed, and the violence continued because there was a fundamental imbalance of power, resources, and status between the two. This is true for cops. I was witnessing the DOJ tout community policing and diversity in Ferguson to increase the benevolence of individual cops instead of reducing their power to be violent. *The End of Policing* author and sociologist Alex Vitale explains that "a kinder, gentler, and more diverse war on the poor is still a war on the poor." A force with officers who looked like Michael Brown could continue to do the bidding of white property owners nearby. Perhaps the new recruits would not shoot down another Black teenager for jaywalking. They might politely ask him to walk in single file on the sidewalk with his friend, or offer him a ride home. Many of us would celebrate that kindness because it's how we think cops are supposed to behave. We'd ignore that at any point, those cops still have the power to inflict the same violence as Darren Wilson did. We just hope that they won't

use it. We would also forget the underlying problems of that encounter: the criminalization of jaywalking that gives cops power to stop people; the sidewalks
that are too narrow for poor pedestrians to walk alongside each other; and the
segregation in Ferguson that concentrates poor, Black people into the apartment complexes where Michael's grandmother lived.[77]

On August 9, 2015, exactly one year after Michael Brown was killed, I was
attending a "Ferguson Is Everywhere" benefit concert featuring rappers Tef Poe,
Talib Kweli, and Bun B. I was there with Justin Hansford and Nyle Fort. I had met
Nyle a few days earlier at a protest in front of the police department. He was a minister and activist who was starting a doctoral program at Princeton later that
summer. He had come to St. Louis the year before on a bus ride that his friend,
writer Darnell Moore, had planned to support the Ferguson Uprising. Darnell
helped orchestrate the constellation of people who created freedom rides to Ferguson from all over the country. On the way back to their home cities from Ferguson,
many people on the bus rides started the first Black Lives Matter chapters. Nyle
had met Tef Poe, a founder of HandsUp United in Ferguson. Fort was inspired and
launched a books and breakfast program with several others in a group called
"The Maroon Project" when he returned to Newark, New Jersey. Before we all met
in person, Darnell, Nyle, and I had all contributed to the same issue of the *Harvard Journal of African American Public Policy* in 2013. I wrote about disparate
impact discrimination from my research with Mickey. Nyle had written about ending mass incarceration:

> For many intellectuals and activists, prison abolition is not only
> progressive it is also practical. For many others, prison abolition is too
> extreme and not realistic. No matter where one stands on the issue, one
> must confront certain historical facts. At the height of American slavery,
> abolition was viewed more as a fantasy than a policy. So deeply embedded
> in the fabric of American society, chattel slavery was considered both
> normal and "natural" while abolition was viewed as extreme and
> unrealistic. However, if history has revealed anything at all, it is that
> "normal" is not always moral and "unrealistic" is not always unattainable.
> As radical as prison abolition may seem to some, centuries from now,

citizens of this country may laugh at how astonishingly normalized and immoral the American prison system once was.[78]

Years later, I asked Nyle whether he had also believed in police abolition at the time of the article. He wasn't sure; when he wrote it, mass incarceration dominated the criminal justice reform conversation. He had learned about prison abolition in seminary after political prisoner Mumia Abu-Jamal called into Nyle's class and delivered a lecture. Before then, Nyle remembered being explicitly against police practices, including stop and frisk and racial profiling like the rest of us. Yet his ideas about police abolition as part of prison industrial complex abolition were unexamined until the Ferguson Uprising, like mine. Our political ideas about how to change the world were not linear because we were always learning and unlearning the history, purpose, and functions of various systems of oppression. Or as Nyle simply put it: "A person's political journey is dynamic as the social justice movement itself."

At the concert, the crowd, once lively and joyous, grew thick and enraged. Tef announced on stage that the police had just killed someone in Ferguson. Nyle and I ran to Justin's car with Marbre Stahly-Butts. Marbre was a lawyer with the Center for Popular Democracy. She and I would reconnect again later as the founding members of Law for Black Lives. When we arrived in Ferguson, tanks were already moving on a growing crowd on West Florissant. A Black woman started shouting, "Take out your contacts, they are about to start shooting at us!" *She's been through this so many times that she already knows when they are going to tear-gas before they announce it.* Others echoed her commands. The crowd was emotional and angry. Montague Simmons, longtime St. Louis organizer and executive director of the Organization for Black Struggle (OBS) at the time, was calling for us to link arms and face the tanks. One woman started shouting and screaming and walking toward the line of cops in armor, asking why *they* kept killing *us*. I instinctively ran to her and wrapped my arms around her. She burst into tears.

Standing in the middle of the road, I embarrassingly expected some change from the cops in the year that I'd gone off to law school, especially since the police's previous militaristic display had become an international embarrassment to the country. Additionally, ArchCity Defenders and Advancement

Project had successfully sued the police to stop tear gassing and shooting rubber bullets indiscriminately during protests. This lawsuit was a major win toward constitutional policing. The court required the police to broadcast a warning before dispersing the crowd with chemical agents and rubber bullets. Here's how the police complied.[79]

Nyle, Justin, and I hurried to a gas station nearby to purchase milk in case the woman was right about the tear gas. We knew to purchase milk because Palestinians living in the militarized occupied territories in Gaza and the West Bank had been tweeting survival tips to us from their own protests against Israel's military forces. Upon our return, cops inside the tanks advanced with the dispersal order. I don't remember what they said, but as soon as they said it, they started shooting the tear gas cannisters. Nyle and I ran toward the crowd and mistakenly into the poisonous cloud to pass out the milk. We first had to pour it on each other's faces to soothe our own choking, gagging, and coughing. Everything was burning. The litigation to make the police warn us did not stop their reckless behavior that night. If that was supposed to be "constitutional policing," then it hurt just as badly as the so-called unconstitutional policing. Hours later, when I made it home, a thin film of the gas and milk covered my skin and locs. My eyes watered uncontrollably and tears burned my cheeks when they fell. I could not believe that protesters inhaled these fumes every night. I never wanted to experience anything like this again.[80]

The next day, interfaith clergy activists staged acts of civil disobedience against the police department in downtown St. Louis. Dr. Cornel West joined dozens of other protesters as they sat on the ground and edged forward, about six inches at a time, toward the building. Like my time in Baltimore, I was there as a legal observer to monitor police behavior. They were threatening to arrest the ministers and people of faith. Legal observers are usually permitted to walk around freely and gather information about the protesters, cops on duty, and any potential for escalation and de-escalation. There was one other legal observer, a tall and skinny white person who was doing the same thing that I was, recording the police who stood in a line facing the crowd of onlookers. Cops started yelling at me to leave, not the white person. "But I'm a legal observer, I can be here," I answered back. The other legal observer continued to walk closer and closer toward the police without incident. To my surprise, a high-ranking cop walked from the back and threatened to arrest me if I did not leave. I turned my back to comply with this demand and began walking to exit the police line. Suddenly a cop, a Black man, walked behind me and yanked my arm so hard that I instantly buckled. He had physically assaulted me for no reason. I stood up and started yelling, "Why did you just hurt me? I was leaving! You saw me leaving! You're a coward! Fucking coward!" He just smirked. I started walking back toward him when lawyer and law professor, Brendan Roediger, came and grabbed me to calm me down. He just kept saying, "You can't go to jail right now. I can't let you go to jail right now." Brendan probably saved me from God knows what. If that cop was bold enough to assault me in front of hundreds of people, I cannot even imagine what he would have done if we were alone.

My arm throbbed for a week because pain doesn't appreciate diversity. I had not felt any less of it because the cop was Black. Writing for the *New York Times* in 1967, James Baldwin explained, "'If you *must* call a cop,' we said in those days, 'for God's sake, make sure it's a white one.' We did not feel that the cops were protecting us, for we knew too much about the reasons for the kinds of crimes committed in the ghetto; but we feared black cops even more than white cops, because the black cop had to work so much harder—on *your* head—to prove to himself and his colleagues that he was not like all the other niggers." There, I had been the other *nigger*. Research shows that employing Black cops can actually increase police violence against people of color, and the diverse police departments in Chicago, Philadelphia, New York, Oakland, Detroit, Los Angeles, New Orleans, and San Juan had not prevented the police's acts of assault, torture, and murder of people of color in those cities.[81]

A week later, I found myself protesting, resisting, and calling for justice for yet another police killing in St. Louis. Kayla Reed, a field organizer with the OBS, Tef Poe, and I were in front of the St. Louis Circuit Attorney's Office with the family of Kajieme Powell. Exactly one year earlier, two St. Louis police officers shot and killed Kajieme as he paced back and forth holding a small knife. The police chief said that he quickly advanced toward the officers with his hand raised above his head as if he was going to attack them. In a video captured by witnesses, Powell did no such thing. Clearly experiencing a mental health crisis, he walked toward them slowly, telling them to shoot him. They fired twelve times. The entire encounter lasted thirty seconds. He was killed about a week after Michael

Brown and the three of us were there a year later demanding that the district attorney charge the police. While I was on the stairs, I saw a friend from high school who had become a cop and asked him why. He shrugged his shoulders and mouthed, "I don't know. I didn't know what else to do after school." He was on a line of cops who were blocking us from entering the courthouse. A few of them started running to their cars. Tef and I overheard on a cop's radio that there was a police shooting at a location in West St. Louis. Protesters started running to our cars, too, to beat them there.[82]

After eighteen-year-old Mansur Ball-Bey clocked off his UPS job and went to his aunt's house, cops and federal agents raided the home. Ball-Bey ran and was shot in the back. Cops said he shot at them first; the family and witnesses said that he did not have a gun. When I arrived at Walton and Page with a car full of activists, a crowd was growing and demanding answers from the cops about the shooting. Brittany Packnett was there. We had both attended West Side Missionary Baptist Church when I was in high school and we were standing in front of the building when the pastor, Rev. Dr. Ronald Bobo walked over. He was stunned that cops not only couldn't constrain themselves during the anniversary of Michael Brown's killing but were also actively killing more people.[83]

Police tanks and squad cars started speeding down the block toward us, forming a horizontal roadblock the entire width of the street, from sidewalk to sidewalk. Behind us, more cop cars sped down Page, sandwiching protesters in the middle. Without warning or provocation, the police suddenly started shooting canisters that contained different chemical agents into the crowd. One of the agents did not have the smoke and gas that I experienced the week before, but it caused us to start sneezing excessively. One military guide explains that "invisible tear gas cannot be seen by rioters once it first emerges from a grenade or mechanical dispenser and therefore produces a greater psychological panic producing effect than tear smoke." It was unbearable. I jumped inside the car because the cops turned the scene into chaos. Shooters in the tanks fired rubber bullets and canisters directly at people and cars, including the one that I was in. Block by block, the St. Louis Metropolitan Police Department catapulted cocktails of chemical agents against the entire Fountain Park neighborhood for hours. Police attacked residents sitting on their porches. They gassed park-goers completely unaware of the gathering. Clouds of smoke from the regular tear gas hindered visibility for people who ran and drove. Several school-bus drivers panicked and dropped kids off at incorrect stops. I took pictures of some blasted tear-gas canisters and uploaded them on Facebook; they were the most toxic kind, CS, that causes vomiting, skin burning, immediate closure of the eyes, and heightened sensitivity from repetitive exposure. A veteran online told me that it could melt contacts in your eyes.[84]

By nightfall, the police were still raining terror, and the protesters gathered in the area were emboldened to fight back. They threw sticks and rocks; I saw a few set a car on fire. The car that I was in was being followed by white vans for about an hour. The vans were the same ones next to the police tanks in a picture that an activist posted online. I was in the car with two Ferguson activists and feared what might have happened if we were isolated and captured. Earlier that summer, a cop in Texas had stopped Sandra Bland for allegedly failing to use a turn signal as she drove to start her new job at an HBCU, Prairie View A&M. He took her to jail. Three days later, Bland was found dead in her cell. Her family outright denied the possibility of suicide and maintained that the jail was trying to cover up her murder. Bland's life and death catalyzed the #SayHerName movement to highlight Black women who died in police custody. So when I realized that we were being followed, I wrote online what other Black activists wrote when we entered the streets: "If something happens, I was not violent. I did not commit suicide."[85]

That evening, the police held a press conference and stated that the cops were responding to attacks initiated by the protesters. It was a complete lie.

Kayla and I organized a door-knocking campaign to interview residents about the neighborhood tear gas shooting spree. After I took legal declarations from community members on the events, OBS, Advancement Project, and the National Lawyers Guild held a police brutality clinic at West Side where the rampage had begun. We wanted to create space for community members to process what happened and learn about potential civil suits against the police departments. Brendan spoke, as well as my supervisor from the Advancement Project, Denise Lieberman. Thomas Harvey, one of the founders of ArchCity Defenders, discussed legal options. He had gathered declarations from me and Nyle about a week earlier because the police had tear-gassed us in violation of the dispersal order that ArchCity won in court. I facilitated the clinic and realized that most of the residents who came really just wanted a place to talk about what happened to them. Some community members explicitly wanted police demilitarization; most wanted the cops to completely leave them alone. Everyone agreed that the violence had to stop.

RESISTANCE TO POLICE violence, systemic racism, and colonization were booming across the world by the time I returned to law school in 2015. That fall, the International Fellowship of Reconciliation, an interfaith organization dedicated to nonviolence, awarded me and Nyle a fellowship to discuss police violence in the Netherlands and Belgium. I had no idea how much I would learn about police and colonialism. We lectured and attended community-based teach-ins two or three times a day. In the evenings, we broke bread and held storytelling nights with activists, artists, and academics. We even met with law enforcement officials who greeted us with Stroopwafels. At one meeting in Amsterdam, a police chief assured us that what happened in Ferguson would have never happened in their country because their police do not racially profile. A police captain of Curaçao descent mostly echoed this sentiment and explained that when people of African or Caribbean descent held protests, the police department sends a captain to the protest who shares the ethnic backgrounds of the dissidents. I found this ironic, since this is exactly what had happened in Ferguson—the department hired and sent a high-ranking Black cop to manage protests, but he still had no power over the command that attacked us those nights. Additionally, I realized that by sending Black captains, departments were using the colonial tactic of installing a member of the colonized group to diffuse dissent among the colonized. They would receive our grievances but could not disrupt the unequal treatment, just like the Black school cops who'd comfort students on the way to detention.

I could not believe how many Stroopwafels I ate. I also could not believe the Dutch cops' assertation that anti-Blackness and racial profiling were American problems. Mitchell Esajas, an activist from The New Urban Collective based in Amsterdam, sent me reading materials on the histories of colonialism and racism in the country. The Dutch had maintained a slave trade in the Caribbean Ocean, including on the currently colonized islands that became Curaçao and Aruba. Inhabitants of those islands are Dutch citizens like Puerto Ricans are US citizens. Mitchell included literature on *Zwarte Piet*, a mythical blackface creature that Black Dutch have been organizing to have removed from national celebrations. Mitchell connected the character to the treatment that Black people received from the cops. He explained that resistance groups like Nederland Wordt Beter, Stop Blackface, and Zwarte Piet Niet, organized protests and freedom rides against racial injustice. In 2014, the police had violently arrested activists, including children. Jeffrey Afriyie, one of the Kick Out Zwarte Piet organizers arrested in 2014, had been arrested before in 2011 for wearing a T-shirt that read "Zwarte is Racism," and again in 2016 for a freedom ride to Rotterdam, a city that had decided to ban protests altogether.[86]

Anti-Black racism is obviously not a problem unique to the US, and neither were other forms of marginalization. Between our meetings, lectures, and dinners, we'd take the tram. At each platform, volunteers held signs welcoming refugees without documentation. I'd been reading about the Syrian civil war that forced people to flee to Europe. In 2015, the Netherlands recorded almost nineteen thousand asylum requests from Syrians, out of a total of forty-four thousand. We met with a group of teenagers and young adults who were immigrants or children of immigrants from North Africa and Syria. Some were undocumented. The group explained that they faced immense police surveillance and violence, and that Europe's heightened xenophobia and Islamophobia made them and their families susceptible to street violence from white Europeans. Police in The Netherlands were carrying out the will of the government *and* the white Dutch—protection for their borders from the brown people crossing over. The Dutch passed significant measures to exclude undocumented migrants from healthcare and the economic sectors. Border patrol was a global phenomenon. I was not in Kansas anymore.[87]

Historically, Belgium, the Netherlands, and France heavily recruited and coerced Africans to fight in their wars and labor in their cities. Between World War I and the 1970s, millions of Africans went to these countries as a result. By the economic recession in the 1970s, many European nations started closing their borders to the Black and brown immigrants whose labor they had been exploiting for decades. Thus, people from the Middle East and Africa fleeing violence, persecution, or economic devastation as a result of Western imperialism have increasingly resorted to asylum-seeking as a route to immigration. Police have been subsequently tasked with managing the rising right-wing Islamophobic and xenophobic criticisms that the immigrants would drain the resources of European nations. The fallout has been most acutely felt among contemporary refugees and laborers fleeing climate catastrophe and war in Syria, and political instability in North Africa. The Netherlands increased police power to question and apprehend people they suspect to be undocumented, akin to Arizona's SB 1070 racial profiling law that I had protested against in college. Moroccan youth are less than 2 percent of the population, yet Dutch police have charged more than half of them with one or more criminal offenses by the time they are twenty-three years old.[88]

The racial justice struggles in the Netherlands and Belgium surprised me. After high-profile police killings, some activists and policymakers would suggest that the US should look to Europe for police reform because cops there rarely kill people. For example, in 2019, cops in the US killed civilians at a rate more than 16 times higher than cops in the Netherlands, and killed over a thousand more people than their Dutch counterparts. The low numbers abroad are a testament that the US could have significantly fewer cop killings if we committed to have fewer guns, fewer cops, and lower inequality. But fewer shootings did not necessarily mean *good* policing, as explained by the Black, Syrian, and Moroccan people we met during the trip. The violence just manifested differently.

Adopting police reforms from other countries could be a start to save some lives, but cities could run the risk of adopting other problems. Instead of slavery, police across the globe were often birthed under other oppressive systems, like monarchies and colonialism. In the northeast United States, the modern police force drew heavily from Britain's patrols, which were developed through the colonization of Ireland. Britain colonized India and established a police force in the 1860s, modeling it after the commonwealth's colonial paramilitary police during its occupation of the Irish. Canada's and Australia's police departments were also rooted in British colonization and the forced genocide of Indigenous peoples. Indonesia's police force developed under Dutch occupation; the Japanese maintained the Dutch's model when it took over Indonesia and established their colonizing police force. Mexico's oldest police forces were derivative of Spain's Guardia Civil. The police force in Rio de Janeiro in Brazil was modernized under Portuguese colonization in the early 1800s to prevent slave uprisings after modern day Haiti. The first national police force in Nigeria was established in

1930 by the British colonial government to stifle dissent against colonial rule; Nigeria has maintained the basic structure of the police even after they gained independence in 1960. Policing is a settler colonial creation to control native populations and is exported abroad to teach other empires how to do the same.[89]

Simply pointing to Europe as a bastion of possible reforms is insufficient to change the institution. Police in Europe were still managing inequality, labor, race, immigration, and borders. Cops provided temporary protection to some immigrants from white people when the government and capitalists benefited from exploiting Turkish and North African laborers. But when their labor was no longer needed after the war, cops apprehended, expelled, and banned their descendants. The United States should absolutely aspire to Europe's relatively low arrest and incarceration rates, but by undoing racism, classism, ableism, and xenophobia, not by concentrating it.[90]

Protests were happening globally. While still in Amsterdam, I learned about students in South Africa who were conducting sit-ins and marches against national tuition fee increases. We discussed their protests at a conference that concluded our delegation called "Decolonizing the University," held at the University of Amsterdam. U of A students were also protesting tuition raises, anti-Blackness, and xenophobic behavior and policy in the region; they held a student occupation for months and supported each other through mutual aid while they crafted their demands. Nyle, Adam Elliott-Cooper, and I along with other participants at the conference took a picture of solidarity to send to the movement happening in the motherland. Adam was one of the most brilliant people that I had ever heard present. He was an organizer and doctoral student in geography at University of Oxford. At first, my very African American, midwestern self, who had only been out of the country once before, was obviously obsessed by a Black person with a British accent. But once I'd gotten over that, I absorbed his analysis on policing, class, and the Caribbean. He introduced me to the works of Black scholars like Paul Gilroy and Stuart Hall, who increased my understanding of empire, African diasporic culture, and class exploitation. When Adam, Mitchell, and the other students spoke about decolonization, I felt as if they were speaking another language full of possibility and struggle. Both were descendants of Caribbean parents, and lived in countries that maintained colonies, so their relationship to colonialism felt fresher than mine. But if students in the Netherlands, the United Kingdom, and South Africa were in solidarity in using a decolonization framework to confront class, policing, and anti-Blackness, then I definitely wanted to be in a global struggle with them, too.

WHEN I LEFT Amsterdam in October 2015, I dreamed of going to South Africa to learn about their student movement. I knew it was a risk. I was still having nightmares from being tear-gassed, assaulted, and shot at from the previous summers. And even though South Africa was much farther away from Cambridge than St. Louis, I did not expect that the police violence would be so familiar to what I experienced at home.

This would be my very first time travelling abroad alone. I had only traveled out of the country for the first time earlier that year; Geuce and I received our passports at the same time. I had traveled a bit throughout the US because of high school camps and college conferences, rarely for leisure. However, Harvard provided resources and a network to enable different kinds of travel. Earlier that year, in March, I had attended a BLSA cultural trip to Mozambique and South Africa. In Maputo, at our first hotel, the front page of the capital's newspaper featured a headline about Ferguson and a picture of a military tank. In October, I went to Dubai, the Netherlands, and Belgium. By November, I was in Paris with Geuce and Grandon when suicide bombers and gunmen killed 130 people at restaurants, a stadium, and a theater, including Le Petit Cambodge, where I had almost dined at the recommendation of my friend Keaton. She encouraged me to go to South Africa, even though I was afraid from all that I experienced through the protests, shootings, and now bombings. The student protests eventually brought me over.

Before I left town, Keaton and I joined students who were organizing under "Royall Must Fall," a decolonization campaign to retire the Harvard Law School's shield, which bore the crest of the slave owner whose bequest founded the school. The initial group of students were from South Africa or had also just returned from studying abroad there. We all discussed how much we were impacted by the "Rhodes Must Fall" and "Fees Must Fall" decolonization movements, and our movement grew to a diverse coalition of US and international students who demanded that Harvard remove the shield. A legal historian who wrote a book about Harvard's history rejected the idea, stating, "I understand why the students are upset, but this is just a fact of the school . . . if we started renaming things and taking down monuments of people linked to slavery, you would start with Washington. You don't want to hide your history. A great institution can tell the truth about itself." His fear was precisely a goal of decolonization: to remove the symbolic, political, and cultural manifestations of the people who destroyed Indigenous symbols, cultures, lands, and peoples. We did not need to start with George Washington; people who are committed to decolonization should organize to remove these legacies where they are. For activist Bree Newsome, it was physically removing the Confederate flags that flew over South Carolina's state capitol. We did not want to hide our history. We wanted to reclaim what was underneath it and decolonize our present. Symbols were a start, but as I would soon realize, institutions needed to go too, like police.[91]

During our campaign against the shield, my friend and fellow activist Rena Karefa-Johnson called me early one November morning to tell me that someone had committed a "hate crime" at Wasserstein Hall: they had used black tape to cover the portraits of Black professors in the hallway. Student activists had been agitating for months for responses from the university around police violence, racism on campus, faculty diversity, the curriculum, and now the shield, and we faced constant backlash. The black tape incident was a tipping point for a lot of students who were not involved in any activism. One group, led by two Black students, walked into the dean's classroom while she was teaching and requested that she end her class to host a community meeting.[92]

At the meeting, Black students, staff, and faculty poured out tons of racist experiences that we had had on campus and in the world. There were lots of tears, frustration, and anger in the packed room. I think the dean was trying to speak in good faith about the moment that we were in and had probably been caught off guard by the incident. Some of my white classmates, in the deepest sincerity, hugged me and told me to "hang in there." Some women on the faculty did the compassionate head tilt, using their right hand to caress my shoulder and elbow to reassure me that "things will get better one day." Two cried. I did not want them to feel sympathy for me. I wanted them to know that racial violence was bad for them, too. An ally sympathizes. I wanted less sympathy, and more commitment, risk, and sacrifice to eradicate white supremacy.

A classmate had a relationship with Melissa Harris-Perry, and MSNBC reached out to me through her to attend the show. I had helped Nyle with his talking points for his slot on the show earlier that year, reminding him to emphasize that our movement was "not anti-police, but anti–police brutality." He had said it, but teased me years later because we'd eventually evolved enough in our politics to become against the institution of policing. We were condemning the idea that activists hated individual cops, and our thinking had developed into condemning the system of policing as a vestige of slavery, colonialism, and capitalism. When I went on *Melissa Harris-Perry*, I blamed legal education for not preparing future lawyers with a racial justice analysis, suggesting that if they had one, they would learn to send cops to prison in their roles as prosecutors and judges. I would come to significantly disagree with myself later on this point. Growth requires us to constantly evaluate the ideas we hold dear.

BY DECEMBER, I was packing my bags to spend a month traveling between two cities in South Africa—Johannesburg and Cape Town. I had applied for a one thousand dollar research grant to learn about the active decolonial student movements, and write comparatively about the protest infrastructures in South Africa and the US. I arrived late on December 31st because that's when flights were cheapest. Police at the airport demanded a tip because they had walked me to a woman cab driver, reassuring me that I was definitely going to be safe because "she is a lady." I watched the clock strike midnight in the back of her cab. I told her "Happy New Year!" She did not even say it back right away because I said it too fast and too excitedly. Then she called a friend and started speaking in Zulu with so much cheer that I wanted to know, to be even, the person on the other end of the phone.

We became lost trying to find Justin Hansford's apartment at Witwatersrand University. I felt lucky that he was there on a Fulbright scholarship studying Nelson Mandela because he'd built relationships with many students and faculty who belong to the Fees Must Fall movement. But we could not find him that night, and my chances dimmed each time I reduced the brightness on my phone to preserve the battery. I didn't have service. She dropped me off at a hotel on a strip filled with parties and negotiated the thirty-dollar room rate to make sure that I was safe.

The next day, Justin and I found each other and he took me to Soweto. I visited Nelson Mandela's home and spent hours at a museum dedicated to the Soweto student uprisings in 1976. The white apartheid government passed a law that required Black South African children to be taught in Afrikaans, a language forged through white Dutch colonial settlements and the enslavement of Africans and South Asians. Along with this law, Black students were mostly restricted to a "Bantu" education: how to be a good African servant in a white home and a white-dominated country. Two teachers were fired because they refused to teach in Afrikaans. Students went on strike to protest the firings and the law requiring the educational program. Protesting was illegal; students did it anyway.[93]

I discovered many parallels between the protests and the government's response to the resistance. Students rebelled for two months and in the pictures on the museum walls, their hands were up, showing that they were unarmed, like we had been doing back in Ferguson. In Soweto, students threw rocks at the cops, like the students in Baltimore, except the South African students were being fired upon with real bullets. The apartheid government claimed that some activists who died in police custody had committed suicide to no fault of the police, just like Texas officials declared about Sandra Bland. Their signs read, "Don't Shoot!" and "Free our Brothers and Sisters!" like ours did, in St. Louis, Boston, Baltimore, and New York City. Signs also read: "Afrikaans Must Be Abolished." Cops used tear gas, rubber bullets, and real bullets. Over six hundred Blacks, some as young as seven, were murdered by police during uprisings.[94]

One photograph of the uprising had gone viral long before the internet. Photojournalist Sam Nzima had captured Mbuyisa Makhubo carrying the body of Hector Pieterson, a thirteen-year-old casualty of police violence on June 16, 1976. Nzima explained, "I saw a child fall down. Under a shower of bullets. I rushed forward and went for the picture. It had been a peaceful march, the children were told to disperse, they started singing 'Nkosi Sikelel.' The police were ordered to shoot." Cops claimed that a bullet ricocheted off of the ground and stuck Hector. An autopsy revealed that the boy was hit directly. Students retaliated against the police and Nzima photographed what happened next: "The students got hold of one policeman and they put him down on the ground and they slaughtered him like a goat . . . They set him on fire. He was burnt beyond recognition." Police forced the photographer to resign from his post at the newspaper for capturing the photos and planned to kill him on-sight. He fled, only for the police to find him, put him on house arrest, and raid and destroy his equipment months later. The police shut down the entire news organization he worked for, the only national Black paper in South Africa at the time.[95]

The police that had opened fire on the schoolchildren were a part of a special unit to quell protest over the course of several months. During South Africa's Truth and Reconciliation process decades later, government officials explained that the police's Riot Unit was set up in the country with the help of Israel a year and a half before the Soweto Uprising:

> The Riot Unit was initially based in several centres around the country and drew on the skills of the Special Task Force—a new elite unit—set up with Israeli assistance. Recruits were drawn from those with counter-insurgency training. One such recruit was Colonel "Rooi Rus" Swanepoel who led a fifty-eight-strong task force into Soweto during the first twenty-four hours of the 1976 riots and took charge of operations in Alexandra during the same period.[96]

Just months before the apartheid South African police cracked down against students that killed Pieterson, Israel military units shot down and wounded Palestinians who were protesting repression and land theft in the West Bank, a political event that came to be called "Land Day." Per South Africa's Truth and Reconciliation Commission, the two governments shared police and military tactics to repress resistance from people fighting for liberation. Colonel Theuns "Rooi Rus" Swanepoel led the forces into Soweto that day and gave the order to shoot the schoolchildren. He told the Commission, "I made my mark. I let it be known to the rioters I would not tolerate what was happening. I used appropriate force. In Soweto and Alexandra where I operated, that broke the back of the organisers."[97]

Similar to how patrols grew in response to slave resistance, and how police became more militarized to suppress Black activism, colonial policing engaged in repressive tactics to stop Indigenous peoples from rising up and overthrowing apartheid rule. It did not have to be this way; at any point, the British and the

Dutch could have ended their oppressive regimes, repatriated land, and paid reparations. They chose not to. The occupying government did not deserve the diplomatic and nonviolent efforts from Black South Africans who repeatedly appealed to the hearts and minds of the apartheid government for freedom after continued rejection. For them, the land, wealth, and resources were more important than human life. And as organizers continued to fight back with more tactics, the apartheid government chose more police, more militarism, more guns, and a stronger occupation. In addition to Israel, apartheid South African police joined cooperation agreements with Argentina, Italy, Chile, France, and Taiwan to learn and share oppression and torture tactics against colonized people across the world. Colonel Swanepoel and others specially learned torture tactics from the French police and military who occupied Algeria; other police learned from Alfredo Astiz, the notorious torturer in Argentina called "the Blond Angel of Death."[98]

Once again, I was mortified to learn about the centuries-old police suppression tactics shared across the globe to maintain oppression, slavery, and in this case, colonialism. In Ferguson, I remembered Palestinians tweeting tips about how to flush tear gas from our eyes, and how to craft makeshift gas masks. I heard rumblings that the St. Louis County police in control of the military equipment used in Ferguson were trained by the Israel's police and military units, along with thousands of other US law enforcement officials, in a program specifically designed to respond to terrorism and civilian protests. I really did not understand the full implications of the claim and was quite dismissive during the Ferguson Uprising. It all felt too conspiratorial that the United States was funding police and defense forces in Israel, and then the police departments in the US would be training with them. But reading South Africa's Truth and Reconciliation documents revealed that governments across the globe have a long history of sharing torture and anti-protest measures against Black and Indigenous peoples fighting for freedom. This history made me appreciate why activists practiced internationalism, a political commitment to support oppressed people in other parts of the world: resisting police violence in the US could help activists elsewhere resist police violence under colonization.[99]

I SPENT EVERY day on campus with students at Witwatersrand and the University of Cape Town. At Wits in Johannesburg, students were actively occupying the premises. They renamed the main hall "Solomon House" and decorated it with posters that read "*Asinamali.*" *We have no money.* They invited me to their plenaries, and nominated a chair to run the meeting. These students were sleeping on the cafeteria floor, partly as an occupation, partly because many of them could not afford to go home for the summer break. Cups and hats collected just enough *rand* to purchase slices of white bread for them to share. *Asinamali.*[100]

While eating the bread, or before fighting the men who sometimes stole the money to buy beer, the students read and strategized together, and debated which theorists and revolutionaries informed their demands. Frantz Fanon. Stephen Biko. Karl Marx. Thomas Sankara. Black women were pushing the space to include more Black feminism and radical queer theorists. Student demands toward the university, and toward each other, grew from these conversations. Their demands evolved from condemning an increase in school fees, to a much broader decolonial project that included calls for free education; protection for women, trans women, and gender-nonconforming students; free university housing; the end of police brutality; and amnesty for charged student activists. Much to my shock, students were also still fighting to abolish classes and exams that were taught only in Afrikaans, the colonial language that the Soweto students had resisted decades earlier. I was most inspired by their demands to end contract and outsourced labor at the university so that the Black dining and custodial workers could receive full medical and tuition benefits.

I spent full days on campus, leaving around midnight and returning at nine the next morning. One morning when I arrived, groups of Black men dressed in all-black uniforms with weapons lined the stairs to Solomon House. Student organizers were crying, bleeding, and running. They explained to me that early that morning, while they had been sound asleep inside the hall, private police quietly entered and forcibly removed activists without warning. The private force woke the men with punches to their faces and bodies, and ripped the shirt off of at least one woman, grabbing and fondling her breasts. Another officer dragged a student outside by her locs. All of the guards were Black, and so were all of the students. Regardless of the shared race, the private guards had still been tasked—by a public university—with the punitive social control of Black people. I tried to help them find each other to regain communication and plan how to regroup. We decided to meet at a private location to do a headcount and debrief about what happened. On my way there, I saw two teams of white students playing cricket on the most serene field I'd ever seen. Two Black women activists who were attacked earlier also saw them play. Rather than walk around the field, they walked directly through the match, glacially, one pausing to smoke a cigarette. A coach yelled at them to hurry and the players started moving with agitation. The activists outright retorted, "This is our land."

The next day, I flew to Cape Town to continue my trip. I almost cancelled my flight because of the violence at Wits, but students at UCT were also still actively protesting, and I wanted to learn about police violence in the township near Cape Town, Khayelitsha. On my way to the airport, I kept reliving the bloody scenes from the messy hall. I tried to think about a different time in Solomon House to replace the images, like weeks before when a lead student organizer told the circle that their fallism movement was not about moving Black people from Soweto to Sandton but transforming the entire racial and economic sphere of the land. Sandton is one of the wealthiest, whitest suburbs of Johannesburg where I happened to be staying at the time for free because a friend from my teaching days had arranged for me to borrow her friend's flat who was summering elsewhere. I began laughing in the back of the Uber because I hadn't known what the student organizer was talking about until I whispered to Justin, "Is that the same Sandton where I'm staying?" Justin had nodded, smiled, and shushed me.

I kept that message close. I had to let go of what so many Black people believed we needed to be free and safe in the United States: the idea that the police, private property, and capitalism were the way to protection and mobility. I didn't want what white people had to be the basis of our liberation. I wanted to be free. White people weren't even free. They were bound to rotten fruits of slavery, colonialism, and genocide, and found culture and identity in flags, borders, and badges. The police reforms that promised us equal protection under the law were equally protecting the violence that I wanted to eradicate. And Black people, all people, in the US and abroad, deserved so much more than that.

FOUR

LOVE AND ABOLITION

CAPE TOWN SITS nestled between an ocean with crashing white waves and several majestic mountains. The cab driver offered a tour up the hillside to see the clouds—I could not refuse. When I got out of the car to take in the smell of the water, I turned to him and said, "White people in America love telling Black people to 'go back to Africa.' I might let these racists start fundraising to send me." He laughed and answered, "Please keep it a secret. The first white people who found out about its beauty did not leave." Johannesburg boasts a 75 percent Black population; less than 20 percent are white, and the remaining are Asian, Indian, and mixed raced people called "Colored." In Cape Town, about 20 percent of the population is Black; more than half are Colored and a quarter are white.

I stayed downtown in Zelda Holtzman's apartment. I met her son, Dmitri, through Purvi Shah, who had invited me to help launch an organization for law students, legal workers, and lawyers to support Black Lives Matter activism. Purvi and I had been on the same legal rapid-response calls to provide jail and bail support for protests in Ferguson and Baltimore. She encouraged me to visit Dmitri's organization, Equal Education Law Centre, when I flew to Cape Town. Dmitri offered to ask his mother if I could stay in her guest room and she agreed. When I met Zelda, I told her what I'd been through in the movements against police violence in the US, and then about the private security that had violently attacked students at Wits. She replied that while much had seemingly changed on the surface, so many repressive colonial practices had remained in policing. I was not prepared for what she said next. She was a former cop. And not just any cop. Zelda had been the highest-ranking Black woman in the entire police force of South Africa after the fall of apartheid in 1994 and belonged to the group of five that was charged with transforming it nationwide.

Zelda had been active in movements against colonial repression and dispossession of the land since she was fourteen years old. A white police officer shot and killed her friend from high school at a protest they had attended together. The killing devastated and angered her, and she consequently joined the Black Consciousness Movement, the dominant rallying political platform for Black liberation at the time. She was later recruited to the African National Congress (ANC), an organization that the white apartheid government had banned and criminalized membership to at the time. The ANC had been mobilizing the public against the government and for the Freedom Charter, a revolutionary document that compiled and distilled the freedom dreams of thousands of South Africans into a set of measures that included democratic governance; equal rights; equal sharing of wealth; redistribution of land and the freedom of movement; equality before the law; the right to labor, unionize, and take paid maternity leave; the right to free education and cultural resources; the right to housing, safety, and health care; and the call for peace and friendship. The Charter provided tremendous impetus for various individuals and civic, business, religious, and community sectors of society to resist the apartheid government and fight for the future they believed in.

Zelda organized to mobilize these sectors from underground and above-ground at the grassroots level. Above-ground organizing entailed mass political education and working in communities around electricity access, laundry line access, the end to unfair criminal charges, and many more basic rights that were translated into political demands under the United Democratic Front that emerged in 1983. These above-ground organizing structures were interconnected to the underground structures that Zelda belonged to as well. The ANC had been pleading the colonial government and even British royalty for an end to repression, violence, and torture against Black South Africans as early as the 1920s, and by the 1980s, they'd moved past the point of pleading and letter writing to save their lives. She recalled: "Peaceful protests through letters and other means were of no consequence to the apartheid government. They attacked and massacred peaceful protestors at Sharpeville. But whether the ANC would engage in other tactics brought heated debates." The ANC ultimately decided to create a militant wing for political resistance, Umkhonto we Sizwe (MK).

To be an operative in the underground, she emphasized, meant to build the ANC presence among the people through day-to-day struggle around their class positions to make the Freedom Charter come alive through a variety of tactics. Principled armed resistance to apartheid was one tactic, which included attacks and bombings against apartheid military and police installations. The white settler colonial government ultimately collapsed under the resistance of freedom fighters like Zelda; the ongoing student protests; and an international boycott, divestment, and sanctions movement to make companies like Shell and Coca-Cola lose money for supporting apartheid in South Africa.

Under peace and transitional government agreements, the MK and other armed wings of anti-apartheid liberation movements integrated into the military and intelligence departments of the former apartheid government. To promote diversity and inclusion, Zelda was assigned to advance representation and equal opportunity in the South African Police Service (SAPS), which was previously an all-white, male-dominated and oriented command structure. She recalled in a later public event that the SAPS was "the most brutal arm of the state"; it conducted "the general day-to-day oppression" of Black South Africans, including the murderous shootings against protesters and people demanding their basic rights. For almost a decade, she attempted to reform and transform SAPS. She eventually left her post in 2003 with not much hope for the police. She explained to me:

I held an earlier view of police to be a resource for people when they need protection or support, but not for police to remove the agency of people to engage in ways that secure their safety. But police act as if they are the only resource, and their obligation is to the state, property, and people with property. When the state and the people are disconnected, then the police are disconnected from the people and view them as the enemy. The state is not enabling the basic needs, visions, and values contained in the Freedom Charter. People protest the corruption, and the police protect the state, turn the guns on the people.

Police will say "bad apples" and we need trials for these extra-judicial killings. However it is a pattern and not isolation, which led me to think of it not as extra-judicial killings, but as judicial; you put them in uniform, give them weapons of war, and send them to march. Cops don't look to protect our safety at protests—no support, no emergency preparedness. They are out to do battle in a war zone and act at the least provocation. This is a war of inequality, but we need a re-imagination of a resource for people's safety, separate from police as the foundation for that, but embedded in the people; conflict resolution, peace commit-tees, street committees, block committees, democratic expressions of people powered projects.[101]

The #FeesMustFall and #RhodesMustFall student movements echoed her criticisms of police violence and broader systemic inequality. For decades under apartheid, the Dutch and the English dispossessed Black South Africans of their homes and land and sold it cheaply to white farmers, and gave it away in many instances. As of 2019, South Africa was 90 percent Black, but 72 percent of the land owned by individuals was owned by white people. The students I met at Wits were making demands against the ongoing legacies of colonialism and their goals—free education, the end to contractual labor, land—mirrored the Freedom Charter. Zelda was very supportive of the student movements because they cham-pioned decolonization discourse, the removal of statutes, symbols, ideas, and systems that facilitated the theft of their land, labor, and lives. This connected to her involvement in the Black Consciousness movement of the 1970s, where they called for "equal education," but not equal in comparison to whites—"the master"—but equal to the needs of the oppressed people rising up.

PARADOXICALLY, THE MORE I wanted to return to my movement in the US, the less committed I became to my movement's demands. After spending time with Zelda, student and worker activists at Wits and the University of Cape Town, the organizers in the townships, and the lawyers at Equal Education, I had begun to grow weary of saying "Black Lives Matter." People abroad were fighting for land, free education, the end to contractual labor, real democracy, and decolonization. I was inspired by their intergenerational relationships and annoyed that in the US, many of our elder Black liberals in the mainstream media condemned our music for its profane language, and young Black people too easily dismissed the messy yet rich traditions that made us possible. For too many of us in the beginning, "Black Lives Matter" was a response to violence or a non-indictment; South Africa demonstrated that we deserved much more. I felt completely politically undone and inadequate. I'd been reading so much history but had not quite yet developed a political analysis connected to any tradition of organizing. I was getting smarter, not necessarily getting free.

I wasn't alone. Phil Agnew, a co-founder of Dream Defenders, told me he'd felt the same way after returning from a pivotal trip abroad. In the aftermath of Trayvon Martin's death, Phil had zeal for leadership within the Florida-based multiracial organization, but his political analysis was nascent. He was concerned that the younger white college students advocating for socialism in the organization might be patronizing provocateurs, or maybe even government infiltrators. Phil believed racism was the primary issue of oppression, not capitalism, as if the two were not intertwined. He made a pact with another organizer to protect Dream Defenders from the aggressive students and to ensure that DD would focus on ending racial profiling, ending the school-to-prison pipeline, and repealing the Stand Your Ground law.

By the time Phil traveled to Ferguson for the uprising in 2014, Dream Defenders were campaigning to end mass incarceration in the state of Florida and learning about prison abolition. They had just added Michelle Alexander and Angela Davis to their advisory board. Like Nyle, Phil did not quite recall whether police abolition specifically was a part of his vocabulary. After one police killing in Miami, members put up "WANTED" posters around town with the cop's name and face to pressure the prosecutor into bringing charges. His heart was in the right place, but he was trying to sort out which traditions he belonged to as an organizer.

All that changed when Phil joined organizers in Ferguson, Ohio, and Florida to go to Brazil for a week-long political education and solidarity gathering with Movimento Sem Terra (The Landless Workers Movement). Phil went to Brazil, studied, and took classes where he finally learned what the early organizers in Dream Defenders meant by socialism. "They weren't trying to infiltrate. They were trying to improve our class analysis."[102]

The Dream Defenders embarked on a social media blackout and started political education reading groups around anti-capitalism, racism, sexism, and patriarchy. The organization hired Rachel Gilmer, an organizer and researcher with the African American Policy Forum, as their Director of Strategy. By 2016, Dream Defenders had reshaped their members, sharpened their feminist politics, shifted their leadership, and launched new campaigns that were rooted in abolition, socialism, feminism, and internationalism. DD waged statewide campaigns against incarceration and initiated delegations abroad so that young activists could learn from Palestinians who wanted to be free from military occupation. The group transformed from the 2012 activists who inspired millions of people to demand justice for Trayvon Martin. I was evolving, too.

When I returned from South Africa to Cambridge in early 2016, I shared my concerns and hopes with student organizers in a meeting on the top floor of Wasserstein Hall. We were committed to social justice and our demands were well-intentioned, though I feared that we had not yet developed a shared political analysis to make sure we were fighting for the right thing. Between 2014 and 2017, our demands mostly mirrored the students' demands at almost one hundred universities: increase in racial diversity among students, faculty, administration, and curriculum. I had been making the same demands since college. This time around, many students wanted schools to issue statements that condemned police violence and affirmed Black lives. We did not want white professors to ask exam questions where we had to hypothetically defend cops, or as one professor did, list all of the charges that an activist could face for protesting the non-indictment decisions.

Yet, unlike the students in Cape Town and Johannesburg, most of us had not taken the time to undergo political education together to develop an analysis around power and justice. We had never interrogated why we believed that justice meant police convictions and whether a more diverse faculty would eliminate campus racism. Most importantly, we had not taken the time to connect our organizing to the workers on campus, including the clinical, custodial, and dining staff, who were especially vulnerable to marginalization, racism, and exploitation.

Finally, we had yet to confront the fact that our well-written demands were insufficient measures toward our liberation. "What are our politics?" I asked the emotionally tense room. Was our goal for a few women, queer people, Black people to integrate into positions of power to make change? Or did we belong to the traditions of organizers trying to dismantle systemic racism and inequality so that more people can thrive? We did not have an answer.

Rathna Ramamurthi, who would become instrumental in redeveloping our political education and demands, was hesitant. She, like more than half of the room, feared that taking the time to read and debate would cause us to lose momentum. A South African graduate student who had been active in student protests abroad suggested that we do both—continue to organize for our demands and add a political education component to our movement.

BEGINNING IN FEBRUARY 2016, our student formation (which we called Reclaim HLS after the black tape incident) changed again. Several members left after furious debates; they thought we were sacrificing our chance for real change to read and become radical. But radical, which according to Angela Davis means to grasp at the roots of a problem, is good. Fighting for a new society where everyone can thrive is radical in a country built on genocide, land theft, and slavery. We tried to convince those students that we needed to understand radical traditions— decolonization, socialism, abolition—before we could criticize or dismiss them. We split. Our smaller group of activists decided to study and organize in the most visible, beautiful hall on the law school's campus, right downstairs from the meeting. Drawing lessons from the student movements abroad who renamed their campus buildings without the permission of the university, we renamed the space "Belinda Hall," after Belinda Sutton, a Black woman who was once owned by Isaac Royall. Royall was a slave owner who bequeathed the money that founded Harvard Law School. Belinda Sutton sued for a pension when Royall fled the country during the Revolutionary War. She won, which may be the first successful case of reparations in Massachusetts history.[103]

We brought art, decor, even air mattresses into the space. At first, I spent the night regularly. But when I became pregnant with my second child, Garvey, I couldn't sleep on the floor anymore. Each day, we organized a plenary, nominated a chair, and made decisions democratically about the future of our movement.

Rathna stayed. She maintained a daily schedule of events in Belinda Hall, including our political education readings, performances, and speeches. Union organizers and striking dining workers held meetings and rallies there. Despite what we perceived to be punitive threats from the administration, we persisted. Affinity groups began holding their meetings there in solidarity with us. It was the only space on the entire campus where anyone could attend or teach a class, regardless of whether they were custodial staff, dining workers, clinical faculty, professors, students, or even affiliated with the university.

As Reclaim HLS, we initially demanded a critical race theory program. The critical race theory movement is a "collection of activists and scholars engaged in studying and transforming the relationship among race, racism, and power." Derrick Bell was foundational to the movement's creation, scholarship, and activism. Student activism pushed Harvard Law to hire Bell, who became its first Black tenured professor. Bell eventually left Harvard Law in protest because they did not hire and tenure Black women. He never returned and died as a visiting professor at New York University. Students in Belinda Hall wanted professors like Bell, who taught how the law intersected with racial justice, feminism, and colonialism.[104]

We kept that demand and decided to run our own critical race theory program in Belinda Hall. We invited a few scholars and word spread so quickly, some scholars started reaching out to us to come. Legendary organizer and strategist Marshall Ganz expressed interest in leading a workshop. Mari Matsuda, Chuck Lawrence, Catharine MacKinnon, Cornel West, Robin D. G. Kelley, Margaret Montoya, Khiara Bridges, and Justin Hansford all held teach-ins. We held many meeting and events twice to accommodate the schedules of workers. Any given gathering could have from six people to several hundred. Student activists from other universities sent delegations and some started political education programs back on their campuses. And of course, whenever there was a police killing or another tragic event in the world, students, faculty, and staff—even the ones who threatened us with disciplinary action—knew to gather in Belinda Hall for support, reflection, and action the next day.

For our very first political education meeting, we read a soon-to-be published essay by historian Robin D. G. Kelley called "Slipping in the Darkness." A modified version was eventually published in the *Boston Review* as "Black Study,

Black Struggle." More important than giving students the answer to our racial justice fight, Robin's essay reminded us that we come from a long tradition of radical Black activists who engaged in love, study, and struggle toward freedom. There was no "one answer" to stop the violence we encountered on campus and in the streets; we needed to form an analysis to evaluate the issues and determine what we wanted to build. Over time, he explained, the university may soften and concede to our cultural demands, but rarely on the transformational ones: "This is why buildings will be renamed and all-Black or People of Color 'safe' spaces will be created out of a sliver of university real estate, but proposals to eliminate tuition and forgive student debt for the descendants of the dispossessed and the enslaved will be derided as absurd." The law school proved him right. They eventually met our original demands to make administrative diversity hires, to remove Isaac Royall's family shield, and to set up a memorial for those enslaved by the Royall family—a rock near the library stairs. Students are still campaigning to divest Harvard's multi-billion endowment from fossil fuels and private prisons.[105]

Robin's essay confirmed that we were on the right track. Some students and faculty mocked our movement. One day, we'd found surveillance bugs planted underneath the tables. On social media, a law firm partner said he'd made sure not hire us. Two classmates shouted at activists who removed Trump signs from Belinda Hall. *Who were we, a bunch of students at Harvard Law whining about being oppressed?* True, all of us were in very different positions than the unhoused people who slept at the intersections in Harvard Square, and far from the workers who cleaned each table and chair in between classes. Our student loans were going to be burdens when we became attorneys, though differently from the payday loans I suffered in college. Yet many of us had been organizers before law school and lived in the thin, overlapping circle between the exploited and the elite. My first summer home, I picked my mother up from a food and clothes pantry. "I told you, I told all of y'all that I had a daughter who went to Harvard," she said loudly to the volunteers. "Harvard or Howard?" "Harvard, momma. Howard is in DC."[106]

Additionally, critics of our campus organizing did not value what I held dear as an organizer: people who care about changing the world should also change where they belong—families, schools, jobs, and neighborhoods. For us, it happened to be the university. Through experimentation, failure, and growth, we built multi-racial, cross sector unity in creating the versions of society we wanted. Writing from his San Quentin Prison cell, political prisoner and movement theorist George Jackson envisioned liberation projects that required the multi-racial, cross-sector organizing of Black, brown, and white people in factories, universities, and the streets. He considered all of us to be victims under capitalist exploitation and called for campus activists to "counter the ill effects of fascism at its training site." Fascism, according to Jackson, is a dynamic and evolving set of political, racist, militaristic, and police-based responses to anything that threatens the capitalist ruling class. Campuses, including Ivy League schools, can certainly become training sites for fascism because that's partially where the ruling classes are preserved. Donald Trump went to the University of Pennsylvania. Kris Kobach and Joshua Hawley both have Yale law degrees. Rafael "Ted" Cruz went to Harvard Law. So did former press secretary Kayleigh McEnany, who was a student there while we were organizing in Belinda Hall. They tout their alma maters all the way to the courts, Congress, and the West Wing to advance white nationalist agendas.[107]

Through all of the criticism, the organizers persisted. In a large circle in Belinda, we read Robin's paper like a lost biblical text. We especially debated his call for marronage. The word "maroons" originates from the Spanish *cimarrones*, meaning "wild" or "feral." Maroons were formerly enslaved Africans who ran away and formed self-sustaining communities of care, comprised of anywhere from a handful of people to several thousands, lasting less than a year for some to more than a century for others. As soon as the Spanish Crown granted permission for settler colonists to transport enslaved Africans to the Americas in 1501, Black people resisted and ran away when they landed. Colonial governments in response began prohibiting Black people from carrying weapons and assaulting white people, and maroons continued to steal and launch raids against plantation owners. Maroon rebellions and raids toward freedom prompted European colonizers to request more resources for law enforcement and patrols to preempt and stop raids from maroons. Sometimes colonizer governments entered truces to stop the wars, as was the case in 1618 when a Spanish king issued a charter to a large maroon community in Mexico; this eventually established the first officially recognized settlement for maroons in the Americas. Earlier settlements happened, too.

In 1526, enslaved Africans rebelled against their Spanish captors who attempted the first European settlement in what became the continental US. With the additional raids from the Indigenous, and mutinous settlers, the Spanish fled. This was the first recorded instance of Black slavery in North America, and more importantly, the first slave rebellion in North America. Africans then joined Indigenous tribes for refuge. These maroons became the first permanent settlement of non-Indigenous people in the US. Maroons lived freely, or at least unenslaved, throughout the Americas in various capacities nearly a full century before indentured Africans were brought to the shores of a Virginia colony in 1619.[108]

Robin hoped that students would model themselves after the fugitive and interdependent relationships that maroons built among each other. Historian Sylviane Diouf explains that many free Blacks lived in subservience to white society and remained controlled by discriminatory laws and customs that guided their interactions. Maroons however lived underneath a society that accepted slavery—but their secrecy forced them into a set of interdependent relationships with other maroons, animals, and the earth. Robin made a parallel case for students to use the university only to get what they needed. Maroons stole tools from the master's house to create the community they believed in, rather than try to use the tools to fix the master's house. He charged us to build our own loving spaces to study and struggle, where we could experiment with democracy, accountability, mutual aid, and care, paying homage to maroon communities who practiced this for centuries.

Rathna, the organizer who was initially skeptical of our political education journey, later explained that our organizing around the essay changed her thinking more than anything else in her life: "Something about that language helped me understand the difference between trying to make an unjust system more 'inclusive' versus building an alternative vision that can also be used to put pressure on the existing system." We were confronted with a choice: keep organizing to make our school or country live up to the ideals that it claimed or build beloved communities to transform ourselves as we organized in pursuit of liberation. We fused the two to keep organizing and implemented our own demands to create the world we wanted.

Alongside marronage, Robin introduced and re-introduced the concept of "abolition" to many Belinda activists. Of course, we knew of abolition as a project of elimination. The word derives from Latin's *abolere,* "to destroy." Generally, when I had heard the term, it was a call to end an oppressive system. *Slavery abolition. The abolition of child labor. Debt abolition. Prison industrial complex abolition.* But in the draft of his essay, Robin coupled the word with "love" and "future," expanding the possibility of our community-building and transformation:

> James Baldwin understood love as agency probably better than anyone. For him it meant to love ourselves as Black people; it meant making love the motivation for making revolution; it meant envisioning a society where everyone is embraced, where there is no oppression, where every life is valued—even those who may once have been our oppressors. It did not mean seeking white people's love and acceptance or seeking belonging in the world created by our oppressor. In *The Fire Next Time,* he is unequivocal: "I do not know many Negroes who are eager to be 'accepted' by white people, still less to be loved by them; they, the blacks, simply don't wish to be beaten over the head by the whites every instant of our brief passage on this planet." But here is the catch—if we are committed to an abolitionist future, we have no choice but to love all. To love all is to fight relentlessly to end exploitation and oppression everywhere, even on behalf of those who think they hate us. This was Baldwin's point—perhaps his most misunderstood and reviled point.[109]

By suggesting that *we* were committed to an abolitionist future, Robin not-so-subtly called into question the direction our movements were heading. Most people in the movements that I belonged to at the time, from Black Lives Matter to Belinda Hall, had not yet professed a commitment to an abolitionist future. We had been calling for the arrests, indictments, and convictions of killer cops; an assertion of Black life in public spheres; and the diversification of systems that participated in the exploitation we'd been fighting. We initially expected that kinder and browner cops, prosecutors, judges, and faculty would alleviate the violence. In contrast, he explained, students at the University of North Carolina at Chapel Hill were demanding that the university end their ties to prison labor; disarm campus police; provide free childcare for students, faculty, and staff; and offer a twenty-five-dollar-per-hour minimum wage. UNC's demands reflected the revolutionary demands from organizers in South Africa, the Netherlands, and Brazil. It was the tradition of organizing I believed in.[110]

Never before had I read about love and abolition that way. For me, slavery abolition sought to end an evil institution and death penalty abolition sought to end an immoral government practice. But in Belinda, I felt responsible for organizing and molding abolitionist futures with other people, which was much broader than the elimination of any one particular system practice. It was a politic, a paradigm to organize, navigate, and re-create the world. *Love* offered me more agency than resistance or trauma could, and my growing desire to learn and take risks with others became a source of inspiration for my freedom. For our freedom.

Fred Moten and Stefano Harney, whom Robin cites in his marronage essay, illuminated abolition further for us during a reading of their text, *The Undercommons: Fugitive Planning and Black Study*, at Belinda Hall:

> Ruth Wilson Gilmore: "Racism is the state-sanctioned and/or extra-legal production and exploitation of group differentiated vulnerabilities to premature (social, civil and/or corporeal) death." What is the difference between this and slavery? What is, so to speak, the object of abolition? Not so much the abolition of prisons but the abolition of a society that could have prisons, that could have slavery, that could have the wage, and therefore not abolition as the elimination of anything but abolition as the founding of a new society.[111]

Moten and Harney revealed a belief that I hadn't realize I held. At that point, I had been somewhat comfortable with the notion of reforming prisons, police, and prosecutors because I thought that our society *had* to have them. I knew the origins of these systems and that they were working according to their design, but creating new societies felt more daunting than tweaking the terms of the state sanctioned violence, whether it was slavery, capitalism, or police.

Moten and Harney also directly challenged what I was being trained to do as a lawyer, which is to keep everything in its place. *Defend the Constitution, don't question its existence. Zealously represent your clients, don't be an activist against injustice in the courtroom. Champion progressive policies that secure lawyers for people in concentrated poverty; don't bother to eliminate concentrated wealth.* Abolition as the founding of a new society disrupts any allegiance to any republic for which it stands, and begs us to ask, "What should we be standing for?" The US once "stood" for genocide, slavery, disenfranchisement and currently "stands" for militarism, policing, and the concentration of wealth for a few. Abolition destroys the stubborn allegiances keep society so violent and births new possibilities to live under a dynamic democracy led by the people.

LAWYERING IN COURT increased my urgency for these abolitionist futures. As I began my last year of law school in 2016, I started working as a public defender in the Criminal Justice Institute (CJI), a legal clinic at Harvard founded by the legendary Charles Ogletree, Jr. Professors Ronald Sullivan and Dehlia Umunna run the clinic. Sullivan is a storied criminal defense attorney; he's won the release of more wrongfully incarcerated people than anyone else in the country. Before coming to Harvard, Umunna had represented hundreds of indigent clients as a lawyer with the DC Public Defender Service, the most reputable public defender office in the country for legal training and advocacy. In CJI, a team of public defense attorneys trained students to represent indigent clients in the Boston area, regardless of the charge. I had been dreaming of *that* moment, of being trained as a "real lawyer" fighting for justice in court, since my mom told me I had to decades earlier. My suits were fresh because I had just given birth to Garvey and my body weight was fluctuating. The state's letter of approval for me to practice was folded in the pocket of my thick, brown letter portfolio. I was ready to go.

Everything about court was wrong. The parking, the weather, the expectation of justice. As soon as I walked in, I saw a giant glass box that covered the entrance to a jail. The court clerk would call the case and a cop would bring a defendant downstairs to sit inside the cage. A tiny circle was cut into the glass box, and each defendant put their mouth through it to speak to their lawyers, the prosecutor, and the judge, and then swap their mouth with their ear to listen. The demeaning dance—ear, mouth, ear, mouth—was repeated throughout the day. When I visited clients in the jail, it happened again. I had to clinch my skirt as I kneeled on the floor to speak with clients because we could only communicate through the thin slot typically used for food trays. Police killings are horrible. The victims cause us to storm the streets, but the survivors end up here. All of those marches and court battles for improve the criminal justice system did not comfort my clients' knees on that filthy floor.

The defendants weren't perfect. They grew up in the same racist, ableist, homophobic, classist, and patriarchal society that I did. When I would walk to speak with court staff or pick up paperwork from the fax machine, a few Black men waiting for their cases to be called would make comments about how I looked, my body, my "ass" specifically. The first time it happened, I called Marbre and cried about how I did not feel comfortable walking to the front of the courtroom anymore. *Damn, I did not go to law school to become a civil rights lawyer for this. I was on their side!* I soon realized that the men who made those comments knew exactly what they were doing and *who* they were doing it to. The only other Black woman lawyer in the courtroom at the time was a prosecutor. I never heard them make any comments like that toward her, though she had so much more power over their lives than I did. So I started sharply speaking back, "What did you just say?" and "Can you repeat that louder?" Surprised at my response, nobody ever did. They'd stay silent, hold my gaze, or try to laugh it off. Being poor does not make someone less patriarchal just like being queer does not make someone less racist, it all just manifests differently. Tweaking the court with modest reforms focuses too narrowly on improving specific practices whereas building an abolitionist future ends these deep forms of violence that underlie our relationships to each other.

Judges and prosecutors were also problematic. Both almost always automatically accepted whatever was on a police report despite wide knowledge of police fabrication. Defense attorneys prayed for particular judges to preside over their clients' cases based on how racist, reasonable, or realistic they perceived the judge. We had to argue to divert people away from jail and ask for probation as an alternative; prosecutors overwhelmingly opposed these arguments, regardless of the underlying charge. One time, a court psychologist evaluated one of my clients. She found that my client lacked comprehension of the charges and was not competent to stand trial. She told the judge that my client would probably never regain competence to stand trial due to a traumatic brain injury and did *not* meet the criteria to be imprisoned or confined in a psychiatric institution. The prosecutor still argued against my client's release. The judge, technically unable to imprison my client because there had been no trial, issued a "continuance" to schedule another hearing as an excuse to detain my client in jail for several more months. As we chanted in Ferguson, "the whole damn system" was indeed guilty.

Probation brought no relief. I argued successfully to divert my clients from jail and they were still under the watchful presence of probation employees who constantly threatened their freedom. "Corrections" is a misnomer since they spent zero time correcting anyone's behavior and all of their time monitoring and inflicting punishment for anyone who fell short of the stipulations. The stipulations are rife with contradictions. For example, they expected one of my unhoused clients to stay away from police, even though the police disproportionately patrol homeless people. If the police arrive at a homeless encampment, then what should people do? Cops can arrest people for loitering; cops even have the legal power to stop them from walking away under the guise of "suspicious behavior"; and cops can chase or shoot people who run for no reason.

I had a small and racially diverse caseload. Everybody was poor. Whatever trepidations I had about abolition "letting all the lawbreakers" out of jail quickly dissipated because most of the "criminals" were actually just poor people. Because of capitalism, racism, and ableism, the darkest and poorest peoples in the United States are relegated to live precarious lives where they do what they can to survive, sometimes including breaking the law. Police do not and cannot address the society that creates racial and economic exploitation, only punish people who steal, fight, burglarize, and trespass because of it. Rather than eliminating the unjust conditions, cities and the federal government send in police to manage the inequality. Cops lie and make careless arrests, so they often punish people who have not committed any crime at all. Police also have wide discretion to arrest someone they deem disorderly. Justin Hansford described enforcement this way to me: "Law is what's on the books; order is what's in a cop's head." Jails are full of people who are there because a cop decided so, not because anything happened. Certainly, jails are full of lawbreakers, too. So are our homes, schools, churches, and grocery stores. The primary differences are race, class, and police presence. Presidents gloat in memoirs and speeches about smoking weed or inhaling lines of cocaine during their high school and college years while championing legislation that deports or imprisons poor people over same thing.[112]

Cops overwhelmingly arrest economically exploited people like my clients, approximately ten million people each year. Five million of those arrested go to jail once, at least one million go to jail twice, and half a million go to jail three or more times. Half of the people who are arrested and jailed at least twice in one year are unemployed, unlikely to have a high school diploma, and have annual incomes of ten thousand dollars or less. In 2014, people incarcerated in prison had a median annual income of less than twenty thousand dollars before they were imprisoned, 41 percent less than their non-incarcerated peers. Incarcerated white men had incomes 54 percent lower than their non-incarcerated peers; Black men 44 percent lower, Black women 47 percent lower, Hispanic men 34 percent lower, Hispanic women 21 percent lower. [113]

Once facing jail, people who could afford to hire private attorneys usually did. Others who could not afford them had to raise or borrow money, find extra work, or put up their houses to try to avoid jail. The remaining ones found themselves with someone like me to help argue for their freedom, a public defender or a law student in a clinic. My clients weren't inherently bad or evil, even the one who repeated racist lines from Trump said about Black people. We had serious conversations about their language and ideas because I refused to tolerate the racism. Yet I chose to continue representing that particular client because ultimately, as I was learning in Belinda, I had a much larger commitment to fight relentlessly to end exploitation everywhere, even on behalf of those who think they hate us.

The routine violence from cops and the courts reminded me of a quote from an Audre Lorde text that we discussed in Belinda Hall:

> For the master's tools will never dismantle the master's house. They may allow us temporarily to beat him at his own game, but they will never enable us to bring about genuine change. And this fact is only threatening to those women who still define the master's house as their only source of support.[114]

While Lorde was originally criticizing white feminists, I realized that her assessment could be applied to me, too. Many people define, as I did, the current legal system as their sole source of support for justice and safety. If police and jails are the sole sources of support for safety, then someone might feel threatened by abolition and comforted by reforms to improve the system. Lorde's quote is a reminder than genuine change comes from dismantling oppressive systems, not taking tools to fix them to work for everyone. The "master's house" is the problem, not just who can access it or whether people will be treated equitably upon arrival. The criminal legal system is similar. Cops did not need to treat my Black and Latinx clients the same way they treated my white clients, for they were all facing the same glass box inside that Roxbury courtroom, together.

Additionally, some community members resist abolition because they rely on police as a source of employment. Cities use policing as a jobs program the same way that states use prisons to revitalize rural economies.

Many cops, especially the cops that I knew, entered law enforcement because it was the only job in our neighborhood that could help feed their families and maybe buy a small house. Criticizing protesters who wanted to divest money from police, Chicago mayor Lori Lightfoot said that activists were "eliminating one of the few tools that the city has to create middle-class incomes for black and brown folks." In her own words, cops were the master's *tools* that Lightfoot sought to protect. Their protection came along with the destruction of the Black communities in Chicago who have faced sexual violence, ableism, assault, torture, and murder by the police. Black and brown people like my clients did not need more police; they needed different tools that abolition offered to address the root causes of violence.[115]

For people like my clients—and my family, friends, and neighbors—the violence they were accused of stemmed from inequality, patriarchy, and racism. Some stole, some fought, some acted violently on their racist beliefs. As George Jackson argued, "Criminals and crime arise from material, economic, sociopolitical causes." Jackson knew as well as anyone. Police arrested him for a seventy-dollar gas station stickup; a prosecutor charged him with armed robbery, and a judge sentenced him to one year to life in prison. The Black men who made the comments toward me in the court were not evil people. They were patriarchal, but not evil. I'm sure whatever landed them in court likely arose from material, economic, and sociopolitical causes and related to their behavior toward me and others. That did not mean that I had to accept or tolerate it. I rejected it. But I also rejected the power that the police, prosecutors, probation officers, and judges had over them.[116]

Those days in court also revealed a limitation in my understanding of "resources." I'd been trapped in regurgitating that we could make abolition possible by providing resources to the most marginalized groups in our society. This is only partially true. I had witnessed people who have immense resources cause more violence than everyone locked every in jail *combined*. None of my clients started the "War on Terror" that killed hundreds of thousands of soldiers and civilians, nor did they sell lead-riddled toys, makeup, and jewelry that poisoned children and teenagers around the world. I've watched a judge sentence a Black man to nearly a decade over a carjacking, but never imprison an automobile company executive who ignored or hid manufacturing defects that caused thousands of crashes that broke bones, shattered teeth, and burned people alive. People with resources were not necessarily innocent of harming others. Quite the contrary. Their wealth accumulation resulted in environmental violence against the planet and our flesh; economic violence through the labor exploitation that makes their wealth possible; police violence that manages poor people in the projects, on the streets, and at the borders; and wars that lead to casualties over oil, coal, natural gas, and precious metals. All of their violent behavior was perfectly legal, so they weren't lawbreakers. Nevertheless, their violence had to be abolished, too.

WHILE I WAS working in the public defender clinic, I continued organizing in Belinda. There, my decolonization analysis and budding abolitionist politics started to collide and crash. Across the globe, my new friends and comrades were arguing about removing structures and practices left over from colonial governments. But by the time I discovered the concept of "abolition democracy," my ideas about decolonization made me realize that I had to stop romanticizing slavery abolitionists who were committed to racial capitalism and colonialism.

The promise and perils of the short-lived Reconstruction period and "abolition democracy" after slavery informs the inspiration and theory for many scholars of abolition, including Angela Davis. When I finally studied her work on abolition in Belinda, I was grateful for how much it had started to influence a generation of budding, contemporary abolitionists, like the Dream Defenders, BYP100, students in South Africa, and me. Davis uses "abolition democracy," the eponym of her book, to explain that "DuBois thus argues that a host of democratic institutions are needed to fully achieve abolition—thus abolition democracy." Abolition happened in the destruction of slavery and barely even that. The day after the Civil War, four million Black people found themselves in the same position they were in the day before the war ended—on plantations, no economic power, no political power. For *abolition democracy*, she explains, and new institutions "should have been created to incorporate black people into the social order." Abolition democracy has become such a gift to students and practitioners seeking to make the prison industrial complex obsolete.[117]

Where I thought that decolonization and abolition were colliding, I eventually realized that activists from across the world were taking these paradigms and forging new and revolutionary ideas and practices on top of them. We needed abolition democracy, and certainly much more.

In *Black Reconstruction*, W. E. B. Du Bois uses "abolition democracy" in two ways. First to describe a progressive moral movement for the abolition of slavery by laborers, small capitalists, and politicians. Du Bois described their viewpoint as: "The abolition of slavery meant not simply abolition of legal ownership of the slave; it meant the uplift of slaves and their eventual incorporation into the body civil, politic, and social, of the United States." Right after, he says that "this outlook and theory of the abolitionists received tremendous impetus from the war." Du Bois applauded the courage and sacrifices of this group. He wrote that radical abolitionists such as Thaddeus Stevens were not just calling for the end of slavery, but for education, universal suffrage (for Black men), and most radically, land confiscation and redistribution from southern plantation owners to newly freed Blacks. This way, Black people could gain political, intellectual, *and* economic power to prevent their re-enslavement.[118]

But what did it mean for abolition democracy to take place on top of systems of colonialism and capitalism? The idea of land redistribution for economic power, though progressive, was obviously tortured. It was a recommendation made possible through the white settler slaughter of Indigenous peoples and land theft. For settler colonialism to work, native peoples must be perpetually disappeared and displaced. Yet for some progressive abolitionists, Black people had to benefit from the settler colonial project, too, just as poor white people benefited. Early nineteenth-century free Black land settlements were made possible through federal acts, which were especially important for Black people formerly enslaved by Native Americans. Under President Abraham Lincoln, white settlers and Black freedmen received land through the Homestead Act. And while some abolitionists fought for Indigenous peoples' rights, that did not stop their commitment to colonial and capitalist expansion.[119]

I also had gathered that Du Bois was using "abolition democracy" to describe a set of debates and eventual alliance between two groups of prominent, powerful abolitionists. The first were the liberal small-capitalist abolitionists I have described. The second group were Northern industrial capitalists. Slavery started threatening the profits in the North's industrial sectors and had to be stopped. Northern industry's promise of expansion prevailed over slavery's proven longevity, and large capitalists wanted to abolish slavery so that they could exploit the labor of free Blacks alongside poor and working-class whites. It was more profitable for companies if they hired workers and paid them a wage because workers sell their labor for income, and then use that income to purchase goods and services. Slaves had no income and could not purchase anything. Black people were a reservoir of laborers and potential consumers. Because of the war, industrialization was spreading quickly and capitalists wanted to grow their wealth by hiring more workers.

Additionally, Northern industrialist abolitionists also wanted freedom and suffrage for Black people because it gave capitalists critical voting power in the South. Industrial capitalists ruled the Republican Party. They planned to prevent the Democratic Party from regaining political control in the South to reinstitute slavery. Ninety percent of Black people lived in the South at the end of the Civil War. With the power of their vote, Black people could presumably stop the rebirth of slavery *and* help the industrial Republican Party stay in power. The longer the

Republican Party could stay in power, the greater the advantage that capitalists would have in the rapidly changing nation.[120]

Between two options to actualize abolition democracy—one by the liberal small-capitalist abolitionists and the other by Northern industrialist capitalists—the latter won. Industry rejected the relatively progressive idea of federal seizures and redistribution of slaveholders' property for Black people. Companies would have been threatened by a government precedent to redistribute other kinds of capital to people who are being exploited, like workers in their factories. Thus, Du Bois explains that abolition democracy *did* happen, a version primarily driven by industrial capitalists:

> Votes for Negroes were in truth a final compromise between business
> and abolition and were forced on abolition by business as the only
> method of realizing the basic principles of abolition-democracy.[121]

Industrialization grew rampantly after Reconstruction. Du Bois explained that "it began in 1876 an exploitation which was built on much the same sort of slavery which it helped to overthrow in 1863. It murdered democracy in the United States so completely that the world does not recognize its corpse." Instead of joining the fight for a more egalitarian society where Black workers and white workers could have had economic power together, these Northern capitalist abolitionists fought for Negro suffrage and the freedom to exploit Black labor.

Though Du Bois affirmed abolition democracy as a courageous viewpoint, he seemed ambivalent about whether it was the correct one. He was critical of the proponents of abolition democracy because they demanded full citizenship for Black people but were "nevertheless instinctively capitalistic; standing on the side of the exploiter . . . scant sympathy for the exploited." He said of Thaddeus Stevens,

> who was at heart the greatest and most uncompromising of abolitionist-
> democrats, but who advocated not only universal suffrage and free
> schools, but protection for Pennsylvania iron; yet in that protection he
> had just as distinctly in mind the welfare of the laborer as the profit of
> the employer.[122]

Thaddeus Stevens's protection over Pennsylvania iron would be analogous to today's police and prison abolitionists' protecting Wal-Mart or Amazon—two major capitalist corporations who take advantage of the people police imprison—poor people, Black people, Indigenous people, and disabled workers.

If the liberal version of abolition democracy had prevailed with its ongoing commitments to capitalism, Black people, poor whites, immigrants, and Indigenous people would have probably been sorted into the most exploited workers today, and thus, the most likely to be policed. I love how novelist Panashe Chigumadzi asks in the *Boston Review*, "What is capitalism if not a system sorting who is most fit for suffering, exploitation, and extraction?" It's possible that some Black people would have been absorbed into high-ranking positions through a more progressive abolition democracy—with the system that we have today, Barack Obama became president with millions of Black people cycling and out of jails, and Kamala Harris became vice-president with cops shooting hundreds of Black people every year. The withdrawal of federal troops from the South during Reconstruction was indeed a betrayal to the promise of protection to newly freed Black people in the United States. But there was also an allegiance to capitalism among the abolitionists that led to the further exploitation of people from all backgrounds, Black, Indigenous, white, and immigrant. Mixing abolition and capitalism was not enough to ensure the full liberation of Black people then, and it is not enough to ensure the full liberation of everyone now.[123]

Abolition democracy did not entail justice for Native Americans, either. On the contrary, the entire project could have been built on Indigenous land to the exclusion of Indigenous peoples. Charles Sumner and Thaddeus Stevens were for land redistribution for Black people, which was laudable. But many abolitionists continued to support land theft from Native inhabitants. Roxanne Dunbar-Ortiz writes in *An Indigenous Peoples' History of the United States* that white abolitionists in the Republican Party advocated for further colonization, genocide, and land acquisition, including arranging the eventual purchase and military control of Alaska, Hawai'i, and dozens of islands in the Pacific Ocean.[124]

Most importantly for me, Du Bois's articulation of abolition democracy focused almost exclusively on the debates of progressive white politicians and Northern industrial capitalists. These debates took place in political settings, congressional hearings, newspapers, and in business meetings. Often, radical

Black abolitionists and runaways rejected these debates, and began forging futures of their own through risk, mutual aid, experimentation, flight, and fugitive struggle. Theoretician George Novack, under the pseudonym William F. Warde, wrote in 1950 in *Fourth International* that we should study these kinds of radical Black abolitionists:

> While this struggle was going on in the governing circles at Washington, the masses in the South were on the move. Direct action by the insurgent people is the most salient feature of a revolution. The Negroes did not always wait for sanction or approval of any constituted authorities or laws to secure these rights, especially in regard to the land and the right to bear arms. In a number of areas they seized possession of the plantations, divided the land amongst themselves, and set up their own local forms of administration. On the Sea Islands off Georgia and South Carolina, for example, 40,000 freedmen each took 40 acres of land and worked it on their own account. When the former owners came later to claim their plantations, these new proprietors armed themselves and resisted. Similar expropriations and clashes took place elsewhere, not only between planters and Negroes, but between land-hungry freedmen and Federal troops. Land seizures would have taken place on a far larger scale if the freedmen did not have faith in Republican promises and expected that land would be handed to them as it was to the homesteaders in the West.[125]

For years, I was told by elders and Black leaders that our ancestors fought and died for the right to vote. That is a fact but not the full truth. Black suffrage was a laudable compromise. Many of our radical abolitionist ancestors, alongside people of all races, fought and died for much more, including self-determination, an end to capitalism, the return of Indigenous land, the redistribution of land for newly freed Black people, and for autonomous regions where communities could test their independence. I wanted to be in the tradition of those abolitionists who were committed to ending oppression of all people, and who built interdependent relationships rooted in care, democracy, and accountability to each other.

When I review the campaigns and platforms of most major civil rights organizations, I can find commitments to end the vestiges of slavery, like mass incarceration, prison labor, police violence, and voter disenfranchisement. These are symptoms of oppression, not always the cause. Rarely can I find commitments to undermine or abolish a root cause of violence, like capitalism, patriarchy, militarism, and ableism. Eradicating these root causes is what it's going to take if we seriously want to eradicate its manifestations.

Thus, abolition was a gift from the past for inspiration and lessons. It is an essential paradigm to think and organize with, and has to evolve to avoid perpetuating other forms of oppression that we might have to end later. For me, decolonization had been another important paradigm, initially because of my time in the Netherlands and South Africa, and later because of lessons that I've learned about colonization in the United States, Australia, Puerto Rico, and Martinique. In Belinda Hall, maroonage was another paradigm. We did not drop out and withdraw from the university, but we stopped making appeals to the university for inclusion and created the democratic space and practices that we believed in. From revolutionary feminists, like Audre Lorde, Toni Morrison, and the Combahee River Collective, I learned to be in principled struggle toward freedom with Black men and people of other races who were trying to do the right thing, even if they were wrong, or may have said something awful, or accidentally harmed me, as long as we were both committed to accountability and a resolution, because I would want the same. The more I studied and organized with others, the more I found abolition in conversation with radical feminism, socialism, environmental justice, and disability justice.

Belinda was just one of my political homes that honed these views. We studied Black and multiracial formations that resisted manifestations of capitalism to build economic power, too. We studied texts like the Combahee River Collective's statement, the League of Revolutionary Black Workers' *General Program*, and the August Twenty-Ninth Movement's *Chicano Liberation and Proletarian Revolution*. We learned how Black people resisted slavery; how multiracial formations organized against industrial capitalists who exploited workers; about Indigenous people launched attacks to resist their own slavery and genocide; and about white immigrants who resisted violence from white American business owners. Much of the resistance in the United States was directly connected to the resistance from people abroad, just as our student movement had been inspired.[126]

I DISCOVERED CRITICAL Resistance in Belinda Hall. The abolitionist organization was founded in the late 1990s after a national convening of more than three thousand people interested or engaged work to dismantle the prison industrial complex. I had learned about the prison industrial complex (PIC) well before going to law school. According to Critical Resistance, the PIC describes "the overlapping interests of government and industry that use surveillance, policing, and imprisonment as solutions to economic, social, and political problems." The overlapping interests of government and industry is precisely where capitalism lives. If it did not, then corporations would not spend billions of dollars to lobby and fund candidates through political action committees for the purposes of minimizing regulation, taxation, and accountability, and maximizing profit, corporate influence in government, and access to the Earth's natural resources. Plainly, what creates concentrated wealth also creates what my clients, my loved ones, and I experienced on a regular basis: concentrated poverty, homelessness, migration, hunger, despair, and anger. Concentrated wealth is celebrated, concentrated poverty is criminalized. Cities use police, prisons, and prosecutors to manage the space in between the two.[127]

What I did not initially understand about the prison industrial complex, however, is that it included police. Before the Ferguson Uprising in 2014, prison closure campaigns and books like Michelle Alexander's *The New Jim Crow* catapulted the notion of "mass incarceration" into the mainstream, raising public consciousness that mass criminalization and imprisonment were wrong. Many activists, nonprofits, and legislators continued or launched campaigns to reduce mass incarceration by cutting the jail and prison populations and decriminalizing low-level drug offenses, major feats worth celebrating. Incarcerated people were being released and returning to their friends and families. New organizations formed to help people with records find work, housing, health care, and voter registration. By the time the Black Lives Matter movement gained momentum in 2015, I wondered about the seeming incongruence between approaches to prisons and police. Cutting the prison population in half was exactly the right idea, but were we going to keep nearly one million cops to keep locking people up? Leave almost eighteen thousand law enforcement agencies untouched? Permit them to make tens of millions of arrests for jails that we were closing?[128]

For this reason, Critical Resistance organizes to abolish the entire prison industrial complex, not just one of its parts. Prison industrial complex abolition necessarily means abolishing the police. CR describes this political idea as "a goal of eliminating imprisonment, policing, and surveillance, and creating lasting alternatives to punishment and imprisonment." Early Critical Resistance member Rachel Herzing's analysis of police abolition specifically made the political vision more tangible for me by encompassing Moten and Harney's broad conception of abolishing the society that could have the criminal legal system that we have. Writing in 2015, Herzing explained: "Taking incremental steps toward the abolition of policing is even more about what must be built than what must be eliminated. Further, it requires steps that build on each other and continue to clear the path for larger future steps while being mindful not to build something today that will need to be torn down later on the path toward the long-term goal."[129]

She spoke to my concerns directly. Even with all of the studying, organizing, and developing analysis, abolishing the police felt like a mammoth task that initially seemed unfathomable as a pragmatic approach to police violence. We can make policing obsolete in incremental changes, as long as we're moving in the right direction.

Rachel helped me distill police abolition into an organizing praxis: make policing obsolete by reducing the police, reducing the reasons why people need police, reducing the reasons why people *think* they need police, and building a society where we have just relationships to each other, to our labor, to our communities, and to our planet.

Rachel suggests that we first analyze our individual ideas and reliance on law enforcement. What do we think cops do? How do they make us feel? What kinds of situations can we address right now without police? What people, places, and practices do we need to rely on to keep ourselves safe *before* an emergency happens? Questions like these can help us investigate why we think we need police in the first place and prepare to keep ourselves safe without them.

Why people "need" police is often related to why people think they need police. For example, the summer after I graduated law school, I locked my keys inside my car during my move to D.C. Geuce and Garvey were both strapped in their car seats. Panicking, I started calling locksmiths for help, but there were none in my Black neighborhood in South East. The closest shop was an hour away. I considered calling 911, but I feared the dispatcher would send cops who wouldn't have the proper tools to help *and* could escalate the problem for any reason. With my kids in view, I ran toward the fire station at the end of my block to signal firefighters who often sit outside, but they were inside and did not hear me. I then called the non-emergency number to no avail. Breaking the window would have scared my children, so I gave up and called 911. I asked the dispatcher not to send cops and specifically requested the firefighters nearby. Less than five minutes later, cops came. I was mortified. The cop walked to my car and slid a tool down the window.

I told him I needed a firefighter with the right equipment, but he kept going as if he was being chivalrous. When it did not work, he made small talk. *How did this happen? What were you doing?* I did not want to reveal anything that could be used against me. It was a trivial mistake—I did not wake up one August morning with "lock my two small kids in the backseat before work" on my checklist. I asked again for a firetruck, and after he proceeded to ignore my plea, firefighters appeared. They popped the door open in a few seconds. Geuce still teases me about calling the police.

Without an abolitionist analysis, maybe I would have believed I needed cops to rescue my kids from a quickly heating car. But the cops couldn't help, and I deserved more from myself and my community. I could have prepared by having a spare key with a friend, neighbor, or inside a lockbox. My neighborhood lacked basic services and businesses and needed a robust variety of them. A local locksmith could have prevented a police encounter and saved my life. Death might feel extreme. Yet not everyone can afford a locksmith and they rely on calling 911, as my family did when I was a child. What if I was darker, disabled, or large-bodied? Or wasn't wearing a maroon Harvard cap? What if my kids' clothes were borrowed and oversized, like mine were at their age? And what if we slept in the car because that's where we lived? Vehicle living is the fastest growing form of homelessness in the US and the number of cities that criminalized it has doubled in the last ten years. Cops could have used any number of these factors to increase my risk of arrest, death, and losing custody of my children.[130]

Most police calls are for these mundane affairs. Criminal justice reporter Josie Duffy Rice makes it clear: "And yet no matter the call—the loud party next door, the permit for a parade, the expired car tags, the escort for a funeral procession, the elderly welfare check, the frolickers barbecuing in the park, the schoolyard fight, the opioid overdose, the homeless person outside in the cold, the stray dog—the state's answer is to respond with armed agents blessed with the near unimpeachable right to kill." A *New York Times* feature found that only 4 percent of police calls in three major jurisdictions were for "serious violent offenses," and hovered below 2 percent in other cities with available data, including Baltimore, Cincinnati, New Orleans, and Seattle. This is just one way we can use 911 data, neighborhood surveys and relationships, and our own needs to assess, reduce, and eliminate the reasons people call police, and build what we need instead. For me, a locksmith.[131]

Organizing and building community relationships to reduce the reasons why people think they need police could also help decriminalization campaigns. For example, when cities decriminalize drugs, it can remove a basis for police stops, potentially reducing 911 calls about "drug-related activity." This is true for homelessness, sex work, loitering, and any number of police-related calls. That's just one part of abolition; the other requires the short term, intermediate, and long-term building toward the ever-changing solutions we need. Instead of cops, cities could have various housing, health care, and employment options to meet the needs of people experiencing homelessness. An intermediate step could be organizing strong tenant unions to ensure that properties are safe and attractive; to end evictions; and stop the use of discriminatory measures that ban applicants with records. Long-term, community members and organizers could brainstorm and experiment with cooperative land stewardship. Because of my mother, I had always thought that home ownership was an ultimate accomplishment for low-wealth Black women; it's the quickest way to accumulate wealth and equity. However, the more that I've learned about the relationship between private property and policing, the more I try to decolonize my thinking about whether any person or company has the right to own a small piece of the planet. I don't think that's right on Mars; I don't think that's right on Earth. But I do think that we can decide countless other ways for people to live pleasantly with and on land.

We will discover various ways to make police, and the entire prison indus-trial complex, obsolete. Shrinking police budgets by defunding them is one option. Critical Resistance offers one resource to help us analyze which proposed measures lead us to reform or toward abolition with these questions: Does this reduce police funding? Challenge the notion that police increase safety? Reduce tools, tactics, technology police have at their disposal? Reduce the scale of police? As much as we can, we should be ensure that the answers are "yes" to chip away at the pieces of policing.

Activists across the country have been working to close prisons and cut the incarcerated population by half; anti-criminalization organizer Mariame Kaba additionally calls to cut law enforcement by half. Communities can accom-plish this by hiring and budget freezes, budget cuts, and participatory budgeting opportunities to ensure that police will not be refunded in the future. States should stop the construction of new prisons; cities and counties should end the construction of new jails; and both could begin closing remaining ones by freeing the people inside. Campus activists can follow the lead of any number of student movements to remove cops from campus and divest their university endowments from private prisons. No new police academies should be established, and not another soul recruited. Cities that rely on policing as a jobs program, as Chicago mayor Lori Lightfoot does, can create universal basic income pro-grams for residents, or offer green jobs to build rapid, accessible public transit between cities across the country.

These are only a few suggestions from a broader set of abolitionist practices and aspirations. It is important to emphasize again that abolition does not nec-essarily provide singular, generic, prescriptive answers to harm. Nor does it mean that cops will disappear overnight. Rather than thinking of abolition as just get-ting rid of police, I think about it as a way to create and support a multitude of approaches to the problem of harm in society, and, most excitingly, as an oppor-tunity to reduce and eliminate harm in the first place. More than seeking a single solution to one kind of violence, abolition study and praxis requires activists and community residents with political will, imagination, and commitment to exper-imentation, implementation, and evaluation. Local, state, and federal governments have invested trillions of dollars into resourcing police and prisons to manage inequality, rather than creating a set of policies that reduce inequality through redistribution. In response, we must vote, organize, protest, and strike to demand these levels of resources to make our lives free and safe.[132]

During my study and organizing, which continues today, I realized that just because I did not know the answers to questions, that didn't mean that they did not exist. I have been on panels with active and retired police officers who are anti-abolition, not because they have read about it, but because they think common sense is enough to understand what abolitionists want. In good faith, I ask them if they have read anything about abolition. None of them have ever said yes. Since massive protests have catapulted abolition into the mainstream, I have regularly read journalists, scholars, and politicians who are dismissive of the abolition or say that "it does not make sense." It makes me wish that people were more curious than critical because it's so much easier to learn that way. When Geuce says that something "doesn't make sense," I ask him to rephrase it as, "I don't understand this." Once I understood that abolition was not going to realistically result in the end of policing overnight, but rather as Rachel said, with incremental progress toward shrinking the police, abolition made perfect sense. Abolition makes sense if you believe that we should end violence and exploitation. This is a path that we forge. How we get there is up to us.

FIVE

JUSTICE FOR THE LIVING

BLACK MOTHERS ARE impossible. My own had pushed me to become a civil rights lawyer for more than two decades and had flown from St. Louis to Boston to celebrate my law school graduation in May 2017. Torrential rain made most families stand near the building entrances surrounding the quad until their loved one crossed the stage. They'd scream and wave banners and slip back to dry off inside. I found my mother afterward who hugged me like a bear. She said, "I'm so proud of you. You really did it and I knew you would. PhD next?" I laughed but her face remained straight. "Mom, a PhD is not the next step after a law degree." She replied, "So you're giving up? Nobody is ever going to call you 'doctor?'"

Within days of graduation, I was off to study for the bar exam. I spent time between classes reading essays I'd written or published over the last decade about racial justice and criminal justice reform. They'd make me laugh, cringe, and cry. I thought the best that we could win were convictions, consent decrees, and body cameras; political education had converted those ideas into archives. Like my organizing and legal work, my public facing writing had begun espousing abolitionist politics. Messages that poured into my inbox dared me to "ride along" with cops in dangerous neighborhoods to witness what police deal with on a daily basis. None of these white men engaged with the substance of my work and they attributed my criticisms of policing to a big misunderstanding of what cops do.

Others had been more aggressive. They would remind me that Black people polled want more police. I didn't have to assume that these are white men because they literally signed-off their letters with versions of: "Yes, I'm white, cancel me." I dreamed of writing back, "Yes, I know. A Black person has never told me to voluntarily get inside of a cop car to ride anywhere. Even the conservative ones."

When I would read these emails, I did not bother responding about the *other side of police* because I was already on it, and I had known about the *dangerous neighborhoods* because that is where I had lived my entire life—except for the three years in Cambridge. Many of them wrote "dangerous" because to them, it was synonymous with Black. A ride along would have just taken me around my blocks where cops bother the boys who wash windshields for a few bucks or ticket my neighbors for an open bottle. Maybe they would have pointed out the houses with high drug activity and I would have thought about which dorms had the highest drug activities. Counter to the tone of the emails, cops did not stand guard in front of each home at night in dangerous neighborhoods to catch the bullets that crept through windows to keep us safe. They show up after the life has been taken. I wanted to save lives.

When I had written or mentioned that police could not solve community-based violence, it was not speculative. I was specifically recalling people that I'd known who'd been shot and others who pulled the trigger. On my way to Baltimore in 2015, I found out that Korie had been murdered. The night before I went on the Melissa Harris-Perry show that same year, I learned about what happened to Grandon's godsister, Sharae, who was murdered in Ferguson. A couple of months after I had given birth in 2016, my first childhood crush, Jarrell, was assassinated on the highway on his way home from work. He always sent me messages saying how proud he was that I made it out. And when I was studying for the bar exam in 2017, my mother called me with news about my little sister, Courtnie.[133]

Courtnie was twenty-two years old and eight months pregnant. My mother told me that Courtnie's boyfriend, Malcolm, had been murdered. Malcolm, who was twenty-five, was in a car when one person blocked his exit, and another took his life. No arrests were made. No arrests have been made. In St. Louis, cops made arrests for less than 40 percent of homicides in 2017, down from above 60 percent in 2011. Police make arrests for about a third of killings in the area where Malcolm died.[134]

My heart broke into pieces for Courtnie. If anyone had overcome the odds it was her. My siblings and I had been through evictions, homelessness, fights, and foster care, and Courtnie had found a way to finish school and secure a stable life. She was in a program that helped subsidize her apartment. She wanted to go back to school and study fashion, but if she did, she would be kicked out of the apartment program because students were ineligible. Torn between affordable rent and pursuing her dreams, she moved out, worked hard, and saved enough to rent a townhome downtown with Malcolm, who was a supervisor at Target. When we spoke, I could hear how proud she was of her independence. When her belly grew, the hotel where she worked fired her because she was pregnant and moving too slowly to clean each room. She knew it was wrong, but didn't know it was illegal, and didn't tell me about it until months after it happened. Then Malcolm was murdered. She found herself facing eviction because she could no longer afford rent. Freshly grieving her beloved partner, she found herself facing the sheriff, who the landlord had sent to evict her. Her due date was weeks away.

Violence reverberates throughout a family and community, and compounds other forms of violence, like racism, sexism, evictions, and policing. Courtnie's crisis did not matter to the sheriff who was there to enforce the will of the property owner. My little sister had to start picking up all of the pieces again. The same day I finished the DC bar exam, I was walking through the streets half terrified, half excited, listening to her scream over the phone as she gave birth to Mavis in a hospital in St. Louis. My sister and nephew would soon move to join me in DC. Between my classmates, friends, and family, I had witnessed how murder shapes our lives, as much as I had known the inadequacy of police to stop it.

THAT AUGUST, I started working at the Advancement Project National Office (AP), a multiracial civil rights organization that used movement lawyering, organization, and communications to advance social justice. I had interned with them two years prior and loved how they supported grassroots organizing in St. Louis and Ferguson after the uprising. On my first day at work, Thomas Mariadason, my supervisor, asked, "If you could start this job doing anything, what would it be?" Without hesitation, I answered, "political education." My time in Belinda Hall overlapped with my time building and organizing with lawyers in Law for Black Lives (L4BL), a project that Purvi Shah conceived of to provide legal, bail, and jail support to the Movement for Black Lives. L4BL was another of my political homes and affirmed the need for political education for lawyers, law students, and legal workers to develop a power analysis, much like what we were doing in Belinda. So by the time Thomas asked how I wanted to start my legal career, I had already decided to commit to developing some shared analyses around race, capitalism, and policing with my new colleagues. Being a good lawyer was not enough for our freedom, especially since many of the nation's well trained lawyers preserve oppression. And caring about justice was a start, but not if justice meant convictions, prisons, and more police. Much to my delight, Thomas was ecstatic. Our newly formed justice project started reading together.

When Thomas left AP a few months later, debates inside and outside the office increased about whether lawyers in the nonprofit sector should talk about abolition as a part of our work. At the time, many lawyers and grassroots organizers outside of AP considered abolition—just as I had—"elitist," and thought that imagining and building a world without police was a disingenuous academic conversation among people who weren't affected by real violence. One organizer on a panel painfully rebuffed my comments on abolition because I was "just a lawyer," while he had to "look at his brown son every day to tell him something *useful* for his survival." He spoke as if abolition was not conceptualized and practiced by Black, Latinx, and queer survivors and political prisoners as a useful response to violence. As if I hadn't felt police violence against my body, or wasn't raising two Black boys in Southeast DC. And as if my nephew's father hadn't just been murdered weeks before.

The law is a generally conservative space that prides itself in upholding constitutional values rather than interrogating them. Philanthropists overwhelmingly support legal nonprofits to fight for equal rights for all within a constitutional framework. By 2017, philanthropic organizations had received and distributed millions of dollars dedicated to reforming police, bail, and prosecutors. Nonprofits embarked on projects such as increasing community policing, eliminating bias in police, launching bailout organizations, and electing "progressive prosecutors." Large organizations like the American Civil Liberties Union, NAACP Legal and Educational Defense Fund, and Lawyers Committee for Civil Rights Under the Law had received funding for campaigns to improve the legal system in the US, but it was still through the lens of reforming the police and improving their relationships with the community. Smaller grassroots organizations like Community Justice Project, Amistad Law Project, the Abolitionist Law Center, and ArchCity Defenders took on riskier work and were lawyering to eliminate the root causes of harm to stop police contact, close jails, and free political prisoners. The Advancement Project was in the middle, maintaining a national presence while committed to grassroots campaigns. AP was also in a difficult position: none of the major philanthropic organizations were really interested in police abolition. It was publicly considered a radical fringe ideology taken up by activists, academics, and artists who were not realistic or pragmatic about social change. And here I was, a zealot.

But I kept pushing. I continued studying, writing, and speaking about abolition publicly—outside of work and outside of the country. The Advancement Project let me use my professional development funds to attend the International Conference on Penal Abolition (ICOPA) in London in 2018. There, I met Beth E. Richie and Ruth Wilson Gilmore, two longtime prison abolitionists. Richie's scholarship and organizing work through INCITE! specifically focused on police and intimate partner violence against Black women and girls. Wilson's book *Golden Gulag* tracks massive prison expansion in the California as a product of surplus land, capital, and labor. Prisons, she posits in *Futures of Black Radicalism,* were not simply a reiteration of slavery, but the result of racial capitalism. Slavery was profitable and exploitative in a way that prisons are not. Rather, racial capitalism helps to spur the prison industrial complex because locking up massive numbers of people frees up jobs for some people, creates jobs for other people, and functions as a carceral babysitter for people exploited in the economy, education, health care, housing, the environment, and much more. Police functions similarly.

In London, I arranged meetings with Deb Coles and Rebecca Roberts at INQUEST, the only charity providing expertise on state-sanctioned deaths and their investigation to bereaved people, lawyers, advice and support agencies, the media, and parliamentarians. Their focus is on deaths in police and prison custody, immigration detention, and mental health settings, and deaths involving multiagency failings where wider issues of state and corporate accountability are in question. INQUEST sought to eradicate these deaths, and for a few hours, I read through decades-old magazines they had published calling for the end of the carceral state. Their work showed me that it was possible for nonprofit organizations, charities, and non-governmental (NGOs) to practice their work with abolitionists values to reduce state and state sanctioned violence.

I also reunited with my friend Adam, who had graduated Oxford by then and was working as a geographer at King's College London. Outside of work, he organized against police violence and taught classes at a people's university. He was planning events that coincided with ICOPA and invited me to contribute.

The first was the anniversary of the burning of Grenfell Tower, a public-housing apartment building that went up in flames due to state neglect. Grenfell Tower did not have sprinklers installed and contractors used flammable materials in its construction and subsequent renovations. The municipality that owned the public housing used nonprofit contractors to create private units for sale and rent inside the building, making a profit. As a result, the renovations "left the tower with just one staircase and exit—an exit that the management company has failed to keep clear." Adding to the nightmare, managers had a policy of telling people to stay inside their apartments in case of a fire, which ultimately led many to their demise. Forty fire trucks had to extinguish the flames and emergency services also told residents to "stay put." Ultimately, at least seventy-two residents died in the building full of people of color, immigrants, and asylum seekers; undocumented survivors were afraid to come forward for fear of arrest and deportation. INQUEST has been representing survivors of the fire and families of the victims during the investigation. Tragically, residents had been protesting for years because the landlord had not prepared residents in case of a fire, writing a mere seven months before the June 2017 blaze,[135]

> unfortunately, the Grenfell Action Group have reached the conclusion that only an incident that results in serious loss of life of KCTMO residents will allow the external scrutiny to occur that will shine a light on the practices that characterise the malign governance of this non-functioning organisation.[136]

When there is a homicide, we can presumably call the police to report it. When the police kill, or a city is responsible for multiple deaths like at Grenfell Tower, there is no number to call to make an arrest.

The second set of events had to do with the Windrush generation. Black people from former British colonies in the Caribbean arrived in the United Kingdom to fill postwar labor shortages between 1948 and 1971. Because they lived in British colonies, the government considered them British subjects or citizens until 2018, when lawmakers decided that without paperwork, they faced deportation. Adam and others were organizing to stop the additional deportations. The Windrush story reminded me how countries welcomed immigrant labor in Belgium, the Netherlands, France, and the US, and began outlawing migration once it was no longer profitable.[137]

The Skadden fellowship also provided me with professional development funds, and I used every penny to fly to Australia for a biannual gathering by Sisters Inside, an organization that "advocates for the collective human rights of women and girls in prison, and their families, and provides services to address their individual needs." Their work is explicitly abolitionist, seeking to ban and close prisons on the continent, end violence, and end all forms of supremacy. Sisters Inside advocates and organizes explicitly around First Nations, Torres Strait Islanders, and Aboriginal women to free them from prison, set up housing for their return, identify legal needs and assistance, and provide full-time antiviolence support. This was precisely an example of abolitionist and decolonization work that disrupted and prevented police contact and incarceration. That year, Angela Davis was the keynote, and afterward, I said hello and apologized for not knowing her work when I had first introduced her in college![138]

BACK IN THE States, I was able to work with organizers in St. Louis and Ferguson to stop police, prison, and prosecutor violence. I loved that I could do local, national, and even some international work through the Advancement Project. I was eager to do this through an abolitionist framework, one that reduced the carceral state, reduced the reasons why people needed it, and reduced the reasons why people thought they needed it. This was especially important in St. Louis where murder rates are among the highest in the country—rivaling cities like Newark, Baltimore, Detroit, and New Orleans.[139]

In 2017, our local partner was St. Louis Action Council, founded by Kayla Reed and Michelle Higgins. These Black women activists were instrumental in reviving, maintaining, and advancing the organizing culture in the area following the Ferguson Uprising. I'd briefly worked with Kayla before in 2015 during the Ferguson Uprising anniversary events. The day before Darren Wilson killed Michael Brown, Kayla was a pharmacy technician and worked weekends at a furniture store. The day after, she joined thousands of people, including me, calling for Wilson's arrest, prosecution, and conviction. She quit her job and became a full-time organizer with the Organization for Black Struggle, one of the oldest Black-led formations with radical politics in Missouri. She left the organization to attend college at Washington University in St. Louis and launched Action St. Louis, a grassroots racial justice organization that seeks to build political power for Black communities period. Reed was also instrumental in building the Movement for Black Lives' Electoral Justice Project, a program dedicated to supporting progressive campaigns, candidates, and actions to improve the lives of Black people.

Through AP, I supported Action's strategic planning meetings, political education, and various campaigns, including a campaign to close the infamous jail called "the Workhouse." ArchCity Defenders worked closely with Action and their attorneys regularly represented clients who were cycled in and out of St. Louis jails, including the Workhouse. I loved that ArchCity were lawyers dedicated to dismantling every part of the local criminal legal system. They provided wraparound services to meet the needs of the clients they represented; they defended protesters and sued the police during the uprisings; and to support Action's campaign, litigated to close the Workhouse. This was my first lawsuit.

As a kid, I had watched family and friends go in and out of the Workhouse so often that I actually thought that it was a place where you went to get a job. Until somebody did not come home for days.

As early as the 1800s, poor people, Black people, and disabled people were sent to the Workhouse to labor. In 1887, a local barber became a lawyer and made a significant profit through an emerging trend: saving time going to court by getting his poor clients to plead guilty instead of going to trial. Clients who could afford more expensive representation fees would go to trial and receive lighter sentences, if any. The *St. Louis Post-Dispatch* described this as an "awful barter of human liberty." It went on, "No doubt many an unfortunate who is really innocent has been frightened by these sharks into pleading guilty, believing if he did not do so he would be convicted despite his innocence and given a long term." Today, 97 percent of cases are resolved through plea deals. Lawyers and activists primarily discuss this practice as a criminal justice system issue. However, like most practices under the system, it is also a racial capitalism issue. Exploitation creates poor people, who are then more easily exploitable again when they seek basic services like legal representation. Regardless of each individual's culpability, the criminal legal system is guilty of perpetuating this cycle.[140]

Through Action, I'd meet Inez Bordeaux, a straightforward and curious nurse and mother of four whose energy kept the room laughing. Inez had been recently released from the Workhouse. She had fled an abusive marriage and without her ex-husband's income, she could not afford the $1,600 bill for childcare so that she could go to work. The government denied her childcare assistance because she was about sixty dollars over the income threshold. Cutoffs like this were so arbitrary because the government can afford to offer free, universal childcare, and each denial for childcare resources, or a subsidized apartment in Courtnie's case, could be a matter of life and death for people in abusive and precarious situations. Inez lost jobs due to her inability to afford day care and when she finally landed a third job, she paid for day care by continuing to draw unemployment benefits, which was against the law:[141]

> After about a year, I was able to get on my feet and I didn't need to do it anymore, so things stabilized. But I got pulled over for speeding in Oklahoma in 2011. The state trooper told me I had a felony warrant for my arrest for larceny. I was charged with overpayment of unemployment benefits. I was placed on probation. My life took a crazy downward spiral. But by the time I ended up in the Workhouse in 2016, things were better. I had three minimum-wage, part-time jobs that I was using to stay afloat.[142]

Her take home pay was less than $1,000 per month. Inez could not afford to repay the unemployment benefits, nor her $25,000 bail. Nor could most people in the Workhouse. The median bond set is $25,000 in a city where the average per capita income is approximately $30,000. St. Louis is 45 percent Black; the population at the Workhouse is nearly 90 percent Black. Ninety-nine percent were detained until their trial date. Inez often reiterated her hatred for statistics because they do not fully convey the feeling of injustice. Black mold painted the walls and leaking ceilings formed indoor puddles. Roaches and rats overran the floor. Temperatures in the jail reached a sweltering 105 degrees in the summertime and dropped to an icy 30 degrees in the winter. Between 2014 and 2020, jail administrators reported seven deaths and God knows how many hospitalizations. Inside, Inez longed for her children and wept. As a result, jailers put her on suicide watch and in solitary confinement for several days.[143]

When we started our political education sessions, I assumed I had found a natural ally in Inez. Surely, she would be eager to abolish the prison industrial complex. She was not. I should not have assumed that someone who had experienced the horrors of one jail to be on board with closing *all* jails. Abolitionist politics are forged through relationship building, study, and experimentation—not assumptions. Formerly and currently incarcerated people organize with a variety of political analyses and across various traditions. Someone's experience inside informs these traditions and can lead people to different outcomes worth exploring and debating. For example, many families of police violence victims have various demands, including convictions, punishment, accountability, reform, abolition, and even forgiveness. Similarly, currently and formerly incarcerated people use their experiences inside to demand reform; others demand immediate improvements to jail conditions to alleviate suffering, but toward the eventual goal of abolition. The overlap of the traditions vary too. After experiencing the horrible rat- and roach-infested conditions at the Workhouse, Inez was committed to figuring out which traditions she belonged to and trusted the activists in the room who were trying to figure out the same thing.

"What about the murderers?" she asked, holding my gaze steadily until I answered.

She was concerned that abolition would leave our neighborhoods even less safe. Inez had survived domestic violence and it cost her almost everything. Understandably, she wanted to be safe and abolition sounded dangerous. Action has twenty- and thirty-something-year-old members who were vulnerable to violence from their neighbors, strangers, lovers, and police. On any given day, they confront racism, sexism, misogyny, fatphobia, transphobia, homophobia, and economic exploitation. Like all of us, they had been socialized to accept police, prisons, and prosecutors as normal features of society to keep us "safe." And in our strategic planning meetings, I was asking them to let go.

"Which murderers, Inez?" I asked back.

I used to feel threatened by that question, even when it had been my own. By the time of this training, I had been asked this question by enough people who did not inquire in good faith, but who wanted to undermine abolitionist study and organizing. It was a supposed to be a "gotcha" question. Time after time, they demanded an answer for every possible scenario of violence, and when I could not provide a specific one, I would feel bad, uncomfortable, or unknowledgeable. Over time, with more reading and organizing, the pressure to know everything subsided because abolition is a project where we co-create the answers collectively. As Mariame Kaba often explains, the federal, state, and local government has spent trillions of dollars on police and still can't clear murders, but they continue to receive funding regardless of their inability to prove that policing works. Additionally, I cared about murder as much as I cared about ending all premature death, from environmental violence, to the negligence that caused so many to perish at Grenfell Tower.

Inez was not asking in bad faith. Nor were many of the Black people I encountered while organizing and lawyering in St. Louis. When they asked "What about the murderers?" it was because they wondered and worried about their own safety. In 2019, the FBI reported just over sixteen thousand murders. However, as we were learning and debating together, the group came to understand abolition is not the mere absence of police and prisons. It is a paradigm, aspiration, and organizing practice to make those institutions obsolete over time. To do that, we needed new ways to think about harm and solutions to preserve life rather than resorting to punishment after death.[144]

I asked the group of organizers if we could broaden the scope of Inez's question. "What about the murderers?" does not have a singular solution because murders do not have a singular cause. "Why do people kill people?" could be more useful for our brainstorming and I asked if we could start there. They agreed. In small groups, they wrote lists of reasons why people kill people on giant Post-it notes. *Gang violence. Mental health. Racism. Rage and jealousy. Homophobia. Transphobia. Retaliation. The police. Killing someone before they kill you. Access to guns. Stress. Passion. Robberies and carjackings gone bad. Self-defense. Accidents. Bystanders. Cheating. Protection.* We shared consensus that we would not respond to each of these scenarios the same way, not even the murders. By disaggregating homicides into digestible social problems, we could brainstorm various solutions to stop, prevent, and respond to harm now, as we were eradicating the root causes and creating better relationships.

Many of these encounters start as small acts of disrespect. Trivial arguments, control over women, and property-related disputes account for 80 percent of homicides. "Trivial" is a relative term in the belligerent conditions of white supremacy, where small fights over Black kids wearing hoodies or listening to loud rap music turn fatal. "Control over women" functions similarly and is informed by society messaging to boys and men that their healthy, rational emotional response to pain is feminine, girly, or gay, and therefore wrong and weak. In a just society, break-ups and divorce might cause heartaches and headaches, but under patriarchy, men are additionally conditioned to punish women they cannot keep or control, like my ex-boyfriend who stalked me. Inez had to flee her ex-husband's violence to save her own life. When he attacked her, she did not call the cops. A prosecutor pestered her to bring charges against him and she refused. Not because she was an abolitionist at the time, but because she said that taking one of her kids' parents away and putting him in jail for five years would not solve the underlying problem. She just wanted to be left alone. Ninety percent of men commit all homicides in the US, not because they are men, but because of their violent patriarchal socialization to control women.

Each example stemmed from interpersonal violence, or harm that occurs between people. This exercise demystified who becomes a murderer and why people kill. Equally important, I wanted this exercise to help us use our imagination to create lots of different solutions to stop, prevent, and undermine harm, thereby reducing the reasons why people need or think they need police. Abolition requires us to reduce violence as we are reducing the carceral responses to it.

Nobody wrote "Black on Black crime" or "senseless violence." All of the violence in our communities made perfect sense. In *Chokehold: Policing Black Men*, legal scholar Paul Butler confronts Black-on-Black male violence, taking the United States to task for centuries of slavery, Jim Crow, and state sanctioned poverty creation that leads to community-based violence. He explains:

> We have seen that the structural conditions of high-poverty neighborhoods are strongly correlated with people being at risk for violence. In the United States, seven out of eight people who reside in those communities are people

of color. To state the obvious, people don't live in the most deprived neighborhoods because they choose to. They live there because white supremacy severely constrains their choices. One study found that racial inequality raises the rate of black-on-white homicide. Black-on-Black homicide, at the same time, increases the more deprived and segregated a neighborhood.[145]

Economic deprivation and neighborhood segregation do not happen by accident and poverty does not grow from the ground. Whenever Black people in this country have attempted to build self-sustaining communities, they have faced white violence and state interference that threatened their wealth. Fannie Lou Hamer writes in her autobiography that just as her family had accumulated enough livestock to cease sharecropping, a white man poisoned all of their mules and cows to stop them from getting ahead. Racists have torched Black-owned businesses and neighborhoods as a racial and economic intimidation tactic. Banks have denied Black people home, auto, and business loans on the basis of race. The federal government failed to deliver the educational, economic, and housing benefits it promised to more than a million Black veterans through the GI Bill. Black communities have been decimated by highway construction, redlining, and gentrification. Studies show that cities with high rates of inequality and economic segregation leads to high levels of aggravated assaults, robberies, burglaries, and motor vehicle thefts, and as Butler details, homicides. Police arrive to manage the fallout.

White racial and economic violence, government discrimination, successive economic downturns, and cyclical police violence gave rise to the territorial disputes in gangs in the last several decades, including in St. Louis. My friends chose or had to join gangs in the neighborhood to meet their basic needs— money, housing, employment, safety—and in return, they agreed to provide the same basic needs for others in the group. For people who must perpetually protect their lives from police, neighbors, and strangers, possessing a gun against the law might be worth the legal risk of going to prison if it means staying alive. And, if they are caught and sent to prison for gun possession, they will exit with a record that schools, jobs, and housing will use against them. They might be even more precarious than before they went in and more vulnerable to violence, so they need more protection over the few resources they have. The likelihood for violence is cyclical because the underlying causes have not changed.[146]

In the ruins of a drive-by, a child might fall. A cop, preacher, or news reporter will call the acts "senseless," a term that can lead to more police funding, patrols, surveillance, and criminalization. This response is more senseless than the shooting that prompts it. Police have a track record of intentionally disrupting neighborhood ceasefires and dropping off Black and Latinx people in rival gang territories to spark violence. One community's street violence is another community's jobs program. We have to eradicate both.

Additionally, eradicating the community-based violence that Black organizers discussed at the trainings in St. Louis necessarily entails eradicating the prison industrial complex. Police exploit the vulnerability of poor people in our communities, especially people of color who have criminal records. Cops create informants and dangle their freedom in exchange for intel or to force them to lie. During press conferences, cops will condemn Black people for refusing to "snitch," as if telling the police information or even the truth usually sets anyone free. To help release people from prison and death row, witnesses recant their testimonies and, at considerable risk to themselves, confess that cops threatened them with abuse or jail to incriminate another; police departments don't usually rally in support of them.

Nipsey Hussle's death in 2019 is an example of the dangers of police use of informants. The prominent Los Angeles rapper was shot to death in the parking lot of his store, Marathon Clothing. Nipsey had garnered a local and national reputation, even among police, for creating programs and jobs for several neglected communities in LA. He was dedicated to his neighborhood and named his first mixtape "Slauson Boy Volume 1." Journalists immediately attributed his murder to "gang violence." According to witnesses, Nipsey was trying to tell the alleged shooter to be careful because the police "had paperwork" to make him tell on other people. Appearing to have been outed as an informant, the alleged shooter denied it. Being a snitch is such a violation of street code that it could lead to the grave; hence the phrases "snitches get stitches" and "snitches get ditches." The accusation can be deadly, and so can the retaliation as in Nipsey's case. What's lost in the making of any killer is the circumstances that the police created for people to be killed. Nipsey was tragically murdered. His accused murderer is likely heading to prison, and the LAPD is creating a fresh set of informants. One way to stop community-based violence is to end police contact with people coming out of jail and stop the use of informants.[147]

Murders that stem from snitching are also significant because of the history of police repression in Black communities. Much like slave patrols grew in response to slave resistance, police tactics like infiltration and informants grew in response to radical Black activism. For example, the Black Panthers were preaching *and* practicing socialism through Free Breakfast programs; free bus rides so people can visit their loved ones in prison; free community ambulance services; copwatch and armed self-defense against the police; and much more. Many Black Panthers were also secretly part of the Black Liberation Army, the militant political wing of the Black liberation struggle that was birthed to fight repression from the police and federal government. When the police killed Black kids sometimes as young as nine years old in the community, the BLA retaliated. They were designated a "terrorist group," much like the ANC and MK wing in South Africa.

Most interestingly, the BLA also tried to stop community-based violence through militant and educational means. They sought to end murders in the neighborhood by breaking up the drug trade.

Before he was imprisoned, BPP leader Alprentice "Bunchy" Carter was a notorious leader of the Slauson gang. After he met Black Panthers and members of the Nation of Islam in prison, he acquired a political understanding of racism and capitalism. Upon his exit from prison, he helped transform thousands of gang members into activists. Bunchy enrolled in UCLA while he was leading the local Black Panther chapter in LA. He and another Black Panther, John Huggins, were killed on campus after the FBI intentionally sowed discord between the Panthers and another Black organization that the shooters belonged to. Former Panther Elaine Brown explains that the government facilitated the assassination and the only people who LAPD arrested that day were members of the Black Panther Party. Per Brown, the LAPD had murdered a Black Panther member every month and arrested one every day. The shooters escaped the country.[148]

Many cops and federal government agents disrupted positive efforts that raised the consciousness of everyday Black people. The FBI was not just concerned with any Black activism; they were primarily concerned with Black people who were against capitalism. For decades, police and the FBI started several surveillance programs, including the Ghetto Informant Program and Counter Intelligence Program (COINTELPRO). Thousands of Black informants and infiltrators went to meetings, church, parties, and bedrooms with members of radical Black organizations. Police specifically chose precarious, poor, Black people in the ghetto to be informants and infiltrators. Police and federal agents targeted them because they had criminal records and faced jail time if they did not cooperate. The decision to "snitch" came down to their prison time or somebody else's. Snitching, informants, and infiltrators led to cops and federal agents conducting raids on Black families, neighborhoods, and organizational offices. Cops and agents killed and imprisoned members of Black organizations. Some, like Assata Shakur and Pete O'Neal, are still living in exile. When the police speak on television and finger-wag against "no-snitching," we must remember that the police violence contributed to this culture in the first place.

If we are committed to preventing and eliminating homicides in our communities, then we must be committed to eradicating the conditions that give rise to them. In the interim, groups of street violence interrupters who do not work with police are important short-term interventions to stop community-based violence. Because police use rivalries, targets, and snitches to exploit volatile situations and increase community-based violence, street violence interrupters can lose credibility if they join forces with cops. Many interrupters themselves are formerly incarcerated *because* police planted drugs or guns on them and refuse to work with them from personal experience. They may not necessarily be abolitionists, but they know that cops create additional violence. One major problem is that local, state, and federal programs will agree to fund some of these projects on the basis that interrupters work with cops. Private dollars support this, too. Some Black churches belong to "cop and clergy coalitions" to support violent interruption work. Decoupling funding between these programs and law enforcement could increase the legitimacy for the street interventions and save lives.

Organizations like LIVE FREE, Taller Salud, and Cure Violence build relationships with residents who are most likely to kill or be killed by gun violence. Interrupters are trained to deescalate volatile situations, relocate potential targets to safety, organize truces between rivalries, and care for the families of those slain. In St. Louis, churches, nonprofits, and municipal offices host annual events where anyone can sell their guns and clear their warrants, no questions asked. Street violent interrupters and activists campaigning to reduce police budgets and departments have an incredible opportunity to work together to reduce community-based harm. Reductions in police budgets could fund non-carceral employment for the most exploited residents and increase the number of violence interrupters working without the police. These are short-term solutions because we must still tackle the roots of harm, including toxic masculinity and racial capitalism. Coupled with all other kinds of investments and services, these interventions could lead us closer to a future without gun violence and without police.

Those of us interested in decreasing murders that arise out of community-based violence must experiment with different prevention and intervention mechanisms. While working at Advancement Project, I met with organizers who were fighting local and federal government surveillance and infiltration, including at MediaJustice and Stop LAPD Spying. These organizations use open records requests to learn about government spying to protect us from further targeting and incarceration. Reducing and eliminating the use of spying, informants, and infiltrators—alongside criminal record expungements—can reduce community-based violence that occurs as a result of being outed.

The law is another mechanism. Currently, to deter gun violence, prosecutors will charge Black people through the federal system instead of the state system where punishment is harsher and sentences are longer. "Project EJECT" provides an example. The federal government works with the police department in Jackson, Mississippi to "cut off the flow of young people to Jackson's street gangs" by using federal funding to "purchase software, equipment and technology to 'improve their knowledge of the gang structure in our community and target the 'worst of the worst' gang members in Jackson." Jackson is 82 percent Black and has a per capita income of twenty-two thousand dollars. A quarter of the residents live in poverty, more than double the national rate. Rather than proactive, community-based investments in employment, education, housing, and conflict mediation that keeps prevents people from surviving in ways that are criminalized, governments invest in reactive policing and prosecution that imprison poor and working-class people. As a start, ending all federal prosecutions for drug and gun possessions would remove one basis of precarity that federal and local agents can exploit for informants.[149]

Additionally, we must lower penalties for handgun and drug possession with the goal of complete decriminalization, while lifting current restrictions on housing, employment, voting, and financial aid for people who have criminal records to ensure their stability upon being released from prison. When I work with people who are currently or formerly incarcerated, they'll express that they landed in prison because they got "caught up with the wrong crowd." They describe incarceration the same way others describe poverty—as an individualized failure to overcome the odds. Yet as the conversations continue, they'll share that their options were being alone and unprotected from neighborhood violence, or joining others and securing minimum protection from neighborhood violence, or selling drugs for income or using drugs to cope with the loss of a loved one or their own health. Getting "caught up with the wrong crowd" manifests differently based upon race, class, gender, citizenship, disability, and especially, wealth. Hunter Biden, prominent lawyer, lobbyist, and son of the commander-in-chief, writes in his memoir that he had been a regular crack smoker and learned how to cook the drug. He said in an interview about the book, "Most people who've gone through what I've gone through are either dead or in jail." I would add that they are also disproportionately Black, exploited, and working-class. There will be no raids on Hunter's home, though there's enough for a warrant and a SWAT team. Neither will there be prosecutions to put him in federal prison. He did not join a gang for physical protection because he did not have to live in segregated and highly exploited neighborhoods with few jobs and resources. He is on a book tour.[150]

Rather than criminalizing gun possession, activists might consider organizing long-term against the *production* of assault rifles and places a gradual moratorium on the production of guns and bullets. This moratorium could give local and statewide coalitions time to reassess the purpose, function, and utility of weapons. Additionally, lawyers must continue to litigate against the faulty interpretation of the second amendment's right to bear arms.

Instead of repeating tropes about "senseless violence," what could make sense to end murders in divested communities is investment, reparations, and the proliferation of democratic practices where people can self-determine their labor, education, health outcomes, and safety. Tenants can unionize and put pressure on their landlords to maintain any and all units, ramping up the level of organizing that the residents of Grenfell Tower used against their landlord in London. This way, landlords decrease harassment or evictions against individual renters who report grievances, which often happens to people of color, people with little means, and immigrants. For decades, Tenants and Workers United have been organizing thousands of low-income renters in Northern Virginia against evictions, rent increases, landlord abuse. The organization accomplished its ten-year campaign for nearly 300 housing units that are cooperatively owned and "democratically controlled by predominately low-income residents." Cooperatively owned and democratically operated projects can more equitably spread resources for everyone, which minimizes inequality and the violence that can accompany it. Concentrated wealth through capitalist accumulation minimizes the amount of people who benefit from the flow of resources.[151]

COMMUNITY-BASED VIOLENCE transcends gangs, so at planning meetings we discussed other forms of violence that lead to homicides, like transphobia. Kiwi Herring was on the hearts and minds of many Black activists in St. Louis in 2017. Herring was a Black wife and mother of three who had moved from Mississippi to St. Louis to escape transphobia, according to her family and friends. Her neighbor in St. Louis brought no relief. Kiwi's husband explained that their neighbor called the couple homophobic slurs and set their back deck on fire. When Kiwi confronted the man, he threw a punch, and Herring allegedly stabbed him in self-defense. The neighbor called the cops who showed up and within minutes, shot and killed Kiwi. Cops claim that she swung a knife and cut one of them. News of the killing sparked vigils and protests that declared, "Black Trans Lives Matter." In a news story, Kiwi's husband beautifully said the couple was not bound to particular identities: "What is in our hearts is the only thing that matter. We are who we are."[152]

How someone identifies does not necessarily prevent violence against them and transphobia has reverberating consequences that can create and cement harmful laws and policies that abolitionists must also undermine. Had Kiwi survived the police shooting, she could have been charged with attempted murder for a single incident that stemmed from transphobic violence. Her partner was charged with armed criminal action and arrested in the aftermath of shooting. Prosecutors often justify these charges as accountability and deterrence for anyone who might follow in this path. If this is true, then what about the white man who intentionally drove his black Mercedes through a crowd of activists at a protest in honor of Kiwi? He injured three people and could have taken their lives. As he drove alongside a police car, he held up his middle finger. Cops had complete power and authority to shoot him to stop him from causing serious bodily injury to the protesters. They withheld their fire. The man was initially charged with a felony, which was reduced to two misdemeanors. His lawyer said he was "scared and made some poor choices." A judge sentenced him to a year of probation that will disappear from his record if successfully completed. State representatives introduced bills to shield drivers like him from lawsuits and criminal liability if they hit protesters, even if they kill them. None of this undermines the initial transphobia, nor does it save more lives.

Kiwi's life and death is situated in a broader transphobic society that we have to eradicate on all fronts—culture, courts, Congress, schools, churches, and in our families—if we want the deaths to stop. In 2017, Human Rights Watch (HRW) recorded more deaths of trans people in the United States than ever before. The victims were disproportionately trans women from an ethnic minority. The HRW report explained that while each case was unique, they had elements of clear anti-transgender bias and reflected a global trend. In 2018, global violence against transgender people rose significantly with approximately 370 deaths, reportedly an undercount. They died from shootings, beatings, and stabbings. Seventy-five percent of the trans women killed in the US were ethnic minorities, and two-thirds were younger than thirty-five (Kiwi was thirty). The majority of trans people killed in the last decade were sex workers.[153]

But why? Why do people, usually cisgender men, kill trans people? An individual's motives are never simply their own. When asked what to do with cops who kill people, Angela Davis explained that we have to stop assuming that one person is responsible for the violence they perpetuate. The person from my college that discouraged me from talking to Davis was influenced by their church teachings and thought warning me was their Christian duty. Kiwi's neighbor who reportedly used homophobic slurs grew up in a society that overwhelmingly tolerates homophobia. It pollutes the water. Imprisoning individuals does not stop the transphobia because it does not and cannot filter nor cleanse the water; everyone continues to drink it. This is also true for gender-based violence, Islamophobia, xenophobia, ableism, and racism among other categories. We are conditioned to be violent and have to be intentional to recognize and dismantle it in our beliefs and practices.[154]

Transphobia and transantagonism—fear, hatred, and hostility toward trans people, identity, culture, and ideas—also result in the policing of others. Congress and the courts are complicit. Trivial courtroom fights over choosing which bathrooms people can use or what sports kids can play according to their genitalia can impact seemingly benign spectators who are now summoned to "save kids" from trans women lurking in the shadows, a harmful trope with lethal consequences. In reality, kids experience violence overwhelmingly from the people with whom they share their bathrooms at home, particularly cisgender men. Furthermore, transphobia can function how racial capitalism functions—exclusion, extraction, and exploitation. Excluding trans people from bathrooms, classrooms, and school sports frees up space for cisgender people to pee, excel, and cross finish lines. The hatred and bias makes employers more easily exploit trans people's labor if they know that other companies will not pay for the full value of their labor. Navigating this oppression extracts the time and health of trans workers.

Transfetishism and transphilia cause a different kind of policing: a man may be attracted to, curious about, even love trans women, but may also be ashamed, embarrassed, or angry because family and friends, movies and music, even his God teach that this is an abomination. So he polices and punishes her for existing. He is enforcing the various laws, policies, and religious teachings around patriarchal, ableist, and heteronormative ideas around what is healthy, normal, and permissible.

After these types of conversations at the trainings, I would ask, *Can police or prisons prevent or stop this violence?* Responses ranged. "Sometimes." "Never." "Not really." "They do it, too!" For trans violence specifically, this is all true. INCITE!, an organization dedicated to eradicating violence against women of color, explains: "More than one-fifth (22%) of transgender people who had interacted with police reported police harassment, and 6% of transgender individuals reported that they experienced bias-motivated assault by officers. Black transgender people reported much higher rates of biased harassment and assault (38% and 15%)." Nearly half of Black trans women report being incarcerated at some point in their lives. Sometimes, a cop will make an arrest and a prosecutor will secure a conviction following an act of violence and some people will say that this sends a message that you can't kill trans people and get away with it. What's tragic is that most of the murderers remain unknown and free because these forms of punishment have not completely eliminated murders for anyone, and, they are carried out by cops and prosecutors in a system that is overwhelmingly transantagonistic. To stop trans people, or anyone, from being murdered, we can't rely on punishment after someone has already been killed. We must keep people alive by vigorously opposing laws, language, and ideas that impassion people to police each other.

If we fear "murderers," as I explained during the trainings, then we must commit to eradicating the conditions that give rise to homicides and building the society that keeps us all safe. Transphobia, racism, ableism, and other prejudices are not just feelings. They are ideas and acts that can deprive people of their basic needs, simple pleasures, and wildest desires. HRC's report explains that "the intersections of racism, sexism, homophobia and transphobia conspire to deprive [trans people] of employment, housing, health care and other necessities, barriers that make them vulnerable." This discrimination can lead to deadly disputes over where transgender people live and how they acquire income.[155]

Employment is a salient issue. The National Transgender Discrimination Survey (NTDS) examined the experiences of over 6,400 transgender adults across the United States and found that nearly 70 percent of sex workers reported that in the traditional workforce, they were denied employment, promotions or were fired as a result of their gender identity or expression; those fired were almost three times more likely than cisgender people to subsequently engage in the sex trade. Eleven percent of transgender people report being involved in sex work for income. Sex work does not have to be a consequence of anti-transgender discrimination, which is why I believe that it's so incredible that BYP100 and Decrimnow's decriminalization coalition organizes campaigns on the basis of sex worker agency and self-determination, while also demanding full economic, political, and social empowerment. Per one decriminalization coalition, "People trade sex for many reasons, but most often to meet basic needs, and until this economy affords everyone a home, a living wage job, health care, and education, many people will continue to trade sex for survival." An egalitarian, abolitionist horizon may not categorically eliminate sex work, but could alter the reason that people enter it—curiosity, pleasure, boredom.[156]

Housing must also be a site of abolitionist organizing and advocacy to eradicate murders. A shockingly high number of young queer people are kicked out of their homes and wind up in precarious and unsafe living arrangements. A 2015 UCLA study found that 67 percent of young homeless people had to leave their home because of their sexual orientation or gender identity/expression; 90 percent faced family rejection. If someone's parents or lover abuses them as a "corrective" to being transgender, then that encounter can escalate in violence against the trans person and by the trans person in self-defense; the encounter can lead to arrest, incarceration, and homicide. Quality, sustainable housing could minimize risks for emotional, physical violence, and murder for us all, and especially for anyone living in immediate danger where they sleep at night. Housing could also reduce the basis for contact by police who consistently surveil people who are homeless and living in dangerous and undesirable living arrangements.[157]

Universal health care is also important to save lives. Almost weekly, I spot an online GoFundMe campaign for somebody's health-care expenses and services. One part of me feels grateful that hundreds of thousands of people donate to directly take care of someone else's needs; the other part of me remembers the recurring campaigns are an indictment of how much capitalism grips the US health-care system. Who can access care is tethered to who has money and how much. Poor and working trans people seeking gender affirmation care and surgeries face additional barriers. Trans patients are less likely to be insured and Medicare just started covering these procedures in 2014. Between 2009 and 2015, more than seven thousand trans patients had gender-related surgeries; half had incomes about seventy thousand dollars and only four people reported incomes below forty thousand dollars. As a measure of who can access this care, 30 percent of Black respondents in the largest national transgender survey reported incomes less than ten thousand dollars in 2015. Exploitation and health care access can cost lives. Transgender people who experience gender incongruence and desire surgery "were six times more likely to be hospitalized after a suicide attempt," according to one study. Our physical and emotional health should not have to be subject to benevolent measures of people pitching in, but that is what we will continue to do until we accomplish free, universal health care for everyone.[158]

Decriminalization, health care, housing, and income are a few areas where people are organizing and creating a society that is less violent and more liberatory. Mutual aid and care are also indispensable for reducing and preventing violence. I think about this support practice most squarely in the maroonage and abolitionist traditions where Black people did not wait on any lawmaker, soldier, or nonprofit to give them what they needed to survive and thrive. Maroon societies used community-based care and support because relying on the repressive slaveholding government was not an option. Ten generations of maroons living in the Great

Dismal Swamp built intentional-living communities based on support and mutual respect, attempting to combat the labels placed on them that previously led to their enslavement, indentured servitude, exploitation, and death. Runaways and their children relied on each other for safety, nourishment, entertainment, medical aid, and accountability. Abolition and decolonization invoke these histories by reminding us that strong, intentional communities of care and resistance weaken the potential and capacity for violence because there is greater impact for accountability measures. Throughout history, all sorts of vulnerable communities have practiced the direct exchange and sharing of resources through mutual aid to provide for a community's well-being. For survivors, this can include money, shelter instead of a dangerous living arrangement, food instead of starvation, self and community physical defense from a partner or the police, and relocation.[159]

The Black church is a prominent example. According to *Black Marxism* author Cedric Robinson, the Black church serves as one of the oldest, most organized sites of mutual aid in the country, providing direct payments, food, clothing, housing, and medical aid to Black people and other vulnerable populations. To be clear, many churches preach and perpetuate homophobic and transphobic ideas, marginalizing many of the queer and trans activists whom I have organized with, loved, and befriended while in the streets fighting for Black liberation. We must contest and combat these oppressive theologies. Thankfully, there are other traditions of the Black church where Black women clergy, queer clergy, and young people simultaneously criticize the church while fusing progressive theology, loving politics, and day-to-day mutual aid in the community. The bulk of this organizing and distribution of care has been by Black people with little to modest means themselves. Meeting the immediate material needs of people can be a direct response to interpersonal harm and community divestment and can keep people safe by increasing their sources of support.[160]

LGBTQIA communities, especially Black and Latinx, have created and driven mutual aid practices, building homes and social networks for youth and adults ostracized from families, friends, and society because of homophobia and transphobia. Called "houses," these homes and networks developed in the 1980s alongside AIDS/HIV activism in queer communities. The houses served as protection from street violence, sex work-related violence, and intimate partner and family abuse, all of which can lead to murder. Back in high school, I belonged to a local dance company that was founded by a Black woman and mostly run by queer Black choreographers. We were not a "house," but we were heavily influenced by ballroom culture, midnight voguing battles and all. Most of the dancers lived in precarious situations, but the choreographers would make time to pick us up for practice, cover our fees for class, provide food, a home, and paid opportunities to teach and perform. A few dancers regularly brought their babies to practice because they had limited or no childcare. We pooled money when someone needed to cover rent or gas. I wonder who would have been killed or in prison instead of where many of them are now, choreographing for award shows, touring with Beyoncé, and running dance companies of their own for mostly young Black queer kids.

The messy and best versions of these traditions can offer some foundational measures to eliminate the violence that people fear. These are not prescriptive solutions, just some ideas and responses that organizers have been dreaming of and demanding for freedom, safety, and real justice for the thousands of Black trans women who deserve nothing less.

DURING THE ACTION St. Louis trainings, we also discussed other harm that leads to homicides and murder, such as burglaries and robberies. In 2018 in the United States, 1.07 percent of households reported a burglary. Seven percent of people who survive burglaries experience some form of violent act when it happens. Of the 16,214 estimated reported murders in 2018, 75 began as burglaries and 548 began as robberies. The low murder rate stemming from burglaries may be connected to two reasons. One, people usually steal from people they know; "acquaintance" is the largest category of murder victim from these acts. At abolition workshops, I ask participants if someone they know or love has ever stolen from them. Everyone nods or raises their hand. Then I ask if any of them have ever stolen something from someone they know or love. They usually confess with laughter.[161]

Stealing is also often an act of desperation, and poor people—not middle or upper class—are the most vulnerable, like my mom and my grandmother, who have had several things stolen from them by friends, family members, and lovers. Households with higher incomes are less likely to be burglarized than households with low incomes. Homes with incomes of less than seven thousand and five hundred dollars are burglarized at the highest rates, homes with incomes above seventy-five thousand dollars are the least frequently burglarized. Mobile homes, like the first ones I saw in rural Tennessee, and apartments, like the ones I grew up in, experience the most break-ins, not villas and mansions. Yet I have never seen a movie where the entire plot centers on a mastermind devising a plan to raid his neighbor's trailer for cash and coins. Movies and television dramatize the victims of robberies as rich and helpless victims of poor people thirsting for money.[162]

If we don't want people to die during burglaries, we have to reduce and eliminate the range of reasons why people burglarize. We have to ask, what kinds of circumstances condition people to risk their lives, and the lives of others, for money? A study of people convicted of burglaries found that the need to acquire drugs was the underlying reason in more than half of the respondents; 37 percent reported a need for money, including money to support drug habits. Only 12 percent reported planning the burglary in advance. Additionally: "most burglars (79%) reported an interest in acquiring cash during their burglaries, followed by jewelry (68%), illegal drugs (58%), electronics (56%) and prescription drugs (44%)." A 2017 study found that among people arrested for burglary, "approximately 70% to 88% tested positive for at least one illicit drug, with the most common drugs being marijuana, cocaine, and opiates."[163]

Drug use and addiction do not capture the magnitude of the problem. Substance use is pretty consistent across income levels and studies even show that drugs and alcohol are used at higher rates in families at high socioeconomic statuses. The difference is that when they want or need drugs, they can buy them. Or doctors, friends, parents, and neighbors provide them. Rich people aren't breaking into the homes of their neighbors because they need money for food, utilities, medicine, and other day-to-day costs. "Senseless violence" is caused when the government criminalizes drugs, making it harder and more taboo for class-exploited people to use and acquire them, and then punishes them when they are caught. Police cannot solve those problems. Instead, they can only occupy poor neighborhoods and wait to catch people.[164]

What could prevent burglaries, robberies, and the few murders that derive from them? Eliminating poverty, economic exploitation, and trailers as the only housing available because residents cannot afford to live elsewhere. Again, mutual aid, universal basic income, labor unions, and employee protection are also good starts. Eliminating concentrated poverty long term could be accomplished by changing the economy from worker-exploitative to worker-owned. Cities and states sometimes require using minority and women-owed businesses for contracts and services. While I worked with Mickey, I learned that many companies found a loophole and only listed a woman or person of color in charge on the paperwork but the company did not run that way in reality. Cities and states could require their contracts to use cooperatively owned companies with particular emphasis on those that are created by Black, Indigenous, disabled, and queer workers. Worker-owned firms can be significantly less exploitative than large (and small) capitalist corporations because they create and spread wealth for all of the employees. By design, workers who own the former are usually more interested in maintaining long-term operations for employment, better working conditions, and benefits that everyone can enjoy, instead of highly selective perks for a few people at the top.[165]

Quality drug access and decriminalization could also prevent robberies and burglaries that can lead to murder, and also undermine the conditions that lead to violence and police contact. Drug decriminalization permits people to exchange drugs more freely in private, public, and commercial settings. People might be willing to ask for money that they need for drugs instead of stealing it. Sharing drugs and pooling money to buy them already happens; Luniz's "I've got five on it" is a lyrical aspiration and a revelation. The problem is that it happens under criminalization, exploitation, and police if you're poor and Black. In the very same song, the rapper says that he is going to fail the drug test from his probation officer. Lawmakers literally police the savings accounts, drug use, and lifestyles of the poor, as they sit in Congress with multiple homes, quality insurance, generational wealth, net worth in the millions, and incomes at nearly two hundred thousand dollars. They can afford the drugs they want and do not have the fear of any drug-testing lingering over them at work.[166]

"WHAT ABOUT THE murderers?" can reveal the kinds of interpersonal harms that we fear most. In my conversations and political education with Action and others who are curious or critical about abolition, I sometimes wonder whether I had emphasized enough how structural violence, like militarism and policing, can create and shape interpersonal violence, like assaults, murders, and mass shootings. I believe that if we truly want to stop homicides and preserve lives, we have to stop militarism and policing in, around, and outside the borders of the United States.

Abroad, the US government sends the military to invade countries that are financially poor and resource rich. Opposing the draft to fight in the Vietnam War, heavyweight boxing world champion Muhammad Ali said, "Why should they ask me to put on a uniform and go 10,000 miles from home and drop bombs and bullets on Brown people in Vietnam while so-called Negro people in Louisville are treated like dogs and denied simple human rights? No I'm not going 10,000 miles from home to help murder and burn another poor nation simply to continue the domination of white slave masters of the darker people the world over." These military pursuits are launched under the guise of wars on terror, communism, and immigrant invasions. Domestically, this can manifest as temporary police occupations, as I witnessed in Ferguson and Baltimore. Congress authorized the Department of Defense's 1033 program to cycle the military's leftover, gently used equipment through police departments. Cops use these tanks, helicopters, and weapons in SWAT raids against people of color and to violate the rights of protesters. In fact, US soldiers cannot legally use tear gas in war, but police officers are granted free rein to use it against protesters.[167]

Historically, white people have volunteered or have been required to police and control the whereabouts of Black people, Indigenous peoples, and people of color. Today, militarism and policing can inspire civilians to continue mimicking the violence from these institutions. The rate of deadly police shootings among Black people is significantly higher than most ethnic groups and nearly half of race related hate crimes specifically stem from anti-Black racism. Following the wars in Iraq and Afghanistan, civilian hate crimes in the US increased against Muslims, Arabs, South Asians, and Sikhs. Under presidents Bill Clinton, George W. Bush, Barack Obama, and Donald Trump, Immigration and Customs Enforcement (ICE) and border patrol ramped up operations to arrest, detain, and deport undocumented immigrants. The Southern Border Communities Coalition reports that the border militarization under Clinton led to the "death and disappearance of thousands of migrants." Illegal armed militias work in tandem with border patrol and federal agents to capture and kill people attempting to cross from Central and South America. The most notable prosecutions related to immigration battles on the border occurred against compassionate No More Deaths volunteers who left food and water in the scorching desert where temperatures soared above triple digits. Clips of border patrol agents dumping the water still circulate the internet.[168]

I protested against border patrol violence and the accompanying illegal mobs in college, and witnessed the xenophobic rhetoric again following President Donald Trump's election. Trump's repeated racist and white nationalist attacks against people of color inspired my client and reflected the everyday views of other people who chose to act violently based on racial and xenophobic hatred. In 2017, Jeremy Joseph Christian yelled racial, Islamophobic, and xenophobic slurs at two Black teens—one wearing a hijab—on a train in Portland, Oregon, "Pay taxes! Get the fuck out! Go home. We need Americans here!" Three white men, Ricky Best, Taliesin Myrddin Namkai-Meche, and Micah Fletcher, stood up on the train to protect the girls. Christian stabbed and killed Namkai-Meche and Best. Fletcher survived. Christian affirmed his act in the back of a police car: "Think I stab (expletives) in the neck for fun? Oh yeah, you're right I do. I'm a patriot . . . That's what liberalism gets you . . . I hope they all die. I'm gonna say that on the stand. I'm a patriot, and I hope everyone I stabbed died."[169]

During Christian's trial in July 2020, Demetria Hester, one of the African American teenagers he threatened to kill on the train, said on the stand, "I blame the system for creating and facilitating people like Jeremy, and then we, the community, have to deal with them. In my case, the white supremacist got special treatment from the police [who] believed the assault wasn't made by the assailant. He didn't believe me or the two TriMet supervisors. The police captured—not killed—the racist white supremacist known to the police, holding the bloody knife he attacked and killed people with while drinking wine from his Gatorade bottle." Hester is absolutely correct: Jeremy is a product of white supremacist violence who carried out his influences against Black people and anyone who stands with them. He was sentenced to two consecutive life terms in prison, and additional time for an earlier racially motivated attack on a Black woman. Sending people like him to prison will stop him from attacking another Black woman on the outside. But prisons are rife with white supremacist organizations where he might be treated as a hero and inspire other white men to act violently once they are released from prison. The underlying violence will not stop until schools, communities, churches, and politicians began to eradicate the underlying racist beliefs.[170]

Christian was not alone. Two years later, Patrick Crusius said he "targeted Mexicans" when he opened fire at an El Paso, Texas, Walmart. I thought about Kelly Hernandez's essay again, *Amnesty or Abolition*, where she explains that border patrol serves as cover for many white men who live in border states to carry out violence. Crusius lived near Dallas and drove more than 600 miles to a border town to enact violence. He killed twenty-three people and injured twenty-six. Tennessee congressman Steve Cohen tweeted advice in response: "You want to shoot an assault weapon? Go to Afghanistan or Iraq. Enlist!" He apparently did not take issue with the El Paso shooter's desire to slaughter people of color—he merely wanted to redirect the bullets toward Black and brown people outside of the United States.[171]

Members of the US military would use their skills and tactical training to raid US Capitol grounds in Washington, DC, on January 6, 2021. After hearing Donald Trump encourage them to reject the presidential election's outcome in favor of Joe Biden, thousands reportedly pushed through cops to storm ongoing congressional debates and reign supreme over politicians who fearfully scurried out of the halls of power. Draped in American, Confederate, Nazi, Thin Blue Line, and Trump flags, the raiders invaded the House floor, occupied representative offices, and filled balconies and scaffolds that line the windows. Joe Biden took to a podium to respond, cautioning the country that "our democracy is under unprecedented assault." At least 14 percent of the raiders arrested were current or former military personnel; dozens were current or former cops. Police spend years of planning and conducting raids, assaults, and arrests in Black and brown communities; these precedented assaults on local communities prepared hundreds of Capitol raiders to temporarily lay siege to the federal government.[172]

The January 2021 Capitol raid was an anomalous one. As Demetria Hester explained at trial, local communities suffer the bulk of militaristic and policing-inspired violence. I did not realize how much militarism and policing really influenced some people who engage commit assaults and mass shootings until I started conducting research for an article that I wrote about the El Paso shooting. Every time the country witnesses a mass shooting by a white man, two phrases circulate: mental health issues and lone wolf. But as I read about the backgrounds of most of these men, I noticed that they were either in or obsessed with the military. Sometimes they fashioned themselves after soldiers. Other times, they were veterans. Consistently, they used military-style rifles during the act. The overwhelming majority of people who retire or are discharged from the military do not engage in mass shootings. But if we are asking, "why do people kill people," we have to explore the relationships between mass killings, militarism, policing, and patriotism.

When Rep. Cohen tweeted that people interested in shooting military style weapons should enlist, it concerns me that so many shooters tried. Adam Lanza failed to accomplish his dream of becoming a Marine and was further discouraged by his mother from joining any other military branch. He killed her before taking twenty-six precious lives at Sandy Hook Elementary School in Newtown, Connecticut in 2012. Lanza's bedroom was filled with posters of military equipment, his wardrobe stylized after uniforms. He wore one the day of the killing spree. Devin Patrick Kelley also wore black tactical gear and a ballistics vest in 2017 when he conducted the largest mass shooting in a place of worship in modern history at a Sutherland Springs church in Texas—the fifth-deadliest shooting massacre in US history at the time. Twenty-six people died; eight were children. Before the rampage, he was enlisted in the United States Air Force. They jailed him, demoted him, and issued a "bad conduct discharge" before the rampage over domestic violence. Lanza took four semi-automatic firearms to Sandy Hook; Kelley took a military-style Ruger AR-556 to church.[173]

Nineteen-year-old Nikolas Cruz also had military obsessions. The very last time he went trick-or-treating, he donned a soldier's uniform with body armor and a ballistics helmet. The National Rifle Association funded his rifle club at school; he was a "very good shot," per a teammate. Cruz killed seventeen students and wounded over a dozen more at Marjory Stoneman Douglas High School during the tragic Parkland shooting in 2018. Cruz wore his JROTC shirt that day and three of the victims were JROTC students. We, even I, often ask in the aftermath, "What kind of a person could do something like this?"[174]

Law enforcement and mainstream media immediately used social media to paint the picture of Cruz as a violent and disturbing white individual who posted guns and knives. After Parkland, I wanted to know, *What kind of country continues to sell these guns? What kind of a country keeps conditioning people toward violence? Why is it more taboo to post pictures of weapons online than for companies to sell them?* What's often lost in the mental health debate surrounding mass killings is that random acts of violence are rarely random in a broader context of war and militarism. Writing a supporter overseas from jail, Cruz admitted, "It wasn't until I was in JROTC that my shooting skills improved. I was in the marksmanship team in Stoneman Douglas. We used to shoot pellet guns in the classroom. It was really fun. We set up targets the size of quarters. I was really good at it." When I was in JROTC in high school, the airmen at an Air Force base let us hold military weapons during summer leadership camps, but we did not have a shooting team there or at my school. I didn't think that one of the thousands of cadets that I crossed paths with could be inspired to use their training against other students.[175]

Cruz was not the first nor the only one to practice his marksmanship on his peers. As a twelve-year-old child all the way in St. Louis, I remember the DC Sniper filling the country with fear. I just *knew* that the killer was going to be a white man. The police broadcasted a profile that said that he would be white. Sniper John Allen Muhammad was very Black, and he had a Black apprentice. He did not match the racial profile, but he did match the military one. In 1978, Muhammad enlisted in the Louisiana National Guard and later the US Army. He learned excellent shooting skills while he was in the military. He later practiced them in 2002 during a killing spree in the nation's capital.[176]

White American Navy SEAL Chris Kyle also reportedly used his military training to shoot and kill Black Hurricane Katrina survivors. Before his own murder by a military veteran, Kyle was considered the deadliest sniper in US history with a record of 160 kills. He claims that the Navy sent him and another military member to New Orleans to kill "looters." Kyle claimed he killed thirty people. Although this is disputed due to a lack of evidence, a ProPublica special investigation found that Black people were indeed shot from long and close range during the aftermath of the flood. Not all of the shooters are known. They could have been killed by Kyle or any of the local militiamen who also shot Black people with the consent of local police. One militiaman explained to a reporter:[177]

> "Three people got shot in just one day . . . Three of them got hit right here in this intersection with a riot gun," he says, motioning toward the streets outside his home. Janak tells me he assumed the shooting victims, who were African-American, were looters because they were carrying sneakers and baseball caps with them. He guessed that the property had been stolen from a nearby shopping mall. According to Janak, a neighbor "unloaded a riot gun"—a shotgun—"on them. We chased them down."[178]

Murders also happen because of the perceived failures of military and law enforcement. Before October 2017, when Las Vegas shooter Stephen Paddock committed the deadliest mass shooting in US history, he had worked as a letter carrier, and then an Internal Revenue Service agent. For several years, he worked as an auditor on defense contracts and then for a weapons manufacturing firm that became Lockheed Martin. He reportedly was angry at the government for using grotesque military force at Waco and Ruby Ridge, where police or US Marshals fired shots against civilians. Although there was "no motive" established in the Vegas shooting, Paddock's disdain sounded remarkably similar to Timothy McVeigh's, the Oklahoma City bomber who killed 168 people in a federal building as revenge for the police violence at Waco and Ruby Ridge.[179]

McVeigh viewed the United States as a bully for killing innocent people during the Gulf War, where he was deployed as a soldier. During his *60 Minutes* interview, McVeigh explained, "I thought . . . what right did I have to come over to this person's country and kill him? How did he ever transgress against me?" When he was honorably discharged, he too witnessed the government attack on the self-proclaimed white separatists at Ruby Ridge. A US Marshal waited outside the family's cabin and shot the dog as the fourteen-year-old boy followed it. The shooting ignited a standoff that lasted over a week. The boy's father returned fire and a shootout ensued. An FBI sniper injured the father and, while attempting to shoot an additional armed man, shot and killed the boy's mother, who was holding a ten-month-old baby. The government dropped manslaughter charges against the agent. McVeigh explained, "The use of what is no more or less snipers, in a domestic nonwartime situation, federal agents taking on the role of judge, jury and executioner, and then to add insult to injury, you have these people, these federal agents, not held accountable. They become immune from the law."[180]

Stephen Paddock's casualty count surpassed the 2016 record belonging to Omar Mateen, who opened fire at the mostly queer and Latinx nightclub Pulse in Orlando, Florida. At the time of the shooting, Mateen was employed by G4S, a billion-dollar private security company that places armed guards all over the world, from prisons to hospitals to suburban subdivisions. At more than half a million employees, G4S is one of the largest private employers on Earth. Mateen wanted to become a prison guard, then a cop, but failed and entered private security at a courthouse. Mateen was born to Muslim Afghan parents whose identities made them targets in the US during the wars in Afghanistan; he claimed a Persian identity to avoid mistreatment. He was impacted by and subsequently angry about US military violence in the Middle East. More than 800,000 people have died due to recent wars in Afghanistan, Iraq, Yemen, Pakistan, and Syria; more than 310,000 civilians have become casualties since 2001. Thirty-seven million have been displaced. The night of the shooting, Mateen called 911 to demand that the United States stop airstrikes in Syria and Iraq. In 2016, President Obama dropped 26,171 bombs abroad. Mateen killed forty-nine people and injured more than fifty. War inspires retaliatory acts that can make us all vulnerable to violence, even when we go out dancing to feel free.[181]

Mass shooters and vigilantes sometimes view themselves *as* law enforcement and punish people by their own authority. Teenage shooters in the 1999 Columbine massacre were not simply victims of bullying seeking revenge as the media described; they were burgeoning white supremacists who bullied and fought Black kids. Eric Harris, one of the shooters, literally called himself "the law" and expressed excitement when he learned in class that the US government was planning to bomb Yugoslavia. When George Zimmerman was in high school, he joined JROTC in hopes of becoming a Marine one day, shining his boots at night. He did not become one, but studied criminal justice at his local college. Zimmerman, the son of a military veteran who retired from the Department of Defense, was the coordinator of the neighborhood watch in his gated community. Police gave the watch group specific instructions not to follow "suspicious people." Against further precaution of a 911 dispatcher, Zimmerman stalked and ultimately killed Martin in 2012, saying "these assholes always get away."[182]

In 2020, an armed white father-and-son duo chased and killed Ahmaud Arbery, a Black jogger in Georgia. They initially tried to apprehend Ahmaud because they believed he was a burglar. A man who helped the two men chase Ahmaud recorded the entire incident and captured the son using racial slurs toward Ahmaud. The father is a Navy veteran, former cop, and retired as an investigator from the prosecutor's office. Cops arrested both men for the killing. During a bail hearing, the son used his Coast Guard experience as evidence of his good character. The Georgia Bureau of Investigation reported that the son said while enlisted, "I loved my job because I was out on a boat and there were no niggers."[183]

Later that year, during the uprisings in Kenosha, Wisconsin, following the police shooting of Jacob Blake, an armed white militia drove to the protest sites to intimidate the activists. Seventeen-year-old Kyle Rittenhouse allegedly shot and killed two people and seriously injured a third while he was waving his assault rifle indiscriminately at protesters. Minutes before the shooting, the police in riot gear and tanks tossed Rittenhouse and other members of the militia bottles of water, saying, "We appreciate you guys, we really do." If Rittenhouse had been a cop, he probably could have shot protesters without facing charges. He was on his way. *New York Times*'s Neil MacFarquhar wrote, "He signed up to be a cadet in a program for teenagers who aspire to be police officers. He filled his Facebook page with support for Blue Lives Matter. He sat upfront at a rally for President Trump in January, and posted images of it on TikTok. For his 16th birthday, he celebrated by raising funds for a support group for the police called 'Humanizing the Badge.'"[184]

If we truly want to save lives in the US and beyond, we have join in the traditions of activists who fight to end policing, wars and military operations across the globe. In their book *Violence, Inequality, and Human Freedom,* sociologists Peter Iadicola and Anson Shupe explain that increasing US involvement in covert and overt wars may have contributed to a "war mentality" that may inspire homicides during those periods: "As violence is increasingly used by the state to repress and control populations that threaten [structures of inequality], nationally and internationally, violence is learned as an appropriate means to address interpersonal problems." Plainly put, when the federal government uses law enforcement and the military to control concentrated wealth, property, and natural resources, they condition everyday people to accept the violence, replicate it, or rebel against it. In the US, white men have historically been the primary beneficiaries and supporters of militarism and policing, so it's possible that white men with military and law enforcement connections and obsessions might feel empowered to act on that conditioning in particular ways more than others today, particular for the most high profile cases.[185]

What is especially awful is that so many people, including many I know and love, enter the military or police academy to escape violence, poverty, and despair. JROTC was a route for them. In many cases, the program was my refuge, the instructors were my mentors, and the class pushed my leadership development. I took the military entrance exam and considered becoming a military lawyer as late as college because the Judge Advocate General (JAG) Corps sponsored the

Black law students conferences I attended. During visits to St. Louis for court or to meet with Action STL, I visited my alma mater to speak with JROTC classes about all that I'd accomplished. My former instructors beamed with pride. From the front of the classrooms where I used to report on current events as a kid, I noticed an increasing number of tan camouflage backpacks at the feet of each student since my time there. When I asked kids why they enlisted, they responded mechanically. "To pay for college." "To see the world." "To do something with my life." Lines from the commercials and mouths of recruiters. I recalled what Robin Kelley wrote in *Black Study, Black Struggle*:

> We are also talking about a generation that has lived through two of the longest wars in U.S. history, raised on a culture of spectacle where horrific acts of violence are readily available on their smartphones. What Henry Giroux insightfully identifies as an addiction does nothing to inure or desensitize young people to violence. On the contrary, it anchors violence in their collective consciousness, produces fear and paranoia—wrapped elegantly in thrill—and shrouds the many ways capitalism, militarism, and racism are killing black and brown people.[186]

I am not sure whether these kids really knew this. I once heard Rev. William Barber, an architect of the Moral Mondays movement in North Carolina, refer to the military as a "poverty draft." Kids who sat in JROTC were signing up for a military that did not care about individual soldiers and applying for jobs in police departments that compromise the well-being of individuals who become cops. There are better ways to keep the peace than by joining the police and the military. Yet having an armed wing of the state protects capitalist practices like exploitation and wealth accumulation. If the federal and state governments offered free college, day care, or universal basic income, perhaps it would lose recruits who enter the military to have their basic needs met.[187]

Once inside these institutions, people of color face racial violence on the force and in the ranks. Others face assault, sexual violence, and murder by their fellow soldiers. Like in prison, white people have to decide whether to join white supremacist and racist peer groups for community or protection or be ostracized by having friends of other races. As reporter Melissa del Bosque wrote for *The Intercept*:

For the last four years, the *Military Times*, an independent publication that caters to military readers, has polled active-duty service members about whether they've personally witnessed white supremacy and racist ideology in the military. In 2020, 57 percent of minority troops surveyed said they had, up from 42 percent in 2017, when the survey was first conducted. The *Times* noted that the troops surveyed "classified white nationalism as a national security threat on par with al-Qaida and the Islamic State, and more worrisome than the danger posed by North Korea, Afghanistan or Iraq."[188]

White supremacists enlist in and recruit from the military and law enforcement because both institutions are filled with marginalized and class-exploited white people who are in the business of surveilling, targeting, and killing people of color. Most soldiers, seamen, airmen, and police do not benefit fully from the exploitation that they protect, no more than any manager of Whole Foods gets to live lavishly like owner Jeff Bezos. Yes, the capitalists and the political establishment will pay for their college and world travel at the risk of bloodshed. And back in the United States, men will mostly emulate militarism as they open fire in schools and churches and concerts.[189]

HAMID KHAN HEARD these violent military stories thirty-five thousand feet in the air for twenty-five years. I'd met Hamid at an organizing meeting at this campaign base in Skid Row in downtown L.A. in 2018 and we connected again two years later at a convening in Miami. Before he became Campaign Coordinator with the Stop LAPD Coalition, Hamid pursued his dream of becoming a pilot when he came to the US from Pakistan in the late 1970s. His co-pilots were usually white men who'd recently exited from the military. They'd share war stories about bombing brown countries and used denigrating language to describe the souls on the other end of the blasts. He told me, "Sometimes Derecka, they'd talk about watching hardcore, triple x movies to get all amped up because they wanted to genderize the enemy. Simone Browne talks about 'unvisibility,' you are there, so they see you, but you're invisible, too." Hamid was one of the few pilots who were not white, and the men would drop epithets about Black and Middle Eastern people and argue against gay people enlisting in the military, which caused arguments in the cockpit.[190]

His co-pilots had not known that Hamid was also a full-time organizer while he was flying. He'd founded South Asian Network in 1990, which was the first grassroots organizing in LA to empower immigrants from South Asia, India, Sri Lanka, Bangladesh, and Nepal to fight discrimination in solidarity with other communities resisting oppression. As early as 2006 they had been calling for the abolition of the Department of Homeland security because of the violence and surveillance against immigrants. Simultaneously, they were organizing within South Asian communities to eradicate homophobia and anti-Blackness. He quit flying at the height of his career to continue cultivating the kind of grassroots organizing work that keeps people safe from prejudice, precisely the kind that can lead to threats, assaults, and homicides.

In 2010, Hamid began tracking and organizing against the military tactics that the Los Angeles Police Department deployed against Muslims and South Asians and was keenly aware that the same counterterrorism and surveillance tactics would be used against Black, Latinx, and Indigenous communities. This was the beginning of the Stop LAPD Spying Coalition, which rejects "all forms of police oppression and any policy that make us all suspects in the eyes of the State." Coalition organizers had various backgrounds and spent many months listening to people in the community to learn which policing and surveil-lance problems to address. They continue to build community-based campaigns and knowledge to keep people safe from police, as well as reduce LAPD's capac-ity to harm the community. Stop LAPD Spying is strengthening relationships across LA, resisting militarism, and stopping police violence all at once.[191]

Contemporary movements for decolonization and abolition were converg-ing or resurging all around us, and Action St. Louis and other bourgeoning organizations had been forming in the wake of progressive coalitions like Stop LAPD Spying. Mijente formed in 2015 after a campaign to end deportations and transformed into a network of grassroots hubs that organize people, campaigns, and technology to build power against, outside, and within the state.

In 2016, the Movement for Black Lives released *Vision for Black Lives*, a policy platform with several demands, including: an end to the war on Black people, reparations, divestment from exploitative systems and investment in Black communities, economic justice, and community control over institutions that govern our lives. The following year, the Red Nation formed a coalition of

Native and non-Native activists to combat invisibility and marginalization in four areas of struggle: defense of indigeneity, Native people, and lands; liberation and return of Native lives and land; anti-colonial resistance; and mobilization of community engagement for coalition building.[192]

The Dream Defenders, who formed in the aftermath of Trayvon Martin's murder to get George Zimmerman arrested, dropped "Freedom Papers" in 2018, a brilliant and colorful campaign demanding freedom from police, prisons, and poverty; freedom of movement; a free, flourishing democracy; freedom of mind and to be; and freedom from war, violence, and environmental destruction. These transformational demands and campaigns condemned war, imperialism, and genocide, and projected visions of possible futures for us all. And ending structural violence can also reduce and eliminate the interpersonal violence that the state inspires.

The Dream Defenders' call to end all wars is an example of how we can prevent murderers domestically. Their "Freedom Papers" profess:

> The US government spends nearly 9 times more on war than it does on education, housing and healthcare and over 20 times more than it does on unemployment. These wars are waged in the name of our safety, but they don't keep us safe—this is a lie they use to keep us fearful of one another so that they can continue to make billions off of destroying the lives of poor people in our communities and around the world.[193]

They are invoking Dr. Martin Luther King, Jr., who called the United States "the greatest purveyor of violence in the world" when he condemned the war in Vietnam. Abolitionist anti-war activism is internationalist, a commitment to solidarity with oppressed people in other countries. It is also anti-imperialist, against the US using the military to spread power and influence in other countries by force. For the ones who made it back, the militarism in other parts of the world not only returned poor soldiers to the ghettos, trailers, and segregated communities that Rev. Dr. King and Rev. Barber described. The militarism may have inspired domestic mass shootings by people who had never been deployed.[194]

College students have long organized to remove ROTC from their campuses. At Harvard, ROTC was banned for forty years due to student pressure around the Vietnam War and "Don't Ask Don't Tell," the military policy that discrimination against gay people. After the repeal of the policy, Harvard welcomed branches back on campus to celebrate the end of the discriminatory policy (The policy did not ban anyone in the military engaging in acts of war against families with queer people in them). New and legacy anti-militarism groups do this work as well. Veterans for Peace and About Face: Veterans Against the War are organizations created and led by former military members who now oppose the global destruction from war and violence. Dissenters is building a youth movement toward ending all wars and toward demilitarization. By calling for the end of war, reductions in military size and budget, and investments in education, employment, and housing, these organizations are saving lives abroad. They are also reducing the possibilities for civilians to mimic police and military violence inside the United States.[195]

TOWARD THE END of our training, Inez sat down at the farthest end of the rectangular table. Her palms were on the sides of her temples. Her fingers grabbed her forehead. "Wow."

I did not know whether this was a good *wow* or a bad *wow*. So I stood awkwardly near the giant Post-it notes waiting for more. Before she spoke again, I nervously repeated what I said at the beginning. I tried to reiterate that abolition is not about knowing all of the answers. That we had to take time to read and brainstorm ideas and learn from what other people are doing to combat violence. We needed to develop an analysis to help recognize our problems before we could jump to solutions. She said it was "a good wow." This was not simply because of me, but because she had started building relationships with the organizers in Action and trusted them to fight for the liberation of Black people in St. Louis. If abolition was going to be one framework that they were going to use to start reducing their reliance on the prison industrial complex, then she was going to earnestly attempt to study it and struggle alongside them to make it possible.

Inez's good faith inquiry pushed us deeper into a conversation about how to prevent homicides and what we could do in response. The overwhelming number of murders can be prevented by changing the society that we live in. As we are paving the road to abolition, we will choose better solutions for accountability and real justice that do not rely on the same systems that murder us, too.

SIX

SEX, LOVE, AND VIOLENCE

COURT AND CAMPAIGN meetings throughout my time in St. Louis brought long workdays and my family made me work overtime. On early mornings I'd be in line at Schnucks grocery store to stock up my mother's refrigerator. On my way to evening community meetings in Ferguson, I'd bring my grandmother fish dinners to her elderly facility down the road from Ferguson City Hall. During our time together in between meetings, my family would ask the same questions about abolition that members in Action STL had been asking. *What about the murderers? What about the rapists?* I was already anxious about whether I'd been intentional enough in having conversations with my own family members about dismantling the prison industrial complex. But I knew that if we were going to build the society that we deserved, I absolutely had to discuss and practice abolitionist politics in my own relationships off the clock.

Additionally, as young, Black organizers began publicly espousing more revolutionary and abolitionist demands to end police violence in the summer of 2017, a movement demanding awareness and accountability around sexual violence catalyzed the national #MeToo conversation. Many of the calls for accountability included calls for imprisonment, which was in part at odds with my work to end reliance on police and prisons as a response to harm. In October 2017, actress Alyssa Milano tweeted, "If you've been sexually harassed or assaulted write 'me too' as a reply to this tweet." Hundreds of thousands, perhaps millions of women eventually shared stories online. When Milano was celebrated as the founder of #MeToo, Black activists and academics organized vigorously to elevate Tarana Burke, a sexual violence survivor and advocate who had created a program called "Me Too" more than a decade before the tweet went viral. Burke said she panicked. "I felt a sense of dread, because something that was part of my life's work was going to be co-opted and taken from me and used for a purpose that I hadn't originally intended." Burke had envisioned "Me Too" as a movement for survivors of sexual abuse, assault, and exploitation to find empathy, support, and empowerment alongside other survivors.[196]

Milano ceded credit to Burke, yet the hashtag continued to circulate primarily as a way to highlight stories that outed powerful men in Hollywood for their predation on women. Many of the calls for accountability included calls for prison time. When NBC fired Today Show anchor Matt Lauer over several allegations of sexual harassment, misconduct, assault, and rape, my mother called me. She had a huge crush on him and made me shudder in embarrassment when she'd playfully say, "Some white boys just got it." After his fall, she apologized for not letting me wear tight jeans as a teen. We were categorically forbidden from getting tattoos and piercings until we were eighteen. Even ear piercings. She feared that clothes or piercings or certain hairstyles would make children likelier candidates for sexual assault and didn't want us to look *fast*. Matt Lauer's downfall due to his colleagues speaking up surprised her. She was used to men taking advantage of poor women, especially men with power, status, and wealth. She had thought that she could protect me until I had enough money or power in society to shield me from what she experienced in so many of her jobs. But when #MeToo entered the mainstream, she realized that sexual violence can transcends degrees, job titles, and race.

With the ongoing Black Lives Matter and #MeToo social movements, on any given day I was in conversation with my family about police violence, neighborhood violence, and sexual violence. Social movements spark conversations and action, inviting people to revisit their previously held beliefs about themselves and the world. We'd revisit old debates and opened wounds about early conversations that had been meant to protect us from sexual violence. After cop and vigilante murders went viral, journalists were obsessed with asking Black parents what we were going to tell our Black sons to keep them from dying. In law school, I grew to hate this question; I wanted them to ask white parents what they were going to do to stop their white children from killing. But the earliest "talks" I had with my mom, aunts, and uncles were not simply about protection from police, but from men. Consequently, up until I began sharpening my political analyses around abolition and the root causes of harm in Belinda Hall, I held unexamined and inconsistent ideas about sex and sexual violence. Men, I'd learned, were protectors and predators. The talk was usually one-sided, focusing on heterosexual violence perpetrated by men toward women. Fathers, husbands, sons, brothers, nephews, cousins, uncles, friends, pastors, bosses, strangers—violated—mothers, wives, daughters, sisters, nieces, aunts, girlfriends, cleaning ladies, babysitters, nuns, neighbors. My relatives told the young kids to resist if we could and use every tool at our disposal to escape. My mother and her boyfriend performed drills to ensure that my brother and I knew to scream loud enough and swing hard enough in case we were abducted. Once, I came downstairs to a sexual assault happening at a family member's house while she was asleep. At eleven, I did not know it was rape, but I knew it was wrong. I screamed. She woke up disoriented and then started swinging at him. So many women tried to prepare me in case it happened to me one day. When it did, I was not asleep.

Watching women and girls fight boys and men also inspired me to resist, too. We ignored teachers who told us that boys were simply beset by their own attraction. I had a dozen childhood fistfights and only two were with girls; the rest were with boys who touched me. During one conversation, my mom reminded me when she pulled me away from an alley basketball court right after I threw a full glass bottle of orange juice at a boy's head. He had fouled me in a way that he didn't foul the boys on the court and called me a bitch when I complained about it. Our parents made us apologize to each other after. At college parties, my friends and I would physically stop men who tugged at our waists, wrists, hips. As I grew up, the violence morphed and so did my refusal and resistance. Boys weren't just touching anymore; it was professors and politicians who'd hug too long, compliment incessantly, or offered me hotels rooms when I'd post online that I was traveling somewhere. As I'd repeatedly decline their advances, they would play it safe by reassuring me that they were just being nice. One woman mentor told me when I sought her help in college, "You're a beautiful girl. These things come with the territory. It's wrong, but men are men. They can't help themselves." I had not possessed the language then to refute her claim, but my body viscerally rejected it.

Neither the state nor the church was on my side. Men in my life were not inherently this way. Church molded them as God molded Adam to have total dominion over women, animals, and Earth; the state protected that dominion through the laws and taxes that determined heads of households by who paid more than half of the financial expenses in the home; and capitalism guaranteed their economic dominion by paying them more than women. In about half of the churches I attended, women could not be pastors, deacons, or ministry leaders. Their exclusion from paid leadership positions conditioned men to believe they had an ordained right to dominate on the basis of gender. This extended from the boardroom to the bedroom. Pastors would quote scripture that commanded wives to submit to their husbands, including for sex. Because I'd married so young, I felt (and was told) that my discomfort to submission was related to my age and rebelliousness. I passionately argued with pastors about this, asking one to delete a social media post describing that when wives don't want sex, they "reject" their husband and his feelings. Regardless of his intent, he was conditioning men to expect sex on demand and virtually removing a wife's ability to consent. After rows of affirming comments from men, and significant backlash from women about the hijacking of our bodies, he deleted the post.

Submission can lead to sexual violence against women and disabled people, and since sex was perceived as a duty, it was not something people called the police about. Many of my married friends would suffer excruciating pain from ovarian cysts, endometriosis, and lupus, and still lie on their backs in agony. Countless times, I would sit in church parking lots with women who wanted to leave their marriages but did not consider their pain to be a justifiable reason. For the ones who left, small groups of women would help them divorce quietly, move, find lawyers, pool money, and babysit until they were safe and stable. On Sunday mornings, I would listen in awe to follow-up sermons about why my generation did not value marriage anymore, or that divorce was the easy route because congregants lacked patience to resolve problems. By continuing to help my friends leave their marriages, I felt like a fugitive sitting in the pews, listening to how I had aided in breaking God's law. But the lengths of marriages can sometimes become shallow measurements for the strengths of marriages. Surely, abusive habits can end in relationships and lovers can undergo transformative and restorative processes to address harm. A commitment to this process should happen freely and can lead to lasting relationships. And similarly, separation and divorce can prevent further abuse and save lives. Sexual violence *contributes* to separation and divorce and men use sexual assault to further punish women who attempt to leave. Inez, who suffered physical violence, and women like my friends who suffered sexual violence, believed that leaving could only free them from harm. If pastors preached against sexual violence instead of against divorce, perhaps they would save more marriages.[197]

In fact, I have only heard one sermon against sexual violence in my entire life. During one trip back home in summer 2017, I attended Rev. Traci Blackmon's church. She delivered a powerful message about the woman whom Jesus saves from being stoned after she was accused of adultery. The biblical law required for the woman *and* the man to be stoned for immorality. Rev. Blackmon pointed out that the man, who was presumably caught in the act, too, was nowhere to be found in the story. Because patriarchy creates the conditions to subjugate non-men to unequal treatment, the mob of rowdy men planned to stone the woman alone. The sermon made me think about abolition. If Jesus would have enforced equal application of the law, then he could have summoned the adulterous man to be stoned alongside her. Instead, Jesus refused to enforce the law, daring any of the anxious punishers to cast the first stone if they did not possess any sins of their own. They dropped the rocks and departed. The pair was spared.[198]

Sitting near the back of the church, I realized that the Old Testament scriptures sounded remarkably similar to the laws governing rape that I'd learned about in law school. Until 2012, the federal policy regarding rape required women to resist, physically, to the utmost of their ability to demonstrate that she did not consent to the encounter. For centuries, the definition categorically narrowed prosecutions toward men if a woman did not physically resist, and failed to recognize other forms of sexual violence against men, women, nonbinary, gender-nonconforming, genderqueer, and agender people. Over time, in the name of protecting victims, the federal government widened the scope of punishment with little regard if more policing and convictions could prevent more survivors.

After the sermon, I'd felt so grateful for all that I'd learned politically from organizing. My experiences in social movements had made me a better person of faith, child, sibling, student, and parent. These lessons had influenced my conversations with my family to locate what needed to change in my own life, because that's what helps to change society. For Christians and churches, this meant my commitment to challenge them when they perpetuate teachings that could cause sexual violence, and supporting people seeking refuge from their relationships. As a child and sister, it meant talking to my mother and siblings about capitalism, sexual violence, and policing and coming up with plans to keep each other safe from these forms of violence. As a parent, I had already been preparing to teach my kids how to recognize sexual violence against their bodies. But because they identify as boys, at least for now, I am especially committed to teaching them how to relinquish conditioning they have to control other people. Rather than forcing them to play together just because one desires it, I have intentional conversations to teach them to respect and affirm each other's decision over their body, time, and joy.

LAW SCHOOL WAS the first place where I had studied sexual violence in any serious depth. Prison was the implicit answer to "what about the rapists?" In reality, prison was not the answer. Police arrests do not match the prevalence of sexual violence and they sometimes make false arrests. Survivors of sexual violence underreport rapes to the police and when they do, they may complete a rape kit to gather evidence for verification or prosecution. These kits collect dust while sitting on the shelves, waiting to be processed, if ever. A 2014 report found a minimum of twenty thousand untested rape kits in police departments in five US cities alone. This figure omits cities that do not keep track of the data, nor does it include how many kits were tested and still awaiting results. For reported rapes, cops make an arrest in 33 percent of cases. Conviction and imprisonment rates are much lower than that. Yet the legal lessons took for granted that prisons had to be the sole answer.[199]

Students weren't just learning about sexual violence in class to become lawyers; it was also reshaping many of our personal experiences with sex and to violence. For example, a hypothetical scenario about someone secretly removing a condom during sex invoked painful memories of encounters for survivors and fresh feelings of trauma for those who had not originally thought of it as sexual violence. A legal theorist told stories in another course about men who realized in class that they had been harming their partners and had not known it because of their limited understanding of rape. During one story, a student repeatedly assured the class that having sex with your spouse when she was asleep wasn't rape because he'd done it himself, several times, to his wife who did not know.

When friends and family members had asked me of abolition, "What about the rapists," I thought about this student and others like him. The moniker "rapist" is typically reserved for strangers, or serial or egregious actors waiting to abduct a helpless soul late at night. But this violence usually happens among our families and friends, spouses and boyfriends. Asking what do we do with people who commit sexual violence could help us ask more specific questions, as in, what about our lovers, partners, siblings, parents, and friends? Of women who have been married, 10 to 14 percent have been raped at least once by their partner; rape among married and formerly married women is four times more common than from strangers. Of women and girls who report being raped, almost half were asleep or at home, overwhelmingly by people whom they know. Nearly 80 percent of sexual violence by boyfriends, husbands, and ex-husbands are not even reported to the police, neither are more than half of rapes by stranger. And we cannot measure the people who don't recognize harm against them as rape, or the people who just don't know that it is happening. The student's wife made me wonder how many victims do not know that they are also survivors.[200]

My legal training confirmed that people were most vulnerable in their homes and gave context to the statistics regarding sexual violence. More than a third of women have experienced physical sexual violence and at least half of women have experienced forms of sexual violence beyond rape. According to the Centers for Disease Control, "12.5% have experienced sexual coercion, 27.3% have experienced unwanted sexual contact, and 32.1% have experienced non-contact unwanted sexual experiences." According to the University of Michigan, "as many as 40% of women with disabilities experience sexual assault or physical violence in their lifetimes and that more than 90% of all people with developmental disabilities will experience sexual assault." Most of the people who caused harm were not strangers. Nearly two-thirds of women who report rape, physical violence, and stalking pointed to a current or former date, boyfriend, partner, or husband. Marital rape, like all sexual violence, is woefully underreported. Almost 20 percent of women have experienced an attempted or completed rape; between 14 and 25 percent of women report sexual assault by their intimate partner. In 2019, ten million people faced sexual violence at work, including almost seven million women at the workplace.[201]

While men account for nearly all arrests for sexual violence, they also constitute victims and survivors. A third of men have experienced sexual violence, physical violence, and/or stalking by a partner over the course of their lives, more than half by the time they are just twenty-five years old. Almost a quarter of men experience sexual violence generally. One in fourteen men report being forced to penetrate someone else. These are not strangers; these are people we know.[202]

I did not need to go to law school to know that spouses and partners do not typically call the police on each other. This fact drove the position in our legal training toward "fixing" this problem. Many lawyers, advocates, and survivors, focused on the fact that police discouraged women from reporting sexual violence by not believing their claims. Congress passed the landmark Violence Against Women Act (VAWA) to send a message to all offenders: if you hurt a woman, then you will be punished. Federal, state, and local dollars poured into policing and prosecution to purchase the commitments of law enforcement agencies to stop sexual violence. But since VAWA passed in 1994, the number of women who reported rape and sexual assault *declined* from 41 percent to 36 percent; the women who did not believe that cops would help more than doubled from 6 percent in 1994 to 13 percent in 2010. Notably, more than half of the women surveyed reported to the police because they wanted the violence to stop, not to send someone to prison; 17 percent wanted to catch, punish, and prevent someone from harming again. Twenty-one percent reported to help cops, or they felt they had a duty to report a crime, a 6 percent drop from when VAWA passed. The resources spent to increase reporting to the police singles out prison as the primary goal of what survivors may want. A larger review of the various responses demonstrates that survivors want protection and for the violence to stop, which is not synonymous with prisons and policing.

In contrast, many activists I'd organize with in Belinda Hall and beyond did not use the law to "send a message" to people who caused harm. They did not consider punishment to be a deterrent from sexual violence in a society that conditions people to be sexually violent. Instead, we discussed safety and changing the conditions and circumstances where people experienced harm, which reminded me of when I supported women from church. Those women did not report to the police solely out of mistrust; they all just wanted the violence to stop, which is not the same as punishment. My church friends did not have to be prison abolitionists to make calculated decisions about their safety and desires. Some wanted acknowledgments and apologies, so we tried using men we trusted at the church to have conversations with their husbands. Other women no longer desired to be in the relationship, but wanted their husbands to co-parent their children, an extremely difficult feat from prison and subsequently with a criminal record. These women were already financially exploited because of capitalism, which devalued their labor in the home, work, and the church and relied on their partners for financial support. Capitalism can keep people in unwanted relationships and contributes to sexual violence. Calling the cops could not deal with the nuances of parenting and income, so we had to find other ways to support each other with time and resources. Until Belinda Hall, I had not realized that what I and many others had already been practicing was part of what abolition requires: reducing our reliance on the prison industrial complex by meeting each other's needs.

CONTRARY TO WHAT teachers and mentors in my life had told me, the explanation for sexual assault was not simply "boys will be boys" and "men cannot help themselves." Decades of increased police funding and longer prison sentences did not send a message to any of the people in my life who caused and experienced harm. The problem is the pipes underneath the surface. Millions of people experience sexual violence every year because of deep, underlying systems, ideas, and laws that police cannot solve, no more than continuously flushing a toilet will solve plumbing issues. For example, if we unearth the layers of seemingly innocuous marital markers that little girls are taught to covet, like changing our last name after we marry, we'll find histories of women as property owned first by their fathers, and then by their husbands. Joining last names was a symbolic gesture and legal arrangement. Women were barred from land ownership and obtaining loans without their husband's permission. They couldn't even legally own their own bodies: the last US state to recognize marital rape did so in 1993, a year before VAWA passed. By law and custom, men could not rape their own wives because they owned them.

I found in political education and organizing what I had not been taught elsewhere, that sexual violence, especially against women, is not mere mistreatment, but a phenomenon that maintained inequality and exploitation. Capitalism fosters sexual violence by creating categories of people who cannot leave abusive relationships, classrooms, and jobs because they do not have resources to sustain themselves. Sexual violence aids capitalism by creating hostile relationships, schools, and workplaces that helps companies more easily pay low wages to people in vulnerable situations, like women, disabled people, undocumented immigrants, and transgender people (as I discussed in the last chapter).

Taunts, catcalling, sexual abuse, and the threat thereof additionally constrains the ability of the people who experience it to move freely in the world. For example, the Black men in that Boston courtroom who repeatedly made comments about my body impeded my ability to represent my clients. I could have quit or requested a different court. The boyfriend who stalked me could have forced me to drop out of school. The women who divorced their husbands at church often left; the men usually stayed and remarried. Sexual violence under capitalism excluded one group from thriving, in this case women, and permitted another group, in this case men, to acquire and hoard the excess jobs, property, church positions, dorm rooms, and class seats. Police cannot prevent sexual violence because they protect the institutions that keep these cycles in place. They can only punish some of the people who are caught. Sexual violence, and resistance to it, does not happen in a vacuum.

It is swept up in all of the other oppressive systems of exploitation, extraction, and exclusion that has to be undermined and abolished. As a kid, my mom had taught me about Black women resisting sexual violence on the plantation. From the shores to the ships to the slave plantations, Black women faced and resisted sexual violence from white men who enacted it out of punishment, thrill, pleasure, experimentation, revenge, curiosity, and breeding—all hostile acts to maintain systems of subordination and violence. Breeding and forced reproduction were needed to perpetuate slavery. And like the activists I'd organized with in law school, organizers I'd worked with as a lawyer emphasized that we needed to resist that violence, as well as the capitalism, colonialism, and patriarchy underneath it.

At the very first Action St. Louis training in 2017, Kayla taught the group about Celia, a nineteen-year-old Black woman who killed her slave master and burned his body for repeatedly sexually assaulting her for five years. A judge issued a call for six "lawful" men to inquire about the death. They arrested and ultimately jailed Celia. She initially denied the act, even when one of the questioners threatened her with a rope. But with the persistence of the threats to her life and her children's lives, they forced her to confess. A judge appointed her a credible lawyer so that the trial would appear fair (her lawyer was a slave owner). The attorney argued self-defense, which did not win over the all-white jury that contained slave owners, too. They found her guilty and sentenced her to death. *Celia, A Slave* author Melton Alonza writes that a sympathetic person likely helped Celia escape from jail but did not intend to free her: "the evidence suggests that Celia's benefactors were not prepared to ignore Missouri law totally, so once her original execution date had passed and it appeared that the supreme court would have an opportunity to hear her appeal, Celia was returned to jail." Since she was pregnant, the courts decided to delay her execution until she gave birth to a third child, who was stillborn. She was then hanged for the murder.[203]

This training had been the first time I learned about Celia and I had to leave the room to gather myself afterward. The law has been a means of sexual violence, toward the end of racial subordination, gender subordination, and wealth accumulation through the reproduction of children. White men were not legally punished for raping Black women under slavery, and in Missouri, Black male slaves could not be charged, either. Missouri rape law required that men of all races were to be punished by castration for raping white women; just as the biblical law that required the same stoning for any adulterers, regardless of sex. Yet in a fundamentally unequal society, there's no such thing as equal application of the law. There is no record of any punishment for white men who sexually assaulted white women, only records of Black men. This was the foundation of the law in the US, the same law that cops and prosecutors purportedly use to keep descendants of Celia and other Black women "safe."[204]

I'd meet Black women organizers at other trainings or campaigns who understood this history, often more intimately than I did. Our conversations were a train ride. We shared so many stops on the way to freedom. We agreed that the law atrociously enabled sexual violence. We applauded the people who fled and fought back. And as we approached the "abolition" stop, passengers started moving to the exit doors. They wanted Black women to be safe and were critical, or at least concerned, that abolition would leave us more vulnerable. I did not want that either, even though I cannot personally recall anyone in my life ever calling the police about sexual abuse. They worried that the police would violate them as well or take their children. Some wanted to end the harm and preserve the relationship. In their words, they did not want to "send anybody to jail," especially a Black man who did not already have a criminal record, and, especially, a Black man who did. These women were negotiating the terms of their sexual violence within a broader context of white supremacy and the system of mass incarceration that had to be eradicated. But beyond my life, many Black women *did* call the cops for sexual assault. In fact, Black and Hispanic victims report violent crimes at higher rates (49 percent) than white victims (37 percent). Of all races, Black women report sexual violence at the highest rates.[205]

Equally important, Black, Latinx, and Asian women are more likely to remain with their partners following rape. Women of color who are vulnerable to sexual violence are not naturally born ride-or-die partners, but as several studies explain, "Economic resources play a particularly significant role in women's ability to leave as those women who are most likely to leave their partners were the ones who are financially independent." Black, multi-racial, and undocumented women have greater risk of being in precarious economic and living arrangements. For example, Immigration and Customs Enforcement and Border Patrol are threats to immigrants, especially undocumented ones, and refugees who risk arrest, detention, and deportation if they report. Immediate resources and long-term commitments to end economic exploitation will reduce sexual violence. And abolishing policing, ICE, and border patrol will eliminate the additional threats to people who deserve relief from violence.[206]

White heterosexual women report sexual violence less and leave their sexually violent marriages more because they have more resources, including wealth, income, childcare, and even the likelihood of meeting new partners in their social lives because white men are not surveilled, policed, and imprisoned like Black, Latinx, and Indigenous men. Centuries of patriarchal, colonial, and capitalist arrangements exacerbates these crises by excluding women from the labor market; exploiting their labor in employment settings; and extracting their labor in the home for unpaid work in families that is disproportionately relegated to them—mothering, partnering, and taking care of parents. Single white men under the age of 35 have a median wealth that is 3.5 times the size of single white women and 224.2 times greater than single Black women.

Those of us who want Black women, all women, and anyone to be safe from sexual violence must also be committed to eradicating the inequality that makes us vulnerable to exploitation and sexual abuse, and create a world where we all can flourish. Celia did not need Black women slaves to have mere equal protection to white women under the law from sexual violence. White women weren't even fully protected. In the short term, she needed to permanently escape the plantation and the jail, instead of the people who returned her because they had faith that the legal system might spare her. Ultimately, Celia and the millions of people who suffered sexual abuse like her, needed the abolition of a society that could have masters who could harm them. They needed the abolition of slavery as a source of sexual violence.

Resistance to European settler colonialism in North America, Australia, and the Caribbean can also serve as resistance to sexual violence. Europeans used sexual violence against Indigenous people as a form of punishment, domination, and control. In the Caribbean, an Indigenous woman viciously fought Christopher Columbus when he kidnapped and raped her; he journaled about it as a part of his colonial conquest. On the mainland, historian Roxanne Dunbar-Ortiz writes, "sexual abuse of both girls and boys was also rampant. Much documentation and testimony attest to the never-ending resistance by children in boarding schools. Running away was the most common way to resist, but there were also acts of nonparticipation and sabotage, secretly speaking their languages and practicing ceremonies. This surely accounts for their survival, but the damage is nearly incomprehensible."[207]

The legacies of sexual violence and policing in Indigenous communities continue today under ongoing conditions of sexual violence. More than one in three American Indian and Alaska Native women will be raped in their lifetime, compared to one in five of all women. While sexual violence usually occurs within race, this is not true for Native American women. Most of the people who violate them are white: 86 percent of reported cases of rape or sexual assault are by non-Native men. And like other women, Indigenous women underreport sexual violence to the police from fear of being assaulted or ignored by them as well. Due to colonialism, reservations have severely limited jurisdiction to prosecute non-Natives, usually white people, for acts of sexual violence. When tribal governments have attempted to use reservation police to stop violence from white men, the US federal government refused to grant them jurisdiction. But states and the federal government maintain the power to police and imprison Indigenous people, who experience arrest and incarceration at double the rate of their white counterparts. Police violence and inaction make the institution ripe not only for abolition, but also purposes of decolonization.[208]

PEOPLE WHO IDENTIFY or are perceived as LGBTQIA are also subjected to sexual violence as a result of capitalism, patriarchy, transphobia, and homophobia. The lack of social safety nets in the US create housing insecurity, employment precarity, stigma, and other forms of marginalization that leave people vulnerable to all violence, including sexual violence. Marginalization creates more precarity and more sexual violence, which lesbian, gay, and bisexual people experience at similar or higher rates than heterosexual people. Bisexual men and women experience the highest rates of sexual violence; nearly half have been raped in their lifetimes. Activists and researchers attribute this violence to people attempting to dominate and control their sexual identities to make them "choose one," or, the violence arose out of the expectation that their attraction to more than one gender means they want sex. This form of policing the sexualities and identities of others and punishing them for it begins early. In middle school, I remember boys who teased my girl teammates on our co-ed football teams for being gay because they hadn't been with a real "man" yet. These ideas are breeding grounds for "corrective rape," a sexual violence phenomenon where straight people attempt to make queer people "straight" through discipline or thrill.[209]

When I started working with Action STL and other organizations around abolition after law school, we discussed how these forced binaries and marginalization led to all kinds of violence. Even though I had started practicing law, it wasn't until I enrolled my kid in pre-kindergarten that I realized how early children were exposed to cisgender norms and sexual binaries. One year, Geuce's teacher sent home a list of kids' names separated into boys and girls for a class Valentine's Day party. First, I laughed. Why did my three-year-old need gender-specific Valentine's Day cards? He was too young to date. But he was subtly being conditioned around a binary that encouraged him to choose blue race car cards for boys and pink fluffy unicorn cards for girls.

The teacher was not being malicious. Everything else in the school was broken into binaries. "Good morning, boys and girls!" sang through the announcement speaker at the top of each day. There were lines for boys and for girls, sports for boy and for girls, and bathrooms for boys and for girls. Each day, these students lived in a world where only two genders existed, and for Valentine's Day, they had to give gifts based on them.

That year, I immediately tried to expand my kid's ideas about gender and sexuality, though at the time, I lacked the courage to say something to the teacher. I wish I had. The following school year, my son sat at a table assigned to boys, as his classmate from his pre-K class pointed to each of them, saying, "You're a girl! And you're a girl!" Each kid was mortified. They laughed and screamed and melted out of their chairs onto the floor because what could be worse? The classmate pointed to curse Geuce. I was late for work, but I hid in the doorway anyway, to observe. Geuce responded in his little voice, "It's okay. Anybody can be a girl." I was so, so proud.

A few months later, I took Geuce to get his first manicure so that we could relax after a hard week. When we arrived, the nail technician initially refused the manicure and pedicure for him. When I asked why, he chuckled and started walking away. I persisted to show that I would not let up until I understood why. After a pause, he mumbled that Geuce was too small for the pedicure massage chair. It wasn't true. The month before, I sat across from a day-care worker who treated her two-year-old girl students to getting their tiny toes scrubbed and painted. Watching them actually inspired me to bring Geuce to the shop. But I didn't feel like arguing. "Fine," I said. "Just a manicure then." He struggled and tried to refuse again. He did not let himself say, *No, he's a boy*, so he did it. Somehow under capitalism and patriarchy, a man can be a nail tech but a boy cannot get a manicure.

After the soak, light clipping, and filing, he asked Geuce if he wanted a clear coating or nothing at all to finish. Geuce looked up and said, "Dark blue."

"Not clear?" The nail tech was either angry or shocked that I walked to the color tray and selected a not-quite-navy OPI paint. With all of the progressive, radical, abolitionist beliefs I thought I held about gender, sexuality, fluidity, and liberation, I felt trapped in that nail salon. Handing the nail tech nail polish was not easy. Tears sat in the corners of my eyes and a thick balloon formed in my throat. Why was this so heavy? The women in the room had been glaring at me, some spinning their black chairs just to see. Here I was, looking like a twenty-something single mom with a two-year-old on her hip, letting her five-year-old paint his nails—with color! It was all true. Grandon and I had recently divorced. Garvey clung to my body during the ordeal. Some women were literally shaking their heads in disgust. Traces of my own fear and the danger of homophobia flooded the room and briefly caught up with me. *Should I actually let Geuce do this? Will he be safe at school? Should I have asked his dad?*

I immediately texted Grandon about what was happening and asked if he could call. I made sure that he was on speakerphone when he affirmed the color choice. *Was I now proving to these people that my son had a daddy who was okay with this? God.* I was so embarrassed. What should have been a harmless, fun activity was now becoming some sort of public spectacle and lesson. Not because Geuce wanted to pretend that he had Spiderman nails, but because people reduced his fun moment to potential claims about his childhood, his sexuality, his gender identity, and my parenting. I felt small. This had to stop. I told his dad thanks and quickly hung up. I stood next to him as the tech did the final coat. "Does it look awesome, Mommy?" "Better than awesome, Sugar." But even before his nails could dry, a boy about ten years old scooted to him and asked me, "Did you let him do this?" "Yes." "He's a boy, though. Now I've seen everything." "Why does it matter that he's a boy? It's good that you've seen this. Hopefully, you'll see a lot more as you grow up and learn a lot more, too." Startled, he shrugged and scooted out of the salon after his grandmother. He only said what every woman in that shop did not say.

Geuce wanted blue nails. Our society socializes babies even before birth with the color blue. Blue baby showers and baby clothes for boys; pink for girls. People bite into their little gender-reveal-party cupcakes and blue icing oozes from the center to let them know a child might be born with a penis. The entire action figure toy aisle is blue. Boys can have blue teeth, blue toy guns, blue hair, and blue Valentine's Day cards. But the second Geuce wanted blue nails, a color that we have been signaling to him for five years is supposed to be his color because "he was a boy," hell broke loose.

I could only imagine other times that Geuce, Garvey, or any one of our kids realize that they desire blue cards instead of pink cards; or that both bathrooms at school were fine for their needs; and that neither line for recess represents who they are. Will teachers or their classmates punish them verbally or physically? We have to be intentional about their relationships to their desires and expression based on their schooling because conditioning them around binaries and heteronormativity leads can turn them into adults that control, punish, and sexually abuse others because of it. It's a matter of violence and justice, and life and death.

WHEN ASKED, "WHAT about the rapists," I also cannot help but to think about the cops who cause sexual violence. Between social movements, political education, and legal study, I became increasingly convinced that police cannot stop sexual violence, and more, that they are a source of sexual violence.

In December 2015, I learned about Oklahoma City police officer Daniel Holtzclaw. Holtzclaw, the son of a police department veteran, targeted Black women for violent sexual acts. Most of the women he exploited were poor and had some record of drug use or sex work. He'd corner them, fondle them, pull out his penis, and force them to perform oral sex. They feared if they did not comply, he would assault, jail, or kill them. He was accused of assaulting more than a dozen women before an elderly, middle-class Black woman reported him to the police. He had assumed that she was like his other survivors, who were more vulnerable to abuse because they were economically exploited. But she was not. He assaulted her as she was driving home through a poor neighborhood that he frequented. Yet she did not live there. Holtzclaw was fired, prosecuted, and sentenced to more than two hundred fifty years in prison.[210]

Holtzclaw's case and imprisonment did not deter other cops from sexually violating poor women of color. I was sitting in the back seat of an Uber Pool when, in 2016, I heard Celeste Guap's story on NPR. Guap was a teenage sex worker in the center of a sexual violence ring with police officers. As many as thirty cops were involved across several law enforcement agencies. My driver, an older Black man, said aloud that the girl "must have really had a shape on her for that to happen." He was suggesting that if cops took advantage of her, she must have had a nice body. "No, she didn't have to have that, she didn't need to have anything for that to happen to her," I responded, angrily. He remained silent. The City of Oakland paid her $1 million in a civil suit after she went public. At least one cop died by suicide, leaving a note about his behavior. Seven cops faced criminal charges, others were fired. Oakland mayor Libby Schaaf famously remarked that she was there to run a police department, "not a frat house." But managing sexual violence and exploitation is exactly what running a police department can entail. Former police chief Norm Stamper wrote in his memoir:

> In my first year I rode with a cop who spent half the shift trying to pick up nurses in the ER, carhops at Oscar's, or women who'd called the police to report a prowler. One summer night I drove into an elementary school parking lot and interrupted a veteran cop having his knob polished in the front seat of his police car. Over the years I would see it all: cops fingering and fondling prisoners, making bogus traffic stops of attractive women, trading freedom for a blow job with a hooker, making "love" with a fourteen-year-old police explorer scout, sodomizing children in a spouse's day care center.[211]

One study found that 40 percent of reported cases of police sexual misconduct involve teenagers. DECRIMNOW, a DC campaign to decriminalize sex work reports that "one in five sex workers (or individuals profiled as sex workers) have been approached by police asking them for sex." From 2005 to 2015, *Buffalo News* sourced media reports to find that a cop was accused of sexual misconduct every five days. Sexual misconduct is the second-highest complaint of police violence, following excessive force, and unsurprisingly, underreported. What happens when you call the cops on the cops? As a former cop explained, "They knew the DAs. They knew the judges. They knew the safe houses. They knew how to testify in court. They knew how to make her look like a nut . . . How are you going to get anything to happen when he's part of the system and when he threatens you and when you know he has a gun and . . . you know he can find you wherever you go?" Since 2005, more than five thousand cops have been arrested for sexual violence, misconduct, and child pornography possession, among other offenses; only four hundred lost their badges.[212]

Why do cops rape? Unlike Norm Stamper, I don't think that there are simply too many rapists who just happen to become cops. I do believe that cops, like all of us, are conditioned by a society steeped in rape culture and gender-based violence. The badge and the baton give cops additional power and protection to act violently. A study found that in more than 70 percent of cases, "officers wielded their authority over motorists, crime victims, informants, students and young people in job-shadowing programs." They especially take advantage of women, trans women, young people, sex workers, prisoners, and others who are class exploited because cops, like Daniel Holtzclaw, deem them less credible as accusers and witnesses. In 2015, 86 percent of trans people who were sex workers, or who cops perceived as sex workers, reported police harassment, attacks, sexual assault, and mistreatment. The figure may be underreported. Cops can technically "have sex" with people they arrest without consequence. For obvious reasons, consent is nearly impossible to give freely when a cop cuffs you and you want to avoid jail. More than half of the states permit or do not prohibit sexual intercourse between a cop and someone in their custody. The reliance on police to stop sexual assault comes at a cost—their sexual assaults of other people.[213]

Police sexual violence and misconduct is reflective of sexual violence in the prison industrial complex. Angela Davis's writing on prisons as sites of gender-based violence challenged my unexamined ideas of sexual violence, and ultimately police sexual violence. Originally, I had learned about prison rape from neighborhood stories, people who were formerly incarcerated, and movies like *Lockdown*. "Don't drop the soap" was a very popular punchline. I unknowingly accepted the violence as entertainment and as part of the punishment. When news in the neighborhood broke about men sent away for child abuse and molestation, what immediately followed was, "You know what they do to them in there." Touching a child violated a code beyond what the law punished. People on the outside expected people on the inside to make them pay with domination and violation. Davis gave political meaning to these stories. Yes, men's prisons were certainly a source of rape and gender-based violence. I almost always envisioned prison rape as a male-prisoner-on-male-prisoner type of violence. Even when I used the word "prison," I only thought of men's institutions. Davis emphasized that this sexual violence occurred at all prisons, women's prisons, too. Furthermore, these acts of sexual violence weren't just between incarcerated people, but also from and among jail and prison guards. There are intentional acts of assault from guards toward the people whom they cage. Sixty percent of sexual violence inside prisons comes from prison staff, including guards.[214]

Almost 40 percent of trans people who have been incarcerated have been assaulted by prison staff and other incarcerated people. The National Center for Transgender Equality found that trans people are more than five times more likely to be sexually assaulted by facility staff than the cisgender US population in jails and prisons, and over nine times more likely to be sexually assaulted by other incarcerated people. Davis explains that the countless routine searches, pat downs, groping, vaginal and anal checks, and much more by guards are nonconsensual and also constitute sexual assault, battery, and rape. Abolishing the prison industrial complex abolishes another site of rape and sexual violence. If we want to address sexual violence, closing prisons and reducing contact with police is a start.[215]

PATRIARCHY UNDERGIRDS SEXUAL violence among police and prisons, and as I'd come to understand, the military. In January 2020, I met Ejeris Dixon at an abolition convening I helped organize in Miami. A little over a hundred organizers and activists gathered to strategize, dream, and discuss the state of our demands. Organizer and activist Rachel Herzing asked the panel, including Ejeris and me, to discuss how we became abolitionists. I was the most recent convert. For more than two decades, Ejeris organized in racial justice, LGBTQ, anti-violence, and economic justice movements. Among many efforts, she built national, statewide, and organizing and advocacy initiatives in response to hate violence, domestic violence, police violence, and sexual violence. She encouraged the audience to read the anthology that she just had published, *Beyond Survival*, which included stories and strategies from the transformative justice movement, to help us dream, strategize, and experiment toward a world without police and prisons. So many people I respected contributed to the anthology and I was excited that it was a resource in the world. One particular story stuck with me. A woman, Blyth, described being raped by a close friend:

A few months later he came home. He'd broken down during [a military] boot camp and got sent to the psych ward, a failure. And while he was there, he made a friend, a boy like him. A few weeks later he found that boy in a bathroom stall dead. It confirmed what he thought he knew already, that boys like him were too weak to live. He told me that story the day before he raped me . . . When he raped me, I could see the way he was grasping for power, for some sense of control over his life. Part of me wanted to give it to him. The rest of me wanted to run. But I couldn't. I couldn't for all of the reasons that only a person raped by someone they love can understand. Shock, terror, fear, shock, shame, pity, shock, embarrassment, shock, politeness, love, care, shock, disbelief, disbelief, disbelief.[216]

How could Blyth's friend do this? And how could she still love him? She didn't turn to numbers and statistics, nor punishment. She did not write him off as "crazy," "sick," or "evil." Those labels may help survivors and victims cope and describe the type of person who has harmed them. But when we use them to describe this behavior, we also perpetuate harmful and ableist ideas about people with mental health challenges. Especially since they are disproportionately vulnerable to violence. Calling people evil can legitimize any form of punishment that we want them to face for harm they have caused, and calling people crazy suggests that they are singularly a problem because they have deviated from the behavior of normal people. But under rape culture, sexual violence is normal, not crazy, evil, or deviant. Men constitute almost 100 percent of arrests for rape. Those are just the ones accused or caught. Less than 5 percent of men were psychotic when they raped someone. What does that suggest about the other 95 percent? Blyth said this of her friend: "The violence of poverty, white supremacy, militarism, assault—they are woven together. No court can ever pull them apart."[217]

She captured so many reasons why people sexually assault each other. Scholars have found that among the several major interpersonal motives that underlie sexual violence are revenge, punishment, access, entitlement, opportunity, and the demand for impersonal sex. For example, people, overwhelmingly men, will rape a woman because a completely *different* woman rejected their advances.

Sometimes the rejection is not even about sex, but about a parent or other figure who has harmed them. In the case of Blyth's assault, she asserts that her friend was looking to feel power or control over his life after being kicked out of the military. She was more accessible than fighting the military, so the revenge was paid forward. Conversely, people also use sexual violence to punish the people who directly turn down their advances. This violence often stems from societal ideas that women refuse men out of politeness or arrogance, or don't always express that they want sex when they really do. Sexual violence is not simply an act perpetuated by deviants; it is a manifestation of race, class, gender, sexuality, patriarchy, and colonial relationships about power, control, and domination.

The sexual violence that Blyth experienced did not just happen in her small town. It was happening all over the country and world, and inside and outside the armed forces. In the US military, all genders experienced more than twenty thousand instances of "unwanted sexual contact" alone in 2018. Women constitute 20 percent of the military, but 63 percent of assaults. One in sixteen reports being raped or groped. Over one hundred thousand men have been sexually assaulted at one of the eight hundred US military bases across the world. After the US invasion of Iraq and Afghanistan, sexual violence increased among civilians and soldiers in the streets and on bases as well. If we want to prevent and better address sexual violence, then we must also reduce war and militarism that cause it.[218]

Militarism and law enforcement manifest domestically as settler colonialism, an ongoing project to displace, incarcerate, and harm the first inhabitants of the country that became the United States. In 2018, I asked Advancement Project if Puerto Rico could become one of my work sites like St. Louis and Ferguson. I had attended a presentation that year where interdisciplinary scholar Marisol LeBron had presented on policing and colonialism on the island. I asked Marisol to connect me to scholars and activists on the island so I could support any activism around police if there was a need or desire. It felt odd that I'd had a better understanding of decolonization through South Africa than of active US colonies. After she sent me a list of resources and contacts, I spent months traveling back and forth to meet activists and lawyers traveling to learn more.

Puerto Rico, a US colony with limited voting rights, has the world's highest per capita rate of women over fourteen killed by their partners. Despite having the second largest police department after the NYPD, the island has a murder rate six times the size of the United States and an intimate partner abuse rate as high as six times as large cities like Los Angeles. An American Civil Liberties Union report stated that the organization expects the rape statistics on the island to be 100 times the figure that Puerto Rico's police department reports, and an estimated eighteen thousand people, mostly women and girls, are raped every year. However, I disagree with the ACLU's framing of the report, that the island's police are inadequately responding to rape and domestic violence. In the exact same report, the ACLU found that the police are complicit aggressors in the violence because cops commit and underreport the violence. This is not a failure of policing; this is policing.[219]

After much research, I could not find any specific data for the US Virgin Islands, the tiny Black colony in the Caribbean. The FBI may not collect or publish it. Guam, another US colony, has a reported rape of 64.2 compared to the United States' 25.2 per 100,000 people. Colonialism and economic inequality are a primary driver of gender-based violence in Guam. The obvious story is that wealth inequality makes people with less power, usually women, rely on men who have more economic power. I also try to remind myself that economic inequality and colonialism do significant harm, too, especially on people who initiate the harm. To commit violence is also destructive to oneself, and colonialism and poverty can manufacture additional powerlessness underneath the United States. And, as one Puerto Rican activist responded when I said that Puerto Rico should become a state to get resources to stop the violence: "We don't need to be a state. We need to be free."[220]

TRAVELING BETWEEN PUERTO RICO, Ferguson, and St. Louis, I read a social media post by one of my childhood friends who had become a cop while we were in college. The post explained that the movement and conversation around police violence made them realize the violent nature of the job, which was not what they had signed up to do. They announced their resignation. I was shocked. I'd only learned about cops resigning from the appeals of mayors and police chiefs who begged people to apply or come to work. In 2018 Puerto Rico, cops had still been staging "sick-outs" in the aftermath of the hurricanes because they hadn't been paid overtime to respond to the violence. Others quit in the US. Between protests in response to Trayvon's death and the peak of the Black Lives Matter movement in 2016, the number of total cops dropped nationwide for the first time in sixteen years. Applications were down, early retirements were up. And contrary to what I would have assumed before I began organizing and lawyering, the rate of reported violent crime has been shrinking, too.[221]

The largest nationwide survey of people reporting to be victims of crime shows nearly a 40 percent decrease in violent crime from 1994 to 2000, and from 1994 to 2011, the rate of reported serious intimate partner violence declined 72 percent for females and 64 percent for males. Since 1991, forcible rape dropped by 60 percent. Sexual violence against children ages 12 to 17 reportedly declined 56 percent between 1993 and 2000, including a 72 percent drop in harm committed by family members and acquaintances. Since 2018, violent crime dropped by 15 percent and people who reported being victims of crime dropped by 12 percent. Rates of serious intimate partner violence, including rape, sexual assault, robbery, and aggravated assault against women have dropped by 72 percent since 1994. Excluding simple assault, the rate of violent victimization against women dropped almost 30 percent between 2018 and 2019 (perhaps not so ironically, the peak of the #MeToo movement). In the same year, 30 percent fewer Black people reported being victims of serious crimes. And, among violent offenses like murder, assault, and sexual violence, the rearrest rate is lower than every other offense, including drugs, property crime, and public order disruptions.[222]

Why the decline? It depends on who you ask. There's an arms race to take the credit. At times, the federal government champions law enforcement, criminalization, and incarceration. Government-funded reports boast the number of new laws and sentence enhancements on the books to deter violence. Yet crime and victimization rates that the government touts do not deter people from committing crime. Research finds that "harsher sentences do not serve as effective 'examples,' preventing new people from committing violent crimes, and also fail to prevent convicted people from re-offending."[223]

The federal government also admits that during this period, massive federal spending through the Violent Crime Control and Law Enforcement Act of 1994 has had a positive but statistically insignificant impact on rape. The Government Accountability Office concluded that while there was a 26 percent decline in overall crime from 1993 to 2000, only 1.3 percent of the decline could be attributed to additional police officers. The majority of the decrease in violent crime, including sexual violence, came from other, unspecified factors; other studies have attributed the decline to preschool expansions and access, youth job programs, and much more. Even the federal government admits this. In 1967, the President's Commission on Law Enforcement and Administration of Justice explained:[224]

> The criminal justice system has a great potential for dealing with individual instances of crime, but it was not designed to eliminate the conditions in which most crime breeds. It needs help. Warring on poverty, inadequate housing and unemployment, is warring on crime. A civil rights law is a law against crime. Money for schools is money against crime. Medical, psychiatric, and family-counseling services are services against crime. More broadly and most importantly every effort to improve life in America's "inner cities" is an effort against crime. A community's most enduring protection against crime is to right the wrongs and cure the illnesses that tempt men to harm their neighbors.[225]

And again in 1988, another federal law enforcement commission explained:

> In searching for ways to prevent or control serious crime, the police look for precipitating causes. While it may be useful to examine what some call the root causes of crime (e.g.; social injustice, unequal economic opportunity, poor schooling, weak family structures, or mental illness), such things are relatively unimportant from a policing perspective since the police exercise little influence over them. The police operate on the surface of social life.[226]

These assertions could account for the reductions in violence in the past decades. Overlapping with the decline in sexual violence were significant shifts in society, especially for women vulnerable to sexual violence. Educational attainment and employment drastically increased for women, which can foster independence, economic security, and self-determination. Since 1996, Black, white, Latina, and Asian women overtook men as the most college-educated group, representing a global trend. College-aged students experienced a lower rate of sexual violence than nonstudents. The gender pay gap also narrowed. From 1980 to 2018, the average hourly wage of women increased 45 percent, from $15 to $22, and the wage gap narrowed from 33 cents to the dollar to 15 cents to the dollar. Women have entered the workplace at vastly increasing rates, representing about one-third of the total workforce in the 1950s but almost half of all workers by 2015. Between 2007 and 2016, individual chronic homelessness declined by 35 percent, and since 2010, 20 percent fewer families experienced homelessness. Investments in education, housing, and employment can reduce precarity that makes people more vulnerable to sexual violence. And all violence.[227]

FOR ME, BEING an abolitionist is not a static position, but about learning, dreaming, practicing what we need until we get free. I'm always becoming, and hope to learn new lessons, ideas, and practices decades from now. As we work to eliminate our reliance on policing, and to reduce violence, we can begin to readily identify friends, family members, or neighbors with whom we can seek refuge if an emergency happens. Rachel Herzing asks us to reduce our own reliance on police, reduce the reasons that we think we need police, and cultivate the safety that we need for our protection through "people, networks, organizations, educational materials, financial resources, etc." I believe people already practice this informally and quite regularly. We make sure people leave and arrive safely, let friends and family members know when we are with new people, and confide in others when we experience harm. The women at my church did not have much money individually, but we pooled it when we could and opened our homes for others' safety. I believe that we should enter relationships—employment, sex work, parties, schools, places of faith, and social organizations with a map to help us navigate what's necessary for our individual protection, and we can invite others close to us to determine what that looks like.[228]

Writing in 1989 following the brutal rapes and murders of Black women in Boston, Audre Lorde also demanded that we hold accountable Black men who pointed to white supremacy and racism as the primary causes of intimate-partner violence. Lorde understood the fact and challenged its use: "But I knew that no weapon is so terrible as the ones we use against each other, and that Black women and men had to start speaking to each other and to our children about this wasteful expression of violence, or we would all be lost." She left nobody behind in her poems inspired by this violence, not the Black woman who "bled at the hands of a brother," nor any brother "who has ever hung his head and wept in stunned silence after the fact wondering what had ever possessed him."[229]

Lorde used her poetry as an organizing tool with other revolutionary Black feminists to start these conversations across the country. Through conversation and community care, people who cause and experience harm must also learn how to change it. I believe in a world where we draw from this legacy as much as we draw from the legacy of Black Panthers to invoke community self-defense, mutual aid, and free breakfast programs to inform our organizing today. The first time that we, all of us, learn about sexual violence should not be the first time we feel or witness it.

Sexual and gender-based violence require community-based interventions as well. I was in awe of the level of community organizing and interventions in Cape Town in 2020 during the global COVID-19 pandemic. South Africa was particularly vulnerable; following millions of global transmission and deaths, a new, more contagious strain emerged in a country already plagued by stark inequality, drought, police brutality, austerity, housing insecurity, and sexual violence. The national lockdowns exacerbated these ongoing crises. In the United States, police were the primary response. I called Zelda Holtzman to see how Cape Town was faring.[230]

When she turned her video on, Zelda was beaming with excitement—during a pandemic. She was supporting several communities that had completely transformed under the lockdown. They rejected video meetings; the internet is unstable anyway, but as the women organizers she worked with often said, "You can't help women being beaten over Zoom." The community also rejected the police. A week into their national lockdown, cops shot and killed a Black man on his way home for allegedly violating the stay-at-home order. In response, groups of residents, mostly women, organized safety bubbles by block. They took inventory of who was in each house and their needs—medication, food, fresh air, protection from harm. The women created safe houses to take in anyone facing violence, which strengthened community responses to harm and accountability. Using community gardens, these residents harvested and shared food to build up each other's immunity and healthy eating habits. They took their teens on meditative wellness retreats to reduce stress and encourage safe recreation. And yes, of course, they distributed masks and soap, and led teach-ins about how to properly use personal protective equipment and sanitizer. In the United States, the primary message campaign for safety was "social distancing." With the communities that Zelda supported: "physical distancing, social solidarity, relief is revolutionary."[231]

LGBTQIA-SPECIFIC INTERVENTIONS AT the community level are indispensable for police abolition as well. Casa Ruby does similar work year-round in Washington, DC. I learned about the organization in 2018 when I attended a dinner and theater presentation by The Tenth, an independent Black queer media company. For its print magazine, The Tenth wanted to feature letters around LGBTQIA and the criminal legal system. They invited people across fields to contribute to the issue, including two staff members from Casa Ruby. They shared all of the support services and solidarity that the organization offered. Ruby Corado, a transgender Latina immigrant, had founded the organization in 2012 after years of organizing and mutual aid with LGBTQIA communities. The organization boasts providing social and human services to thousands of people every year, including support for sexual and reproductive health, housing, employment, and immigration. Casa Ruby also provides therapeutic and mental health support, including counseling, for people who survive sexual, physical, and emotional violence.[232]

Black and Pink provides another example, but explicitly through an abolitionist framework. In March 2019, I sat on a panel with executive director Dominique Morgan, a formerly incarcerated trans woman who wore a bright pink shirt listing the number of days she was incarcerated in Nebraska. She had recently assumed leadership of the organization, which was founded in 2005 by Unitarian Universalist minister Jason Lydon. Black and Pink was not only abolitionist, but founded explicitly as an anarchist project of mutual aid and support. They do not rely on police and prisons for safety because they recognize both as forms of danger. Instead, Black and Pink works independently to build community and organize with people who are incarcerated, or formerly incarcerated, and/or living with

HIV/AIDS. The organization provides down payments and two months' rent for members transitioning into housing, bypassing the traditional background and credit checks that bar people with records from securing apartments. Growing from one hundred fifty members and one chapter in 2005, to more than eleven chapters and twenty thousand members nationwide, their work to close prisons, cultivate relationships with people inside prisons, launch campaigns against the criminal legal system, and serve as community for people returning home disrupts the cycles of violence from the community and the prison industrial complex.[233]

Organizations such as Assata's Daughters also work explicitly from an abolitionist lens. The Chicago-based group was founded in 2015 by Black women, femmes, and gender-nonconforming people to "carry on the tradition of radical liberatory activism encompassed by Assata Shakur, to train up others in the radical political tradition of Black feminism, and to learn how to organize on the ground around the demand for Black liberation, particularly a demand for abolition." While they initially were volunteers who focused on political education and organizing with women-identified, femme, and gender-nonconforming teens, they expanded to teach and organize with young men and boys "on toxic notions of masculinity, dismantling patriarchal systems of oppression, and understanding the impact of both on interpersonal relationships." We need more community-based organizations that aim to teach children, teens, and young adults in this tradition. It could reduce and prevent sexual violence, gender-based violence, and affirm young people with a range of genders and sexualities.[234]

Teaching about violence and systems of patriarchy is exactly what Audre Lorde called us to do in her poetry. We need the proliferation of programs and projects that encourage and incentivize people of all ages to unlearn violence and harm toward each other, and practice new ways of being in relationships. These efforts are as important as racial, ethnic, gender, and queer studies programs that give students of color a sense of pride about their history and the contributions of their peoples. But often lacking is an analysis of how to dismantle systems of oppression. Learning about women's contributions is not necessarily *feminist*, no more than learning about Black history necessarily fosters racial justice. We need students to learn about stories of resistance more than they learn about oppression; to experiment with democracy, more than watered-down lessons on suffrage; and to fight patriarchy, more than replicating it.

Within abolition, decolonization, and socialism, the hope for societies free of sexual violence is bright. Organizers in the movements who influence me find it and forge it. In the United States, organizations such as Black Youth Project 100 and Dream Defenders—both originally founded in the wake of calls to send George Zimmerman to prison—have adopted internal processes for transformative and restorative justice models for sexual violence. The restorative and transformative models they use are not romantic or perfect, but through deep experimentation, their members have embarked on efforts to restore relationships between each other after someone has caused harm, and to transform the conditions in which the harm was made possible in the first place. Without law enforcement, and with the help of restorative and transformative justice practitioners, young, Black-led organizations are not only fighting racism, sexism, capitalism, and militarism in the country, but also attempting to hold their members and leaders accountable for violence inside the organization.

Common Justice provides another example of restorative and transformative justice work among people most directly impacted by violence. The founder, Danielle Sered, operates under the assumption that the people who cause harm and violence are usually victims first. The organization employs a five-step model to meet the needs of everyone involved in the harm, including services, coping strategies, and accountability. Common Justice operates the first "alternative-to-incarceration and victim-service program in the United States that focuses on violent felonies in the adult courts." In New York City where Common Justice operates, 90 percent of survivors of violence choose their restorative justice process over sending someone to prison. All over the country, smaller independent restorative and transformative processes occur to varying degrees of success. However, because they are usually private to protect the parties involved, rarely do people talk publicly about how wonderful their individual processes went. It is usually when they are not successful, or when harm recurs, that they become public. We shouldn't shy away from that fact, but use it as a lesson to improve our approaches.[235]

IN ADDITION TO community-level approaches, police abolition and eliminating sexual violence also require deep legal change that is fully within our grasp. Organizations such as Survived & Punished work at the intersection of ending law enforcement and gender-based violence, with a focus to release all incarcerated survivors who are imprisoned because they defended themselves from harm. According to the American Civil Liberties Union, 60 percent of women in all state prisons and as many as 94 percent in particular populations have experienced physical or sexual abuse. In 2012, a Black woman in Florida, Marissa Alexander, fired a warning shot in the air to stop her husband from abusing and threatening to kill her. She was arrested, prosecuted, convicted, and sentenced to twenty years in prison. Alexander unsuccessfully tried to use "Stand Your Ground" as a defense to her actions. In the thicket of advocating against Stand Your Ground because of Trayvon's murder that year, some popular civil rights organizations chose to remain silent about Alexander, instead of highlighting the gender and racial disparities in its application. Thanks in part to the growing movement demanding her release, Alexander finally came home in 2017. Survived & Punished was founded as a coalition initially tasked to free Alexander from prison, and the project evolved to raise awareness, resources, and advocacy for other survivors, too, including people who have defended themselves from sexual violence. Cyntoia Brown spent more than fifteen years in prison after killing a white real estate agent and youth minister who had picked her up as a teenage sex worker from a Sonic. By the time Brown was twenty-nine, organizations like Survived and Punished and thousands of individuals advocated for the Tennessee governor to grant clemency. She was released in 2019, and started an organization to help teenage sex workers.[236]

BYP100 and the Sex Workers Project among others organize decriminalization campaigns to protect sex workers from their employers, their customers, and the police—which could all be the same person sometimes. Sex worker collectives want to repeal criminal laws because "policing and criminalization of sex work is one of the primary sites of racial profiling, police violence, and mass incarceration of Black and brown women, girls, and trans and gender-nonconforming folks." Police, prison, and criminalization do not stop sex work; they push it into the shadows where people are even more vulnerable to abuse. Instead, these collectives use a human rights approach emphasizing housing, health care, income, and the right to self-determination to make their work free from physical, verbal, and sexual coercion.[237]

In addition to decriminalization, parts of the Violence Against Women Act that fund law enforcement must be repealed, as well as any state, federal, and local grants that require partnerships between cops and social service agencies. VAWA is hard for me to discuss, especially since so many people with good intentions believed that criminalization and police could provide for women's safety. Yet one woman's police protector is another woman's perpetrator. According to the National Center for Women and Policing: "Two studies have found that at least 40 percent of police officer families experience domestic violence, in contrast to 10 percent of families in the general population. A third study of older and more experienced officers found a rate of 24 percent, indicating that domestic violence is two to four times more common among police families than American families in general." Good intentions don't always keep us safe. Legal scholar Aya Gruber explains in her book, *The Feminist War on Crime*, that even the feminists most sympathetic to end mass incarceration will draw the line around people accused of domestic and sexual violence, as if the same reasons precipitating other harm do not also account for these forms of interpersonal harm. They do. And between limited gains from police intervention, the harm that cops cause, and the levels of robust sex and gender-based organizing, we deserve and require investments beyond law enforcement.

Included in the decriminalization is an expectation that sentences for survivors of sexual violence, as well as people convicted, must start shrinking as we close prisons, cut the size of police departments, and especially as we reduce sexual violence. As I mentioned before, long sentences do not deter people from sexual violence, especially when it happens unintentionally, unknowingly, in secret, in our homes, or by people who rely on their power and status to protect them. If anything, law enforcement exposes people who cause harm to sexual violence, continuing the cycle of rape rather than eliminating it. Abolition of the prison industrial complex eradicates the sexual violence that prisons and policing create and maintain.

There is no singular answer to "what to do with rapists." We decide it. Equally urgent, we must continue to challenge the societal arrangements that leads to preventable pain and suffering. Marriage can be quite beautiful and sacred, for example. Marriage can also privatize dependence: it encourages people to enter relationships for resources and benefits, like health care, savings, and tax deductions. I was nineteen years old when I got married, mostly informed by my faith tradition. I was also in love, but very poor, and marriage offered me a stability that I never had as a child. I was so lucky that the person I married was kind, thoughtful, and also very much trying to figure out his relationship to Christianity and his evolving manhood. When we divorced nine years later and became friends and co-parents, I realized how the marital benefits I once aspired to have did not make sense. I could remove him from my health insurance to account for the divorce, but I couldn't add any of my uninsured siblings, whom I would be related to forever. And our children had two options for insurance because they had parents who went to college and worked jobs that offered it, but independent contractors in my family did not have an option that wasn't a financial sacrifice. If we focused on meeting the healthcare, employment, educational, and housing needs of people in society, then those who want to marry could more freely enter those relationships on their terms, and people who needed to escape because of violence could more easily leave without worrying what will happen if they get sick and need to see a doctor.

We should heed to calls for investment in the programs, opportunities, and laws that make everyone free and safe. Here too, universal basic income can help, allowing people to meet their basic needs and not rely on potentially sexually exploitative intimate relationships for income. Removing benefits from marriage accomplishes this, too. With universal health care, and other programs like free and quality childhood education, people vulnerable to violence have more free range to move, live, and practice healthy lifestyles.

SEVEN

DEHUMANIZATION, DISABILITY, AND RESISTANCE

WHEN I START reading a new book, I write a short letter to myself on the inside cover. The letter usually includes dates, what's going on in the world, where I am and how I'm feeling. I don't regularly journal, so these notes have become my greatest archive and literary gift. On the inside cover of Teju Cole's *Known and Strange Things*, I'd written "I am a custodian of my black body." A custodian is a guardian, someone who has the responsibility to protect and provide for something, in this case, a black body. Cole writes this of himself in the book while comparing himself to James Baldwin. He concludes his list with:

> . . . and I, too, left the church; and I call New York home even when not living there; and feel myself in all places from New York City to rural Switzerland, the custodian of a black body, and have to find the language for all of what that means to me and to the people who look at me.[238]

Church teaches that the spirit is separate from the flesh. *Absent with the body, present with the Lord*, we offer to each other as comfort after losing a loved one. But being a "custodian of a black body" had taught me that my humanity is separate from the tender body and mind that I occupy, and I am obligated to protect it. A slave trade made that body racial; patriarchy made that body gendered; and the heights of sidewalk curbs, kitchen cabinets, and door handles made that body abled. There's more. My children made that body swell; music made that body dance; friends made that body laugh. This was the body in my custody. The note I wrote inside the cover a few years ago helped me grapple with what it meant to be human, and to reject the language I once used regarding my black body: dehumanization.

I did not know what *dehumanized* meant until someone told me that I could be. To condemn centuries of police violence and racial subjugation, many activists have used "dehumanized" to describe what their bodies mean to themselves under white supremacy, and how others—especially cops and white people—treat them. "Less than human." "They hunt us like animals." "They treat us like property." "When they see us." And after Sean Bell's killing in 2006, I accepted and repeated this language. I repeated it because I found resonance with the activists and community members who described our treatment this way. With good reason. Darren Wilson said that Michael Brown had the face of a demon, the *New York Times* called the teen "no angel." The paper apologized after a backlash. In the wake of other viral violent incidents, the public will frequently discover that local cops depict Black people as apes and gorillas in their group chats, as they discovered for the LAPD in the nineties. During the trial of the cops who beat Rodney King in 1991, the prosecutor asked one cop, "He deserved to be treated like a human being, didn't he? All right, he wasn't an animal, was he?" The cop answered, "No, sir. Just acting like one." Novelist and cultural theorist Sylvia Wynter wrote in an open letter to her colleagues:[239]

> The [news] report stated that public officials of the judicial system of Los Angeles routinely used the acronym N.H.I. to refer to any case involving a breach of the rights of young Black males who belong to the jobless category of inner city ghettos. N.H.I. means "no humans involved."[240]

Cops used this description for everything from disturbances in Black neighborhoods, to Black gang members who had been murdered. "No humans involved" is arguably worse than dehumanization because it denies the possibility of any humanity at all. It's not something removed, but something that was, is, and always will be, non-existent.

While I was working with Action STL, I also had been supporting activists in Ferguson around the Dept. of Justice's consent decree with the Ferguson Police Department. There, I'd listen to organizers pour their heart out during community meetings about how dehumanizing police, courts, and jails were in St. Louis. Testimonies were powerful rallying cries against the oppressive and death dealing institutions that we needed to abolish. The DOJ adopted this language, writing in the investigative report that documented racial bias in the police department: "In email messages and during interviews, several court and law enforcement personnel expressed discriminatory views and intolerance with regard to race, religion, and national origin. The content of these communications is unequivocally derogatory, dehumanizing, and demonstrative of impermissible bias."[241]

Yet the DOJ and the community were not invoking dehumanization for the same reasons. Community members wanted the police to stop ticketing, harassing, and jailing poor, Black people. The DOJ wanted FPD to do it constitutionally. By focusing on the views and content, the government lawyers obscured that law enforcement and court officials still possessed the power to act on those beliefs, regardless of whether they verbalized them anymore. The consent decree has explicit goals: rebuild relationships with the communities it serves and protects; ensures protection of the constitutional and other legal rights of the community; improve Ferguson's ability to prevent crime; enhance officer and public safety; and increase public confidence in police. Ferguson's police department could meet all of these goals, and still subject Black people to "dehumanizing" treatment. "In order to try to prevent the Ferguson police from treating African-American residents unfairly, their constitutional powers have to be curtailed," Paul Butler explains. "Not only is the Constitution, as interpreted by the Supreme Court, insufficient to protect black people from police abuse, it actually aids and abets the abusers."[242]

As I'd felt with "Black Lives Matter," I'd started becoming worried that the people we were fighting against could simply use our language against us because it did not challenge the power they possessed. Dehumanization is subjective and can mean everything, anything. Sometimes it is a precursor to violence; many of the activists I organized with believed that since *they* don't consider *us* human, then they can justify their violence against us; that if the cops who beat

Rodney King saw him as human, then maybe they would not have beat him back down each time he attempted to stand. Consequently, I was realizing that when we invoked dehumanization as a problem, we often invoked *humanization* as a solution. We accentuate the fondness of the fallen—what kinds of family, friends, and lovers they were before the police cut their lives short. Family reunion and graduation photos start circulating. Lezley McSpadden said of her son, Michael Brown: "I just want them to know who Michael Brown was. That's my purpose. My son was not a bad person, he was not a thug, he didn't have a rap sheet, he didn't tote a pistol, he was not like that at all." Time and time again, families to come to the defense of their loved ones, as I would for mine. This defense of Black life resonated with me deeply as a parent. And I was navigating my concern of it as an organizer and lawyer.[243]

Dehumanization and humanization have deep roots in many debates surrounding Black life. A 2018 *Boston Review* essay by historian Walter Johnson helped me reckon with that note I'd written inside Teju Cole's book cover, as well as the histories of the appeals to humanize Black people. Johnson was fiercely critical of the scholarly claim that slavers needed to "dehumanize" Black people in order to enslave them (this was *it*, exactly what I'd been feeling about police). He explained that slave owners depended on enslaved Black people's *human* capacities in order to enslave them, their capacities to think, labor, obey, love, fear, feel pain. He asked, "Who is the judge of when a person has suffered so much or been objectified so fundamentally that the person's humanity has been lost? How does the person regain that humanity? Can it even be regained? And who decides when it has been regained?"[244]

The questions struck me. Activists charged the police with dehumanizing us all of the time. Why did we bestow them with omnipotence? Was it temporary? Everlasting? Were we human again after the cop wrote us the ticket? While reading the essay, I thought about Stokely Carmichael's 1966 quote on Black Power: "Now, then, in order to understand white supremacy we must dismiss the fallacious notion that white people can give anybody their freedom. No man can give anybody his freedom." And I believe the same of our humanity. In order to understand white supremacy, policing, or any other system of oppression, we must dismiss the fallacious notion that anybody can give us our humanity or take it away. Even if police treated us perfectly "human," the job is still problematic. The school police who walked kids to in-school suspension treated them with compassion on the way to unfair punishment. Dehumanization language obscured the real problem: police power. Not how they view or treat us, but the institution itself. We must focus on reducing police power, more than humanizing ourselves.[245]

FROM WALTER JOHNSON, I'd also gathered that just as activists attempted to humanize victims of police violence, abolitionists, and anti-slavery advocates attempted to humanize enslaved Black people. These forms of humanization were often bound to ableist ideas about class, intelligence, physical fitness, and beauty. Physical and mental fitness were used both to justify slavery, and to end slavery. The slave industry relied on pseudoscience to prove that Black people were inferior and incapable of surviving outside the violent plantations. Much of this science at the time was mainstream and accepted widely. Pseudoscientific and racist depictions were so virulent that white abolitionists responded by portraying Black people as erect, attractive, and intelligent as evidence of their humanity. Abolitionists in the United States spread images of Black men portrayed as strong and healthy to offset pro-slavery depictions of Black people as animals or deformed. Slavers also attempted to *humanize* slaves for profit. Auctioneers described whether slaves on the block were of "sound body and mind," and owners would force enslaved Black people to "humanize" themselves by hiding disabilities. Both depictions obscured important realities: slavery was a disabling system and made many Black people ill. The problem was slavery and the power to enslave, not bondspeople.[246]

In Jamaica, planters used the health and appearance of the Maroons to justify slavery and "explain away the achievements of Maroons as exceptions to the institutionalized rule of African disability, which consigned them to forced labor." Maroons had a reputation among English planters for strength, wisdom, and physical attractiveness. The planters begged the British crown for more money to fund more patrols and militias to fight what they described as the unassailable runaways who waged attacks on them; planters sometimes fabricated and exaggerated the raids to strengthen its patrols, just like police do today. Some British abolitionists used these descriptions inversely to argue against slavery; bio-archaeologist David Ingleman explains that they supported abolition so that Africans could start "looking and behaving more like Europeans," which they believed slavery prevented.[247]

As I was grappling with this history, I realized that what often remained consistent under dehumanization or humanization was the power to control and dominate Black people with all kinds of bodies and minds. Slavery and capitalism exploited—continues to exploit—sight, mobility, smell, hearing, and taste for profit. For example, a slave's ability to run fast might be profitable if an owner needed to quickly transport produce from the plantation, but a slave who could run away to chase freedom was a liability. At any given point, slavers had the *power* to sever limbs. Potentially lost in the focus on dehumanization under slavery then, and policing now, is this exact power to disable people.

This is a matter of life and death, freedom, and exploitation. Attempts to humanize Black people left many disabled Black slaves on the cotton fields and in the masters' houses. In reading more about Northern industry and abolition democracy, I discovered that capitalists eagerly awaited Black emancipation because former slaves could toil in the factories. More workers meant more goods could be produced and sold, and therefore higher profits for the bosses. So, during the Civil War, the Union Army initially did not rescue or protect Black people they perceived to be disabled and refused to let them into military camps because they could not work. These were supposed to be the soldiers on the runaways' side and fighting for freedom. Historian Jim Downs emphasizes that these soldiers did not rescue these disabled Black people because they did not want them to be a burden on the federal government. As Lincoln's soldiers traveled throughout the South, they *recorded* which plantations had "helpless slaves" under the *care* of slave owners rather than freeing them. In "The Continuation of Slavery," Downs offers an example:

> Consider Hannah, a blind slave who lived in the Natchez district. Her owner continued to find work for her in both his garden and in his home despite the ending of the institution of slavery. But Hannah was not alone. On a neighboring plantation in Natchez, two blind slaves remained enslaved on William Newtown Mercer's plantation. Not just in the Natchez district, but throughout the postbellum South, scores of disabled freed

slaves remained enslaved. Their continual enslavement varied according
to the wishes of their owners and their own physical predicament.[248]

Freedom was not for all Black people, just those who could run, physically toil,
and prove their worth as human beings in a capitalist society.

When slavery became against the law, it didn't just end. Owners tricked or
forced newly emancipated Black people into working on plantations for several
months or years. I had even celebrated Juneteenth, the holiday honoring slaves
in Texas who learned of their freedom two years after the Emancipation Procla-
mation. But it wouldn't be until I was a lawyer that I learned some of the specific
failures of abolition and emancipation for disabled Black slaves. As Downs
argued, "if a discourse of equality truly emanated throughout the South, then
all slaves would have been free, not just those who could work or those who
were connected to wage-earning freedpeople." No Juneteenth celebrations
for them. Northern abolitionists eventually found many "free" Blacks in jail or
on abandoned plantations because they had nowhere else to go.[249]

Humanity had not been bestowed or removed by slave owners, and many
disabled Black slaves and their loved ones resisted slavery and capitalism's valu-
ation of the body and mind based on ability. Black parents hid their disabled
children from being abused or sold; other Black parents relied on disabled Black
slaves to babysit their children. Slaves physically carried each other into the
woods to escape the plantation, including elderly slaves, slaves experiencing pain
from rheumatism, and those who had been mutilated as punishment for a prior
escape. During Reconstruction, Black families appealed for help to rescue their
loved ones from plantations and later lobbied for federal funds to help cover
someone who had been denied employment because of age or a disability, real
or perceived.

Toward the end of slavery, flight, more than rebellion and raiding, was
the predominant form of resistance. The conditions of slavery fostered nearly
impossible choices for Black people who could physically escape. Run alone.
Run with others. Return. Never return. Not everybody could run, including many
children, the elderly, and some disabled slaves. Many ventured anyway. Harriet
Tubman did. Tubman is perhaps the most famous abolitionist. She was injured
as a teen after she refused an overseer's demand to tie down a Black man who

had left the plantation without permission. When the Black man started running away again, she tried to stop the overseer from catching him. When the overseer threw a two-pound weight to stop the runaway, it hit Harriet in the head. This head injury caused her to fall into deep sleep at random throughout the rest of her life, including when she ran away from the plantation.[250]

Like Black children during Black History Month, at some point in my life teachers taught me that Tubman made several trips to the South to rescue Black people. I knew that she had had a head injury, and that slave catchers and patrols had an advantage over her because of it. I did not conceive of her as a disabled slave until law school.

When a museum purchased a photo of the younger Tubman sitting upright, the director explained, "All of us had only seen images of her at the end of her life. She seemed frail. She seemed bent over, and it was hard to reconcile the images of Moses leading people to freedom." He continued, "I also think that one of the real challenges of history is that sometimes we forget to humanize the people we talk about . . . and I think that [younger] picture humanizes her in a way that I would have never imagined." Once again, the desire to *humanize* obscured the full range of how human beings look, even our abolitionist heroes.[251]

My perception of her completely changed after learning about the Harriet Tubman Collective, as well as my understanding of her commitments to liberation. I read or reread stories, newspaper clippings, and books about her. Tubman did not solely rescue "able-bodied" people who could run. She created the conditions for people to survive. She gave opioids to infants and children so that they could sleep and be carried on the journey. She created a wagon to rescue her elderly parents who could not run at all. Once free, Tubman became the first woman, and the first disabled woman, to lead a US military raid when she led black Union Army troops to free more than 750 slaves during the Combahee River raid in South Carolina. According to historical records, she did not leave anyone behind. For three decades, the US government denied her a pension for her military service, even first paying her a small pension as a widow because her late husband had fought in the Civil War. Tubman supported her family and runaways with next to nothing in her old age. She shared a home with "the lame, the halt, and the blind, the bruised and crippled little children, and one crazy woman," according to her biographer. A blind woman living there had spent two decades caring for the elderly Tubman. They did not need to be *humanized*; they were humans who needed an end to the racist, sexist, and ableist conditions that created slavery and their subsequent economic suffering.[252]

Prompted by Johnson's essay and disabled slaves' lives and resistance, I try to remember the limitations in humanizing victims under police violence without trying to reduce police power. This is challenging. Families want their loved ones to be remembered as more than just victims who were shot and killed in the street; protestors condemn the violence because victims were somebody's parent, friend, or child; and lawyers who sue the police want to portray victims as appealingly as possible to win their lawsuits. But law enforcement re-packages these calls for humanization in attempts to further legitimize themselves. When we invoked dehumanization as a problem, they invoked *humanization* as a solution—this manifests as more funding for community engagement, so they can practice seeing us as humans on basketball courts and in boxing gyms to jog their memory on how to treat us when they encounter us in the field. The 2016 consent decree in Ferguson goes further. While the DOJ investigation recognized the "dehumanizing" treatment from Ferguson officials, it provided cops with mental health services, counseling, free physical fitness resources, adequate time off during uprisings, and competitive salaries—no reparations, services, counseling, or physical fitness opportunities for the communities they assaulted, arrested, and tear-gassed for years.

FOLLOWING THE DOJ investigation of the Ferguson Police Department in 2016, I was introduced to the Harriet Tubman Collective. I was the editor-in-chief of the *Harvard Journal of African American Policy* (*HJAAP*) and soliciting essays, lectures, art, and syllabi on the Movement for Black Lives (M4BL), an ecosystem of organizations that formed as a policy arm of the protests. M4BL's policy table released "A Vision for Black Lives: Policy Demands for Black Power, Freedom, and Justice," a comprehensive and visionary policy agenda for the liberation movement that was catalyzed in Ferguson, Missouri, following Michael Brown's death. The Vision featured six areas: ending the war on Black people, reparations, divestment and investment, economic justice, community control, and political power. A policy brief accompanied each pillar, with demands, ideas, proposals, and model legislation. Our editorial board wanted to display the breadth and depth of the Vision in the journal, as well as responses to it. After I revised and released *HJAAP*'s call for proposals, I read Kerima Çevik's submission. She is a blogger, advisor, legislative advocate, and parent activist for autism and social justice. Police are especially dangerous toward Black disabled people like her son Mustafa, a tall, neurodivergent, nonspeaking Black boy. Çevik powerfully penned:[253]

> Ironically, it seems that the way to protect our son is to have him steer clear of those who have sworn to protect and serve him. The best policy solutions for reducing catastrophic encounters with law enforcement for neurodivergent Black and brown males are those that limit their encounters with law enforcement in the first place. I never imagined that I would teach my son to avoid police. Yet he stands at the intersection of racism, ableism, and disability in a society that empowers police to respond to his black body and his neurodivergence with aggression.[254]

Çevik recounted the story of Arnaldo Rios Soto as an example. In July 2016, behavioral therapist Charles Kinsey left a facility to retrieve Arnaldo Rios Soto, a patient resident who had walked out to wander the streets with his toy fire truck. Soto towers more than six feet and several hundred pounds; his skin is the color of butterscotch wrappers at the bottom of a church lady's pocketbook, his mental capacity described as the level of a four-year-old eager to find the candy. Police allege they thought the twenty-something-year-old was holding a gun, despite repeated pleas from his caregiver Kinsey, to stand down. Kinsey laid flat on his back and raised his arms high to show that he was unarmed. North Miami cop Jonathan Aledda fired, intending to hit the quietly and calmly sitting Soto, and missed. Aledda shot Kinsey instead. Aledda's first trial ended in a hung jury. In his second, he was acquitted on two charges and found guilty of negligence on the second.[255]

The shooting impacted Çevik. She had experience organizing for better police training and spent time lobbying the Maryland state legislature for an autism-training bill for first responders. First responders, unfortunately, include cops. In 2013, three off-duty deputies in Maryland handcuffed and fractured Robert Ethan Saylor's throat. A twenty-six-year-old white man with Down syndrome, Saylor was at a movie theater with his caretaker and attempted to re-watch a film by re-entering the theater without paying a second time. A theater manager called the cops. Ethan's caregiver repeated pleas to the police to not touch Ethan and to let her de-escalate the situation. Ethan died. A grand jury did not indict the cops and they returned to work. Contrary to popular notions, cops are not safe for all white people, and more training does not make people less committed to protecting capitalism. Three cops accosted Ethan over a ten dollar movie ticket. Ethan's family reached a civil settlement in 2018. His mother lamented, "It's been four years of gut-wrenching reports and judges' opinions and depositions and defending my son's right to be seen as human, to be seen as valuable."[256]

Police in Maryland began receiving training in a program named after Ethan. But Çevik witnessed police *with* training continue to assault, shoot and kill disabled people, including autistic people like her son. Police with more training would still be a risk. By the time she wrote her essay, she had espoused more transformational demands: retraining emergency dispatchers; eliminating encounters between neurodivergent Black and brown people and the police; training parents to request emergency vehicles instead of police; removing cops from schools; prohibiting school administrators from calling police on students in crisis; reporting student arrests to civil rights offices; and establishing grassroots mental health crisis support. Some of these were policy demands and others were rooted in community-based practices of keeping each other safe. We are each other's custodians, too.

I had not been expecting a journal submission on disability. I assigned Çevik's piece to an associate editor for review and went to check my email to read the next submission. There was another one. And another one. Two more authors had submitted pieces on disability, race, and police violence. A group of disabled Black organizers called the Harriet Tubman Collective contributed a searing submission on erasure and marginalization within the contemporary Black freedom struggle. Their writings introduced me to disability justice, a framework that queer radical disabled activists Mia Mingus and Patty Berne began exploring as a paradigm in 2005. With other disabled activists, these women of color accounted for many of the omissions that they experienced from disability rights movements and racial justice movements. Members within the disability justice and performance project Sins Invalid have distilled the framework into principles that include commitments to racial justice, abolition, anti-capitalism, decolonization, cross-movement solidarity, and collective liberation. The Harriet Tubman Collective and Sins Invalid departed from the slavery abolitionists who left disabled people on the plantation; from the civil rights movement that often privileged attractive young light-skinned college students who could march and participate in sit-ins; and from some Black Lives Matter activists who attempted to humanize victims of police violence based on education, body size, and parenting skills. These disability justice activists offered more depth by recognizing that "all bodies are unique and essential."[257]

The Harriet Tubman Collective's submission critiqued the first version of the M4BL platform because it omitted disability justice when half of the people who police kill have disabilities. M4BL had mentioned disability in one section, but the Collective explained:

> The Platform employed the term "differently abled," which is considered offensive within disability communities. The phrase "differently abled" suggests that we are the locus of our disability when we are, in fact, disabled by social and institutional barriers. Use of this term reifies the marginalization that Black Disabled/Deaf people face within our own communities and oppressive state institutions.[258]

They were right. Not just about the omission from the platform, but the general practice of disability's omission and marginalization in broader movements for racial justice and freedom, just as it had been for the abolition of slavery. I had lacked intention in many organizing spaces from neglecting to account for representation from all kinds of organizers, to choosing to have actions and marches without considering various ways that people can participate. It wasn't until Belinda Hall that I was pushed to ask these questions; for example, disabled student activists and those who knew about disability justice tried to ensure that our furniture was arranged so that wheelchair users could navigate the space and that we demanded that the school close, record lectures, or properly clean the sidewalks during heavy snowfall so that all students could make it to campus. When we invoked the police trauma and violence that we experienced in the streets and on campus that induced anxiety, depression, and other mental health challenges, we criticized professors for their ableist assertion that we were "snowflakes." Between 2014 and 2018, "the percentage of Harvard undergraduates reporting that they have or think they may have depression jumped from 22% to 31%, and the percentage reporting that they have or think they may have an anxiety disorder increased from 19% to 30%." Harvard found that these figures were higher for Black students, graduate students, and students with children like me. We were living under constant racism, ableism, and exploitation in one of the most expensive cities in the country with the reputation for being the most racist.[259]

The inverse was true, too: disability rights movements have often obscured racial and economic exploitation in its advocacy. Talila Lewis, a member of the Harriet Tubman Collective, wrote a separate essay that challenged the disability rights movement to apply an intersectional analysis and praxis to state violence: "Disabled people of color are disproportionately impacted by state violence. Even still, most resourced disability rights organizations refuse to take action to end the crisis of racialized people with disabilities dying in our schools, streets, homes, and prisons, while resourced non-disability civil rights entities dishonor the lives of the same people by failing to uplift their whole humanity." Black feminist scholars have faced and combat similar singular approaches to freedom in social movements. Black men dominated leadership and decision-making power in Black liberation movements and white women fought against gender-based oppression without regard to race. Black women organized against formations that excluded them in both spirit and practice. Black feminists and radical lesbians marooned and forged new activist spaces for themselves, too. Similarly, the Harriet Tubman Collective, including Lewis, challenged the Movement for Black Lives for perpetuating ableism, and called out the disability rights movement for perpetuating racism. M4BL worked diligently to revise the platform, which now includes a demand to "End the War on Black Health and Black Disabled People."[260]

IN 2016 AND beyond, as activists and protestors fought against police violence that disproportionately impacted Black people, disability justice activists raised awareness around the intersections of ableism and state violence. I knew then that the police primarily capture, cage, or kill poor people, Black people, and Indigenous people. I had not realized that racism, capitalism, and ableism pushed more than half of disabled people into long-term poverty, increasing the chances of violent police encounters. According to the American Psychological Association, people with low vision have unemployment rates that exceed 70 percent, and intellectually and developmentally disabled people have unemployment rates higher than 80 percent. One government report estimates that employers pay more than 220,000 disabled people with intellectual/developmental disabilities less than the already low minimum wage. The government permits this superexploitation, while also banning disabled people who receive government support from saving more than two thousand dollars total. This cap keeps disabled people in poverty and economically vulnerable positions.[261]

Disabled people are excluded from the labor market (and forced out of schools), not because they cannot work, but because capitalists are not interested in, and are minimally required to, paying for the costs of accommodations. On the plantation, slavers would sell disabled slaves by the dozen at a bargain when it was cheaper than accommodating them and they could not derive profit another way (playing "the dozens"—when Black people make fun of each other until one person wins, and what sourced my mother's comedy—comes from slaves who were coping with being regrettably sold among the bunch). Under capitalism, it is cheaper to exclude disabled workers who could otherwise work in an non-ableist environment. And by capping savings, and refusing to provide universal health care, universal basic income, and adequate protection against exploitation, the federal government chooses businesses over disabled workers. Writer and activist Marta Russell explains, "If workers were provided with a social safety net that adequately protected them through unemployment, sickness, disability, and old age, laborers would gain a stronger position from which to negotiate their conditions of employment." These cycles of exclusion from work, schools, and housing creates more jobs, seats in class, and apartments for people without disabilities. Disability justice is also labor, health, and housing justice.[262]

My family did not have insurance and our community lacked basic clinics, which is why we relied so heavily on 911 for basic medical care. Disabled people and their loved ones or neighbors call the police for help during a crisis when their options for support are limited. Tragically, police contact can result in involuntary commitment to psychiatric hospitals, arrests, and death. Afterward, the police or family might issue a statement saying that the victim was off of their medication at the time of the shooting or tasing. These statements often place the blame solely on the victim. Millions of people skip their medication and are not killed by the police. Additionally, rich people can afford the best prescription mental health drugs and purchase them at the highest rates of any income bracket. If the rich disproportionately use mental health prescriptions, does that mean that they are disproportionately diagnosed with mental health issues? They rarely die during police encounters, even rich Black people. Yet a third of disabled poor people on Medicare "skipped medication, reduced the dosage, or failed to fill prescriptions because of the medication's cost." Abolishing a society that relies on police requires the abolition of the inequality that makes disabled people susceptible to police violence, including economic exploitation.[263]

Even if nobody calls, the police routinely patrol poor segregated neighborhoods where disabled people, like Freddie Gray and countless others, live. The police contact in our neighborhoods have dire consequences. Talila Lewis writes:[264]

> Disabled/neurodivergent people comprise just 26% of the United
> States population—but represent up to half of the people killed by police,
> over 50% of the incarcerated adult prison population, up to 85% of the
> incarcerated youth population, and a significant number of those incarcerated in medicalized carceral spaces like nursing facilities, group
> facilities, and civil commitment, "treatment" facilities, and "hospitals."[265]

Twenty-two thousand people are involuntarily committed in various institutions and many without any determined release date.[266]

Disability justice is more than humanizing disabled people, or simply replacing cops with crisis intervention workers. It changes the conditions upon which everyone can thrive. Because disabled people like Freddie Gray are often excluded from the labor market, capitalism finds creative and cunning solutions to profit from them still. A labor market exists predicated on the exclusion of disabled people from the workforce. The clearest examples are elderly facilities where my grandmother lived: they provide jobs for workers who assist people who could otherwise be independent and interdependent in communities that have resources. For others, especially poor, Black and Latinx disabled people, it's policing and imprisonment. When companies, schools, and landlords push disabled people out, police are then tasked with patrolling and surveilling their daily lives.

LIKE SLAVERY, POLICING also disables people. On a global scale, the US exports policing tactics and militarism that inflicts disability as a tactic to gain imperial and colonial advantages. Women and gender studies professor Jasbir Puar describes this as *debility*, "bodily injury and social exclusion brought on by economic and political factors." Death and the fear of debilitation can discourage and dissuade occupied peoples from resisting the nations that colonize them. Domestically, shootings, beatings, tasings, high-speed chases, and tear gas create and trigger physical impairments, blindness, depression, anxiety and psychological trauma. During residential raids, cops use stun grenades that cause blindness, deafness, and other injuries. Criminal justice journalist Radley Balko argues that the injuries are not accidental because "even when used and executed as intended, flashbangs cause injury *by design*, and when used by law enforcement, that injury is inflicted on people who have yet to even be charged with a crime, much less convicted of one."[267]

In May 2014, a SWAT team conducted a no-knock raid to find a young man who was accused of making a fifty-dollar drug deal. Police broke down the door to a home where he did not reside. They threw a flashbang grenade and it exploded inside nineteen-month-old Bounkham Phonesavanh's crib. The grenade put a hole in the baby's small chest. Seeing a pool of blood and hearing her screaming baby, Bounkham's mother, Alecia Phonesavanh, said police told her to calm down because the child had only lost a tooth. Doctors put him in a medically induced coma to save his life and cover his exposed ribs. Phonesavanh wrote in an essay:[268]

I know that SWAT teams are breaking into homes in the middle of the night, more often than not just to serve search warrants in drug cases. I know that too many local cops have stockpiled weapons that were made for soldiers to take to war. And as is usually the case with aggressive policing, I know that people of color and poor people are more likely to be targeted.[269]

According to his family, the child had eighteen surgeries before his fifth birthday. The sheriff's deputy who authorized the raid was acquitted of charges, and Bounkham family settled a civil suit for $3.6 million. Since 2010, an investigative reporter found at least thirty lawsuits a year stemming from SWAT raids that caused injuries. A South Carolina man received an $11 million settlement after a SWAT raid left him paralyzed. He sold fifteen grams of weed to an informant, enough for police to secure a warrant for a drug raid on his home. Not a single cop was criminally charged because their actions were legal.[270]

Police disables people in the streets, too. At protests, police shoot rubber bullets and hit activists and bystanders in the eyes, many believe intentionally. Tear gas and mace have triggered asthmatic reactions. In November 2016, police launched a concussion grenade at Sophia Wilansky when she was bringing water to activists who were protesting Dakota Access Pipeline construction. Wilansky survived but her arm was nearly severed. In 2017, pastor and soon-to-be-congresswoman Cori Bush told me during an interview that officers kicked and punched her until she was unconscious. Police cause physical and psychological violence that impair people every day and long after the initial encounters. Clinical psychologist Jennifer Sumner explained in the *Huffington Post* that police assaults on the community during protests can trigger Post-Traumatic Stress Disorder:

Quite a large body of evidence suggests that both trauma exposure and PTSD are associated with developing a wide range of physical health disorders down the line. Chronic diseases of aging like cardiovascular disease, like having a heart attack, having a stroke. Developing blood clots in your veins. All of these are associated with trauma and PTSD.[271]

Police ambushes also causes migraines, high blood pressure, diabetes, sleep disruptions, and stress that impacted activists' bodies and minds long-term. Many of us in the streets, including myself, may not yet know the full impact for years to come. I started getting migraines in 2018. As a child, I'd play with the colorful accessibility functions on the Dell from Rent-A-Center that my mother paid for in small weekly installments, and at a price three times the computer's value. I would invert the colors to make the screen's background black and all of the text white. Now, with my recurring migraines, I need the color inversion to alleviate the pressure on my brain when I write, even as I write this book. When my migraines are most severe, I must be in a completely dark room and underneath a pillow for days, for any light is too much to bear. I'm dizzy and disoriented. There's evidence that suggests that migraines might be hereditary. My mother has never had them, and I wonder if my time in the streets over the last fifteen years is why I have them now. And I pray that I do not pass them on to my children.[272]

AROUND THE TIME I gave birth to my second child, Garvey, in October 2016, I read about a sixty-six-year-old Black woman named Deborah Danner. Danner was an information technology specialist who took pride in her intelligence and found solace in her church. She lived with schizophrenia and called it "a curse." Hauntingly, she wrote in a 2012 essay: "We are all aware of the all too frequent news stories about the mentally ill who come up against law enforcement instead of mental health professionals and end up dead." This did not have to be her fate. Four years later, a neighbor called 911 because Danner was ranting loudly in the hallway. Medics came first. Brittney Mullings, an emergency medical technician, testified that Danner was holding scissors in her own home. Danner insisted on only talking to medics, rather than law enforcement, and agreed to put the scissors down. Mullings entered the apartment and Danner was empty-handed. According to a *New York Times* feature, Danner had physically calmed down but remained agitated because someone had called the police on her. While Mullings and Danner were speaking, Mullings heard the cops behind her ask each other, "Are you ready?" Next, NYPD sergeant Hugh Barry rushed from behind Mullings and shot Danner twice. He did not say anything to her before he killed her. The officer was charged with second-degree murder, manslaughter, and criminally negligent homicide. A judge acquitted him.[273]

Deborah Danner's essay is so powerful and revelatory about the US. She indicts the society that refuses to meet the unique needs of everyone, including people with mental illness who deserve housing, employment, relationships they desire, and the right to refuse confinement in prisons, hospitals, and elderly facilities. Danner said she endured stigma in society and lost a job after confiding in a coworker about her condition. To save her life and others, she demanded what Kerima Çevik had demanded years before: better training for law enforcement to prepare them for encounters with "the mentally ill in crisis." What's tragic is that the training that the police had for these encounters did not save her life. The prosecutor argued that the sergeant ignored his training and provoked the confrontation instead of patiently waiting until specially trained people arrived. Instead, the cop disrupted the conversation between Danner and the medic, then escalated the violence by shooting.[274]

Danner's tone in the essay shifted when she wrote about the strong support from her church: "They know I suffer and still accept me . . . They trust and support me, offer assistance financially and emotionally and bring me ever closer to a God who I know loves me. I've begun therapy with the wonderful Naomi— a mental health professional—who listens, converses with and advises me and has me convinced that I am still a person of worth." This is what I believe is the best tradition of the church, friendships, and mutual aid networks. I had known the church to be a messy place with regard to disability. Sometimes, pastors will use the Bible to talk about disabilities as a curse or punishment. And I've seen the same pastors say, *For those who are able, please stand to read the word of God*, and ensure that church members visit and support disabled members with food, transportation, clothing, and Communion. We did not only pray for the "sick and shut-in"; we were commanded to create the conditions for everyone's participation in fellowship with each other. As I've aged, I've observed pastors shift from praying away mental illness as an evil spirit to encouraging therapy and medication for those who want it. Every major Black church where I have been a member used captioning for sermons or rotated between Black women who preached the message and interpreted the choir's songs in American Sign Language. The love, acceptance, kindness, care, support and accountability that

Danner had was the exact opposite of everything that the police provided. More accurately, police are incapable of providing that support system because they are empowered to arrest, assault, incarcerate, and kill disabled people. [275]

Danner's essay also referenced the murder of Eleanor Bumpurs (whom she mistakenly calls "Gompers") as a failure of law enforcement's response to someone in crisis. Eleanor was a sixty-six-year-old Black mother of seven and grandmother of ten who lived in New York public housing in the Bronx. Her neighbors described her as a woman who loved children. Historian LaShawn Harris wrote an extraordinary article around Eleanor that details a long history of resilience, migration, parenthood, and economic exploitation. She was born in North Carolina and migrated to New York to live, love, and parent. She worked as a domestic at the Waldorf Astoria until she underwent a major surgery in her forties and was forced to leave her job. She received very little government assistance because she was "disabled." Her daughter said in court that her mother began facing mental health challenges and needed support so badly that her older sister once lied to the police so their mother could be committed to a psychiatric ward. Her sister was desperate for help and like many families, depended on calling 911. Eleanor spent almost a year in prison well before she went to New York and faced arrests and involuntary commitments throughout the rest of her life. She still parented and took care of her neighbors' children, who described her as "nurturing."[276]

The picture most shared online of Eleanor shows her arms folded and face dreary. I made it my profile picture on social media for more than a year before I discovered the back story in Harris' article. The projects where Eleanor lived caught fire and all of her belongings became ashes. News reporters went to the scene and took pictures of the poor, Black people standing outside who had just lost everything. After police shot her, this was the widely circulated picture in the media that probably confirmed for some people that she was a large, aggressive old woman. One picture after a fire. What I found remarkable is that her daughter founded the "Eleanor Bumpurs Justice Committee" afterward and used the same picture for the logo. Presumably, she had other pictures that "humanized" her mother. But I wonder if she used this image because of the widespread circulation, or because police should not have the power kill anyone, regardless of how we perceive them.

By the time Eleanor was living in her own place again, she developed cordial and good relationships with her neighbors, even babysitting their kids so they could go to school or work. She owed a few hundred dollars in rent. Like my mother before we were evicted, and my grandmother before she was evicted, and countless other poor Black women that I knew, Eleanor made several complaints about the condition of the apartment and withheld rent in protest. Pipes broke. The toilets flooded. At one point, she said that she was withholding rent because her stove and lights did not work. At times, she refused entry to maintenance workers. Other times, she let them in and held a knife for protection. The public housing agency sent a psychiatrist to interview her. He determined that she was not aggressive and held a knife "defensively" like a "security blanket." He also determined that she should be evicted and then hospitalized. A group of police officers went to announce the eviction order. The *Washington Post* reported that the cops arrived with "helmets, bulletproof vests, gas masks, Plexiglas shields, a six-foot pronged restraining pole and a shotgun."[277]

This was the NYPD's Emergency Service Unit. ESU is a special unit that was "specially trained to deal with emotionally disturbed people." They kicked down her door. She stood there, naked, approximately 5′8″ and almost three hundred pounds. She waved a knife at the ESU unit that advanced toward her with a metal bar. Officer Stephen Sullivan, a white ESU cop—the person trained for these situations—shot her in the hand that was holding the knife, and then shot her in the chest. NYPD then carried her naked body outside, uncovered, bleeding. She died en route to the hospital. New York City's chief medical examiner altered her initial autopsy report to support the police's story that the officer only fired once; it was not uncommon for newspapers to report that he and other examiners tampered with police cases, destroying and misconstruing data that might have revealed more details about police killings. Sullivan was charged with criminally negligent homicide and faced fifteen years. Eleanor's neighbors expressed joy at the indictment announcement and hoped for "justice." Many were angry, saying Sullivan "shot her twice like she was a dog" and that she had trouble walking as proof why she was not a threat. During the trial, white police and white citizens attacked and killed Black people out of anger and retaliation. One paper reported that ten thousand cops surrounded the courthouse to rally against the charges, a figure that the paper considered the largest cop protest in

US history. The entire Emergency Services Unit—250 cops—demanded transfers out of the unit in defiance of the indictment. A judge acquitted Sullivan. The department reinstated him and sought funding to purchase stun guns as a reform for future encounters.[278]

The more I studied the case the more I could not believe it. Black NYPD commissioner Benjamin Ward said that Eleanor Bumpurs "looked like my mother." That was a lot like the line President Obama used decades later for Trayvon Martin. Both Black men responded to racist violence with reforms that did not eliminate the root causes of racial violence. For Obama it was My Brother's Keeper and community policing. For Commissioner Ward, the *New York Times* reported that he "noted that some good had come from the case because it had brought about a change in police procedures for handling emotionally disturbed people . . . The new guidelines emphasize negotiation and non-lethal devices such as shock guns, and require the presence of a precinct commander or duty captain to decide how such a person should be restrained." Eleanor Bumpurs was killed in 1984. Deborah Danner was slain in 2016. Police who had been part of special mental health procedures shot and killed them both.[279]

I wanted to know where the special Emergency Service Unit (ESU) that killed Eleanor came from. It was *already* intended as a reform measure against police violence. The reform was killing people. On August 22, 1979, five white NYPD cops shot Luis Baez twenty-one times for making a slashing motion with a pair of scissors. Activists and organizers demanded accountability because witnesses said that he was unarmed and clearly in mental distress. Others speculate that he did not understand their English commands because he only spoke Spanish. Consequently, NYPD created the ESU. A week after Baez's killing, white NYPD officer Michael Latimer shot and killed Elizabeth Magnum, a thirty-five-year-old Black woman, whom he claims slashed him in the arm when he tried to evict her from her apartment. Because she had been flagged as "emotionally disturbed," the ESU was on the way to her apartment to assist in the eviction. He killed her before they arrived. There were no civilian witnesses to explain what happened.[280]

NYPD reported that cops responded to approximately 34,000 calls in 1984 for "emotionally disturbed individuals"; 18,997 were eligible for ESU. The ESU says it acted in 844 cases and only Eleanor was killed. NYPD underscored her death as a tragic departure from the routine behavior of the specialized unit. This is complicated for several reasons. One, NYPD regularly assaulted, shot, and killed Black, brown, and poor residents in the city. At the time of Eleanor's death, a medical examiner tampered with autopsy findings that tainted the data on police killings. It's unclear how many homicides actually resulted from police violence. Second, the report did not include any data on the outcomes of the remaining cases. How many "emotionally disturbed people" did the NYPD injure or kill outside of the ESU? Baez and Magnum, for example, would not have counted toward the ESU data had they been killed in 1984. And finally, if we accept the police's depiction of Eleanor as one death in 844 interventions, we still have to ask, what were the circumstances of the other 843? I did not consider non-killings a success for the police, who were still tasked with managing public housing, private property, racism, inequality, and mental health. What the city invests to evict people with police could be a starting investment to pay for rent and quality mental health options, not violence. This is why the kind of abolition that I believe in does not aim for the police to politely evict elderly Black grandmothers from their government-subsidized apartments. Rather, it aims to eliminate the police contact by addressing the root of the problem, and ultimately policing.[281]

Eleanor Bumpers's daughter Mary Bumpers organized the Eleanor Bumpurs Justice Committee (EBJC) to demand justice for her mother and other victims of police violence. The committee consisted of "tenant leaders, welfare mothers, workers and grassroots community activists." EBJC's work was so much more comprehensive than the reforms that New York City offered its residents. In a press release following the acquittal, EBJC wrote:[282]

> Very disturbingly, if one didn't know the history of the case, one would think it was Eleanor Bumpurs and her family on trial. There has been a systematic attempt by Sullivan's lawyer to portray Ms. Bumpurs as an emotionally disturbed person and dangerous, and cast aspersions on her family as the ones responsible for her death . . . What is the strategy? Why has there been no case made of the fact that the police should not have been involved in an eviction, or that they tied her apartment

door, so even if she wanted to come out, she couldn't have. Or why was the police so insistent in storming Ms. Bumpurs' apartment when they could have sought some civilized alternative?[283]

In their organizing, EBJC demanded the firing and prosecution of Sullivan and other police officers who have killed people in the city *and* moratoriums on evictions that were underlying the initial police contact. They knocked on doors throughout the public housing communities and fought for the rights of poor people and senior citizens.[284]

EBJC worked with the Welfare Action Coalition and the New York chapter of the National Lawyers Guild to fight state violence and combat homelessness and the housing crisis, a crisis that New York City treated with additional police funding. The New York City Housing Authority is the largest public housing authority in North America, and the second-largest landlord in the United States after the military. Police primarily patrol poor Black and brown tenants in the buildings and EBJC was fighting back. At an event sponsored by the Communist Party, Mary Bumpers and other families of police violence victims gathered to condemn racial violence, "from Soweto to Harlem." In the year following the elder Bumpurs's death, nearly one thousand South Africans had been killed in protests against apartheid schools, police, and military. Bumpers encouraged the crowd to fight police terror everywhere. This level of organizing in EBJC was dedicated to eradicating the conditions that made police violence possible.[285]

WHEN FRIENDS OF mine or people I grew up with die, I reread all of our texts and social media messages. Sometimes, I'll send a message even though I know they will not respond. I don't know why, but it feels related to my kindergarten seances to bring my father back to life. I find myself searching for clues left behind or messages from the other side. My friends archived pieces of their lives online so that's where I visited them instead of their graves. I don't know whether this is right or wrong but it's the truth. When he was killed in 2016, I went through every picture of Jarrell. I watched him in pictures twisting his fingers with other Black boys in our neighborhood. I saw him enter the military to avoid jail or the grave and watched him come home and get a good job with the city and wear church clothes on Sundays. Like a flashing deck, I flipped and saw him turn into a man with a round belly and full beard. I laughed at his story of buying a hamburger from Steak 'n Shake and then putting a slice of cheese on it when he got home because he did not want to pay the extra quarter. I watched the birth and growth of his two beautiful daughters, again. The family gatherings with his big sister Shay whom I adored and his little sister Trina who got on my nerves and his mom who used to live next door to my grandmother. These colorful digital archives became perpetual obituaries that mixed the living and the dead.

I don't know why or how but I found myself in a wondrous and painful rabbit hole with hairstylist Korryn Gaines. Like any of us who curate and archive our lives online, I know what she shared does not represent all of her. She just felt so familiar to me. She lived in Maryland, but she felt like the natural hairstylists who twisted my locs in St. Louis and Kansas City. I would sit in the chair and they'd talk about racism and how Black unity was the answer to stopping white supremacy. Before I had children, I would listen to them talk about raising their Black sons to protect themselves from violent white men and police officers. On any given day, I could hear traces of pan-Africanism or Black nationalism: "Black women protect and provide for Black men and Black men must protect and provide for their families and communities." In post after post, Gaines made clear that she was compelled to spread messages like these. But the farther I went back, I noticed a remarkable shift.

Like Jarrell's pictures, I saw beautiful portraits of Gaines's family. I watched her belly grow with her children, a son and a daughter. She was fly. The hairstylist seemed to love stripes and lip color. Her pictures were mostly selfies, kids, and positivity memes until April 2015. She then made a political post about Freddie Gray, who had been killed by the Baltimore Police Department. When police surrounded hundreds of Black kids to stop them from protesting or going home after school, the kids retaliated by throwing rocks. Cops threw rocks back. Often first. Gaines lived in Baltimore. She criticized the contradictory calls for the children to be mature when the police taunted and teased them.

On March 20, 2016, Gaines honored Sandra Bland online, saying that she saw herself as a younger version of her. Bland, who lived with epilepsy, had also been very critical of police and white supremacy online and had inspired Gaines to start sharing and posting messages to raise consciousness for Black people facing racism. Gaines, like Bland, was pulled over for a traffic violation. Her son and daughter were in the car. She began recording immediately. Gaines did not want to raise children who submitted to racial violence and pushed them to be vocal about how the police killed Black people. When the cops told her son that they were his friend and his mother was lying about police killing Black people, Gaines became angrier, saying "I don't have to lie to him. I can pull up a video right now of you killing people for no fucking reason. People that look like his uncle, his brother, his sister—anybody." The cop just responded with, "You don't realize what you're talking about." Here is a Black mother, witnessing a movement against police violence, being told by a white cop that she is lying about police violence to her children. Cops took her to jail for resisting arrest because she did not want them to tow her car for having improper plates. She was in jail for two days and she said she was denied food and water while she was there. Police transported Gaines to the hospital where she says the doctors told her she had miscarried while she was in jail. My heart broke watching her videos.[286]

Police went to Gaines's house to issue a warrant for her arrest because she had missed court, and to issue a warrant for her fiancé, even though his address on file was different. She did not open the door when they knocked. Agitated for being ignored, cops picked open the lock but the chain lock stopped the door from opening all the way. When they kicked the door down, Gaines was sitting with a gun in her lap to defend herself. Her fiancé and daughter eventually walked out of the apartment. Gaines was streaming the encounter on Facebook live for safety and transparency. Cops told Facebook to cut the feed from the public and the social media site complied. A cop shot Gaines when she walked to the kitchen toward her son. The bullet also hit her child, who survived. She died. The district attorney declined to bring charges. A jury awarded her son $38 million in a civil suit.[287]

I found it all profoundly confusing and unjust. Gaines's fiancé told the police that she had been battling mental illness and had not taken her medication. But was that it? Why was it supposedly "crazy" for Korryn Gaines to be a custodian of her Black body, to defend herself against the police, who had told her that she was lying to her children about viral police killings? Who took her to jail where her treatment caused her to have a miscarriage? Who had severed Freddie Gray's spine? The

Baltimore Police Department was the subject of a federal investigation and prosecution because cops had been planting BB guns next to people they killed and planting drugs in illegal raids they conducted. During a trial against BPD officers, some cops shared that they and others illegally entered homes to see what was inside first before obtaining warrants. This is the context in which Gaines found herself in her apartment surrounded by cops.[288]

I do not deny the fact of schizophrenia, depression, bipolar disorder, and much more. I have been pushed to understand that those diagnoses are only one part of people who are complex beings. However, I wonder how these diagnoses would manifest in a society that is not racist, capitalist, ableist, and carceral. I do not believe that it's mere coincidence that Korryn Gaines, Deborah Danner, Eleanor Bumpurs, and Elizabeth Magnum were killed in their homes while defending themselves from the cops, no more than it is coincidental when white men commit mass shootings. Patriarchy, militarism, and white supremacy have historically empowered white men to shoot and kill en masse with impunity and with reward. Killing people en masse meant getting slaves, land, oil, coal, votes, power. In contrast, Black women have historically resisted this violence from their partners, white men, slave patrols, and the police. Mental illness cannot explain this away, especially since disabled people are much more likely to be victims and survivors of violence than others who cause it. The society is violent.

This does not have to be the case. We could have a society where Deborah Danner's family and workplace trust and accept her like her church and therapist, and she could share as much or as little about her health without risking being fired. In that society, Eleanor Bumpurs would not have to live in the projects because there would not be any projects, but different kinds of quality housing options where she could choose to live. In 1984, the minimum wage was three dollars and thirty-five cents. That means that she would have sold an hour of her labor and time for less than five dollars and still been poor, regardless of how hard she worked. Instead, Eleanor could have received a guaranteed basic income and could have chosen labor that was not painful and that she enjoyed, rather than a job she was relegated to perform because she was poor. Anyone who lived in apartment buildings as she did would not have cops show up to enforce evictions when tenants complain about repairs. Instead, cities would regularly send weekly cleaning and maintenance crews into apartments and neighborhoods.[289]

In that society, Sandra Bland might be here still, too. When she told the police officer who stopped her that she had epilepsy, he replied, "Good." Bland should not have had to endure racism, sexism, and ableism from that cop and could have started the new job at the HBCU that she was driving toward. Korryn Gaines would no longer have problems with white supremacy and police violence, which we must continue to eradicate. Without racism and viral police shootings, I wonder if her social media would have continued to show her babies, her bright lip colors, her striped outfits.

I MET DUSTIN GIBSON in January 2020 at the same abolition convening where I had met Ejeris Dixon. We were in a few small group sessions together. I realized that he was a member of the Harriet Tubman Collective and had submitted the critique of M4BL when I was the editor-in-chief of the Harvard journal years earlier. Dustin told me that he grew up in Southwest Wyoming and had family who lived in a small Missouri town called Kinloch. Decades ago, white homeowners in Ferguson had set up a mini municipal apartheid wall to prevent Black residents from Kinloch from coming over. Kinloch was originally a commuter town for white business owners and politicians. They let Black servants live on a separate plot of land nearby and this became Missouri's first Black town. Kinloch had a thriving social, civic, and political community until white people nearby prohibited its expansion and sold off homes to a developer for an airport runway that never happened. My aunt's home on Dade in Ferguson bordered Kinloch. I'd look from the back seat on the drive there and see grass grow taller than the car. Apartment buildings had tenants, gates, and gaping square holes that windows should have filled. All of those memories rushed back when Dustin said Kinloch. Due to racial zoning and segregation, it had become one of the poorest suburbs in North County.

Dustin moved around after several evictions and a year spent living out of his truck. He moved to Pennsylvania, secured jobs at Goodwill and Staples, and started volunteering at the Center for Independent Living, a community-based, cross-disability, nonresidential private nonprofit agency that is designed and operated within a local community by individuals with disabilities. The Ferguson Uprising happened while he was volunteering. His family was still in North County so the protests took place near their homes.

Dustin told me that Michael Brown's death and the subsequent activism surrounding it made him start paying attention to disability, policing, and incarceration. He explained that after the Uprising, police shot two people whom he worked with at the Center in Pennsylvania; both men had been diagnosed with schizophrenia. The first one lived and is now a wheelchair user. Dustin was conscious of disability, but not as a consequence of police violence. Community members organized around this particular shooting, which occurred after several high-profile acts of police violence in Pittsburgh, including Johnny Gammage. Following the aftermath of the protests for Rodney King, Congress authorized the Department of Justice to sue local and state agencies over patterns and practices of discrimination. These lawsuits often become settlements called consent decrees, like the one in Ferguson. The very first consent decree was with the Pittsburgh Police Department after local cops killed Gammage, a Black man they pulled over because he was driving a Jaguar. The autopsy listed homicide by asphyxia due to the stop of airflow to his chest and neck. His last words were, "I'm thirty-one." According to Dustin, Gammage's death in 1995 and the police beating of Black high school student Jordan Miles in 2010 had laid the foundation for subsequent protests that he joined.[290]

The second person from the Center in Pennsylvania, Bruce Kelley, Jr. did not live. Dustin said that in January 2016, Kelley and his father were drinking beers at a public gazebo a few blocks away from the Center when the police approached them. Kelley resisted an officer when she tried to arrest him. He then went for a walk away from the neighborhood for twenty minutes. Per Dustin, when police from three different departments found him, ten cops surrounded him and used pepper spray and batons, and tased him five times. They threatened to send a K-9 dog to bite and retrieve him. Kelley threatened to stab the dog in self-defense if it attacked him. Police sent the dog to attack him and shot Kelley several times in the back when he began to stab it. The kill shot was in the back of his head. Like Michael Brown, Dustin said Kelley's body was left in the street for hours, uncovered, and police had to direct traffic around it, including a school bus. Cops took Kelley's father to jail on charges, most of which they dropped—but did not release him for his son's funeral. The police department had a grand televised funeral procession for the canine.[291]

The murder angered and devastated Dustin. He said that the police who killed Kelley were trained for encounters like those and failed miserably. Or so he thought. He had originally accepted the recommendations of President Obama's Task Force on Twenty-First Century Policing for more police crisis intervention training. He believed that raising awareness in police departments could be a solution to stop the violence from the police at the time. But in this case, Dustin emphasized that the police who killed Kelley were aware of his psychiatric disabilities, but he still tried to work within the confines of the criminal legal system for change.

When Dustin went to St. Louis in the aftermath of the Ferguson protests, he joined other organizers to arrange for community members to meet police officers to put an end to the violence. He assisted with a crisis intervention training at the police academy. He was not particularly enthusiastic about accepting these training reforms wholeheartedly, but they were *a* solution, which was seemingly better than no solution. I felt deep resonance when he said that he thought fixing the police was a solution to violence—until the *trained* police kept killing people. His friends. People who lived in Pennsylvania. Strangers. He started organizing with other disabled activists, studying abolition for political education, and working full-time to end the institutionalization of disabled people, particular in nursing facilities, prisons, and jails. He realized that the police could only exacerbate crises that his community experienced: "I mean, I'm talking about twenty-six year olds that's like, 'Yo, I have diabetes. I'm sleeping in my car. And my girl just kicked me out and I'm about to drive to Florida so I'll have somewhere warm to stay. And my foot is swollen because I can't store my insulin anywhere.' So it's like those types of situations. And then I see, like, just the way in which like the legal system has been a part of perpetuating that."[292]

When I spoke to Dustin again, I watched him fill with stories of people he loved and lost. Samuel was one. He was a "sixty-something"-year-old Black man. "What do you call the shed in the graveyard?" Dustin asked me. "He was living there. He was living in the basement of the groundskeeper in the cemetery." Samuel was in a state waiver program: he had personal care attendant services to assist with daily activities, but he didn't have support for the hours that he actually needed. Dustin explained that the lack of investments in these types of "home and community based services" is one of the main reasons people are forced into institutions. He tried to assist Samuel with moving into a house through a program. They could not start the application over the phone and needed to find transportation to complete the paperwork. Three months after Samuel submitted it, the police arrested him for having heroin. Samuel had cancer and was in constant pain. The program would not let him move into the house without going to court. He was too sick to make the court date. He died a few months later, inside the cemetery. Dustin could not find any of Samuel's family and had to claim the body himself for burial.

By the time we met in person, Dustin said that he was one thousand percent abolitionist. Geographer and political theorist Ruth Wilson Gilmore's concept of abolition as presence rather than absence influenced him to think about dismantling the institutions of police and prisons while also building the world that we want. Specifically, he'd already accepted abolition of asylums and nursing facilities through his work and organizing, and he'd began making the same connections about police and prisons. He was concerned that abolitionists often missed the need to abolish institutionalizing practices, which can be as or more carceral than police and prisons. We can accomplish this, too.[293]

Dustin made sure to say that much of what we need is already here. He believes that care for disabled people should be free, and that caregivers should be compensated fairly. By care, he meant that people in our communities should learn how to get somebody out of bed, organize groceries, set schedules, and whatever other daily activities people need for survival. He believes that those who want to receive care should learn independence from people in their peer group as much as possible, and I would add that for me, this is what it means to be a custodian of one's body and mind. Dustin meant independence that is connected to one's self-determination, so they can learn how to use the phone, catch a bus, drive, ski, cook, whatever they would like to do. I thought about Rachel Herzing because she often discusses how abolitionists should practice building skills for their own survival and thriving. Dustin was echoing a similar sentiment, noting that when we discuss abolition, it's largely to imagine different societies and systems. But he wanted to emphasize that we all have to imagine and become different kinds of people, too.

I told Dustin that I completely understood. My grandmother went into an elderly facility when I was fifteen and she was sixty-eight. She had two strokes and her lung collapsed. The facility that she went to did not assist her properly to regain strength and she became a wheelchair user. Nobody in our family had space or resources to take care of her. In St. Louis and other cities, Black and Latinx women overwhelmingly perform care work and are grossly underpaid, if at all. Working class women and migrants often do this labor for free in their families. Inside the facility, my grandmother became blind and was diagnosed with breast cancer. Dustin laughed when I told him that that did not stop her from having boyfriends that she would sneak off with inside. "Really, Grandma?" I said after the facility called and said she had temporarily gone missing. "Child, I am grown!" she cackled back.

Dustin, Kerima Çevik, Mary Bumpurs, Deborah Danner, and others demonstrate what is possible with disability justice and abolitionist frameworks. They have called for independence, acceptance, love, solidarity, and trust with and among disabled individuals of all backgrounds. Proactive planning, independence and self-determination, and community-based care work can meet the unique needs of everyone's body, mind, and spirit. I agree with Dustin that we already practice much of it. We must share best practices, skills, and resources between individuals, families, friends, and communities to strengthen this support. Housing crises, gentrification, and residential displacement can disrupt close-knit blocks and neighborhoods. Tenant groups, homeowners, and block associations must oppose these when possible and attempt even harder to keep the community close through organizing, accessible events, and mutual aid.

Disability justice activists and the families of police violence victims have also organized moratoriums on evictions, and demanded an end to police violence, and housing and voluntary treatment for people who need it. Scholars must conduct research in furtherance of these demands and stop trying to improve relationships between cops and the people whom they surveil. They can start by examining the nature of 911 calls to help shift resources to accomplish the goals of disability justice organizers. More than two hundred million calls occur each year—for everything. Suspicious activity. Bad food. Heart attacks.

Loud music. The data could offer specific, foundational understanding on why people think that they need police, and help communities get to the bottom of their problems without cops. More urgently, the data could show why people rely on the police for themselves or others during a mental crisis. Community-based organizations can do this through door-knocking campaigns and surveys to inform concrete responses or alternatives to real and perceived harm.[294]

Critical Resistance's "Oakland Power Projects" (OPP) does a version of this by building the capacity for "Oakland residents to reject police and policing as the default response to harm and to highlight or create alternatives that actually work by identifying current harms, amplifying existing resources, and developing new practices that do not rely on policing solutions." I spoke with a former OPP organizer, Onyinye Alheri, who was in an early training cohort. She said that OPP interviews residents for their "Know Your Options" workshops. Early cohorts primarily consisted of residents, doctors, nurses, paramedics, therapists and other health-care workers who wanted to be responsive in emergencies without calling the police. Trainers conducted the sessions on different issue areas through an abolitionist framework, including behavioral health crises, acute emergencies, and opioid overdose prevention. Critical Resistance provided medical kits and compiled emergency and preventative resources for the participants based on the interviews. The members of the cohort were trained sufficiently to replicate the training in their organizations. OPP helped participants develop concrete responses to different scenarios to eliminate contact with police and reduce the potential for violence. Onyinye joined Critical Resistance after she completed OPP and helped update the curriculum to make it widely accessible. Utilizing the train-the-trainer model, Critical Resistance and OPP health-care worker cohorts have offered over fifty "Know Your Options" workshops in Northern California.[295]

As individuals and communities are building preventative and emergency responses, cities must also stop dispatching cops to people in mental distress, especially since the police use the word "crisis" to escalate their violence. For more than three decades, the Crisis Assistance Helping Out on the Streets (CAHOOTS) program in Eugene, Oregon, has handled nearly 20 percent of the city's 911 calls without police. CAHOOTS is staffed by a local clinic and dispatches unarmed, non–law enforcement medics and crisis workers for mental health-related crises, including conflict resolution, welfare checks, substance abuse, suicide threats, and more, relying on trauma-informed de-escalation and harm-reduction techniques. More than 60 percent of CAHOOTS's clients are homeless, and "30% live with severe and persistent mental illness (SPMI)." In 2019, they responded to twenty-four thousand calls and called for police backup 150 times—less than 1 percent of the time. Other cities are following Eugene's lead, cities as large as San Francisco and Los Angeles. While these programs can be a step toward reducing our reliance on police, they are not necessarily abolitionist. The cities that have these alternatives will still use cops for evictions or to respond to theft, sexual violence, etc. Which is why it is especially important to undermine the conditions that give rise to violence and displacement in the first place.[296]

Additionally, if we want to reduce and eliminate ableism and disabling injuries, then we have to reduce and eliminate police. Media and police dismissed Korryn Gaines for calling the police "kidnappers," but cops have a long history of kidnapping Black, brown, Muslim, and poor people for detention and torture. In Baltimore, police conduct life-altering "rough rides" to intimidate and injure the people they arrest. In 1997, four NYPD officers violently cracked Abner Louima's teeth and sodomized him with a broomstick. Louima had to undergo several intestinal surgeries. A decade later he was still having issues from his previously perforated bladder, and pain from the horrific memories. Louima received $8.75 million, the largest payout for a police brutality case at the time. He used the money to open hospitals and fund educational opportunities in his homeland, Haiti. Between 1972 and 1991, Chicago Police Department commander Jon Burge allegedly led a torture ring against Black Chicagoans, using "racial epithets, electric shock, suffocation, and brutal beatings." The Chicago Torture Justice Center offers healing resources to the Chicago Police Department victims and their families who suffered physical and psychological torture. The center was founded as a result of the organizing efforts of We Charge Genocide, a coalition of activists who won financial reparations and free tuition as a result of the campaign. Middle-school students across the city will also learn the history of this torture and the campaigns to stop it. Aislinn Pulley, the center's director, emphatically says that the police torture justice center that she runs should not be the only one in the United States, and not even the only one in Chicago: "We know that Burge was not the first police officer to use torture techniques and he's not the last." We need local communities to fight to ensure the collective memories of the policing behavior and serve as a resource for healing, justice, and reparations.[297]

Torture, policing, prisons, capitalism, and colonialism attempt to control and suppress the lives that we desire. Lives full of care, curiosity, reflection, intimacy. When Audre Lorde returned home after receiving breast cancer treatments, she wrote, "At home I wept and wept and wept, finally. And made love to myself, endlessly and repetitively, until it was no longer tentative. Where were the dykes who had had mastectomies? I wanted to talk to a lesbian, to sit down and start from a common language, no matter how diverse." She credits the love and care of women for keeping her alive for as long as she lived. Even women she did not know and sometimes women she did not like. The support and self-determination reminds me of Deborah Danner.[298]

We seek and forge these communities of care and struggle, and can provide them for others, too. These communities will be especially important to prepare for and politically resist what's ahead. As Sins Invalid explains, "Each day the planet experiences human-provoked mudslides, storms, fires, devolving air quality, rising sea levels, new regions experiencing freezing or sweltering temperatures, earth-quakes, species loss and more, all provoked by greed-driven, human-made climate chaos. Our communities are often treated as disposable, especially within the current economic, political and environmental landscape." Without resistance and organizing, the destruction of the planet will have catastrophic consequences on all of our bodies, minds, and souls. And the police help facilitate the destruction of the Earth by advancing and facilitating the torture, displacement, ableism, and death that makes it easier for companies to make a profit from our commu-nities. We must not let them.[299]

EIGHT

"WE ONLY WANT THE EARTH"

CLIMATE CATASTROPHE SCARED me. Phrase and phenomenon. A mere mention of global warming could fill my throat with pebbles and palms with sweat beads like when I first learned about hell in the church basement near Lafayette Park during Sunday school as a kid. But hell felt better. It was in a speculative afterlife, and if it was a real place, God would not send me there as long as I confessed with my mouth and believed in my heart that Jesus died for my sins and was raised from the dead. If it was not real, then I would live a chaste life and die a decent person. By my early twenties, I realized that I could become a better Christian if I forfeited the idea of hell and heaven. I was no longer comforted by the belief that we had to endure suffering until we cross over into the afterlife; I wanted to end suffering now. My urgency increased to learn how. This required me to understand the physical world around me, including climate change. Unlike hell, it was not a matter of my faith or fear. I could not will it away nor repent. God could not save me from it.

Rising temperatures would invite violence to our doorsteps. I knew this before learning anything about abolition or the changing Earth. My grandmother had taught me. In St. Louis, she shared a grayish-brown concrete apartment porch with Ms. Yvonne, her neighbor to the west. The 90s and early 2000s were filled with their quiet feuds. For Thanksgiving, my grandmother displayed

"Happy Fall!" on her windows and Ms. Yvonne put brown and orange turkey cutouts on hers. When Ms. Yvonne wrapped green Christmas lights around the peeling black steel bannisters, my grandmother wrapped red ones on her side. Fourth of July was the worst. Ms. Yvonne put countless tiny flags in corners on each stair. My grandmother would answer by alternating red, white, and blue plastic table weights with shredded ends from the Dollar Store. Mail carriers and Jehovah's Witnesses feared the wrath of these women and carefully avoided knocking any decorations over on the way up. But they were allied for our safety. My grandmother would sit outside, opposite Ms. Yvonne, and say, "It's getting hotter and hotter outside. Y'all better be careful." Ms. Yvonne would rock and nod in agreement.

After warning me for so many years, she didn't have to explain anymore. Summer meant Black joy, pleasure, stress, and death. Gunshots and heat strokes alongside games like freeze tag and kickball. The ice-cream trucks sold fruity "bomb pops" and played "The Entertainer," the famous ragtime number that Scott Joplin composed in St. Louis. We chased lightning bugs whose neon bulbs lit the dusk sky and the insides of our hands. I rarely see them now. Our apartments had central air conditioning but we couldn't use it because we could barely afford the electricity bills. If we dared to reenter the house when the AC was on, we forfeited going outside again that day. So, everyone opened the windows and went outside to stay cool instead. On the hottest days, kids would play with water hoses and even fire hydrants if we were lucky. Union Electric Company completely cut down several of my favorite shady trees because the branches interfered with the electricity poles. I thought it was wrong because the trees were there first and that the electricity poles were interfering with the trees. Years later I discovered that the tree cuttings, shootings, strokes, high bills, and disappearance of lightning bugs were something new under the sun. The planet was burning.

To warn each other when cops were nearby, we'd say, "the block is hot." Our block had literally become hotter, which lead to violence, including by police. It was cyclical. Racial capitalism relegated Black people to poor, overcrowded housing. We would go outside for space, air, and ironically, privacy. Police patrolled our relief using laws against loitering, trespass, and idleness. So back into the house we'd go until we needed temporary relief again. If the block continues to get hot, it might be even worse. By one prediction in David Wallace-Wells's *The Uninhabitable Earth*, "climate change in the United States would bring about an additional 22,000 murders, 180,000 rapes, 3.5 million assaults, and 3.76 million robberies, burglaries, and acts of larceny." Federal and local governments will consequently increase budgets for police and prisons to respond. Yet the problem will continue because cops will not and cannot stop the underlying causes of these waves of violence caused by the flood of corporate, state, and human pollution that warms the Earth and poisons us.[300]

Heat bakes industrial chemicals and metals into our soil, water, plants, and animals. Paint on our homes and playgrounds peel and expose us to toxins that make us sick with preventable illnesses. Coastlines are swallowing islands due to melting ice caps and oceans fill with waste from crude oil and cruise lines. Rather than protecting us, laws will continue to protect the rights of companies to destroy the Earth for profit; cops will be the first responders to arrest activists who protest the destruction, detain displaced people seeking refuge, and jail homeless people who can no longer live in their homes because of climate gentrifiers— coastal people who replicate their neighborhoods in inland communities by displacing locals. Fighting for abolitionist futures means that we have to undermine climate change and environmental degradation, and resist policing and militarism as solutions to these problems.

CLIMATES—WHETHER RACIAL, ECONOMIC, or environmental—have forced migration within US history. All three shaped how my grandmother Virginia landed in St. Louis. My great-grandparents and grandmother were one family among the six million Black people who moved from the South to the North, Midwest, and West between 1916 and 1970. Virginia's mother, Rosie, my great-grandmother, was born in 1918 in Arkansas, five years after Harriet Tubman died and two years before white women gained the right to vote. In 1936, at seventeen, she became pregnant with my grandmother and gave birth in Memphis, Tennessee. This era was marked by Jim Crow, Juan Crow, and Jane Crow—laws that legalized racial and gender segregation throughout the US. Police enforced these laws with the help of white residents, students, and business owners. Even celebratory functions remained segregated. Memphis still held onto cotton as a major crop in the 1930s, so much so that residents tried to revive the economy through a whites-only Cotton Carnival. Black people responded with their own version, Cotton Maker's Jubilee. Neither was enough to stimulate the economy and unemployment rose significantly around the time of my grandmother's birth.

My family left to find work and flee white supremacy. They found labor in the factories above the Mason-Dixon line where they worked until companies decided to move their operations overseas to more easily exploit Black and brown workers in other countries. Jobs decreased and policing increased. Economist Ellora Derenoncourt found that cities with the largest flow of Black migrants began increasing in the 1940s and continued for decades: compared to cities with fewer Black migrants, local governments in Great Migration cities spent a larger share of public expenditures on police, increased the number of cops, and increased incarceration rates. They did not increase public services such as fire-fighting, education, income-based programs, or jobs programs. Derenoncourt explains that these political and economic spending decisions under the Great Migration contributes to a 43 percent of the "upward mobility gap between black and white men in the region today." Migration was not the problem; it was the local government's response.[301]

Police violence had also been catastrophic to poor, white people. During the Great Migration, governments used cops to stop the mass migration of exploited white people fleeing environmental disaster and climate change. The dust bowls were one example. I have no idea how my great-grandmother Rosie survived being pregnant with my grandmother Virginia during the summer of 1936, which delivered some of the most severe temperatures in modern history and one of the deadliest ecological disasters in North America. Between June, July, and August, Tennessee had forty-six days of temperatures at least at one hundred degrees, much higher than normal. By comparison, Florida, a much more southern state, only had five such days. That summer, five thousand people across the country died due to a heat wave brought on by the dust bowls.[302]

Dust bowl scenes mimicked Old Testament plagues. Men in cities cornered and clubbed to death hundreds of thousands of rabbits. Thousands of grasshoppers would swarm crops at a time. The government bought cattle from farmers as economic relief but killed half of them because they could not be consumed by people. This heat wave was not simply a natural disaster, but a consequence of settler colonialism. According to meteorologist and climate specialist Jeff Berardelli, the federal government gifted or cheaply sold land to entice settlers to the Midwest. The settlers destroyed the deeply rooted native grasslands by setting up wheat and cattle farms to meet the demand for meat and bread. During droughts, the native grasslands usually maintained enough moisture to offset the heat in the summer. Settlers disrupted this environmental chain by harmful farming practices and the Great Plains suffered when droughts hit during the 1930s because winds removed millions of tons of topsoil that had been covered by the grasslands. Thousands of people died from "dust pneumonia," heat strokes, and more.[303]

Millions of people fled west to escape death and destruction. California criminalized poverty by passing state laws that banned people from entering who were poor and punished anyone living in California who tried to help climate migrants cross. Officials directed police and prosecutors to threaten and arrest migrants and their supporters. Police did what police do. *LA Times* journalist Cecilia Rasmussen reported, "For a few months in 1936, the Los Angeles Police Department launched a foreign excursion of sorts—a 'Bum Blockade' on the state's borders. The LAPD deployed 136 officers to 16 major points of entry on the Arizona, Nevada and Oregon lines, with orders to turn back migrants with 'no visible means of support.'" Some people paid the police everything they had to be let in. Thousands were denied entry. Police caught people on commercial trains and told them to either leave California or labor in the workhouse for six months. The American Civil Liberties Union sued Los Angeles to stop the police and the city complied. A decade later, the United States Supreme Court ruled in *Edwards v. California* that states could not ban citizens from entering on the basis of poverty. Once again, these were not refugees fleeing Latin America, Asia, or Africa, but poor, white US citizens who California fought for the right to banish.[304]

The millions of people who experienced police violence and discrimination during the "Bum Blockade" and beyond were internally displaced people, a category of climate migrants who are forced to move about inside a nation's borders due to environmental events (as compared to refugees who normally move across borders, and stateless people, who are excluded from nation states altogether). Dust bowls were the catastrophic event, and police were used as a solution to address the migration, even though arrests and detentions do not solve climate crisis nor cool the planet.

Not only have the catastrophic climate events continued, they've become worse over the course of my grandmother's lifetime. The United Nations reports: "Hazards resulting from the increasing intensity and frequency of extreme weather events, such as abnormally heavy rainfall, prolonged droughts, desertification, environmental degradation, or sea-level rise and cyclones are already causing an average of more than 20 million people to leave their homes and move to other areas in their countries each year." Without concrete climate interventions, the World Bank estimates that more than 143 million people will become internally displaced by 2050 in the three regions most exploited by western imperialism: Sub-Saharan South Africa, South Asia, and Latin America. This mass movement will shape public policy, conflict, militarism, and policing to control the flow of people, just as there had been during the Great Migration and the dust bowls.[305]

Organizing for abolition alongside climate justice is imperative because policing and carceral responses will continue to manage internally displaced people, especially Black people, Indigenous people, and people of color who are constantly displaced from colonialism, capitalism, and climate change. As in California during the dust bowls, in the US during the Latin American migrant caravans, and in Europe during the drought and migrant crisis in Syria, political leaders will discuss migration as a drain on a nation's resources. This scares the public over scarcity and leads to hostility, violence, and arrests toward people seeking help. Yet the actual resource problem is that governments permit and encourage companies to build massive wealth by exploiting the Earth's finite resources, and then permits them to use the profits to hoard food, land, and even time.

Many Black people have already been relegated to live near places that are especially susceptible to floods, droughts, and environmental toxins. Increasingly, pollution from humans and companies heats the planet, which melts polar ice caps and raise sea levels that encroach on native coastal communities who rely on the land for their livelihood. Low-income Black and Latinx people are more likely to live in neighborhoods prone to flooding following storms, as compared to white and Asian people. Atmospheric scientist Dr. J. Marshall Shepherd cautions that southern Black and rural residents might be more vulnerable to storms and tornadoes because they have fewer radars in their region to track the weather; in the west, these gaps disproportionately impact people who are Latinx and Indigenous. Our most marginalized groups will lose acres upon acres of land because of corporate greed, and they will not be able to call the police to stop this massive theft.[306]

Growing up in the Midwest, I was used to tornado drills as a child. At school, we'd rush into the hallways and those who could kneeled on the floor with our hands covering our heads. At home, we'd run into the basement in case a twister toppled a tree on our apartment. In 2011, I had to recall all of these safety measures while attending a summer leadership program for women interested in public policy and politics. We had a special lunch at the governor's mansion in the state capitol, Jefferson City, and his wife sat at a table across from mine. A host welcomed us and introduced the dozens of men wearing sharp tuxedos who would be serving our food and cleaning our tables. They were in prison. Since 1871, Missouri prisoners have worked for the governors' families by providing laundry, cleaning, catering, and whatever the job demands. The women in the room clapped and remarked on how well-mannered the men were; I could not help but to think how enslaved these men were. I'm sure the time out of prison may have been a break or even something they looked forward to, but the exploitation of their labor was worse than the optics of so many Black men "serving" tables full of upwardly mobile white women.

Then, the tornado warning came. At moment's notice, the governor's wife was rushed away by security and our leadership academy was rushed to the basement. Just a couple of days before, one of the deadliest and most financially damaging tornadoes had just hit nearby Joplin, Missouri. Thousands of homes and businesses were flattened. By the time we were in the basement, we were still under a state of emergency from the devastation. President Obama did the commencement speech at the high school graduation the following year to commemorate the devastation and triumph in the community. We left the basement without any incident that time around.

After Joplin's tornado, the governor, local leaders, and the president repeatedly assured us that "we are all in this together." In spirit, this is mostly true. Donations, volunteers, and gifts pour in from across the country to ensure that people who have lost everything will at least have some relief. Yet disaster recovery is disproportionate; it mimics the inequality that capitalism creates. Researchers have found that "the more natural hazard damages accrue in a county, the more wealth white residents tend to accumulate, all else equal. Blacks, on the other hand, tend to lose wealth as local hazard damages increase." White disaster survivors in places like Joplin, where the population is nearly 85 percent white, accumulate more wealth than Black disaster survivors, *and* even more wealth. Increased wealth for white people could increase access to relief such as housing, school, health care, and clean air; and decreased wealth for Black people following disastrous storms could equate to precarious living arrangements, employment, and health outcomes. The disproportionate financial outcomes have carceral consequences: the precarious lives and downward mobility of internally displaced Black migrants increase their contact with cops during times of survival.[307]

In addition to dust storms and tornadoes, preventable fires create internally displaced migrants in the US. By the time my grandmother was eight years old, the federal government had created one of the most recognizable advertisement campaigns in the US: Smokey Bear. *Only You Can Prevent Forest Fires!* I remember the soft brown bear with the judgmental finger from my youth, too. Like deserts, swamps, and oceans, forest fires only existed on television for me, my mom, and my grandmother living in the Midwest. Still, even I felt an obligation. Sociologist Kari Marie Norgaard explains that the campaign was used to deter fires and as propaganda to protect capitalists who wanted to cut down acres upon acres of timber to sell. Trees provide shade and absorb carbon dioxide to keep the planet cool, the losing trees to corporations warms the planet. Fires threatened their business, and their business of cutting down trees caused more fires. So, Smokey Bear was a sort of colonization campaign to discourage Indigenous peoples from setting fires to the land where trees could be sold for profit. Since 1850, California had banned ritualistic and cultural burnings of forest land by tribes. Before these burnings were criminalized, tribes had set small intentional fires to clear decaying parts of the forests that were likely to catch fire later in dry seasons. These burnings controlled fires and decreased the kind of wild raging fires that now occur every year on the West Coast. Corporations and the state helped destroy the forests and threatened Indigenous peoples with arrest and jail for trying to save it. More than twelve thousand years of native land management systems and environmental flourishing nearly all went up in flames.[308]

I did not know this history until I read a 2017 *New York Times* article about California's prison labor problem. In February of that year, the state paid four thousand prisoners less than two dollars an hour to extinguish wildfires. Then state attorney general Kamala Harris's office opposed the early release of prisoners due to overcrowding because it "would severely impact fire camp participation—a dangerous outcome while California is in the middle of a difficult fire season and severe drought." When Harris herself found out about the argument, she told the lawyers in her office to stop using it to oppose the release, but not to oppose the release itself. The argument was cruel, but not as cruel as creating other politically palatable arguments to keep people locked inside, especially when prisons were already 200 percent beyond capacity.[309]

So first, California created a problem by outlawing an Indigenous tradition to save forests. California and the federal government exacerbated their own problem by permitting companies to cut down millions of trees that contributed to fires. Then, instead of solving the underlying problems of deforestation and capitalism, California responded by putting a cute bear on television and capitalizing on its exploding prison population to force laborers to handle the fires. The failure of state and federal fire suppression only started forcing officials to decolonize their land-management practices and decriminalize some intentional burnings in 2019. Yet as of this writing, organizers are still demanding that California stops using prison labor for firefighting.[310]

Hurricane Katrina's climate migrants were policed and incarcerated, a sharp contrast from the "we're all in this together" that I witnessed later for Joplin. When I reported on Hurricane Katrina as a high school student in JROTC, it was called a "natural disaster." The major story then was that the government had built insufficient levees to stop the flood. It would be almost fifteen years before I learned from scientists that the hurricane's impact was also a consequence of climate change and environmental degradation: burning fossil fuels and heating the planet melted ice caps and dramatically raised sea levels. When French settler colonists landed in Louisiana, they destroyed wetlands that absorbed and prevented flooding. Oil companies further destroyed the gulf and engineers built on top of disappearing native land, which sank half of New Orleans below sea level. The combination of colonialism and capitalism leads to increased sea levels, extra water for high winds to carry, more flooding into Black neighborhoods that were already prone to flooding, and fewer wetlands to stop it.[311]

Five days into the disaster, the state built a makeshift jail as "a real start to re-building" New Orleans. Police primarily arrested people for looting. The warden of the jail remarked: "They might spit on you. They might have AIDS . . . a looter to me is no different than a grave robber." For six weeks, police managed the crisis by arresting people and accusing them of car theft, curfew violations, and public intoxication. Some people saved themselves from the flooding jail cells and escaped. Police caught others and turned them back. Organizers responded, too. Even though Katrina had destroyed Critical Resistance's Southern regional office, they still organized and demanded amnesty for more than a thousand people who had been arrested in the first six weeks after the storm. CR reported that thousands of prisoners were either left in their cells to drown or sent to thirty-five prisons across the country. CR demanded amnesty in hopes that "no one should be arrested, charged, tried, sentenced, fined, imprisoned, jailed, detained, involuntarily relocated, or deported." In addition to amnesty, CR had three other demands: they challenged the use of the prison industrial complex in the disaster, while structural disasters such as racism and poverty continue to be ignored; they challenged the imprisonment of people whose cases had been impacted by Katrina; and they publicized the dangers of rebuilding New Orleans on top of jails and military-occupied streets.[312]

Lawyers also resisted the simultaneous environmental devastation and police violence in New Orleans. I listened to Colette Pichon Battle speak at a Law for Black Lives conference in 2015 at Riverside Church. She was a DC corporate lawyer who went to Louisiana, where she was from, to volunteer in the aftermath of the hurricane for a few weeks. She eventually quit her job and became a climate activist. Battle demanded pay for the capitalist ventures that destroyed the earth, pay for the Black people whom the New Orleans Police Department killed, and pay from the Jefferson Parish Sheriff's Office, which, "in the middle of the storm, [as] people literally tried to leave the city [to] get away from the water that was slowly rising," had deployed "armed sheriffs on the bridge of the

Crescent City connection telling people that they could not get out, and [they] sen[t] them back into Orleans Parish." She concluded her speech by demanding federal recognition for the United Houma Nation, an Indigenous tribe in Louisiana. The government, she explained, does not recognize them because the tribe is entitled to land full of oil and natural gas. Her "rad talk" made all the connections at the intersection of abolition, anti-capitalism, decolonization, and racial justice.[313]

WHEN POLICE MAKE arrests in the wake of environmental and climate destruction, they put people in jails and prisons that are also sites of environmental devastation and climate violence. In 2018, I met organizer Jordan Mazurek from the Campaign to Fight Toxic Prisons (FTP), a collective that uses grassroots organizing, advocacy, and direct action to challenge the prison system on the grounds of environmental justice and earth liberation. We were speakers at a Students for Prison Education and Reform (SPEAR) at Princeton. At the FTP session, Jordan called a currently incarcerated member of the campaign, Bryant Arroyo, to discuss their joint organizing efforts at SCI-Mahanoy in Pennsylvania. Arroyo, whom Mumia Abu-Jamal has called the first "jailhouse environmentalist," spoke of the toxins surrounding the building full of cages and flowing through the water at the prison. Jordan echoed this point, explaining that governments build prisons near and on top of hazardous waste sites because the land is cheap to buy. People who are detained in toxic jails and prisons risk diseases, cancers, and death as a consequence and often guaranteed outcome of their confinement. And remarkably, Bryant had led a campaign from behind bars that successfully stopped the construction of a coal and liquid gas refinery adjacent to the prison.

Unlike free-world climate migrants who can attempt to leave dangerous conditions, incarcerated people obviously face considerable obstacles and punishment if they attempt to make demands, and especially if they attempt to leave prison. So instead, many of them organize against the conditions inside alongside campaigns while Fight Toxic Prisons organize on the outside to close carceral facilities and to prevent new ones from opening. As the FTP Collective puts it, "Every prison is toxic. Whether environmentally toxic to the people inside it and the land on which the prison is built, or socially toxic to our communities deemed disposable by capitalism, white supremacy, and settler colonialism and thus targeted by the criminal punishment system."[314]

It was only three months later that I understood the context for rising water during my work trips to Puerto Rico. I had not viewed the island as, in effect, a modern-day colony until the year before, when I visited Martinique. My Airbnb host had explained that the small French island is a colony where the Black inhabitants work and the white French party. I felt this as soon as I headed to the beach. The restaurant staff were always Black. The customers, except for me and my friend Christina, were usually white. Our host said that some of the local Black people took pride in having French passports, even if it meant not having local democracy or self-determination. Not her. She seemed indifferent to French patriotism and was more saddened that highly educated Black Martiniquans, like her son, left for France, only to find menial work. "The mediocre white French come here and thrive, unfortunately." And that's when I realized that Puerto Rico was not a US territory, but rather a colony where the people, land, and resources were drained. "Territory" sounds more neutral than "colony." Guam, US Virgin Islands—not territories. But colonies.

I asked AP if Puerto Rico could become one of my work sites because I wanted to support organizers on the island and learn more about policing in the current colonial context. Puerto Rico has several law enforcement agencies with overlapping jurisdictions. The Puerto Rico Police Department (PRPD) is the island's main local law enforcement agency and operates as a state or national police force. In 2011, PRPD had approximately seventeen thousand police officers, which made it the second-largest force after the New York Police Department. Today, the department has plummeted to a figure that hovers around twelve thousand. The police have historically repressed activism with tear gas, beatings, and assassinations. AP agreed. I stayed at a very cute, small beachfront hotel and fell asleep to the sound of waves softly thumping against my room. When I woke up, I opened the shutters to search for the sun. Outside, to the left of my window, a concrete staircase led right into the ocean. *Why would they build stairs that drop so suddenly?* My coworker Ricardo laughed sadly when I expressed confusion about the mystery steps. He said that the stairs used to lead to a wide, sandy beach. Now, that land was completely under water. In an essay about resisting police violence and climate catastrophe, teenage activist Isabel Valentín wrote, "Though no one ever said it, there was an unspoken understanding of what happens to small bodies of land surrounded by water when water levels rise too much. And when that body of land is inhabited by people of color like me, the situation is even more precarious for the archipelago's inhabitants." The Atlantic was drowning the hotel.[315]

Two hurricanes devastated the island before I went. Hurricane Irma technically missed, yet the winds still left more than a third of the island without power. Hurricane Maria landed. The death toll is underreported at more than three thousand lives. Puerto Rico received a quarter of its annual rainfall in one day. This rain triggered floods, mudslides, and contamination of the drinking water. Scientists found that the hurricane produced the "single largest maximum rainfall event since 1956," and that global warming changed the water and air temperatures to produce the hurricane. More than two hundred thousand people fled the island and will not likely return. What I found especially tragic is that the island's colonial status forces the local government to rely on US-based fossil fuel companies that are responsible for global warming. Naomi Klein writes that the "island gets an astonishing 98 percent of its electricity from fossil fuels. But since it has no domestic supply of oil, gas, or coal, all of these fuels are imported by ship . . . The whole behemoth is monstrously expensive, resulting in electricity prices that are nearly twice the US average."

During Maria, islanders lost power. Puerto Rico and the federal government relied on the police department to work overtime in the aftermath to attempt to quell the violence that occurred in the dark, but due to pay constraints, many cops refused. Normally, about five hundred cops call in sick every day on the island. After Maria, it had risen to almost three thousand cops every day. They did "sick-in" protests because the governments did not pay them for overtime to stop crime, primarily theft of generators and other resources for survival. Rather than spending the money on generators for the people, the governor of Puerto Rico paid tens of millions of dollars to compensate police for their labor.[316]

In the aftermath, the local government issued curfew and cops who continued to work made arrests for curfew violations and robberies. Jails and prison flooded inside. During one of my trips, I learned that the prisons were deliberately placed on the coastlines. The government had no evacuation plan. During storms, prisons flood and people inside risk drowning and contamination from poisons, animals, and bugs that pour into the cells. The jail's lackluster response during the recent hurricanes especially threatened disabled incarcerated people who have to navigate the cell-crowding tactics that prison officials used to move people to higher ground. At the Puerto Rico Federal Detention Center, one detained person explained that the toilets filled with human waste and could not be flushed for more than a week. Everyone was locked in their cells and guards displayed a complete disregard for their health. When the water levels increased at night, detainees feared that they were going to drown. The power was out. During a surprise raid, prison guards entered cells and made detainees get on the floor. One detainee explained:[317]

> Because every cell's floor was covered in feces and urine infested water most inmates were hesitant and the ones who refused or stalled to get face down in the dirty water were either pepper sprayed or shot at close range with a machine gun type weapon that fires rubber bullets. Several inmates were shot multiple times and had bleeding and severe bruising from the close proximity of the fired shots . . . So much pepper spray was used that every inmate was coughing, choking, and blinded. The cloud of pepper spray was so large that even the officers were coughing despite some of them wearing masks . . . No mercy was shown for my cellmate who is a sick elderly man in his sixties and who is blind out of his glass eye.[318]

And like California, Texas, and Florida, government officials used prison labor to clean up debris on the roads and in communities after the storms.[319]

For me, Critical Resistance's work in Louisiana, Fight Toxic Prison's work across the country, and the incarcerated organizers in Puerto Rico illuminated a possibility to do abolitionist activism alongside climate justice. I thought that these campaigns would be wonderful entry points for people who cared deeply about climate and environmental justice or disability justice, but are still curious or skeptical about abolition. They could find common ground that rejects police putting people in flooded cells during an environmental catastrophe, or that refuse allowing anyone to live or work on toxic waste sites. Because these issues and campaigns intersect with environmental justice, disability justice, and climate justice, activists who primarily organize in those fields can contribute to making the prison industrial complex obsolete.

IN ST. LOUIS, MANY of the people held in toxic jails like the Workhouse first lived in neighborhoods fixed with hazardous waste and pollution. My great-grandparents Rosie and Odell migrated northwest with my grandmother to St. Louis. During World War II, the Black population in the city increased by 41 percent. It was also the only time in modern history when the globe temporarily cooled. Postwar industrialization in Europe and the United States was so immense that particles from the burning fossils fuels may have absorbed the sunlight for several decades. Aerosols cause cancers, asthma and type 2 diabetes. When people ask abolitionists, "What about the murderers?" I wonder if they realize that climate change can kill us all. Quickly *and* slowly.[320]

My grandmother was twelve years old when the Supreme Court decided *Shelley v. Kramer* in favor of a Black St. Louis couple trying to buy a house in a white neighborhood. The decision ended the legal use of racial covenants nationally. Within two years, white people began a mass exodus from the city to the county. Over two decades, 60 percent of white people left St. Louis City. During this exodus, the federal government, in conjunction with cities and states, destroyed several thriving Black communities to build highways. In 1955, a St. Louis board voted to destroy Mill Creek Valley, a vibrant Black neighborhood with homes, apartments, shops, stores, dance halls, and clubs. More than twenty thousand Black people were displaced, and forty churches were bulldozed. The construction made way for the highway that ran next to the apartments where my mother, grandmother, and I lived. These routes made it easier for the white suburban workers to drive to their jobs in the city over newly unemployed Black people displaced by the construction. Highways are not neutral passageways and the violence would reverberate in our bodies for generations to come. Traffic pollution causes asthma, lung impairment, cardiovascular diseases, and premature death. Cars unleashed lead into the air that was absorbed into Black people's lungs, yards, parks, schools, and playgrounds.[321]

Middle- and upper-class Blacks fled next. My great-grandfather was a welder and his sons, my grandmother's younger brothers, got jobs working at McDonnell

Douglas after they had been honorably discharged from the military. They moved to the county—Ferguson, Florissant, Bellefontaine Neighbors. My grandmother could not afford it. She persevered in the crumbling city with her six children. She worked as a tailor at a clothing store for more than a decade and resigned because the men expected her to clean. Her resignation letter listed eight reasons for leaving, including filthy floors and toilets, lack of extermination for the pests and rodents, and mold and "the falling plaster in the back room" where she went to retrieve items for customers. She'd written that she had breathing problems inside the store and regularly fell ill. Her beautiful sleek skin would break into hives and rashes. "P. S.," she wrote in cursive, "I am a sales clerk, not a porter or maid."

"Black flight" from St. Louis had been attributed to everything. Underperforming schools, rising crime rates, high unemployment. Racism. Climate change and environmental degradation also displaced Black people—the highways, rising temperatures that contributed to rising crime and the toxic conditions my grandmother detailed in her resignation letter. She had withheld rent for the same toxic conditions at home. Writing to the court in 1979, she criticized her landlord, a white woman who owned the multi-family unit a few blocks from highway 70, for failure to keep the building up. My grandmother lived in the downstairs unit. Before she signed the lease, the landlord assured her that the apartment would be fixed, painted, decorated, and ready to move in. After my grandmother signed the lease, the landlord disappeared: when she left, she did not even give my grandmother her phone number or any contact information for anyone at all. For five years, my grandmother made all of the repairs that she could by herself. She fixed broken pipes that she had not burst; paid for painting to cover the peeling lead paint; and boarded floors and stairs to cover gaping holes. The upstairs unit was vacant yet unlocked. My grandmother chased out men and dogs sleeping there and and boarded it up herself. When that unit's pipes broke, the water made my grandmother's kitchen ceiling cave and flooded her basement. The water sat there for three years because the repairmen she called refused to drain the basement because of the poorly wired gas and electrical systems. In the letter, my grandmother wanted reimbursement for her expenses, injuries, stolen valuables, and labor. She also demanded compensation "for embarrassment of odor from the basement which could be smelled for a block away."

The landlord had exploited my family's low wealth and race and created dangerous living conditions where they suffered for five years. Her negligence and misfeasance exposed my family to noxious fumes, lead, mold, and mildew. She only showed up to sue my grandmother for back payment of rent. My grandmother could not call the police on the landlord for any of this, but the landlord could call the sheriff to evict my grandmother. As Professors Shupe and Iadicola explain, "While the government focuses its attention on the violence that occurs from street crimes, it tends to ignore the violence that occurs from the chemical assault on the environment. More is lost in money and health through pollution than crimes of street violence, yet only the latter is defined officially as violence. This is also true of property ownership. The landlord had not only been negligent, but her inaction had been violent against the bodies of that home."[322]

My mother, grandmother, aunts, and uncles were always yelling at kids in the family about peeling paint and lead poisoning. This is partially why. They had grown up in homes that constantly assaulted their bodies and minds. It's not really as if they could simply move. In his "I Have a Dream" speech, Dr. Martin Luther King Jr. acknowledged that "We cannot be satisfied as long as the Negro's basic mobility is from a smaller ghetto to a larger one." Lead and other toxins were all around them. Withholding rent, just as Eleanor Bumpurs had done, was a tactic to address the conditions. Police often came instead of maintenance workers. Sometimes to arrest and evict the parents, sometimes to arrest and harass the lead-poisoned children and throw them in the Workhouse. None of it removed the lead, only the survivors.[323]

When I was in my late teens, I heard my grandmother say that police would be waiting outside in the streets to catch the kids who were "underdeveloped." It felt ableist, eugenic even. I argued viciously with my uncle Phil about it behind her back. "That's bad racial science! That not real." But as I grew older and listened more closely, she was actually explaining pieces of the St. Louis activists' campaigns against lead poisoning.

Ivory Perry began lead testing homes in my family's neighborhood in the 1960s. My softball team practiced in a park named after him in that neighborhood but I did not know who he was until I became a lawyer. He organized under the Union-Sarah Gateway Center. Black tenants living in conditions like my family's and worse called him to put pressure on white landlords to make repairs. Perry had helped organize rent strikes and fight police violence and was a local coordinator for the Dr. King's Poor People's Campaign. In *A Life in the Struggle: Ivory Perry and the Culture of Opposition*, historian George Lipsitz explains that Perry noticed that children in the oldest and poorest sections of the city suffered rashes, constantly running eyes and noses, and persistent colds, especially in homes with peeling paint and fallen plaster. Every house he tested for lead in my grandmother's neighborhood returned with positive results. Heat made it worse. Perry explained, "Most poor people don't have air conditioning, and they raise the windows in the summertime, and most of the little kids put their mouths on the windowsill." The federal government only banned lead paint in new homes built after 1978 and did not require landlords to remove any lead paint from current homes. At once, white people were moving into lead-free homes in the county and renting substandard lead-ridden homes to poor Black families in the city.[324]

When my grandmother said "underdeveloped," she was referring to the consequences of lead poisoning. Neither she nor my mom ever told us what lead *was*, only what it *did* based on what they had learned from the campaign. I did not understand the science until the Flint water crisis. Per the World Health Organization, child lead poisoning can lead to "temper tantrums, argumentativeness, active defiance and refusal to comply with adult requests and rules, deliberate attempts to annoy and upset people, frequent anger and resentment, mood instability, substance abuse, aggression toward people and animals, destruction of property, and deceitfulness, lying or stealing." No amount of lead is safe in our bloodstreams. Bioethicist Harriet A. Washington's *A Terrible Thing to Waste* details how lead causes several different illnesses and can reprogram young, developing brains. Per Washington, the reprogramming can increase aggressive behaviors such as bullying, slow down mental processing, and pass on these mutating genes to the next generations; she and other scientists suggest that lead was the primary cause of the violent crime wave in the 1980s and '90s. In one study, "childhood blood lead was the single most predictive factor for disciplinary problems and juvenile crime. It was also the fourth largest predictor of adult crime." States and the federal government invested heavily in police and prisons instead of lead detoxification and safe environments. The United States eventually banned lead from gas and violent crime rates dropped.[325]

What's so frustrating about research is that it happens on top of a racist, carceral terrain. Spending for policing and prisons have been increasing since the 1940s, which provides more resources to cops to patrol and surveil Black communities. Lead *may* lead to disciplinary problems and juvenile crime. But discipline and crime are social constructs that we give meaning. For example, there were juveniles who committed drug crimes because drugs were criminalized. As the federal government explained during the peak of "juvenile crime":

> Usually there is no complainant, so the police must be proactive in finding drug offenders. They choose when, where, and how often to look for drug activity and, as a result, drug enforcement activity affords the police an opportunity to apply coercion when and where they see fit.[326]

Cops made more arrests for particular behaviors, which is not necessarily a marker of increased crime and disciplinary infractions. So even if lead does impact our bodies and minds, it doesn't impact them in a vacuum, and for the poor and dispossessed, cops will be the primary response.[327]

Especially insidiously, Washington explains that General Motors decided to use lead in gas because the company could not patent and profit from the widely available ethanol; GM knew and disregarded the risks and exposed millions of people to lead poisoning, which "may be the cause of the biggest childhood poisoning epidemic ever." In the 1970s, Ivory Perry had tried explaining this fact to everyone he could, alderman, businessman, scientist. According to Lipsitz, even Black doctors initially rebuffed the claims, so Perry set up a makeshift office in the back of a Black-owned bar and recruited college students to administer lead tests to poor Black children with the funds he raised. After years of protesting, shutting down conferences, and public shaming, Perry and Black parents forced the city and local health officials to fund initiatives to fix the lead problem. More than twenty thousand Black children at the time had tested positive for poisoning that was completely preventable. As of 2021, more than one million children in the United States have lead poisoning and 800 million globally, about a third of all children.[328]

Lead poisoning does not manifest neutrally. Black children and Mexican American children have the highest rates of lead exposure. Almost 67 percent of Black children born between 1985 and 2000 were raised in high-poverty neighborhoods compared to 6 percent of white children; these communities are likely to have significant lead presence. Korryn Gaines had sued landlords from her childhood over lead poisoning. The lawsuit stated that a "sea of lead paint" in their properties had caused her to display "signs of neurocognitive impairment" and loss of "significant IQ points as a result of that exposure." Gaines and other tenants had sued the landlord who owned the property where she believed she was poisoned. Freddie Gray's family had also filed a lawsuit over lead poisoning and won. Upon discovering these legal cases, journalists used the lead poisoning claims as evidence Gaines and Gray's behavior toward the police was erratic; using their lawsuits subtly blamed the victims for how they died instead of criticizing the police for escalating the violence against them.[329]

Lead poisoning impacts policing and immigration as well. New York state mandates that parents get their children tested for lead poisoning at ages one and two years old. A team of researchers found in a 2012 study that South Asian residents had elevated blood lead levels "in 20% of the adults and 15% of the children, as compared to 5% of adults and 2.5% of children citywide." The scientists associated the blood lead levels with recent repair work, the inability to speak English, belonging to Bangladeshi or Indian ethnic groups, and occupational risk factors. The two greatest risk factors were having recent repair work done at home that exposed lead paint, and not having health insurance. In response, the mayor acknowledged the lead paint, but with an important caveat that blamed the people who had been poisoned: "Some traditional consumer products used in the South Asian community can contain lead." The city announced five hundred thousand dollars on a multilingual campaign to warn South Asians about the dangers of lead. Awareness is absolutely important. But it appears that these communities needed the city to require landlords to also safely detoxify lead from the premises, and for the federal government to ensure their health-care coverage to treat the exposure.[330]

The heat from corporate and human greenhouse gas emission will continue to warm the planet and unless we stop it, the lead violence will continue. Lead is still present in millions of homes and goods, especially older homes where landlords cheaply painted over it. Most of the hottest summers in recorded history have occurred since 1998 and heat will primarily force poor people of color to cool down and lead them to lead- contaminated windowsills, doorways, streets, and parks. Without climate justice, environmental justice, and abolition, police will continue to arrest, capture, and kill lead poisoning survivors.[331]

MY GRANDMOTHER HAD become severely depressed from her unhealthy living and work conditions. My mother arranged for her to move to the apartments on Hickory Street and I was born a few months later. She'd say to me, "I was very depressed. I was in a dark, dark place. You were my light." I think it was the change of scenery, too. My uncle said she was so happy that her life was turning around and she didn't have to deal with racist landlords anymore. First we lived with her, then next door for about seventeen years. Kids in the neighborhood stopped by and played in her hair, makeup, pearls, and elaborate wardrobe. When I was late to school, she'd grab her cane and walk me half way to L'Ouverture and would not turn back until I went inside the building. She had the beautiful stereotypical Black-grandmother living room: the couches were gold paisley with red specks and the armchairs were green. *Everything* was in plastic except for the wooden television set with the built-in record player. I had memorized the order of the vinyls on the rack near the entrance. She teased me about rap music. I teased her about the blues. "Grandmomma, what kinda song is 'Your Husband Is Cheating on Us?'"

I did not know my grandmother had diabetes until my brother and I got in trouble for stealing her orange sherbet ice cream. She'd prick herself at the kitchen table with tiny plastic covered needles. My mom was sick, too, and could never get rid of a cold. Courtnie always had nosebleeds. Corey, her twin, had asthma. I had severe eczema that made my skin bleed and peel. Then my grandmother's strokes came. She lost her penmanship and I started writing her correspondence for bills and filling out her checks. The second stroke came in 2006. I was heading to my boyfriend's junior prom when the ambulance carried her off. Since we used the ambulances for everything, it felt normal. We didn't really have our own doctors or dentists because we didn't have insurance. (Roy, a Black boy across the street from us, pulled my mother's aching wisdom tooth out with a pair of pliers). This time, my grandmother's lung collapsed. She did not come back home. She went to an elderly facility that her Medicaid covered, one right next to a highway.

Our neighborhood was a newish development and a far cry from the dilapidated housing my family had moved from. Still, it sat nestled near the polluting highway, like every other neighborhood my grandmother lived in since her family migrated to St. Louis. Wholesale commercial floral distribution chains occupied LaSalle, one block north of us. A fish-seasoning manufacturing company sat two blocks north, and Praxair, one of the largest industrial gas companies in the world, sat one block east. The military airplane junkyard was three blocks down and across from my middle school. Sometimes I still go on Google Earth and look at the side-by-side images of exposed broken airplanes and children on the playground where I once had gym class. The grocery stores closed down and we had to rely on corner stores with overpriced and expired goods because we never had a car.

We were always taking care of each other because we were getting sick all the time. Sick meant missing school, and my absenteeism alerted police, social workers, and foster care. When cops and social workers came to our house, we were poor and physically ill. Not abused. They removed us from our home and it did not stop us from getting sick. Ironically, my second foster home was on the same street where my grandmother, mom, aunts, and uncles lived and many of the issues had remained: lead, concentrated poverty, and economic exploitation. Our foster parent beat my brother and I our first night there because we fell asleep, crying, in the same bed. "Boys and girls don't sleep in the same bed!" she screamed after midnight while swinging a broom at our seven- and nine-year-old bodies. We were literally being punished for being poor, for being sick, and for being Black.

Our mother fought vigorously for our return. When we came home, the dying started. Shootings and asthma attacks claimed my friends, heart diseases and cancers claimed our parents. By the time I reached law school, many of my mother's neighborhood friends were gone or dying. We lost Michael, who was short and lean, often shirtless with a big smile and a brown paper bag wrapped around a can. We lost his son first, Mickey, to a shooting. Michael and his brother Emory beat on my family's door to warn us about the exploding Praxair gas tanks. We also lost Ray, my mother's frenemy. On weekends, they'd start singing and drinking on the front porch and often ended by cursing each other out. Our neighbor Ms. Brenda took us to the grocery store when we needed to do big shopping trips, and I helped her program her AOL account in return. She'd die from cancer. Her daughter, Jenny, too. Jenny was a bubbly triplet with two brothers who all befriended my mom. They were the first Black triplets I'd ever seen. She had six kids and did not live to see fifty. Their big sister Jennette is battling cancer as I write. Trina didn't see fifty either and her children are my two little sisters' ages. These were the parents, lovers, Spades partners who'd argue with each other and later loan money. Right before Christmas 2017, my grandmother was diagnosed with cancer, too. I was heartbroken and terrified.

Was it the climate? A lifetime of living near highways? Decades of lead exposure? Stress from racism, sexism, classism from her landlords and bosses? The smoking because of the stress? The military junkyard down the road? The exploding Praxair tanks? Bad food? The multitude of possibilities demonstrated the depth and breadth of oppression.

Familiar diseases and ailments had become more than enough reason for me to want to reclaim our planet in the name of abolition, environmental justice, and climate justice. But this reclamation was especially important for what is to come, the unfamiliar. If capitalists and countries do not reduce and end their reliance on fossil fuels and environmental toxins, our families will continue to become sick and die. Police and prisons will continue to manage survivors of the devastation.

AT NEARLY EVERY opportunity for progressive change to preserve our planet, the police have been on the opposite side. Nationally, police have enforced evictions against tenants who complain about environmental hazards because police protect private property owners; my grandmother could not call the police on the landlord whose property nearly killed her. Internationally, police arrest and beat prisoners who complain and organize against conditions because cops maintain the order inside prisons. In Flint, Michigan, cops arrested activists who complained about the lead in the water at a city council meeting, not the governor or any official whose administration used pipes that poisoned the poor Black community. In South Dakota, police shot rubber bullets, tear gas, and water cannons at Standing Rock Sioux tribe members and other activists who organized to stop the Dakota Access Pipeline, a $3.8 billion pipeline to carry five hundred thousand barrels of fossil fuel a day more than 1,100 miles from North Dakota to Illinois. Spills and leaks would destroy the water supply and contaminate soil; successful passage would lead to burning more fossil fuel and warming the Earth. Kelcy Warren, the billionaire CEO of the majority share-holding company for DAPL bragged, "I'm going to be a little boastful here. Nobody has built more pipelines in the last fifteen years than Energy Transfer." Activists cannot call the police on the capitalists because the police are there to protect the capitalists. After four years of protests, organizing, and litigation by activists, a federal judge halted the pipeline in 2020 and ruled that it must be emptied of all oil while the government undertakes an environmental review of the potential impact. Though a victory, the fight is not over.[332]

Black organizers had a history of resisting this police violence, as well as fighting environmental devastation to their neighborhoods and to their bodies. Ivory Perry's organization was just one example. MOVE is another. I cannot exactly remember when I learned about them but I remember how I felt to learn that the City of Philadelphia dropped a bomb on a house full of Black people in 1985. For more than ten years before the bombing, the family and other people had been living and organizing together using the revolutionary religious teachings of John Africa. Mike Africa Jr., who was raised in the MOVE family before and after his parents were imprisoned following a political prosecution, stated in an interview:

> When we say life, we're taking about people, animals and the environment.
> In the '70s, the organization began protesting against institutions that
> were enslaving life, bartering life and mistreating life. MOVE people
> demonstrated against Barnum and Bailey Circus, the Philadelphia
> Zoo, the East Park Reservoir (to protest pollution), and also the prisons
> themselves for detaining people, particularly Black people, on unjust
> charges and with extremely high prison terms for crimes that other people

served little or no prison time for. Because of this, the group was met with extreme opposition.[333]

MOVE charges that people "will do all in their power for a breath of air, because air is a necessity and money is worthless. Over the last century, industry has raped the earth of countless tons of minerals, bled billions of gallons of oil from the ground, and enslaved millions of people to manufacture cars, trucks, planes and trains that further pollute the air with their use." They practiced communalism and lived healthy lifestyles, mostly consuming a raw diet; they even kept hundreds of pounds of food for birds, dogs, and squirrels. They counseled their children for accountability instead of delivering physical punishment and whippings. They opposed intimate-partner violence as well, and believed that people could become revolutionaries without discipline and intention.[334]

MOVE did believe in self-defense and engaged in armed self-defense against the police who constantly harassed them. They also organized against capitalism, and were critical of Jesse Jackson, the Southern Christian Leadership Conference, and other Black leaders whom they believed promoted it. The combination agitated capitalists, traditional civil rights leaders, and law enforcement alike. The FBI was created to target groups who wanted to destroy capitalism, and agents went undercover in MOVE's rapidly gentrifying neighborhood to spy on Black and left-wing groups. On March 28, 1976, MOVE threw a welcome-home celebration for family members returning from jail. Cops showed up and attacked them, and crushed the skull of Janine and Philip Africa's newborn baby, Life Africa. Because she had been delivered at home and did not have a birth certificate, police denied the baby existed. Neighbors and local politicians confirmed that Janine indeed had Life. Some people expressed sympathy, but still, their neighbors, and Black middle-class people around the city, found their lifestyle and activism nuisances, which increased their vulnerability to police violence.[335]

After years of standoffs and fights, MOVE and the police entered an agreement in 1978, per Mike Africa Jr. Cops exchanged political prisoners for MOVE's weapons, then broke the agreement during a random raid a year later. A cop was killed during the raid and nine MOVE members went to prison for nearly forty years, including Janine. The cop was killed by a single bullet, and Guardian Chief Reporter Ed Pilkington explains that during trial where they were found guilty of third-degree murder, "no forensic evidence was presented that connected the MOVE 9 to the weapon that caused the fatality," which the defense argued came from another cop. MOVE's Del Africa told Pilkington during an interview: "There was no shooting from our side . . . No one in the house had any gunshot residue, none of us had fingerprints on any of the weapons they claim came out of the house."[336]

In 1985, the first Black mayor of Philadelphia labeled them a terrorist organization and ordered them to be bombed during another police standoff at their home. The department had already fired ten thousand bullets in an hour and a half at their home; two people survived and eleven died, including five children and founder John Africa. Police killed another of Janine's children, twelve-year-old Phil. Sixty-five homes eventually caught fire from being in proximity to the burning building, leaving over two hundred people homeless. The police commissioner stopped firefighters from saving houses and instead let the fires burn.[337]

Sometimes, abolition critics will tell me that we—Black people, oppressed people, whomever—first need to organize ourselves before we address police violence. The problem with this criticism is that the police have a history and practice of destroying progressive communities, ideas, and programs that build up our neighborhoods and MOVE is a primary example. They prevented other radical and progressive organizing as well. Chicago Police Department destroyed the meals for the free breakfast programs that the Young Lords used to feed children, and law enforcement across the country threatened the Young Lords and Black Panthers who used tuberculosis and lead poisoning screenings to keep their communities safe and healthy. Cops attempted to destroy MOVE, too, because they were mostly Black people with leftist politics who were practicing their beliefs, engaging in their rights to protest, practice self-defense, and raise their children according to their values of healthy living and appreciation for all life. Police attacked and imprisoned MOVE because they practiced protecting themselves and the planet, which threatens capitalism and policing. We cannot wait until we build everything to begin abolishing the prison industrial complex because the police will just destroy it. We have to build and dismantle at the same time.

Incredibly, MOVE people were still politically active while in prison and after four decades of incarceration and still held onto their beliefs. Guards targeted them for keeping their MOVE identities and maintaining their innocence. They withstood. Janine Africa, Janet Africa, and Debbie Africa supported each other inside and trained a dog that helped disabled people. Janine Africa was the minister of education and published articles critical of US imperialism and policing. Upon their releases, they continued to organize around their beliefs and condemned the criminal legal system. Other MOVE people died in prison. Mumia Abu-Jamal, a journalist who covered the family extensively and adopted John Africa's teachings, remains incarcerated following a political prosecution after a cop was killed during an encounter. Abu-Jamal also maintains his innocence. When I met MOVE members in 2019 in Philadelphia to help organize against the prosecutor keeping him incarcerated, they remained relentless in their pursuit of his freedom.[338]

MOVE's commitment to healthy humans, animals, and the environment, and toward the liberation of all oppressed people is one revolutionary example that I found different from other movements that had not incorporated anti-capitalism and racial justice into their campaigns. Before the Ferguson Uprising, nearly all of the green activism that I learned about was organized around single-issue causes and led by well-intentioned white people. I played softball at Ivory Perry park for three years and did not know about his legacy of organizing against police violence, economic oppression, and environmental degradation for Black families across St. Louis and then the country. I had known about mass incarceration for years; I had not known about the organizing and resistance inside prisons against these toxic sites of violence. And, I did not know about the long history of poor Black and Latinx families, especially Black women, who withheld their rent from landlords over crumbling and poisonous housing conditions. I had to widen my understanding of what counts as resistance to fully appreciate and acknowledge centuries of spectacular and quotidian claims to live a healthy life. From the maroons to Eleanor Bumpurs, from MOVE to my grandmother, as long as there have been people willing to destroy humans for a profit, there have been people resisting. The police have been developed in response to this resistance, and my activism has grown in response to the police. As the title of Mary Frances Berry's book on progressive social movements instructs, *history teaches us to resist.*

I HEARD RUTH Wilson Gilmore once say "abolition must be red, black, and green" at the "Making and Unmaking Mass Incarceration" conference in Oxford, Mississippi. I'd written it on the inside cover of the book I was reading at the time. She later explained on a podcast that "red" meant abolition had to generalize resources for everyone, first to those most vulnerable; I believe the most vulnerable are people most susceptible to exploitation and premature death. "Black" represented internationalism, the commitment to care and organize with people across borders for a better world. And for Gilmore, abolition must be green, "to take seriously the problem of environmental harm, environmental racism, and environmental degradation." In addition to activism toward these aims, several groups have demanded widespread policy proposals to save the Earth, and all of us on it.[339]

Indigenous activists from the Red Nation have demanded "the Red Deal," a policy proposal to stop climate change, end environmental degradation, and advance comprehensive prevention to harm in the first place. Nick Estes, who helped co-found Red Nation in 2014, explains that the deal focuses on "Indigenous treaty rights, land restoration, sovereignty, self-determination, decolonization, and liberation" in addition to the free housing, universal health care, free education, and green jobs already proposed in the Green New Deal. The Green New Deal is a policy proposal that seeks to end climate change and offer a robust set of responses to an array of social problems. The two primary architects of the bill were Rhiana Gunn-Wright and Demond Drummer, two leaders at New Consensus, a Chicago-based policy think tank that tackles "climate change, economic stagnation, racial and rural wealth gaps, and more by proposing solutions modeled after mass economic mobilizations of the past." The Red Deal aligned with particular elements of the Green New Deal, and proposed additional demands to divest from militarism, imprisonment, and policing. These proposals are rooted in decolonization, anti-capitalism, and Black abolitionism. Organizations such as the rapidly growing Sunrise Movement popularized the Green New Deal through activism and a sit-in demonstration against Speaker of the House Nancy Pelosi in November 2018. When the policy entered the mainstream and public imagination, it became a litmus test for presidential and congressional candidates on fighting climate change.[340]

The Movement for Black Lives had completely changed its Vision for Black Lives and created a new campaign, the "Red Black, and Green New Deal." M4BL explained that "Black, Indigenous, and people of color and working class poor communities are hit the hardest, though we contribute the least to what accelerates climate disasters. So in times of crisis, we need our communities aware and strong enough to be our own first responders." By focusing on policy, resources, and activism, the campaign can help build independence among people in the community to identify toxic environments and storms, and begin to prepare themselves in the event of disaster. Additionally, robust agendas can foster interdependence within communities to plan together to prevent and respond to climate change and environmental degradation through discussing the issues mutual aid, and organizing local campaigns. The policy aspects of these campaigns put pressure on elected officials to divest from polluting institutions, including corporations, military, and the police, while also investing in clean energy solutions and neighborhood detoxification to improve our quality of life. By having a diversity of tactics, people interested in saving the environment and ourselves can contribute in various ways that can promote healthy living while abolishing all of the forms of state and corporate violence that causes prema-ture death. The abolition of the prison industrial complex is the minimum for healthy lives that we all deserve to live. We only want the Earth.[341]

CONCLUSION

WE USED TO call 911 for everything except snitching. Now, we have not called in years.

Since the COVID-19 pandemic hit the United States in 2020, my three sisters and I have all been in quarantine together. One evening, two of them, Kayla and Courtnie, were walking home from a grocery store. They saw a man shouting from his car because a toddler, probably younger than two years old, was in the middle of the street with a puppy. No other adult was present. My sisters grabbed the boy's hand and walked him from the street to a nearby house with an open door, shouting inside the house for help. Another boy, maybe about five years old, came down a flight of stairs. He said nobody was home. My sisters told the older boy to please keep the toddler inside.

When my sisters came home, they told me about the toddler, the brother, and the puppy. Courtnie also said that a woman walking down the street stopped to observe and appeared to be taking down the address to call the cops or child protective services. I did not want the state to take anyone's children away or the cops to take anyone's parents away, so Courtnie and I ran back to the kids' home to wait outside. I knocked on the door. The puppy barked and the toddler climbed onto the couch to twist the doorknob. I shuddered. We started shouting into the house again, but nobody answered.

I immediately thought about Atatiana Jefferson, the Black woman in Texas who had left her door open one early morning while playing video games with her nephew. A neighbor called the cops to perform a wellness check. Her nephew reportedly told investigators that his aunt pointed her gun toward a window when she went to check out noises she heard outside; a cop arrived and shot inside the house through the window, killing Atatiana. He could have also killed the boy. The cop resigned and pleaded not guilty to murder charges. I did not want to risk anyone else's life for a "wellness check."[342]

Courtnie and I decided to wait there until someone came home. I walked to the salon on the corner to ask the stylists if they knew the family. A stylist said the toddler had wandered into the shop, alone, about an hour earlier, around the time Courtnie spotted him. The stylist called the shop's owner, who tried to reach the boy's mother to no avail. I returned to their house and a neighbor came outside. I asked if she knew the mother, and she said yes, but defensively and afraid. I asked her to contact the mother, and she said she didn't have the mother's number and hurried back inside. She quickly returned with a bag of food and walked to the house where the boys were waiting. Courtnie and I turned to each other in confusion. The neighbor said that she was the boys' grandmother and asked if I was a social worker. I told her no, that I was a lawyer, but more importantly, that I was afraid that someone would call the cops or a social worker to take the kids.

We were not sure what to do, whether to believe the neighbor in the doorway before us. We wanted to help but didn't want to be overbearing, so we approached the salon stylist who confirmed that the neighbor was indeed the grandmother, who usually watched the kids. We felt a mixture of uncertainty and relief, so we walked back home.

In the days that followed, Courtnie and I went back to the house several times to knock on the door. Nobody answered. We visited the salon again and the stylist said that she would keep her blinds open to watch out for the children. If the boy wandered, she would contact the grandmother and sit him in a chair to wait like she had done before, the day Courtnie walked him out of the street. She also took our contact information in case we needed to come up with a better plan, and told me that she would contact me if she reached the mother. We'll keep going back until she does.

It's absolutely nightmarish, what could have happened to those kids. A car could have hit the toddler, or a stranger could have abducted him off the street. Flames could have engulfed the house, or the mounted television could have fallen. The parent could have lost her children, or, if they'd lived, lost custody. I'm sure that some people believe that the latter is exactly what should happen based on this incident. I offer no specific defense. I can only speculate whether the parent left for an emergency or for leisure. Maybe she trusted her mother to babysit in her absence, and at the exact time that Kayla and Courtnie had been walking down the street, the grandmother had gone inside the house for any number of reasons.

If someone had called the police, it is very likely that the city and the state would have sent cops and social workers to that family's house. The mother probably would have had to spend time in court fighting to get her kids back if she was not prosecuted and imprisoned for child endangerment. A foster parent would get checks to support the boys. And then there's the stigma, shame, and violence associated with losing custody of your children, which simply cannot be measured.

When I became a parent, I remember listening to white parents tell stories, with no shame, about how their young kids went wandering outside or accidentally ate small amounts of household poison about the house. Surely, they had some fear, but police involvement, prison, or losing custody were never a part of the conversation—those were unfathomable. The contrast along racial and class lines is stark. Indigenous lines, too. In law school, we studied *State v. Williams*, a case where Native American parents were prosecuted for manslaughter because they had not taken their toddler to the doctor for a cavity that became infected and led to his death. The parents did not know how serious the infection was, and at the time, the state of Washington, where they lived, had removed custody from Indigenous parents at such high rates and for such trivial matters that it deterred families from seeking help. At the time of the case in the late seventies, states took at least one child from nearly 80 percent of Indigenous families living on reservations. The removal of Indigenous children continues to be a legacy of settler colonialism. Today, they constitute less than 1 percent of all children, but nearly 25 to 50 percent of children removed from families in several states. And for the Black boys my sisters helped in the street, their fate could have been akin to the millions of other Black kids whom the state removed, and who now constitute nearly 25 percent of kids in foster care.[343]

AROUND THE TIME of my first visit to the boys' house, I listened to the jury in the Derek Chauvin trial read the guilty verdict for his murder of George Floyd. The prosecutor asked that the judge detain Chauvin in prison until sentencing, and a cop handcuffed his former colleague to take him away. Many people felt joy—excitement, even. President Obama and President Biden refrained from calling the verdict justice, but affirmed that it was a step in the right direction. Speaker of the House Nancy Pelosi went farther. She thanked George Floyd for sacrificing his life so that justice could be served. But he did not sacrifice his life; he did not want to die at all. He screamed that he couldn't breathe so that he could live. He was executed. As I'd learned with Oscar Grant, Walter Scott, Akai Gurley, LaQuan McDonald, Botham Jean, and any other victim of police violence whose killer had been convicted, a conviction was not justice for George Floyd. We will never know what justice for him might look like because justice requires the participation of the impacted. The dead cannot participate. Chauvin was punished and will fight tooth and nail to appeal the decision, to avoid prison, the place where we send mostly poor, Black and disabled people to suffer.

Moments after the verdict, a cop in Columbus, Ohio, shot and killed sixteen-year-old Ma'Khia Bryant. Ma'Khia and her sister were in foster care. Their mom had taken them to a social worker, seeking help with her teenage girls who she'd felt were rebelling against her. Rich parents send rebellious teenagers to boarding schools and Christian academies, or pay for them to have a gap year to travel the world and decompress between high school and college. Poor, rebellious Black teenagers who are frustrated by precarious lifestyles—moving constantly, switching schools, food and utility insecurity, all of what I'd experienced—get juvenile prison or foster care, often both. After a court hearing, cops detained Ma'Khia's mother because she was found guilty of neglect, and also detained the children, the supposed victims, in a police van.[344]

Cedric Robinson describes Western civilization as "neither." Foster care is also neither: it is a system of family punishment rooted in slavery and settler colonialism. And like with the police, parents will seek support from the system when they are in dire need of resources.[345]

After being removed from their mother's home, the sisters had lived with their grandmother, but a landlord kicked them out of the newly crowded apartment. A *New York Times* feature explained that Ohio pays licensed strangers ten times more than relatives for foster care, and a social worker took the Bryant children away from their grandmother, who had asked if they could spend a few nights at a hotel with her until she sorted out a new living arrangement. The girls were put in five different homes and faced bullying. The day of Chauvin's verdict, Ma'Khia's sister called the police for help because she said that adult women were at their house trying to fight them. Cops arrived during the altercation just as one of the adult women spat at the girls. Ma'Khia ran toward the woman with a knife, and a cop fired in the direction of the family, killing Ma'Khia. Columbus police quickly released the body-camera footage in defense of the cop.[346]

After several high-profile police killings, the same lawyers and pastors flock to the families who have the best chance of winning civil and criminal suits. George Floyd had three celebrity-studded funerals; Ma'Khia had none. No fanfare or eulogy by a famous Black preacher. No Black lawyer promising to secure justice for the family or the child. A petition that circulated online to demand "justice for Ma'Khia" failed to reach five thousand signatures; Trayvon Martin's petition surpassed one million signees. The most transformative action happened at Ohio State University, where students organized a sit-in to demand that the school cut ties with the local police department.[347]

Exponential amounts of money, time, and energy were spent to "correct" Ma'Khia's mother, including several thousand dollars a month paid to strangers for taking temporary custody, social workers' salaries, judges' salaries, court costs, the cost of the dispatcher who answered the 911 call, and the salary and benefits of the cop who took Ma'Khia's life. Family removal and the criminal legal system create jobs for the middle class to manage the poor. Instead, all of that money, time, and energy could have paid for quality housing in a neighborhood without high concentrations of crime, economic inequality, deindustrialization, and violence; it could help eliminate those neighborhoods altogether. Ma'Khia and her sisters could have kept their friends and community. Instead of a landlord who kicked them out of their grandmother's apartment, their grandmother could have had her own home where they had sleepovers on floors and couches for fun, not out of necessity. If the teens argued with their mother over bedtimes, the family could have talked about it at therapy sessions on a Wednesday after school. Maybe the mother would have learned that the girls were really good at TikTok and obsessed over the app, or that it was the only time when they had privacy. We would not have known Ma'Khia's name unless she went viral for another reason.

THAT'S THE ABOLITIONIST present and future that I'm forging, one that eliminates the possibility of policing and family punishment for children like the boys in the street, Ma'Khia and her sister, and even my siblings and I when we were kids. But it's not just any abolitionist future. Historically, it has been possible to be abolitionist while also being capitalist, ableist, patriarchal, and colonialist. More than ever, we need dynamic abolitionisms that depart from all forms of oppression, and for each generation to decide their own fight and future.

For me and many of my peers, our abolitionist fight and future is committed to decolonization, disability justice, Earth justice, and socialism. All of these require mass political education, a commitment to understand and debate these issues with people who we love and organize within our communities.

Through abolition study and praxis, we explore and understand why millions of people in the US call the cops every year and how to begin reducing our reliance on them for help. An estimated 21 percent of people sixteen or older in the US had some contact with police in 2015, approximately 53 million people. Residents initiated approximately 10 percent of the contact with cops and only 6 percent of that figure was to report a possible crime. Calls for "violent crime" constitute 4 percent or less of calls to cops. This is true in cities with the highest homicide rates. In Memphis, 20 percent of 911 calls are a mistake; of the 130,000 emergency calls in 2016, at least 25,000 were for everything ranging from misdiagnosed stroke symptoms to simple sore throats. In New Orleans, 15 percent of 911 calls fall into the category of "other," 24 percent are calls for area checks, and 14 percent are for a generic category of complaints. For further context, in 2020 the top four categories for calls were area check (104,004), complaint (47,419), business check (25,527), disturbance (25,240), as compared to theft (12,865), suicide threat (1,650), death (292), simple rape (61), and simple assault (13). St. Louis, my hometown, currently tops the list for the highest murder rate, and the top calls there are for disturbance, domestic disturbance, and suspicious person. Contrary to popular belief, cops are not spending the bulk of their time responding to dangerous streets in urban communities.[348]

One tentative suggestion to reduce our reliance on police is to make 911 and 311 data publicly available and accessible everywhere. Progressive organizers and activists could sort this data, which would reveal what kinds of calls are made, which neighborhoods, and whether anyone was arrested. I anticipate that most people need social services and businesses, not cops. For example, if 20 percent of calls in a neighborhood are for wellness checks because someone left their door open, then hopefully neighbors could begin knocking, as my sisters and I did. However, if for other reasons neighbors cannot, volunteers from an organization or neighborhood association could perform checks. If the calls reveal harm, the organizers can use that information to place street violence interrupters, mediators, and resources for families of victims as proactive measures for conflict resolution and de-escalation—without police. The goal is not to replace cops with other people to police our neighborhoods; the goal is to begin eradicating the reasons we call cops in the first place, and organizers and community members must be tasked with completely changing the dynamics of the area, not just the people who respond to calls. That is partly what abolition is: eradicating the prison industrial complex *and* harm, at the same time, over time, to make both obsolete.

Organizers and activists do not, and ought not to, rely on 911 data alone. Conflict mediation centers, organizers, or the block associations that exist right now could begin taking inventory of the needs of the residents on each block and help them prepare for emergency and non-emergency situations. This could be done by canvassing and going door-to-door to collect information, and meeting and organizing with homeless people who experience high police contact. Hamid of Stop LAPD Spying Coalition, for example, met with Skid Row community members for several months to learn about their contact with police. The organization documented the various contacts, created a people's history of police violence to display in the streets there, and then created campaigns based on that information to reduce surveillance and contact. Critical Resistance and the Audre Lorde Project help people proactively prepare for emergencies to reduce their reliance on and contact with police.

Organizers and communities are demanding a reduction of the carceral state. We have to dismantle the structures as we build solutions and alternatives to harm because cops have a long record of disrupting progressive community-based organizing. We need people dedicated to organizing for decriminalization, decarceration, and divestment from the prison industrial complex. Decriminalization is the process of removing criminal punishment from laws, such as repealing alcohol prohibition laws and drug crimes. Decriminalization removes causes for police encounters. Marijuana decriminalization in California, for example, gives cops one less excuse to stop and arrest someone who they suspect has it. Police forces are already declining in number because of public pressure; cities must halt recruitment, freeze budgets, and cede to campaigns like Assata's Daughters' call to close cop academies. Additionally, all federal funding and programs for local police departments must end, including COPS and 1033, as well as funding for immigration and customs enforcement and border patrol, which organizations like Mijente have called to be abolished. Federal government funding to local departments began in the 1960s and can easily be rolled back. Republican-led states have no issue with withdrawing from federally funded programs such as unemployment and health care; they should direct the same energy toward police.[349]

THE POSSIBILITIES ARE endless with abolition, which is why, more than anything, I hope that people join or start grassroots organizations to get in where they fit.

Robust movements for socialism, decolonization, disability justice, and Earth justice are equally or perhaps more important than a singular movement for abolition. Capitalism creates concentrated poverty, especially for people who are Black, Indigenous, disabled, women, migrants, or young. This exploitation makes people less safe. Socialism is mystifying, and because it threatens capitalism, business and government work together to make it sound scary and dangerous. They'll point to Cuba or the Soviet Union as failures of socialism or communism, even though the US has been responsible for the deaths of millions upon millions to preserve capitalism through slavery, war, environmental degradation, prison violence, police violence, and state-sanctioned violence through mass shootings and extra-judicial killings by white people. But an economy controlled by workers would increase resources and wealth for everyone, not just the billionaires like Jeff Bezos, Bill Gates, Mark Zuckerberg, and Elon Musk. Big businesses use cops to break up strikes and labor movements because once workers unite against bosses, it's harder for companies to exploit their labor.

The Democratic Socialists of America and Dream Defenders both organize for socialist demands. Dream Defenders describes that in a socialist world, "everyone would have a decent place to live, enough food to eat, clean water to drink, clean air to breathe, medical attention when they need it, warm clothes for the cold weather, a good education, and the ability to develop to their fullest potential. Under Socialism, everyone would be free and equal regardless of gender, race, nationality or religion." Both groups organize for demands including quality, free universal health care, free education, and strong labor movements. These demands strengthen the social safety net so that workers can be in a better bargaining position to demand higher wages from their employers. This is especially salient for disabled workers who are exploited the most in the workplace and have a weak social safety net, which makes all of us vulnerable to exploitation. Companies will not raise wages for people who depend on them in desperation to survive. Capitalism is an inequality-making machine. And using socialism to eradicate inequality reduces the purpose of police to manage people who are locked out of schools, housing, health care, work, and social life.[350]

Until we have a completely people-centered economy, activists have called for various measures to move us in that direction. One measure is mass public education to demystify capitalism and socialism, and to debunk the mainstream notion that poverty is an individual person's decision or fault, and that people become billionaires by virtue of their hard work and good ideas. This simply is not true. If it was, then Fannie Lou Hamer, who was a sharecropper and wanted to destroy America to build a free, integrated society, would have been rich, and not just the seven Black Americans who became billionaires—Oprah Winfrey, Michael Jordan, Tyler Perry, Kanye West, Jay-Z, Robert Smith, and David Steward. Slaves and sharecroppers who toiled for hours and invented medicines and machines worked hard, and capitalists stole their earnings on the fields, then stole their children's earnings in the factories, then stole their grandchildren's earnings in the penitentiary. Meanwhile, the people whose families stole the earnings benefited from generational wealth, their great-great grandparents' right to enslave and steal land, their great-grandfather's right to vote, their grandparents' right to inherit homes, their parents' right to pay for college, and their child's right to admission as a legacy applicant. Taxation to begin redistributing wealth is very important, but to gain the traction we need for widespread support, we have to tell the truth about capitalism. As Professor Manning Marable writes: "The choice for Blacks is either socialism or some selective form of genocide; for the US proletariat, workers' democracy or some form of authoritarianism or fascism."[351]

Global decolonization movements tie many anti-capitalism and abolition strands together. For example, the Red Nation's "the Red Deal" calls for abolishing colonialism, capitalism, occupations, law enforcement, and child protective services, which would have kept Ma'Khia Bryant and many Indigenous children alive. Modern colonial territories and occupations, from tribal reservations to Western Sahara, against Puerto Ricans and Palestinians, are enforced by police and militaries that create more violence and cannot keep people safe. Palestinian women and girls report high rates of violence from Palestinian men, and Palestinian men report sexual violence and rape while detained by Israeli's military. Similar to the lack of police and prosecutorial jurisdiction for Indigenous people in the United States, Palestinians have no authority to prosecute Israelis (and even within Israel's military, 91 percent of sexual assaults happen against women; more than half are not reported). Palestinian women have to cross borders illegally and hide from military forces to seek refuge from sexual violence in women's shelters. Police cannot stop the violence and sometimes contribute. There are no shelters in Gaza and survivors cannot flee for help. Ending occupations and the legacies of settler colonialism not only ends violence from nation-states, but also changes the terrain upon which all violence occurs, and improves our ability to prevent, eliminate, and respond to harm.[352]

Rather than further displacement and land dispossession, the Red Deal echoes calls for free and sustainable housing, education, health care, and transit that is accessible by all, as well as the end of violence against oppressed peoples, animals, and the planet. The Deal's details for each demand are rooted in love, healing, and research. They emphasize the importance of political education around budgets for the sake of liberation. For instance, the Deal criticizes the federal government for spending 80 percent of transportation appropriations on highways and 20 percent on public transit and calls on us to wage campaigns against this disproportionate spending in order to improve movement for poor, rural, and working-class people:[353]

> The vast majority of these funds line the pockets of private contractors who make a profit from infrastructure projects and automobile corporations who lobby to improve highways so that consumers will continue to purchase and drive private vehicles. This means that the majority of public money—our money—goes towards inflating the profits of the ruling class. We must advocate for public money to go to operational costs like driver wages, gas, and bus maintenance, which creates stable employment for thousands of working-class people.[354]

The stable and sustainable employment for accessible green jobs in housing and transit cuts across decolonization, anti-capitalism, environmental and climate justice, and disability justice. These intersectional platforms and policy demands are in conversation with abolition: housing, jobs, and transit reduce precarity, violence, carjackings, theft, and arguments that become physical. This is the right idea: building the thriving societies that we want by dismantling the oppressive societies that we have.

ACTIVISTS OR ABOLITION-CURIOUS people will often ask me, "What does abolition look like to you?" My answers change all the time during conversation, especially since I believe that the dreaming and practicing should happen together. This is what I'm thinking about today as I'm writing the conclusion to this book. Every neighborhood would have five quality features: a neighborhood council; free twenty-four-hour childcare; art, conflict, and mediation centers; a free health clinic; and a green team.

COUNCILS

Neighborhood councils and block associations would have meetings where people make impactful decisions about the community. Many communities already have these, but few people participate in them because they don't have time, resources, or interest. These associations would be different; private property owners would not dominate them, and since everyone who wanted quality living space would have it, anyone who had time and an interest could help facilitate the council. I don't care much about races, but if people wanted to run them, then they all would be funded equally so that voters would not think that a candidate was stronger simply because they had bought more yard signs or cool T-shirts. The councils would make quick and impactful decisions about traffic, pollution, and construction, and act as incubators for people to try different ideas around quality-of-life improvements such as streetlights, solar panels, block parties, and festivals.

At these councils, everyday residents would take up particular causes to keep their communities safe from all kinds of violence. In the mid-eighties, a group of mostly poor and working-class Black mothers started attending city council meetings to protest a measure that would have put a trash incinerator in their neighborhood. They began meeting with each other and eventually formed Concerned Citizens of South Central Los Angeles. They waged a two-year campaign against the placement of the dump, and won. They had not previously trained organizers self-identifying as environmental justice activists, but as parents who committed time, energy, and resources to meeting regularly because their lives, and the lives of their children and neighborhoods, depended on it. There are countless examples of organizations and ad hoc committees like these that win campaigns against companies and governments, but because they are at the local level, the history is often overlooked. In my future, if there were difficult decisions to be made in a neighborhood, the council would be responsible for hosting town-hall meetings, distributing literature, and acting on the community's response to local problems.[355]

The councils and block associations would strengthen our communities, which is especially important because abolition requires us to begin creating safe spaces where we are. We'd spend time cultivating current and future generations to be invested in their local communities. No more excitement about gaining value according to how many followers, likes, retweets, and shares we accumulate online. Our social media profiles will no longer be commodities that we are incentivized to package and sell, and we would focus on building relationships with our neighbors that could save our lives by protecting us from fires, performing wellness checks, watching our kids in a pinch, and working in gardens—none of which we can accomplish online.

But people are not fighting over trash dumps and corporations in the world that I ultimately want. There, in some tomorrow, I hope that neighborhood councils mainly fight over color themes for street festivals, not whether the bulk of spending needs to go to police and permits for security. I want council members to be annoyed with each other because the community garden is running out of space for new fruits and vegetables, and it's taking longer than expected to determine whether to expand the smallest garden or open a third location. I want new kinds of controversies for the democratically elected boards, like reserving a town hall to discuss lowering the age for voting on neighborhood issues so that more youth can be eligible to participate. We deserve new kinds of problems.

CHILDCARE

Every neighborhood would also have free twenty-four-hour childcare centers for people who wanted or needed it. Every day in law school, I watched dozens of older Black women push white babies in strollers through Harvard Square. Full-time and part-time childcare should not be available only to those who have wealth; it should be, and can be, available to us all. Currently, cities pay cops around the clock to arrest people who are primarily poor. Cities can afford to provide free twenty-four-hour day care to help millions of people prevent harm. Ma'Khia Bryant's mom, my mom, the parent in our neighborhood whose baby Courtnie helped get home, Courtnie herself, me—whoever needs to run errands, go to work, go to school, or even have a break, should at least have the option. It would minimize stress and create sources of income for people who are excited about watching children. If the median income for a cop is seventy thousand dollars, then surely we can at least pay that to a multiracial, multigenerational corps of childcare workers, a far cry from what the underpaid, hyperexploited Black, brown, Indigenous, immigrant, poor, and elderly women who disproportionately provide childcare make now.

Well-funded, well-resourced, bright, and beautiful childcare spaces could alleviate lots of violence in the home. Inez could have left her marriage and still

had support for her children. Other people with children would not have to
rely on an abusive partner's income or babysitting anymore. Instead, they would
have an option to drop the kids off somewhere if they needed to work and go
to school, much like parents who work during the day when their kids are at
school now. My teacher friends used to say that "we aren't babysitters," and
they are right. We were not. But we should *have* babysitters, and it would be
great for everyone. Work and education will enable people who have children to
try new careers, find time to do things they love, and build skills to take care of
themselves as well. The families could work together to help shape the expectations of the center, like whether there should be weekly or daily limits on the
program. In my neighborhood, I would want the childcare center to give each
parent two consecutive weeks of childcare so that parents or whoever is raising
kids could take a vacation or spend time fixing up their home.

People who are raising children deserve leisure and downtime, too, and free,
around-the-clock childcare could help. The United States has such a warped
sense of reality. Many people praise people who accumulate so much wealth that
they can afford nannies and full-time workers to take care of their children. We
will praise Beyoncé, whom I love and often pay to watch perform, for being
one of the greatest international superstars to ever live, while also being a wife,
entrepreneur, and mother. Her work ethic has become a measuring stick for so
many women, and my friends and I joke with each other, "Girl, you have the same
amount of hours in a day as Beyoncé." It's funny, until I need to go to the grocery
store for breakfast and I have to get two sleeping kids up and dressed. When
Beyoncé tours, she has private childcare. If her labor seems more important than
all of the essential workers who watch our children, work at grocery stores, make
our clothes, and fix our cars, then try living one day without Beyoncé, and then
try living one day without the labor or products of essential workers.

We can pilot these childcare centers in different kinds of communities and
zip codes to test them. Cities do not technically have to lead the charge, childcare could also happen in the form of mutual aid through community-based
organizations. We could build sustainable dorms into neighborhood schools,
revitalize storefront churches, gut the insides of prisons, jails, and police
departments and flip them into something useful. If children are better served
at home or in smaller groups, the childcare centers could send people to homes

dividual circumstances. Additionally, the center would be able
nmodate anyone who came, worked there, and needed services,
guage, disability, sleep schedules, and religion.

ART, MEDIATION, AND CONFLICT RESOLUTION

n of communities that have art, mediation, and conflict-resolution
e can expand or build these practices and centers now by reducing,
ng our reliance on, police, patrols, surveillance, and calls. Reducing
ce on police involves many of the practices and campaigns that I've
roughout the book, from conflict mediation, to emergency prepared-
uilding interdependent networks to mediate and provide some relief
entially violent encounters. The Safe OUTside the System Collective
another example: the anti-violence program is led by lesbian, gay,
, trans, two-spirit, and gender-nonconforming people of color under
re Lorde Project, and they are "devoted to challenging violence against
NC POC, specifically hate and police violence in Central Brooklyn by
ommunity-based strategies rather than relying on the police or state sys-
They teach people how to recognize violence from police, and from other
, and internalized forms of violence to our own bodies, as well as how to
independent and interdependent plans toward preventing violence, inter-
g in and deescalating violence, and responding to violence if it happens at
es. These devoted community-based projects that keep people safe from
e and from community-based harm and can offer lessons and support to
r communities that are building similar projects.[356]

My art, mediation, and conflict (AMC) resolution center would have each
mmunity develop people's histories of protests, activism, art, and culture.
ighborhood archivists would work and volunteer there for multigenerational
rojects. Elders would record family and community histories and fill in each
other's stories. The archives and art would rotate to other AMC centers so that
we could learn from other neighborhoods about our shared struggle and resistance, and also never forget that we used to have a world that put people in metal
shackles, cages, and institutions of confinement. We'd remember that we used
to live in a world where some people had to press a button to enter a building

instead of using the sliding doors that we have now. We would host Freed
Fellows, the descendants of people from all formerly occupied territories to g
updates on how they melted barbed-wire fences into metal sculptures and men
rials for their ancestors.

Trained mediators, therapists, and restorative justice practitioners wou
offer dispute and conflict-resolution training, and engage in restorative justi
and transformative justice processes between family members and blocks, ar
across neighborhoods. What Zelda and other organizers created in Cape Tow
under the COVID pandemic was remarkable because building cohesive neigh
borhoods creates the basis for strong measures of accountability and healing
which are more sustainable long-term than punishment. Abolishing the priso
industrial complex does not mean that there will not be emergencies or harm; i
recognizes that the vast majority of harm is preventable and can be eliminated

AMC centers would also help us navigate harm that remains using true mea
sures of accountability that our communities can decide, rather than the violen
system of policing that we currently have, and including for murders. Today,
approximately four hundred thousand people die worldwide from homicides,
which is less than 1 percent of all deaths. Cardiovascular diseases claim seventeen million lives by comparison. In the abolitionist future that I hope to
build, for now, the number of murders has dropped drastically. Not in a magical
sense, but in a material sense. Whoever wants to work can and will receive their
fair share of what they produce instead of a wage, which will prevent murders
resulting from property, theft, robberies, and burglaries. We've learned how to
have healthy breakups, so people we used to call men don't kill people we used
to call women over leaving relationships. Heated arguments turn into headaches
sometimes, not shootouts, because we've eliminated most guns. (We may keep
a few guns for sport only, but they cannot leave the arenas where we used them
for play.)

In the rare case that a murder would happen, it would shock our communities, the entire world. We could more appropriately grieve, memorialize, and
honor the fallen, unlike the way we barely absorb the lists upon lists of names
from the news or online now. For the person who killed, we could spend time
learning the circumstances and reasons underlying the murder for the purposes
of rehabilitation, repair, and reparations. We could gather different options for

rom the victim's family, the community, the council, AMC work-
ie person who did the killing. The hearings and decisions would
cratic, and what we would decide could range from temporary
loss of privileges to further inclusion and additional support for
needs, and the family's needs. The process could be roughly the
AMC centers, and the democratic aspects would account for the
f the circumstances.

HEALTH CLINICS

cs are pretty self-explanatory. Members of the Rainbow Coalition
provided health care in the city and tested poor and working-class
color for illnesses and lead poisoning, just as Ivory Perry did in
would expand this, and every community would have a place where
ould go for checkups, from preventative health to standard outpatient
s. The clinics would provide different options for health care and
ring so people with different needs could have different choices for
-being. The clinics would be on the upper levels of the building, and
dios, and workout facilities would be on the main level, fusing a clinic
MCA-style building. But there would be few people utilizing the clinics
gencies because the food, air, water, and working conditions would be
and people would not be dying from preventable diseases, cancers, and
ated injuries. So the local clinics would become spectacular at repair-
ins and bones because sports would be inclusive and people would more
lly active. We'd laugh about the days of big pharmaceutical companies
ove up the cost of medicines that were in demand, and we'd mourn the
we lost because they could not afford the insulin that the clinics now kept
tribution on the shelves.[357]

GREEN TEAMS

neighborhood would have a green team. They would do trash pickup and
ng on every block. After dinner several times a week, workers would get
to collect food-waste bins to turn into a neighborhood compost filled with

terrific soil and worms, which I'm too afraid to be around. No more shipping and burning waste abroad—we would do our best to reuse materials and food locally, donating plastics, metals, paper, and glass to the art, mediation, and conflict-resolution center. The green team would also prioritize maintaining trees and flowers on each block so that people could live in shady environments which would keep us cool and keep violence down. The neighborhood council would have to consult with them if anything needed to be cut down to build something. In almost every city that I visit, the downtown center has people in bright yellow vests who replace flowers and pick up trash. I want this for my neighborhood, too. Not parks and recreation guards who shoot children, but park-keepers and protectors who teach children how to keep spaces neat and clean.

Our green teams would report to a regional council of sustainability. Because we would flip the budget allocations for highways and transit, 80 percent of the spending would be for high-speed trains that relied on renewable sources of energy, and 20 percent of the spending would go toward roads and cars for people who live, work, and play in remote areas. Train stops would be collectively decided and voted upon by the people. Bye Uber, bye Lyft—the few drivers that we would have would collectively own a company called "Swoop." They'd keep track of how many people they carried safely between destinations, appointments, excursions, clinics, and parties. Reducing our current use of cars would drastically cut pollution and save the lives of those suffering from asthma, diseases, and cancer because we live near highways and major roads. Carjackings would drop, too.

EVERY TIME SOMEONE moved into a community, the neighborhood council would prepare a welcome package with a unique gift and information about the local council, neighborhood, twenty-four-hour childcare center, green team, clinic, and art, mediation, and conflict-resolution center.

I'm going to cheat and offer a sixth feature: dream centers. We do not have to wait for this; we can start imagining and believing that we can create the world that we want and deserve. The greatest threats to our freedom are hopelessness, helplessness, and the criminalization of rebellion. Dreaming and joining others fights hopelessness because it reminds us that we develop the world that we want. As novelist Ursula K. Le Guin remarked, "We live in capitalism, its power seems inescapable—but then, so did the divine right of kings. Any human power can be resisted and changed by human beings." Dreaming also fights help-lessness. Our only option is not to sit idly and weep at the viral videos of police killings. Those of us who care about freedom, justice, and safety are obligated to ensure that there will be no more videos. If we can dream of that world, then we can create it, too.[358]

And finally, our freedom dreams are the greatest threat to capitalism, colo-nialism, and the carceral state. Which is why after every uprising, states quickly pass laws to stop our dissent. Since the 1960s, protests have become more safe for police, yet police violence against civilians continues. Between 1976 and 1998, cops averaged about four hundred "justifiable homicides" every year, and nearly eighty cops were murdered each year in the line of duty. Since the uprisings in 2014, cops average nearly one thousand homicides each year, and the number of cops killed in the line of duty has hovered around forty-eight. Homicides by cops have nearly doubled, while homicides of cops have nearly halved; yet the mainstream notion is that we are in an anti-cop environment. This could not be farther from the truth, and the violence must decline on all sides. We need rebellions and riots as much as we need sit-ins and marches. We privilege "peace," but peace alone has never gotten anyone free. We need nonvi-olent direct action and a diversity of tactics because we have lives, communities, and a planet worth fighting for.[359]

It is not a question of "if" abolition will happen; abolitionism is being prac-ticed every day. The question about total abolition is "when." And we have to do everything that we can right now so that our future children, elders, and activists will not be behind when they fight for whatever abolition they need in their lifetimes. We have to decide if we will delay their liberation, or if we will give them a head start by forging our freedom dreams right now.

ENDNOTES

1. Heather Ratcliffe, "Family of Woman Who Died after Praxair Blast Files Suit," *St. Louis Post Dispatch*, May 25, 2007; Trisha Howard and David Hunn, "Ten Years Ago Today: Explosions at Praxair Inc. Rattled Lafayette Square," *St. Louis Post Dispatch*, June 24, 2015.
2. William Pagano, "Rip Off," Stlreporter.com, accessed June 2021, https://stlreporter.com/tag/william-pagano/.
3. Mike Maciag, "Law Enforcement Officers Per Capita for Cities, Local Departments," Governing.com, August 31, 2012, https://www.governing.com/archive/law-enforcement-police-department-employee-totals-for-cities.html; "Death by the State: Police Killings and Jail Deaths in St. Louis," ArchCity Defenders, January 2021, https://www.archcitydefenders.org/wp-content/uploads/2021/01/ACD-FSV-report.pdf.
4. Shaila Dewan, "Few Police Officers Who Cause Deaths Are Charged or Convicted," *New York Times*, September 24, 2020.
5. Nicole Wetsman, "There Isn't Enough Research to Know If Tear Gas Causes Early Periods," The Verge, June 22, 2020, https://www.theverge.com/2020/6/22/21295159/tear-gas-menstural-cycle-miscarriage-period-protests; Gina Martinez, "Tear Gas, Miscarriages, and Breastfeeding: Is It Safe to Protest While Pregnant?" Rewire News Group, June 9, 2020; "Breastfeeding after Exposure to Tear Gas," Centers for Disease Control and Prevention, accessed April 2021, https://www.cdc.gov/breastfeeding/breastfeeding-special-circumstances/environmental-exposures/tear-gas.html.
6. Elizabeth Alexander, "The Trayvon Generation," *New Yorker*, June 22, 2020.
7. Robert Coles, "James Baldwin Back Home," *The New Yorker Times*, July 31, 1977, https://www.nytimes.com/1977/07/31/archives/jamesbaldwin-back-home-james-baldwin.html.
8. "Convict Leasing," Equal Justice Initiative, November 1, 2013, https://eji.org/news/history-racial-injustice-convict-leasing/#:~:text=After%20the%20Civil%20War%2C%20slavery,and%20often%20deadly%20work%20conditions; "A Brief History of the Drug War," Drug Policy Alliance, accessed June 2021, https://drugpolicy.org/issues/brief-history-drug-war; "Violent Crime Control and Law Enforcement Act of 1994," Govtrack.us, accessed June 2021, https://www.govtrack.us/congress/votes/103-1994/h416; Joseph Ax, "New York City Will Pay More Than $330,000 for Occupy Wall Street Pepper Spray Incidents," Reuters, July 6, 2015; "'Occupy Wall Street' UC Davis Protests Escalate After Pepper Spray Use Sparks Anger," *Washington Post*, November 21, 2011.
9. Naomi Murakawa, email with author.

10. "Number of People Shot to Death by the Police in the United States from 2017 to 2021, by Race," Statista.com, June 1, 2021, https://www.statista.com/statistics/585152/people-shot-to-death-by-us-police-by-race/; "Fatal Force," *Washington Post*, June 10, 2021, https://www.washingtonpost.com/graphics/investigations/police-shootings-database/; "Crime Clearance Rate in the United States in 2019, by Type," Statista.com, October 1, 2020, https://www.statista.com/statistics/194213/crime-clearance-rate-by-type-in-the-us/; "National Police Misconduct Reporting Project 2010 Annual Report," Cato Institute, accessed June 2021, http://policeprostitutionandpolitics.org/pdfs_all/COPS_DAs_JUDGES_PED_PORN/2010_CATO_National_police_misconduct_report.pdf; "Number of Reported Forcible Rape Cases in the United States from 1990 to 2019," Statista.com, September 28, 2020, https://www.statista.com/statistics/191137/reported-forcible-rape-cases-in-the-usa-since-1990/; Jeff Asher and Ben Horowitz, "How Do the Police Actually Spend Their Time?" *New York Times*, June 19, 2020; German Loopez, "There's a Nearly 40 Percent Chance You'll Get Away with Murder in America," Vox, September 24, 2018, https://www.vox.com/2018/9/24/17896034/murder-crime-clearance-fbi-report; Charles Wellford and James Cronin, "Clearing up Homicide Clearance Rates," *National Institute of Justice Journal* no. 243 (April 2000).

11. Olivia Eubanks, "Here Are Some Commonly Used Terms That Actually Have Racist Origins," ABC News, July 30, 2020, https://abcnews.go.com/Politics/commonly-terms-racist-origins/story?id=71840410; "Texas Rangers," Bullock Museum, accessed June 2021, https://www.thestoryoftexas.com/discover/campfire-stories/texas-ranger.

12. "Peculiar Institution," Encyclopedia.com, accessed June 2021; "Abolition of Slavery," Constitution Center, accessed June 2021, https://constitutioncenter.org/interactive-constitution/amendment/amendment-xiii#:~:text=13th%20Amendment%20%2D%20Abolition%20of%20Slavery%20%7C%20The%20National%20Constitution%20Center.

13. Cathy Girouard, "Fact Sheet: School Resource Officer Training Program," U.S. Department of Justice, March 2001, https://www.ncjrs.gov/txtfiles1/ojjdp/fs200105.txt.

14. "George Vashon: First Black Person to Graduate from Oberlin College," Black Then, September 11, 2020, https://blackthen.com/george-vashon-first-black-person-graduate-oberlin-college/.

15. "Liddell v. Board of Education," Casetext, accessed June 2021, https://casetext.com/case/liddell-v-bd-of-educ-city-of-st-louis-mo-2; Malcom Gay, "She Takes Control of Troubled Public Schools in St. Louis," *New York Times*, March 23, 2007.

16. Kim Bell, "Two Women Found Shot to Death in St. Louis Duplex, Two Toddlers Found Inside Unharmed," *St. Louis Post Dispatch*, April 30, 2015.

17. Josh Terry, "Ten Years Ago Today, Kanye West Said 'George Bush Doesn't Care About Black People,'" *Chicago Tribune*, September 2, 2015; A. C. Thompson, "Post Katrina, White Vigilantes Shot African-Americans with Impunity," ProPublica, December 19, 2018, https://www.propublica.org/article/post-katrina-white-vigilantes-shot-african-americans-with-impunity; Ken Wells, "The Nomads of Esplanade," *Wall Street Journal*, September 4, 2005; Scott Gold, "Trapped in the Superdome: Refuge Becomes a Hellhole," *Seattle Times*, September 1, 2005; Joan Brunkard et al., "Hurricane Katrina Deaths, Louisiana, 2005," *Disaster Medicine and Public Health Preparedness* 2, no. 4 (2008); Carl Bialik, "We Still Don't Know How Many People Died Because of Katrina," FiveThirtyEight.com, August 26, 2015, https://fivethirtyeight.com/features/we-still-dont-know-how-many-people-died-because-of-katrina/.

18. Howard Witt, "For Marchers, Destination Jena," *Baltimore Sun*, September 20, 2007.

19. "Thousands 'March for Justice' in Jena, Court Orders Hearing on Teen," CNN, September 20, 2007, http://www.cnn.com/2007/US/law/09/20/jena.six/; Howard Witt, "Part of 'Jena Six' Conviction Dropped, Charges Reduced," *Chicago Tribune*, September 5, 2007, https://www.chicagotribune.com/nation-world/chi-jena_05sep05-story.html.

20. "Frequently Asked Questions About the Arizona Racial Profiling Law," ACLU, accessed June 2021, https://www.aclu.org/other/frequently-asked-questions-about-arizona-racial-profiling-law.

21. John Milburn, "Arizona Sheriff Arpaio Stumps for Kobach," *Wichita Eagle*, July 14, 2010.

22. "Pete O'Neal," Profiles in Kansas City Activism, accessed June 2021l, https://info.umkc.edu/kcactivism/?page_id=209.

23. "Race and Justice News: One-Third of Black Men Have Felony Convictions," The Sentencing Project, October 10, 2017, https://www.sentencingproject.org/news/5593/.

24. "Remarks by the President on Comprehensive Immigration Reform," The White House Office of the Press Secretary, July 1, 2010, https://obamawhitehouse.archives.gov/realitycheck/the-press -office/remarks-president-comprehensive-immigration-reform; Serena Marshall, "Obama Has Deported More People Than Any Other President," ABC News, August 9, 2016, https://abcnews .go.com/Politics/obamas-deportation-policy-numbers/story?id=41715661.

25. Eamon McNiff, "Witnesses Now Say They Lied in 1991 Trial That Sent Troy Davis to Death Row," ABC News, June 23, 2010, https://abcnews.go.com/TheLaw/witnesses-helped-convict -man-death-row-now-recant/story?id=10995816.

26. "Georgia Executes Davis, Supporters Claim Injustice," Associated Press, September 22, 2011; "Troy Davis Amidst 11th Hour Plea to Hugh Court," CBS News, September 21, 2011, https:// www.cbsnews.com/news/troy-davis-amidst-11th-hour-plea-to-high-court/.

27. Sherry Wolf, "Why Did Obama Let Troy Davis Die?" SocialistWorker.org, accessed April 2021, https://socialistworker.org/2011/09/22/why-did-obama-let-troy-die; Joy Freeman-Coulbary, "Obama Silent on Troy Davis," *Washington Post*, September 21, 2011; William Sessions, "Should Davis Be Executed?" *Atlanta Journal-Constitution*, August 10, 2012; John Rudolph, "Troy Davis Execution: Former FBI Chief William Sessions Calls on Georgia to Stay Order," HuffPost, September 15, 2011, https://www.huffpost.com/entry/troy-davis-execution-william-sessions_n_963366.

28. Frances Robles, "Records Show George Zimmerman Got D's in Criminal Justice Classes," *Miami Herald*, August 9, 2012.

29. Bill Chappell, "Zimmerman Arrested on Murder Charge in Zimmerman Case," NPR, April 11, 2021, https://www.npr.org/sections/thetwo-way/2012/04/11/150449405/zimmerman-arrested-on -murder-charge-in-martin-case; Sarah Childress, "Is There Racial Bias in 'Stand Your Ground' Laws?" PBS Frontline, July 31, 2012, https://www.pbs.org/wgbh/frontline/article/is-there-racial -bias-in-stand-your-ground-laws/.

30. "Sanford Police Chief Fired in Wake of Trayvon Martin Case," CNN, June 21, 2012, https://www .cnn.com/2012/06/20/justice/florida-martin-case-police-chief.

31. Ta-Nehisi Coates, "How Stand Your Ground Relates to George Zimmerman," *The Atlantic*, July 16, 2013.

32. Tiffany D. Cross, "Mother of Jordan Davis Running for Office," The Beat, October 4, 2017, https://www.tiffanydcross.net/top-news-stories/2017/10/4/mother-of-jordan-davis-running-for- office; Penny Dickerson, "From Father to Foot Soldier," *Florida Courier*, June 19, 2015, https:// pennydickersonwrites.com/2020/08/22/ron-davis-father-and-foot-soldier-for-justice; Lucy McBath, *Ballotpedia*, https://ballotpedia.org/Lucy_McBath.

33. "Transcript: President Obama's Remarks on Trayvon Martin and Race," NBC News, July 19, 2013, https://www.nbcnews.com/politics/politics-news/transcript-president-obamas-remarks -trayvon-martin-race-flna6C10689424; James S. Brady, "Remarks by the President on Trayvon Martin," The White House, July 19, 2013, https://obamawhitehouse.archives.gov/the-press -office/2013/07/19/remarks-president-trayvon-martin.

34. Alyssa Newcomb and Dean Schabner, "Michael Dunn Trial: Mistrial Declared on Murder Charge in Loud Music Killing," ABC News, February 13, 2014, https://abcnews.go.com/US/michael -dunn-trial-mistrial-declared-murder-charge-loud/story?id=22503778.

35. Attom Data Solutions, "Nearly 1.5 Million Vacant US Homes in Q3 2018 represent 1.52 Percent of All Single Family Homes and Condos," press release, October 30, 2018, https://www .prnewswire.com/news-releases/nearly-1-5-million-vacant-us-homes-in-q3-2018-represent-1-52 -percent-of-all-single-family-homes-and-condos-300739953.html#:~:text=States%20with%20 the%20highest%20share,and%20Indiana%20(2.45%20percent).

36. David Hunn and Kim Bell, "Why Was Michael Brown's Body Left There for Hours?" *St. Louis Post-Dispatch*, September 14, 2014.

37. Derecka Purnell, "Why Does Obama Scold Black Boys?" *New York Times*, February 21, 2019; Stephen Pulvirent, "The $15,000 Detail Hidden in Obama's Official Portrait," Bloomberg, February 15, 2018, https://www.bloomberg.com/news/articles/2018-02-15/the-15-000-rolex-hidden-in -president-obama-s-official-portrait.

38. Julia Dahl, "Stop and Frisk: AG's Report Says Only 3 Percent of NYPD Arrests Using Tactic End in Conviction," CBS News, November 14, 2013, https://www.cbsnews.com/news/stop-and-frisk

-ags-report-says-only-3-percent-of-nypd-arrests-using-tactic-end-in-conviction; Eric T. Schneiderman, "A Report on Arrests Arising from the New York City Police Department's Stop-and-Frisk Practices," New York State Office of the Attorney General, November 2013, https://ag.ny.gov/pdfs/OAG_REPORT_ON_SQF_PRACTICES_NOV_2013.pdf. https://www.baruch.cuny.edu/nycdata/population-geography/pop-demography.htm, https://www.nyclu.org/en/stop-and-frisk-data

39. James Baldwin, *The Fire Next Time* (New York: Vintage, 1997).

40. "BYP Announces National Call for Video Testimonials from Young Black People Criminalized by Police," Black Youth Project, June 9, 2014, http://blackyouthproject.com/byp100-announces-national-call-for-video-testimonials-from-young-black-people-criminalized-by-police/; Randell Stevens, "Trayvon's Law—Bill Summary," NAACP, https://docplayer.net/12514588-Trayvon-s-law-bill-summary.html.

41. R. H. Taylor, "Slave Conspiracies in North Carolina," *The North Carolina Historical Review* 5, no. 1 (January 1928); Cedric J. Robinson, *Black Movements in America*, 1st ed. (New York: Routledge, 1997).

42. Robinson, *Black Movements in America*; David Correia and Tyler Wall, *Police: A Field Guide* (New York: Verso, 2018); Matthew Restall, "Black Conquistadors: Armed Africans in Early Spanish America," *The Americas* 57, no. 2 (October 2000).

43. Taylor, "Slave Conspiracies in North Carolina," 20–34; Sir Hilary Beckles, "On Barbados, the First Black Slave Society," Black Perspectives, accessed June 2021, https://www.aaihs.org/on-barbados-the-first-black-slave-society/.

44. Gary Potter, "The History of Policing in the United States, Part One," Eastern Kentucky University Policy Studies Online, accessed June 2021, https://plsonline.eku.edu/insidelook/history-policing-united-states-part-1; "The Connection," The Barbados and the Carolinas Legacy Foundation, accessed June 2021, https://www.barbadoscarolinas.org/the-connection-1; "Slave Codes," South Carolina Encyclopedia, accessed June 2021, https://www.scencyclopedia.org/sce/entries/slave-codes/.

45. Sally E. Hadden, *Slave Patrols: Law and Violence in Virginia and the Carolinas* (Cambridge: Harvard University Press, 2001), 23.

46. Hilary McD. Beckles, "A 'Riotous and Unruly Lot': Irish Indentured Servants and Freemen in the English West Indies, 1644–1713," *William and Mary Quarterly* 47, no. 4 (October 1990).

47. Harmeet Kaur, "Kanye West Just Said 400 Years of Slavery Was a Choice," CNN, May 4, 2018, https://www.cnn.com/2018/05/01/entertainment/kanye-west-slavery-choice-trnd/index.html; Sam James Ervin, *A Colonial History of Rowan County, North Carolina, Volumes 16-19* (Chapel Hill: University of North Carolina Press, 1917).

48. W. E. B. Du Bois, *Black Reconstruction in America, 1860–1880* (New York: Free Press, 1997).

49. Walter Rodney, *How Europe Underdeveloped Africa* (Brooklyn: Verso, 2018).

50. "Slave Patrols," NCpedia.com, accessed June 2021, https://www.ncpedia.org/slave-patrols.

51. Hadden, *Slave Patrols*.

52. The Wars of Reconstruction, 550; Keri Leigh Merritt, "Private, Public, and Vigilante Justice, Part Four," Black Perspectives, February 12, 2017, https://www.aaihs.org/private-public-and-vigilante-violence-part-4/; Kristian Williams, *Our Enemies in Blue: Police and Power in America* (Chico: AK Press, 2015).

53. Du Bois, *Black Reconstruction in America*.

54. "Walter Scott Had Bench Warrant for His Arrest, Court Documents Show," NBC News, April 10, 2015, https://www.nbcnews.com/storyline/walter-scott-shooting/walter-scott-shooting-warrant-over-child-support-court-records-show-n339151; "Why Was Walter Scott Running?" The Marshall Project, April 10, 2015, https://www.themarshallproject.org/2015/04/10/why-was-walter-scott-running.

55. Lauren Sausser, "Walter Scott Was Dogged by System That 'Criminalizes' Debt," *Post and Courier*, April 9, 2015.

56. Meghan Keneally, "Officer Charged with Murdering Walter Scott Has Been Fired," ABC News, April 8, 2015, https://abcnews.go.com/US/walter-scott-shooters-insurance-continued-jail/story?id=30160301; "Quick Facts, North Charleston City, South Carolina," United States Census, accessed June 2021, https://www.census.gov/quickfacts/northcharlestoncitysouthcarolina.

57. "'They Tasing Me': Walter Scott's Mother Tells Jurors in Cop's Murder Trial About Son's Last Words, Collapses," NBC News, November 3, 2016, https://www.nbcnews.com/storyline/walter-scott-shooting/they-tasing-me-walter-scott-s-mother-tells-jurors-cop-n677696.

58. Michael Schmidt and Matt Appuzzo, "South Carolina Officer Is Charged with Murder of Walter Scott," *New York Times*, April 7, 2015.

59. Nayyirah Waheed, "The Color of Low Self Esteem," *Salt* (self-pub., 2013).

60. "Our Demands," Black Lives Matter, accessed April 2021, https://web.archive.org/web/2013105040012/http://blacklivesmatter.tumblr.com/demands; "#BlackLivesMatter National Demands," Black Lives Matter, accessed April 2021, https://web.archive.org/web/20141023044545/http://blacklivesmatter.com/demands/.

61. German Lopez, "Feds Tell Ferguson Police to Stop Wearing 'I Am Darren Wilson' Bracelets," Vox, September 28, 2014, https://www.vox.com/2014/9/28/6854987/Michael-Brown-protests-Justice-Department-Ferguson-Police-Darren-Wilson-bracelets; Jonathan Allen, "New York Medical Examiner Testifies Chokehold Led to Eric Garner's Death," Reuters, May 15, 2019.

62. "PDF: Charging Documents for Freddie Gray," *Baltimore Sun*, April 20, 2015; Baynard Woods, "'Rough Ride': Practice Linked to Freddie Gray's Death at the Center of Latest Trial," *The Guardian*, June 6, 2016.

63. "Accused Ferguson Looter Found Dead Two Days After Being Charged," Fox News, May 5, 2015, https://fox2now.com/news/woman-charged-for-looting-during-ferguson-grand-jury-decision-night/.

64. "President Obama on Freddie Gray's Death: 'This Is Not New, and We Shouldn't Pretend That It's New,'" The White House, President Barack Obama, April 28, 2015, https://obamawhitehouse.archives.gov/blog/2015/04/28/president-obama-freddie-gray-s-death-not-new-and-we-shouldn-t-pretend-it-s-new.

65. Marisa Franco and Carlos Garcia, "The Deportation Machine Obama Built for President Trump," *The Nation*, June 27, 2016; "Fact Sheet: Strengthening Community Policing," The White House Office of the Press Secretary, December 1, 2014, https://obamawhitehouse.archives.gov/the-press-office/2014/12/01/fact-sheet-strengthening-community-policing; Kimberly Kindy, "Some US Police Departments Dump Body-Camera Programs amid High Costs," *Washington Post*, January 21, 2019; Quentin Hardy, "Taser's Latest Police Weapon," *New York Times*, February 21, 2012; Alex Pasternak, "We Spent a Fortune on Police Body Cameras," *FastCompany*, June 17, 2020.

66. Phil Rogers, "Video from Burger King Near Laquan McDonald Shooting Released," NBC News Chicago, December 4, 2015, https://www.nbcchicago.com/news/local/video-from-burger-king-near-laquan-mcdonald-shooting-released/61527/; Jeremy Borden, "How a Little-Known, Uber-Driving Freelancer Brought the Lawsuit that Forced Chicago to Release Police Shooting Video," *Columbia Journalism Review*, November 25, 2015; Morgan Winsor, "Four Chicago Police Officers Fired Over Alleged Cover-Up of Laquan McDonald Shooting," ABC News, July 19, 2019, https://abcnews.go.com/US/chicago-police-officers-fired-alleged-cover-laquan-mcdonald/story?id=64433067; "One Million Per Shot," *Chicago Sun Times*, June 24, 2016; Chip Mitchell, "Four Chicago Police Officers Fired in Alleged Cover-up for Jason Van Dyke," NPR/WBEZ, July 19, 2019, https://www.npr.org/local/309/2019/07/19/743412353/4-chicago-police-officers-fired-in-alleged-cover-up-for-jason-van-dyke.

67. Andy Newman, "Jury Deadlocks in Trial of Ex-Officer in Killing of Unarmed Black Driver in Cincinnati," *New York Times*, November 12, 2016.

68. "University of Cincinnati Reaches Settlement with Family of Samuel DuBose," NPR, All Things Considered, January 20, 2016, https://www.npr.org/2016/01/20/463740319/university-of-cincinnati-reaches-settlement-with-family-of-samuel-dubose; Kate Murphy and Mark Curnutte, "University of Cincinnati Pays $250,000 to Ex-Cop Who Killed Sam DuBose," Cincinnati.com, March 22, 2018, https://www.cincinnati.com/story/news/2018/03/22/university-cincinnati-pays-cop-who-killed-sam-dubose/450587002/.

69. Jon Schuppe, "Justice Department Won't Charge Six Officers in Freddie Gray Death," NBC News, September 12, 2017, https://www.nbcnews.com/storyline/baltimore-unrest/justice-department-won-t-charge-six-officers-freddie-gray-death-n800786; Tricia Bishop, "Uneven Justice for Baltimore's Rioters," *Baltimore Sun*, March 3, 2016, https://www.baltimoresun.com/opinion/op-ed/bs-ed-bishop-0304-20160303-story.html.

70. "National Census of Fatal Occupational Injuries in 2019," Bureau of Labor Statistics news release, December 16, 2020, https://www.bls.gov/news.release/pdf/cfoi.pdf; Chelsea Bailey and Daniel

Arkin, "Ray Tensing: Ex-Police Officer Won't Be Retried for Third Time in Murder Case," NBC News, July 18, 2017, https://www.nbcnews.com/news/us-news/ray-tensing-ex-police-officer-won-t-be-retried-third-n784111.

71. Graham v. Connor, 490 U.S. 386 (1989), https://supreme.justia.com/cases/federal/us/490/386/.

72. Frederick Douglass, *Narrative of the Life of Frederick Douglass*, PagebyPageBooks.com, accessed June 2021, https://www.pagebypagebooks.com/Frederick_Douglass/The_Narrative_of_the _Life_of_Frederick_Douglass/Chapter_X_p5.html.

73. Frederick Douglass, *My Bondage and My Freedom*, Lit2Go.com, accessed June 2021, https://etc .usf.edu/lit2go/45/my-bondage-and-my-freedom/1458/chapter-11-a-change-came-oer-the-spirit -of-my-dream/.

74. Aamer Madhani, "No Charges in VonDerrit Myers Shooting in St. Louis," *USA Today*, May 18, 2015; Lauren Raab and Christine Mai-Duc, "St. Louis Police Officer Who Killed VonDerrit Myers Won't Face Charges," *Baltimore Sun*, May 18, 2015.

75. Race Forward, "Ferguson's 'Lost Voices' Speak," YouTube video, November 24, 2014, https:// www.youtube.com/watch?v=1yc4JxGeeCw.

76. "Investigation of the Ferguson Police Department," US Department of Justice, Civil Rights Division, March 4, 2015, https://www.justice.gov/sites/default/files/opa/press-releases/attachments/2015/03 /04/ferguson_police_department_report.pdf; "Executive Order 14-14," Secretary of State John Ashcroft website, accessed June 2021, https://www.sos.mo.gov/library/reference/orders/2014/eo14 _14; "Justice Department Announces Findings of Two Civil Rights Investigations in Ferguson, Missouri," United States Department of Justice press release, March 4, 2015, https://www.justice.gov /opa/pr/justice-department-announces-findings-two-civil-rights-investigations-ferguson-missouri.

77. Alex Vitale, *The End of Policing* (Brooklyn: Verso, 2018).

78. Nyle Fort, "Prisons, Pot, and Profit: The Plight of Post-Emancipation," *Harvard Journal of African-American Public Policy* (2013).

79. "Settlement Reached with Ferguson Over Court Fees," ArchCity Defenders press release, March 25, 2020, https://www.archcitydefenders.org/for-immediate-release-settlement-reached-with -ferguson-over-court-fees/; Leon Neyfakh, "St. Louis Police to Limit Use of Tear Gas in Response to Ferguson Lawsuit," Slate.com, March 27, 2015, https://slate.com/news-and-politics/2015/03/ferguson -tear-gas-lawsuit-michael-brown-protesters-win-concessions-from-st-louis-police.html.

80. Thomas Gorton, "Palestinians Tweet Tear Gas Tips to Ferguson Residents," Dazeddigital.com, August 15, 2014, https://www.dazeddigital.com/artsandculture/article/21289/1/palestinians -tweet-tear-gas-tips-to-ferguson-residents.

81. James Baldwin, "Negroes Are Anti-Semitic Because They're Anti-White," *New York Times*, April 9, 1967, https://archive.nytimes.com/www.nytimes.com/books/98/03/29/specials/baldwin -antisem.html?_r=1; Tracy Jan, "Study: Hiring More Black Cops Won't Stop Fatal Police Shootings of Black Citizens," *Washington Post*, January 5, 2017.

82. Chris McGreal, "Police Release Video of Fatal Kajieme Powell Shooting in St. Louis," *The Guardian*, August 21, 2014.

83. Brakkton Booker, "Autopsy Reveals St. Louis Police Shot Mansur Ball-Bey in the Back," NPR, August 21, 2015, https://www.npr.org/sections/thetwo-way/2015/08/21/433540554/autopsy -reveals-st-louis-police-shot-mansur-ball-bey-in-the-back.

84. Robert J. Bunker, ed., *Nonlethal Weapons: Terms and References*, INSS Occasional Paper 15 (Colorado: USAF Institute for National Security Studies, 1997).

85. Jorge L. Ortiz, "'Open up the Case': Sandra Bland's Family Wants Answers After New Video Surfaces," *USA Today*, May 7, 2019.

86. "Police Violence Alleged in Anti-Zwarte Piet Activist's Complaint," *NL Times*, November 22, 2016; "Dutch Police Arrest around Two Hundred Protesters against Controversial 'Black Pete,'" *Global Times*, November 13, 2016, https://www.globaltimes.cn/content/1017581.shtml.

87. Joanne Van Selm, "Migration in the Netherlands: Rhetoric and Perceived Reality Challenge Dutch Tolerance," Migration Policy Institute, May 1, 2019, https://www.migrationpolicy.org/article /migration-netherlands-rhetoric-and-perceived-reality-challenge-dutch-tolerance.

88. Moha Ennaji, "Patterns and Trends of Migration in the Maghreb," Middle East Institute, May 2, 2010, https://www.mei.edu/publications/patterns-and-trends-migration-maghreb; Morgan Meaker, "For Dutch Moroccans, a Campaign of Fear," *Politico*, March 14, 2017.

89. https://dmc.tamuc.edu/digital/collection/p15778coll7/id/458/; Marieke Bloembergen and Ellen Klinkers, "Dutch Colonial Police," in Gerben Bruinsma and David Weisburd, eds., *Encyclopedia of Criminology and Criminal Justice* (New York: Springer, 2104); "Civil Guard," *Encyclopedia Britannica Online*, accessed June 2021, https://www.britannica.com/topic/Civil-Guard; "History of Rio de Janeiro's Military Police Part One: Nineteenth-Century Beginnings," RioOnWatch.com, accessed June 2021, https://www.rioonwatch.org/?p=13506; "History of the Nigeria Police Force," Nigeria Police Force online, accessed June 2021, https://www.npf.gov.ng/aboutus/History_Nigeria_Police.php#:~:text=The%20British%20merged%20Lagos%20colony,Nigeria%20Police%20Force%20(NPF).

90. "States of Incarceration: The Global Context," PrisonPolicy.org, accessed June 2021, https://www.prisonpolicy.org/global/.

91. Jacob Gershman, "Harvard Law Students Want School's Link to Slaveholder Scrubbed from Official Seal," *Wall Street Journal*, November 3, 2015.

92. David A. Graham, "Black Tape over Black Faculty Portraits at Harvard Law School," *The Atlantic*, November 19, 2015.

93. "16 June 1976: The Day Hector Pieterson Died," *Brand South Africa*, June 15, 2004.

94. Aryn Baker, "This Photo Galvanized the World against Apartheid. Here's the Story Behind It," *Time*, June 15, 2016; William Claiborne, "Massive Boycott Marks 1976 Soweto Uprising," *Washington Post*, June 17, 1987, https://www.washingtonpost.com/archive/politics/1987/06/17/massive-boycott-marks-1976-soweto-uprising/e5829fda-be52-452c-8152-e1549cf88263/.

95. "Hector Pieterson," South Africa History Online, accessed April 2021, https://www.sahistory.org.za/people/hector-pieterson; Chris Barron, "Sam Nzima, Photographer Who Made History," *Sunday Times*, May 20, 2018; Baker, "This Photo Galvanized the World Against Apartheid."

96. "TRC Final Report," Truth Commission Special Report, Sabca Radio, accessed April 2021, https://sabctrc.saha.org.za/reports/volume3/chapter6/subsection20.htm?t=%2BPolice+%2Bbrutality&tab=report.

97. "Notorious 'SOWETO' Policeman Dies," South African History Online, July 7, 1998, https://www.sahistory.org.za/dated-event/notorious-soweto-policeman-dies; "Hector Pieterson Gets His Memorial," Joburg.org, accessed June 2021, https://www.joburg.org.za/play_/Pages/Play%20in%20Joburg/Culture%20and%20Heritage/Links/Hector-Pieterson-gets-his-Memorial.aspx#:~:text=Swanepoel%20told%20the%20TRC%3A%20%22I,the%20back%20of%20the%20organisers.%22.

98. Helen Popper and Karina Grazina, "Life Sentence for Argentine 'Blond Angel of Death,'" Reuters, October 27, 2011, https://www.reuters.com/article/us-argentina-rights/life-sentence-for-argentine-blond-angel-of-death-idUSTRE79Q0D020111027.

99. Kristian Davis Bailey, "The Ferguson/Palestine Connection," *Ebony*, August 19, 2014.

100. Erik van Ees, "'Asinamali' Invites Whites on Rare Tour into the Heart of Black," *Chicago Tribune*, April 13, 1986.

101. The Social Change Initiative, "Zelda Holtzman: Challenges of Delivering Change in Post-Conflict South Africa," Vimeo, August 24, 2018, https://vimeo.com/286536528.

102. Phillip Agnew, interview with author.

103. "Belinda Sutton and Her Petitions," Royall House and Slave Quarters, accessed June 2021, https://royallhouse.org/slavery/belinda-sutton-and-her-petitions/.

104. Richard Delgado and Jean Stefancic, *Critical Race Theory: An Introduction* (New York and London: New York University Press, 2001).

105. Robin D. G. Kelley, "Black Study, Black Struggle," *Boston Review*, March 7, 2016; Maya Rhodan, "Harvard Law School Supports Removing Shield with Ties to Slavery," *Time*, March 4, 2016; Jamie D. Halper, "Law School Unveils Slavery Monument, Reflects on History," *Harvard Crimson*, September 6, 2017.

106. Randall Kennedy, "Black Tape at Harvard Law," *New York Times*, November 27, 2015; Lindsay Church and Brianna Rennix, "Recording Device Allegedly Found in the Lounge," *Harvard Law Record*, April 8, 2016.

107. George L. Jackson, *Blood in My Eye* (New York: Random House, 1972), 113.

108. Robin D. G. Kelley and Earl Lewis, eds., *To Make Our World Anew: Volume I: A History of African Americans to 1880* (New York: Oxford University Press, 2005).

109. Kelley, "Black Study, Black Struggle."

110. "A Collective Response to Anti-Blackness," #WeDemandUNC, accessed June 2012, https://docs .google.com/document/d/1r1Rp3Tn8sPlfbn_bO3vQXOVRnDpaDvB_ctaBKXvbpNU/edit.

111. Fred Moten and Stefano Harney, *Undercommons: Fugitive Planning and Black Study* (Brooklyn: Autonomedia, 2013).

112. Michael Medved, "Obama's Cocaine Confessional Won't 'Blow' His Chances," ABC News, January 6, 2007, https://abcnews.go.com/Politics/BothSidesAllSides/story?id=2773754&page=1.

113. "Number of Arrests for All Offenses in the United States from 1990 to 2019," Statistica.com, accessed June 2021, https://www.statista.com/statistics/191261/number-of-arrests-for-all-offenses -in-the-us-since-1990/; Alexi Jones and Wendy Sawyer, "Arrest, Release, Repeat: How Police and Jails are Misused to Respond to Social Problems," Prison Policy Institute, August 2019, https:// www.prisonpolicy.org/reports/repeatarrests.html; Bernadette Rauby and Randall Kopf, "Prisons of Policy," Prison Policy Institute, July 9, 2015, https://www.prisonpolicy.org/reports/income .html; Courtney Connley, "Latinas Earn $.55 for Every Dollar Paid to White Men, a Pay Gap That Has Barely Moved in Thirty Years," CNBC.com, October 29, 2020, https://www.cnbc.com/2020 /10/29/latinas-face-an-ongoing-pay-gap-that-has-barely-moved-in-30-years.html.

114. Audre Lorde, "The Master's Tools Will Never Dismantle the Master's House," *Sister Outsider: Essays and Speeches* (Berkeley: Crossing Press, 1984).

115. David Marchese, "Lori Lightfoot, Mayor of Chicago, on Who's Hurt by Defunding Police," *New York Times Magazine*, June 22, 2020. This comment came years after a coalition, We Charge Genocide, won reparations for some survivors of Chicago police torture. They took their name from the 1951 petition to the United Nations edited by William Patterson, signed by W. E. B. Du Bois, Claudia Jones, Paul Robeson, and Mary Church Terrell among others, to seek relief for Black people from state-sanctioned violence.

116. George Jackson, *Soledad Brother* (Toronto: Lawrence Hill Books, 1994).

117. Angela Y. Davis, *Abolition Democracy: Beyond Empire, Prisons, and Torture* (New York: Seven Stories Press, 2011).

118. Du Bois, *Black Reconstruction in America*.

119. Smith, "Heteropatriarchy and the Three Pillars of White Supremacy," Campus Compact of Oregon, accessed April 2021, http://www.oregoncampuscompact.org/uploads/1/3/0/4/13042698 /undoing_racism_-_three_pillars_-__andrea_smith_.pdf; Roxanne Dunbar-Ortiz, *An Indigenous Peoples' History of the United States* (Boston: Beacon Press, 2015).

120. "The Civil War Era," *Encyclopedia Britannica Online*, accessed June 2021, https://www .britannica.com/topic/African-American/The-Civil-War-era.

121. Du Bois, *Black Reconstruction in America*.

122. Du Bois, *Black Reconstruction in America*.

123. Panashe Chigumadzi, "Who Is Afraid of Race?" *Boston Review*, March 11, 2021.

124. Henry Louis Gates, Jr., "The Truth Behind 'Forty Acres and a Mule,'" PBS, The African Americans, accessed June 2021, https://www.pbs.org/wnet/african-americans-many-rivers-to-cross/history /the-truth-behind-40-acres-and-a-mule/.

125. William F. Warde, "The War Deal's Economics," *Fourth International* 2, no. 3 (1950).

126. Kristian Williams, *Our Enemies in Blue: Police and Power in America* (Chico: AK Press, 2015).

127. "What Is the PIC? What Is Abolition?" Critical Resistance, accessed June 2021, http:// criticalresistance.org/about/not-so-common-language/#:~:text=The%20prison%20industrial%20 complex%20(PIC,economic%2C%20social%20and%20political%20problems; Karl Evers-Hillstrom, "Lobbying Spending Reaches 3.4 Billion in 2018," OpenSecrets.org, January 15, 2019, https://www .opensecrets.org/news/2019/01/lobbying-spending-reaches-3-4-billion-in-18/.

128. Duren Banks et al., *National Sources of Law Enforcement Data* (Washington, DC: US Department of Justice, Bureau of Justice Statistics, 2016).

129. Gabriella Paiella, "How Would Prison Abolition Actually Work?" *GQ*, June 11, 2020; Rachel Herzing, "Big Dreams and Bold Steps Toward a Police-Free Future," *Truthout*, September 16, 2015.

130. Jonathan Berr, "More Americans Are Forced to 'Reside' in Their Vehicles," CBS News, July 31, 2018, https://www.cbsnews.com/news/more-americans-are-living-in-their-vehicles-amid-high-housing -prices/.

131. Josie Duffy Rice, "The Abolition Movement," *Vanity Fair*, September 2020; Asher and Horowitz, "How Do the Police Actually Spend Their Time?"

132. Polly Mosendz and Jameelah D. Robinson, "While Crime Fell, the Cost of Cops Soared," Bloomberg, June 4, 2020, https://www.bloomberg.com/news/articles/2020-06-04/america-s-policing-budget-has-nearly-tripled-to-115-billion.

133. Shawndrea Thomas, "Man Charged for Murdering Ferguson Woman after Facebook Meeting," Fox News, December 1, 2015, https://fox2now.com/news/man-charged-for-murdering-ferguson-woman-after-facebook-meeting/; "Police Believe I-55 Killing in St. Louis Is Unrelated to Others," *St. Louis Post-Dispatch*, December 6, 2016, https://www.stltoday.com/news/local/crime-and-courts/police-believe-latest-i-55-killing-in-st-louis-is-unrelated-to-others/article_d460601f-b2c4-535a-813b-af7a8132f80e.html.

134. "Homicide Database," *Washington Post*, accessed April 2021, https://www.washingtonpost.com/graphics/2018/investigations/unsolved-homicide-database/?utm_term=.a1848ca73e91&city=st-louis.

135. "Grenfell Tower: What Happened," BBC News, October 29, 2019, https://www.bbc.com/news/uk-40301289. Fergus O'Sullivan, "The Grenfell Tower Fire and London's Public-Housing Crisis," *The Atlantic*, June 14, 2017; Ed Davey, "Grenfell Contractor: Sprinklers Would Have Saved Tower," BBC News, September 27, 2017, https://www.bbc.com/news/uk-40301289; "Grenfell Inquiry: Stay-Put Advice 'Good' Says Firefighter," BBC News, September 4, 2018, https://www.bbc.com/news/uk-45411551; INQUEST, accessed April 2021, https://www.inquest.org.uk/.

136. "KCTMO—Playing with Fire!" *Grenfell Action Group*, November 20, 2016, https://grenfellactiongroup.wordpress.com/2016/11/20/kctmo-playing-with-fire/.

137. "Windrush Generation: Who Are They and Why Are They Facing Problems?" BBC News, July 31, 2020, https://www.bbc.com/news/uk-43782241.

138. "About Sisters Inside," Sisters Inside, accessed June 2021, https://www.sistersinside.com.au/.

139. "Thirty Cities with the Highest Murder Rates in the US," *Rapid City Journal*, November 13, 2017; John Gramilch and Drew DeSilver, "Despite Recent Violence, Chicago Is Far from the US Murder Capital," Pew Research.org, https://www.pewresearch.org/fact-tank/2018/11/13/despite-recent-violence-chicago-far-from-u-s-murder-capital/.

140. "For Very Grave Offenses in the Criminal Court," *St Louis Post Dispatch (Vol. 38, no. 16)*, July 21, 1887; "Report: Guilty Pleas on the Rise, Criminal Trials on the Decline," The Innocence Project, August 7, 2018, https://innocenceproject.org/guilty-pleas-on-the-rise-criminal-trials-on-the-decline/.

141. "Close the Workhouse! An Interview with Inez Bordeaux," Ben and Jerry's, September 12, 2019, https://www.benjerry.com/whats-new/2019/09/inez-bordeaux.

142. "Close the Workhouse!" Ben and Jerry's.

143. "Activist's Work Pays Off: St. Louis Votes Unanimously to Close the Workhouse Jail," Ben and Jerry's, July 17, 2020, https://www.benjerry.com/whats-new/2020/07/st-louis-closes-workhouse#:~:text=Black%20people%20make%20up%2047,to%20keep%20the%20Workhouse%20running; "Quick Facts, St. Louis City, Missouri," United States Census, accessed June 2021, https://www.census.gov/quickfacts/stlouiscitymissouricounty; "'Unspeakably Hellish' St. Louis Workhouse Targeted in Class Action Suit," *Riverfront Times*, November 13, 2017; https://static1.squarespace.com/static/5ada6072372b96dbb234ee99/t/5e1e370f8460a6689db212e5/1579038479212/Sources+-+CTW+Report+2.0.pdf.

144. "Total Number of Homicides in the United States in 2019, by State," Statistica.com, accessed June 2021, https://www.statista.com/statistics/195331/number-of-murders-in-the-us-by-state/.

145. Paul Butler, *Chokehold* (New York: The New Press, 2017).

146. Gun access is generally problematic in the United States. Guns outnumber people and most murders involve firearms. Stricter laws on gun purchase, sale, and possession might reduce gun violence. DC and Chicago both operate under strict gun laws but the murders remain nearly constant: "There Are More Guns Than People in the United States, According to a New Study of Global Firearm Ownership," *Washington Post*, June 19, 2018; "District Crime Data at a Glance," DC Metropolitan Police Department website, accessed June 2021, https://mpdc.dc.gov/page/district-crime-data-glance; Rob Arthur, "Chicago's Murder Rate Is Rising, but It Isn't Unprecedented," EightThirtyEight.com, January 25, 2017, https://fivethirtyeight.com/features/chicagos-murder-rate-is-rising-but-it-isnt-unprecedented/.

147. Callie Ahlgrim, "Nipsey Hussle Used the Money He Made from Rapping to Give Back to His Hometown," Insider.com, April 1, 2019, https://www.insider.com/nipsey-hussle-dead-legacy-charity

-work-investments-south-la-2019-4; Eric Leonard and Doha Madani, "Nipsey Hussle Murdered After Snitch Remark, Grand Jury Transcripts Say," NBC News, June 27, 2019, https://www.nbcnews .com/news/nbcblk/judge-rules-unseal-grand-jury-transcript-nipsey-hussle-murder-case-n1023341; Nancy Dillon, "Murder Case for Nipsey Hussle's Alleged Killer Pushed Out Again As Judge Retires," *Daily News*, January 21, 2021, https://www.nydailynews.com/snyde/ny-nipsey-hussle-alleged-killer-eric -holder-appears-in-court-20210121-gvmerfeza5g5tladub4i7ppybi-story.html.

148. "The Black Panther Party: Challenging Police and Promoting Social Change," Smithsonian.com, accessed June 2021, https://nmaahc.si.edu/blog-post/black-panther-party-challenging-police-and -promoting-social-change; Akinyele Omowale Umoja, "Repression Breeds Resistance: The Black Liberation Army and the Radical Legacy of the Black Panther Party," *New Political Science* 21, no. 2 (1999): 131–155, 10.1080/07393149908429859, "Elaine Brown Shares Context behind Events Surrounding Huggins and Carter Deaths," *Daily Bruin*, December 28, 2012, https://www .youtube.com/watch?v=w4FpEEgAAME; Abhishek Shetty, "Throwback Thursday: Fifty-Year Anniversary of 'Bunchy' Carter, John Huggins Shooting," *Daily Bruin*, January 17, 2019, https:// dailybruin.com/2019/01/17/throwback-thursday-fifty-year-anniversary-of-bunchy-carter-john -huggins-shooting.

149. "US Attorney's Office Announces Project EJECT," US Attorney's Office, Mississippi, press release, March 22, 2020, https://www.justice.gov/usao-sdms/pr/us-attorney-s-office-announces -project-eject-project-safe-neighborhoods-and-project.

150. David Oliver, "Hunter Biden Says He Was 'Smoking Crack Every Fifteen Minutes,' More Jaw-Dropping Moments from *Beautiful Things*," *USA Today*, March 31, 2020; "Hunter Biden Opens Up to CBS About His Roller-Coaster Life," *Los Angeles Times*, April 5, 2021.

151. "Our History," Tenants and Workers website, accessed June 2021, https://www.tenantsandworkers .org/about.

152. Nassim Benchaabane, "One Year After, Family and Friends Remember Transgender Woman Shot by St. Louis Police," *St. Louis Today*, August 25, 2018.

153. "Report: Violence Against the Transgender Community in 2018," Human Rights Campaign, accessed April 2021, https://www.hrc.org/resources/violence-against-the-transgender-community -in-2018; "Murders of Transgender People Rising Worldwide," Thompson Reuters Foundation, November 20, 2018, https://news.trust.org/item/20181120075803-0k6vn/.

154. Cisgender: a person whose sense of personal identity and gender corresponds with the sex they were assigned at birth.

155. "Reforming Police and Ending Anti-Transgender Violence," *Blueprint for Equality* (Washington, DC: National Center for Transgender Equality, 2016); "Violence against the Transgender Community," Human Rights Watch, accessed June 2021, https://www.hrc.org/resources/violence -against-the-transgender-community-in-2018.

156. Jaime Grant et al., *Injustice at Every Turn: A Report of the National Transgender Discrimination Survey* (Washington, DC: National Center for Transgender Equality, 2011); Erin Fitzgerald et al., *Meaningful Work* (Washington, DC: National Center for Transgender Equality, 2015); Nina Luo, "Decriminalizing Survival," Data for Progress, 2020, https://www.filesforprogress.org/memos /decriminalizing-sex-work.pdf.

157. Soon Kyu Choi et al., *Serving Our Youth* (Los Angeles: Williams Institute, UCLA School of Law, 2015).

158. "Report of the 2015 US Transgender Survey," National Center for Transgender Equality, Summer 2015, https://transequality.org/sites/default/files/docs/usts/USTSBlackRespondentsReport-Nov17 .pdf; "Sex Reassignment Surgery Yields Long-Term Mental Health Benefits, Study Finds," Reuters, November 11, 2019.

159. Richard Grant, "Deep in the Swamps, Archaeologists Are Finding How Fugitive Slaves Kept Their Freedom," *Smithsonian*, September 2016.

160. Robinson, *Black Movements in America*.

161. "2018 Crime in the United States," FBI.gov, accessed June 2021, https://ucr.fbi.gov/crime-in-the -u.s/2018/crime-in-the-u.s.-2018/topic-pages/murder; Rachel E. Morgan et al., *Criminal Victimization, 2018* (Washington, DC: US Department of Justice Bureau of Justice Statistics, 2019); Shannan Catalano, *National Crime Victimization Survey, Victimization During Household Burglary* (Washington, DC: US Department of Justice, 2010).

162. Peter Wagner, *The Prison Index: Taking the Pulse of the Crime Control Industry* (Northampton: Prison Policy Initiative, 2003); Catalano, *National Crime Victimization Survey*.

163. Joseph B. Kuhns, *Understanding Decisions to Burglarize from the Offender's Perspective* (Charlotte: University of North Carolina, 2012); Joseph B. Kuhns et al., "Drug Use and Abuse as Primary Motivators for Involvement in Burglary," *Journal of Drug Issues* 47, no. 1 (2016).

164. Megan E. Patrick et al., "Socioeconomic Status and Substance Use among Young Adults," *Journal of Studies on Alcohol and Drugs* 75, no. 3 (September 2021).

165. Michelle Chen, "Worker Cooperatives Are More Productive Than Normal Companies," *The Nation*, March 28, 2016.

166. "How Much Do Members of Congress Get Paid?" Congressional Institute website, accessed June 2021, https://www.congressionalinstitute.org/2019/02/21/how-much-do-members-of-congress-get-paid-2/; Ben Peters, "Will Members of Congress Ever Drug Test Themselves? They've Certainly Tried," Roll Call, February 22, 2019, https://www.rollcall.com/2019/02/22/will-members-of-congress-ever-drug-test-themselves-theyve-certainly-tried/.

167. "John Legend Reads Muhammad Ali's 1966 Antiwar Speech: 'The Real Enemy of My People is Right Here,'" Democracy Now!, June 6, 2016 https://www.democracynow.org/2016/6/6/john_legend_reads_muhammad_alis_1966.

168. Kuang Keng Kuek Ser, "Data: Hate Crimes against Muslims Increased after 9/11," PRI The World, September 12, 2016, https://www.pri.org/stories/2016-09-12/data-hate-crimes-against-muslims-increased-after-911; John Gramlich, "How Border Apprehensions, ICE Arrests, and Deportations Have Changed Under Trump," Pew Research Center, March 2, 2020, https://www.pewresearch.org/fact-tank/2020/03/02/how-border-apprehensions-ice-arrests-and-deportations-have-changed-under-trump/; "Operation Gatekeeper and the Birth of Border Militarization," Southernborder.org, accessed June 2021, https://www.southernborder.org/operation_gatekeeper; Kevin Krause, "North Texas Militia Vigilante Who Rounded Up Migrants at Border Found Dead After Months on the Run," *Dallas Morning News*, January 10, 2020; Derek Hawkins and Marisa Leti, "Texas Militia Leader Went into Hiding. Months Later He Turned Up Dead," *Washington Post*, January 12, 2020, https://www.washingtonpost.com/nation/2019/01/20/they-left-food-water-migrants-desert-now-they-might-go-prison/.

169. Bianca Quilantan and David Cohen, "Trump Tells Dem Congresswomen: Go Back Where You Came From," Politico, July 14, 2019, https://www.politico.com/story/2019/07/14/trump-congress-go-back-where-they-came-from-1415692; Madison Park and Stephanie Becker, "Portland Train Suspect: 'I Hope Everyone I Stabbed Died,'" CNN, May 31, 2017, https://www.cnn.com/2017/05/31/us/portland-train-stabbing-what-happened/index.html.

170. Oregonian, "Jeremy Christian Threatens to Kill Victim During Outburst at Sentencing," YouTube video, June 23, 2020, https://www.youtube.com/watch?v=Cw1DrzcQBHA.

171. Julio-Cesar Chavez, "Death Toll Reaches Twenty-Three from Last Year's Mass Shooting in El Paso, Texas," Reuters, April 26, 2020, https://www.reuters.com/article/us-texas-shooting/death-toll-reaches-23-from-last-years-mass-shooting-in-el-paso-texas-idUSKCN22901V; Ben Norton, "This Is Terrorism," Twitter, August 4, 2019, https://twitter.com/BenjaminNorton/status/1158103710742065152.

172. Steve Doig, "It Is Difficult, If Not Impossible, to Estimate the Size of the Crowd That Stormed Capitol Hill," The Conversation, accessed June 2021, https://theconversation.com/it-is-difficult-if-not-impossible-to-estimate-the-size-of-the-crowd-that-stormed-capitol-hill-152889; "Our Democracy Is under Unprecedented Assault, Biden Says," *New York Times* online, January 6, 2021, https://www.nytimes.com/video/us/politics/100000007537323/our-democracy-is-under-unprecedented-assault-biden-says.html; Sara Sidner et al., "Disproportionate Number of Current and Former Military Personnel Arrested in Capitol Attack," CNN, February 4, 2021, https://www.cnn.com/2021/01/31/us/capitol-riot-arrests-active-military-veterans-soh/index.html.

173. Sarah Pulliam Bailey, "The Charleston Shooting Is the Largest Mass Shooting in a House of Worship since 1991," *The Washington Post*, June 18, 2015, https://www.washingtonpost.com/news/acts-of-faith/wp/2015/06/18/the-charleston-shooting-is-the-largest-mass-shooting-in-a-house-of-worship-since-1991/; N. R. Kleinfeild et al., "Newtown Killer's Obsessions in Chilling Detail," *New York Times*, March 28, 2013; Dave Altimari and Jon Lender, "Sandy Hook Shooter Wore Earplugs," *Hartford Courant*, January 6, 2013; MariAn Gail Brown, "Newtown Shooter Dreamed of Being

Marine," *CT Post*, December 19, 2012; David J. Phillip, "Autopsy Confirms Sutherland Springs Church Gunman Died by Suicide," NBC News, June 30, 2018, https://www.nbcnews.com/storyline /texas-church-shooting/autopsy-confirms-sutherland-springs-church-gunman-died-suicide-n888051; David Philipps, Richard A. Oppel Jr., and Serge Kovaleski, "In Air Force, Colleague Feared Church Gunman Would 'Shoot up the Place,'" *New York Times*, November 11, 2017; "Names of Victims Killed in Sutherland Springs Church Shooting Released," Associated Press, November 8, 2017; "What Adam Lanza Took, and Didn't Take, to Sandy Hook Elementary," Coalition to Stop Gun Violence, accessed April 2021, https://www.csgv.org/adam-lanza-took-didnt-take-sandy-hook-elementary/.

174. Brittany Wallman and Megan O'Matz, "Parkland Shooter Scrawls Childish Love Letters from Jail: 'I really want kids . . . You know the joy they bring,'" *South Florida Sun Sentinel*, April 8, 2019; Michael Biesecker and Collin Binkley, "National Rifle Association Shooting Suspect Was on School Rifle Team That Got NRA Grant," Associated Press, February 16, 2018.

175. "Leader of White Nationalist Group Says Florida Shooting Suspect Was a Member," PBS News-hour, February 15, 2018, https://www.pbs.org/newshour/nation/leader-of-white-nationalist -groups-says-florida-shooting-suspect-was-a-member; Wallman and O'Matz, "Parkland Shooter Scrawls Childish Love Letters."

176. Tanika White, Laurie Willis and Linell Smith, "African-Americans Grapple with Race of Sniper Suspects," *Baltimore Sun*, October 25, 2002; "Sniper Suspect's Military Record Revealed," *Time*, October 24, 2002.

177. Erik Hedegaard, "The Body, Slammed," *Men's Journal*, n.d.; Jarvis DeBerry, "Inside an 'Ameri-can Sniper's' Preposterous Post-Katrina New Orleans Story," NOLA.com, January 20, 2015, https://www.nola.com/entertainment_life/article_2057a37f-1fd0-505e-ab2b-1e9ebfeee7be.html; Thompson, "Post-Katrina, White Vigilantes Shot African-Americans with Impunity."

178. Thompson, "Post-Katrina, White Vigilantes Shot African-Americans with Impunity."

179. Jennifer Median, Richard Pérez-Peña, and Adam Goldman, "Meticulous Planning by Las Vegas Gun-man Before He Opened Fire," *New York Times*, October 3, 2017; Vanessa Romo, "FBI Finds No Motive in Las Vegas Shooting, Closes Investigation," NPR, January 29, 2019, https://www.npr.org /2019/01/29/689821599/fbi-finds-no-motive-in-las-vegas-shooting-closes-investigation; Jessica Chia, "Las Vegas Shooter Stephen Paddock Claimed Americans Need to Wake Up to Government Plot to Seize Guns," *New York Daily News*, May 17, 2018; Tess Owen, "Las Vegas Shooter Ranted about Gun Control and Right-Wing Conspiracies Weeks before the Massacre," Vice News, May 17, 2018, https://www.vice.com/en/article/kzk8dx/las-vegas-shooter-ranted-about-gun-control-and-right -wing-conspiracies-weeks-before-the-massacre.

180. 60 Minutes, "Timothy McVeigh Speaks," YouTube video, March 11, 2018, https://www.youtube .com/watch?v=wJUn3XkGZVg; "McVeigh: Gulf War Killings Led Him on Path to Disillusion-ment," CNN, March 13, 2000,https://www.cnn.com/2000/US/03/13/mcveigh/.

181. Adam Chandler, "What Exactly Did the Company Omar Mateen Worked For Do?" *The Atlantic*, June 14, 2016; "The Costs of War," Brown University website, accessed June 2021, https://watson .brown.edu/costsofwar/costs/human; Madea Benjamin, "America Dropped 26,171 Bombs in 2016," *Guardian*, January 9, 2017; Ryan Felton and Oliver Laughland, "Orlando Shooter Was Fired for Making a Gun Joke Days after Virginia Tech Killings," *Guardian,* June 17, 2016.

182. Paul Duggan et al., "Shooter Pair Mixed Fantasy, Reality," *Washington Post*, April 22, 1999; Ish-mael Reed, "The Pundits Misfire on School Shootings; Causes: The Media Offer Uninformed and Often Racist Reasons for Violence by US Students, a Critic Charges," *Baltimore Sun*, March 30, 1999; Joel Achenbach and Dale Russakoff, "Teen Shooter's Life Paints Antisocial Portrait," *Wash-ington Post*, April 29, 1999; Chris Francescani, "George Zimmerman: Prelude to a Shooting," Reuters, April 25, 2012; Michael Muskal and Tina Susman, "Rules for Neighborhood Watch Dis-cussed in George Zimmerman Trial, *Los Angeles Times*, June 25, 2013; Meghan Keneally, "Zimmerman Charged with Stalking Man Working on Trayvon Martin Documentary," ABC News, May 7, 2018, https://abcnews.go.com/US/george-zimmerman-charged-stalking-man -working-trayvon-martin/story?id=54995405; Abby Rogers, "Zimmerman Called Trayvon Mar-tin One of 'These Assholes' in 911 Call," *Business Insider*, June 21, 2012.

183. Larry Hobbs, "Friends, Family Testify on McMichaels' Behalf," *The Brunswick News*, Novem-ber 12, 2020; Richard Fausset, "What We Know About the Shooting Death of Ahmaud Arbery," *New York Times*, February 28, 2021; Minyvonne Burke, "White Man Accused of Killing Ahmaud

Arbery Allegedly Used Racial Slur after Shooting, Investigator Says," NBC News, June 4, 2020, https://www.nbcnews.com/news/us-news/white-man-accused-killing-ahmaud-arbery-allegedly -used-racial-slur-n1224696; "Ahmaud Arbery Case: Suspect Travis McMichael Used Racial Slur after Shooting, Investigators Say," Action News Jax, June 4, 2020, https://www.actionnewsjax.com /news/local/glynn-county/ahmaud-arbery-case-3-men-accused-murder-appear-court-thursday-morn ing/UOMM5JLMGZBL7IPI2CBZZA3QQM/.

184. Eric Litke, "Fact Check: Police Gave Kyle Rittenhouse Water and Thanked Him before Shooting," *USA Today*, August 29, 2020; Neil MacFarquhar, "Suspect in Kenosha Killings Lionized the Police," *New York Times*, August 27, 2020.

185. Peter Iadicola and Anson Shupe, *Violence, Inequality and Human Freedom* (New York: Rowman and Littlefield, 2012).

186. Kelley, "Black Study, Black Struggle."

187. Rev. Dr. William J. Barber III, "The Necessity of Moral Resistance in the Face of Militarism," Kairos Center website, accessed June 2021, https://kairoscenter.org/sermons-bible-studies -liturgies/barber-moral-resistance-miltarism/.

188. Melissa del Bosque, "The Military's Failure to Reckon with White Supremacy in Its Ranks," The Intercept, March 7, 2021.

189. "Number of Mass Shootings in the United States between 1982 and May 2021, by Shooter's Race," Statistica.com, accessed June 2021, https://www.statista.com/statistics/476456/mass-shootings -in-the-us-by-shooter-s-race/.

190. Hamid Khan, interview with author, 2020.

191. "Stop Lapd Spying Coalition—Campaign to Rescind Special Order 1(1)," Stop LAPD Spying Coalition, Los Angeles, CA, https://stoplapdspying.org/about-slsc/.

192. "About," The Red Nation, accessed April 2021, http://therednation.org/about/.

193. "Freedom Papers," Dream Defenders, accessed April 2021, https://dreamdefenders.org/freedom -papers/.

194. "Transcript: Beyond Vietnam," April 4, 1967, King Papers, Stanford University Martin Luther King, Jr. Research and Education Institute, https://kinginstitute.stanford.edu/king-papers /documents/beyond-vietnam.

195. Kelly Field, "After the Repeal of 'Don't Ask,' Elite Colleges Rethink ROTC," *Chronicle of Higher Education*, January 9, 2011.

196. Alyssa Milano (@AlyssaMilano) "If you've been sexually harassed or assaulted write 'me too' as a reply to this tweet," Twitter, October 15, 2017, https://twitter.com/alyssa_milano/status /919659438700670976?lang=en; Sandra Garcia, "The Woman Who Created #MeToo Long Before Hashtags," *New York Times*, October 20, 2017; "The Movement," Just Be Inc., accessed April 2021, https://justbeinc.wixsite.com/justbeinc/the-me-too-movement-c7cf.

197. Iadicola and Shupe, *Violence, Inequality and Human Freedom*.

198. John 7:53–8:11.

199. Emily Homrok, "How Often Do Rape Kits Go Unprocessed?" *Truthout*, October 3, 2014; "2018 Crime in the United States," FBI.gov.

200. Patricia Mahoney and Linda M. Williams, "Sexual Assault in Marriage: Prevalence, Conse- quences, and Treatment of Wife Rape," Family Research Laboratory, University of New Hampshire, accessed June 2021, http://www.ncdsv.org/images/nnfr_partnerviolence_a20-yearlit eraturereviewandsynthesis.pdf; Michael Planty et al., *Female Victims of Sexual Violence 1994– 2010* (Washington, DC: US Department of Justice Bureau of Justice Statistics, 2013); Callie Marie Rennison, *Rape and Sexual Assault: Reporting to Police and Medical Attention, 1992–2000* (Wash- ington, DC: US Department of Justice Bureau of Justice Statistics, 2002).

201. "Disabled Women and Sexual Violence," Now.org, accessed June 2021, https://now.org/wp -content/uploads/2018/05/Disabled-Women-Sexual-Violence-4.pdf; Kathleen Basile et al., *Stop SV: A Technical Package to Prevent Sexual Violence* (Atlanta: National Center for Injury Prevention and Control, 2016); "Sexual Violence and Intimate Partner Violence among People with Dis- abilities," Centers for Disease Control and Prevention, accessed April 2021, https://www.cdc.gov /violenceprevention/datasources/nisvs/svandipv.html; "The Sexual Assault Epidemic No One Talks About," NPR, January 8, 2018, https://www.npr.org/2018/01/08/570224090/the-sexual -assault-epidemic-no-one-talks-about; "Media Press Kit: Intimate Partner Violence," Centers for

Disease Control and Prevention, accessed April 2021, https://www.cdc.gov/media/presskits/aahd /violence.pdf; "A Quick Guide: Domestic Violence and Sexual Abuse," National Coalition Against Domestic Violence blog, April 4, 2018, https://ncadv.org/blog/posts/quick-guide-domestic -violence-and-sexual-abuse.

202. "National Prevalence of Sexual Violence by a Workplace-Related Perpetrator," *American Journal of Preventative Medicine* 58, no. 2 (2020); "Intimate Partner Violence, Sexual Violence, and Stalking among Men," Centers for Disease Control and Prevention, accessed April 2021, https://www .cdc.gov/violenceprevention/datasources/nisvs/men-ipvsvandstalking.html; Rennison, *Rape and Sexual Assault*.

203. DeNeen Brown, "State of Missouri v. Celia, a Slave: She Killed the White Master Raping Her, Then Claimed Self-Defense," *Washington Post*, October 19, 2017.

204. 96, Alonza; Black men were survivors of sexual violence under slavery, too. Slave owners sexually assaulted Black men, and also forced them to rape Black women for reproduction; Melton Alonza McLaurin, Celia, a Slave (New York: Avon, 1999).

205. Morgan et al., *Criminal Victimization, 2019*.

206. Raquel Kennedy Bergen and Elizabeth Barnhill, "Marital Rape: New Research and Directions," National Resource Center on Domestic Violence, February 2006, https://www.ilcdvp.org /Documents/Marital%20Rape%20Revised.pdf.

207. Dunbar-Ortiz, *An Indigenous Peoples' History*; "When Sexual Assaults Made History," History.com, October 9, 2018, https://www.history.com/news/sexual-assault-rome-slavery-columbus-jim-crow.

208. "Statistics on Violence against Native Women," NCAI Policy Research Center policy paper, February 2013, https://www.ncai.org/attachments/PolicyPaper_tWAjznFslemhAffZgNGzHUqIWMRP kCDjpFtxeKEUVKjubxfpGYK_Policy%20Insights%20Brief_VAWA_020613.pdf; André B. Rosay, *Violence against American Indian and Alaska Native Women and Men* (Washington, DC: US Department of Justice National Institute of Justice, 2016); Sophie Croisy, "Fighting Colonial Violence in 'Indian Country': Deconstructing Racist Sexual Stereotypes of Native American Women in Popular Culture and History," *Angles* no. 5 (2017); Em Loerzel, "Policy, Wellness, and Native American Survivorship," *AMA Journal of Ethics* 22, no. 10 (2020); Andrea Smith, "Not an Indian Tradition: The Sexual Colonization of Native Peoples," *Hypatia* 18, no. 2 (2003); Genevieve Le May, "The Cycles of Violence against Native Women: An Analysis of Colonialism, Historical Legislation, and the Violence against Women Reauthorization Act of 2013," *Portland State University McNair Research Journal* 12, no. 1 (2018); Roxanne Daniel, "Since You Asked," Prison Policy Initiative, April 22, 2020, https://www.prisonpolicy.org/blog/2020/04/22/native/#:~:text=Other %20data%20on%20Native%20Americans,Prisoner%20Statistics%20(NPS)%20series.

209. "Sexual Assault and the LGBTQ Community," Human Rights Campaign, accessed April 2021, https://www.hrc.org/resources/sexual-assault-and-the-lgbt-community; "An Overview of 2010 Findings on Victimization by Sexual Orientation," National Center for Injury Prevention and Control, accessed June 2021, https://www.cdc.gov/violenceprevention/pdf/cdc_nisvs_victimization _final-a.pdf.

210. Jessica Testa, "How Police Caught the Cop Who Allegedly Sexually Abused Black Women," BuzzFeed News, September 5, 2014, https://www.buzzfeednews.com/article/jtes/daniel-holtzclaw -alleged-sexual-assault-oklahoma-city; Phil Helsel, "Oklahoma City Cop Daniel Holtzclaw Found Guilty of Rapes," NBC News, October 20, 2015, https://www.nbcnews.com/news/us-news/ex -oklahoma-city-cop-daniel-holtzclaw-found-guilty-rapes-n478151; "US Supreme Court Rejects Ex-Cop's Appeal of Rape Convictions," Associated Press, March 9, 2020; "Daniel Holtzclaw," The Marshall Project, accessed April 2021, https://www.themarshallproject.org/records/2268 -daniel-holtzclaw.

211. James Queally, "Accuser in Oakland Police Sex Abuse Scandal Settles Claim for Nearly $1 Million," May 31, 2017, https://www.latimes.com/local/lanow/la-me-ln-oakland-sex-scandal-settlement -20170531-story.html; Richard Gonzales, "Sex Scandal Leads to Chaos inside Oakland's Troubled Police Department," NPR, June 20, 2016, https://www.npr.org/2016/06/20/482776880/sex-scandal -leads-to-chaos-inside-oaklands-troubled-police-department; Norm Stamper, *Breaking Rank: A Top Cop's Exposé of the Dark Side of American Policing* (New York: Bold Type Books, 2009).

212. Samuel Walker and Dawn Irlbeck, *Police Sexual Abuse of Teenage Girls* (Omaha: University of Nebraska Department of Criminal Justice, 2003); Isidoro Rodriguez, "Predators behind the

Badge," The Crime Report, March 12, 2020, https://thecrimereport.org/2020/03/12/predators -behind-the-badge-confronting-hidden-police-sexual-misconduct/; "Why Decriminalize Sex Work," Decrimnow, accessed April 2021, https://www.decrimnow.org/why-decriminalize-sex -work; "Sexual Abuse by a Few Police Officers is a Stain That Must Be Eradicated," *Buffalo News*, November 27, 2015, https://buffalonews.com/opinion/editorial/sexual-abuse-by-a-few -police-officers-is-a-stain-that-must-be-eradicated/article_2daeb8de-317b-5d67-9fe3 -b5caa9ad80c9.html; "Want to Understand the Relationship between Police Brutality and Sexual Harm? Here's Where to Begin," Chicago Alliance Against Sexual Exploitation, July 10, 2020, https://www.caase.org/reading-list-police-sexual-misconduct/; Matt Sedensky and Nomaan Merchant, "Hundreds of Officers Lose License over Sex Misconduct," Associated Press, November 1, 2015.

213. Dara Purvis and Melissa Blanco, "Police Sexual Violence: Police Brutality, #MeToo, and Masculinities," *California Law Review* 108, no. 5 (October 2020); James Herman et al., *Report of the 2015 US Transgender Survey* (Washington, DC: National Center for Transgender Equality, 2016); Devon Link, "Fact Check: Sex Between Police Officers and Their Detainees Isn't Illegal in Many States," Associated Press, July 9, 2020.

214. "Perpetrators of Sexual Violence: Statistics," RAINN, accessed April 2021, https://www.rainn .org/statistics/perpetrators-sexual-violence.

215. National Center for Transgender Equality, *LGBTQ People Behind Bars* (Washington, DC: National Center for Transgender Equality, 2018); Herman et al., *Report of the 2015 US Transgender Survey*.

216. Ejeris Dixon and Leah Lakshmi Piepzna-Samarasinha, eds., *Beyond Survival: Strategies and Stories from the Transformative Justice Movement* (Chico: AK Press, 2020).

217. Lawrence A. Greenfeld, "Sex Offenses and Offenders: Bureau of Justice Statistics Executive Summary," US Department of Justice, January 1997, https://www.bjs.gov/content/pub/pdf/SOO.PDF; Iadicola and Shupe, *Violence, Inequality and Human Freedom*; Dixon and Piepzna-Samarasinha, *Beyond Survival*.

218. Dave Philipps, "'This is Unacceptable': Military Reports a Surge of Sexual Assaults in the Ranks," *New York Times*, May 2, 2019; Dave Philipps, "Interactive: Sexual Assault in the Military," *New York Times*, September 10, 2019; J. Hennigan, "More Than Five Hundred Sexual Assaults Happen in a Single Year at Some Military Installations," *Time*, September 21, 2018; Philipps, "This is Unacceptable"; Ruth Rosen, "The Hidden War on Women in Iraq," *Mother Jones*, July 13, 2016; Joseph Goldstein, "US Soldiers Told to Ignore Sexual Abuse of Boys by Afghan Allies," *New York Times*, September 20, 2015.

219. American Civil Liberties Union, *Island of Impunity: Puerto Rico's Outlaw Police Force* (New York: American Civil Liberties Union, 2012); "Top Twenty Largest Police Departments in the United States," Cjusjobs.com, January 25, 2021, https://cjusjobs.com/largest-police-departments/#:~:text =With%20over%2036%2C000%20police%20officers,that%20comprises%208.5%20million%20 people; "Island of Impunity," ACLU.org, accessed June 2021, https://www.aclu.org/report /island-impunity-puerto-ricos-outlaw-police-force; "'Don't Give Up on Us': Puerto Ricans Wrestle with High Crime," NPR Morning Edition, February 7, 2013, https://www.npr.org/2013/02/07 /171071473/-don-t-give-up-on-us-puerto-ricans-wrestle-with-high-crime; American Civil Liberties Union, *Island of Impunity*.

220. Haidee V. Eugenio, "Spotlight on Guam's High Volume of Sexual Assaults," *Pacific Daily News*, January 24, 2017.

221. Simone Weichselbaum and Wendi C. Thomas, "More Cops: Is It the Answer to Fighting Crime?" *USA Today*, February 13, 2019.

222. Shannan Catalano, *Intimate Partner Violence, Attributes of Victimization 1993-2011* (Washington, DC: US Department of Justice, 2013); Rachel Morgan and Jennifer Truman, *Criminal Victimization, 2019* (Washington, DC: US Department of Justice, 2020); "Female Victims of Sexual Violence 1994-2010," Bureau of Justice Statistics, February 7, 2013, https://www.bjs.gov/index .cfm?ty=pbdetail&iid=4927; David Finkelhor and Lisa M. Jones, *Explanations for the Decline in Child Sexual Abuse Cases* (Washington, DC: US Department of Justice Office of Juvenile Justice and Delinquency Prevention, 2004); Morgan et al., *Criminal Victimization, 2019*; "Reforms without Results" press release, Prison Policy Initiative, April 2020, https://www.prisonpolicy .org/reports/violence.html.

223. "Reforms without Results," press release, Prison Policy Initiative.
224. https://web.archive.org/web/20140722020554; United States Government Accountability Office, "COPS Grants Were a Modest Contributor, to Declines in Crime in the 1990s," Report to the Chairman, Committee on the Judiciary, House of Representatives, October 2005, https://www.gao.gov/new.items/d06104.pdf; Derecka Purnell and Marbre Stahly-Butts, "The Police Can't Solve the Problem. They Are the Problem," *New York Times*, September 26, 2019.
225. Commission on Law Enforcement and the Administration of Justice, *The Challenge of Crime in a Free Society* (Washington, DC: US Government Printing Office, 1967).
226. Mark H. Moore et al., "Crime and Policing," *Perspectives on Policing* no. 2 (July 1988).
227. Kurt Bauman, "Shift Toward Greater Educational Attainment for Women Began Twenty Years Ago," United States Census Bureau, March 29, 2016, https://www.census.gov/newsroom/blogs /random-samplings/2016/03/shift-toward-greater-educational-attainment-for-women-began-20 -years-ago.html; Camille Ryan and Kurt Bauman, *Educational Attainment in the United States* (Washington, DC: United States Census Bureau, 2016); Sofi Sinozich and Lynn Langton, *Rape and Sexual Assault Victimization among College-Age Females, 1995–2013* (Washington, DC: US Department of Justice, 2014); Rakesh Kochhar, "Women Make Gains in the Workplace amid a Rising Demand for Skilled Workers," Pew Research Center, January 30, 2020, https://www .pewresearch.org/social-trends/2020/01/30/women-make-gains-in-the-workplace-amid-a-rising -demand-for-skilled-workers/; Mitra Toossi and Teresa Morisi, *Women in the Workplace Before, During, and After the Great Recession* (Washington, DC: US Bureau of Labor Statistics, 2017); Meghan Henry et al., *2016 Annual Homeless Assessment Report to Congress* (Washington DC: US Department of Housing and Urban Development, 2016).
228. Rachel Herzing, "Standing Up for Our Communities: Why We Need a Police-Free Future," *Truthout*, March 7, 2017.
229. Audre Lorde, *Need: A Chorale for Black Women Voices* (New York: W. W. Norton, 1990).
230. "COVID-19 Dashboard," Johns Hopkins Coronavirus Resource Center, accessed June 2021, https://coronavirus.jhu.edu/map.html; Michelle Roberts, "South Africa Coronavirus Variant: What Is the Risk?" BBC News, April 13, 2021, https://www.bbc.com/news/health-55534727#:~:text =Is%20it%20more%20dangerous%3F,have%20significant%20underlying%20health%20condi tions; "Coronavirus: South Africa Eases Strict Lockdown as Cases Drop," BBC News, September 17, 2020, https://www.bbc.com/news/world-africa-54186040.
231. Zelda Holtzman, conversation with author, 2020.
232. Michele Kim, "Trans Latina Activist Ruby Corado Is Eyeing DC City Council Run in 2023," Them.com, January 19, 2021, https://www.them.us/story/trans-latina-activist-ruby-corado-city -council-run-2023#:~:text=Corado%20launched%20Casa%20Ruby%20in,career%20coun seling%2C%20and%20immigration%20aid; "Still Saving Lives 24/7," Casa Ruby, accessed June 2021, https://casaruby.org/.
233. Adam Mahoney, "For Black and Pink Organizers, Decarceration Must Grapple with Constant Violence against LGBTQ People," Shadowproof.com, July 29, 2020, https://shadowproof.com/2020 /07/29/for-black-pink-organizers-decarceration-must-grapple-with-constant-violence-against -lgbtq-people/.
234. "Our Herstory," Assata's Daughters, accessed June 2021, https://www.assatasdaughters.org/our -herstory-2019.
235. "Our Work," Common Justice, accessed June 2021, https://www.commonjustice.org/our_work.
236. "Prison Rape Elimination Act of 2003," ACLU, accessed April 2021, https://www.aclu.org/other /prison-rape-elimination-act-2003-prea?redirect=prisoners-rights-womens-rights/prison-rape -elimination-act-2003-prea; "About S&P," Survived and Punished, accessed April 2021, https:// survivedandpunished.org/about/; Bobby Allyn, "Cyntoia Brown Released after Fifteen Years in Prison for Murder," NPR, August 7, 2019, https://www.npr.org/2019/08/07/749025458/cyntoia -brown-released-after-15-years-in-prison-for-murder; Sharon Lynn Pruitt, "Who Is Johnny Michael Allen, the Man Cyntoia Brown Was Convicted of Killing?" Oxygen "True Crime Buzz," April 29, 2020, https://www.oxygen.com/true-crime-buzz/netflixs-murder-to-mercy-who-was -johnny-michael-allen#:~:text=Johnny%20Michael%20Allen%2C%20a%2043,sex%2C%20 according%20to%20court%20documents.

237. "Background on Decrimnow," Decrimnow.com, accessed April 2021, https://www.decrimnow .org/about.

238. Teju Cole, *Known and Strange Things: Essays* (New York: Random House, 2016).

239. Monstrous descriptions can be dehumanizing, but that's not where Darren Wilson gained his power to shoot. It was the law. "Excerpts from the LAPD Officers' Trial," Famous Trials website, accessed June 2021, https://famous-trials.com/lapd/581-excerpts.

240. Sylvia Wynter, "No Humans Involved," *Forum N. H. I.: Knowledge for the 21st Century* 1, no. 1 (Fall 1994).

241. "Investigation of the Ferguson Police Department," US Department of Justice.

242. Paul Butler, "The System Is Working the Way It Is Supposed to: The Limits of Criminal Justice Reform," *Georgetown Law Journal*, 104, no. 6 (2016), 1419.

243. Madison Gray, "Finding 'Mike Mike': Michael Brown's Mom Shares His Story in New Book," *Ebony*, May 10, 2016.

244. Walter Johnson, "To Remake the World: Slavery, Racial Capitalism, and Justice," *Boston Review*, February 20, 2018.

245. "Stokely Carmichael, 'Black Power,'" Voices of Democracy, Accessed June 2021, https:// voicesofdemocracy.umd.edu/carmichael-black-power-speech-text/.

246. Indigenous people, too, through violently converting them to Christianity and forcing them into schools to de-Indianize them. David M. Turner, "African American Slavery and Disability: Bodies, Property, and Power in the Antebellum South, 1800–1860," *Disability & Society* 29, no. 9 (2013): 1505–1506.

247. D. A. Ingleman, "Kojo's Dis/Ability: The Interpretation of Spinal Pathology in the Context of an Eighteenth-Century Jamaican Maroon Community," in Jennifer F. Byrnes and Jennifer L. Muller, eds., *Bioarchaeology of Impairment and Disability Theoretical, Ethnohistorical, and Methodological Perspectives* (Cham: Springer, 2017).

248. Jim Downs, "The Continuation of Slavery: The Experience of Disabled Slaves during Emancipation," *Disability Studies Quarterly* 28, no. 3 (Summer 2008).

249. Downs, "The Continuation of Slavery."

250. "Harriet Tubman," PBS Africans in America, accessed June 2021, https://www.pbs.org/wgbh/aia /part4/4p1535.html.

251. Allison Keyes, "A Previously Unknown Portrait of a Young Harriet Tubman Goes on View," *Smithsonian Magazine*, March 26, 2019.

252. The Combahee River Collective, the Black socialist feminist group, draws their name from this raid. "Harriet Tubman and the Underground Railroad," National Park Service website, accessed June 2021, https://www.nps.gov/articles/harriet-tubman-and-the-underground-railroad.htm#:~: text=She%20was%20proud%20of%20her,I%20never%20lost%20a%20passenger.%E2 %80%9D; "Compensation for Civil War Services," Harriet Tubman Historical Society website, accessed June 2021, http://www.harriet-tubman.org/compensation-for-civil-war-services/; Sereno E. Payne to George W. Ray, Washington, DC, February 5, 1898; Records of the US House of Representatives 1789–2015, Record Group 60, National Archives Building, Washington DC, https://www.archives.gov/files/legislative/resources/education/tubman/images/payne-xl.jpg; Sarah Bradford, *Harriet: The Moses of Her People* (Mineola: Dover Publications, 2004).

253. "Movement for Black Lives," Vision for Black Lives, August 2016, https://m4bl.org/policy-platforms/.

254. Kerima Çevik, "Standing at the Intersection of Race and Disability," *Harvard Kennedy School Journal of African American Public Policy*, 2017.

255. Erik Ortiz, "Cops Shoot Unarmed Caregiver With His Hands Up While He Helps Man," NBC News, July 21, 2016, https://www.nbcnews.com/news/us-news/cops-shoot-unarmed-caregiver-charles -kinsey-his-hands-while-he-n614106; Scott Neuman, "Miami Officer Acquitted of Attempted Manslaughter in Shooting of Caregiver," NPR, June 18, 2019, https://www.npr.org/2019/06/18 /733621616/miami-officer-acquitted-of-attempted-manslaughter-in-shooting-of-caregiver.

256. Theresa Vargas, "Settlement Reached in Police Custody Death of Man with Down Syndrome," *Washington Post*, April 24, 2018.

257. "What Is Disability Justice?" Sins Invalid, June 16, 2020, https://www.sinsinvalid.org/news-1 /2020/6/16/what-is-disability-justice.

258. Harriet Tubman Collective, "Disability Solidarity: Completing the 'Vision for Black Lives,'" *Harvard Kennedy School Journal of African American Public Policy*, 2017.

259. "Report of the Task Force on Managing Student Mental Health," Harvard University, July 2020, https://provost.harvard.edu/files/provost/files/report_of_the_task_force_on_managing_student_mental_health.pdf; "Boston. Racism. Image. Reality," *Boston Globe*, December 10, 2017.

260. "Honoring Arnaldo Rios-Soto & Charles Kinsey: Achieving Liberation through Disability Solidarity," Talila A. Lewis, July 22, 2016, https://www.talilalewis.com/blog/achieving-liberation-through-disability-solidarity; Derecka Purnell, Aaron Francis, Alexis Morgan, Anneke Gronke, Aya Saed, Caleb Gayle, Elorm Avakame, Malcolm Temple, and Rae Shih, Harvard Kennedy School Journal of African American Public Policy, 2017, http://hjaap.hkspublications.org/wp-content/uploads/sites/14/2018/02/HKSJAAPP-2017.pdf; Movement for Black Lives, End the War on Black Health and Black Disabled People, https://m4bl.org/policy-platforms/end-the-war-black-health/.

261. "Disability and Socioeconomic Status," American Psychological Association, accessed April 2021, https://www.apa.org/pi/ses/resources/publications/disability; "Highlighting Disability/Poverty Connection, NCD Urges Congress to Alter Federal Policies That Disadvantage People with Disabilities," National Council on Disability, October 26, 2017, https://ncd.gov/newsroom/2017/disability-poverty-connection-2017-progress-report-release.

262. Marta Russell, *Capitalism and Disability* (Chicago: Haymarket, 2019).

263. "Do Wealthier People Buy More Prescription Drugs?" Harvard School of Public Health, accessed June 2021, https://www.hsph.harvard.edu/news/hsph-in-the-news/do-wealthier-people-buy-more-prescrip; Talila Lewis, "Disability Justice Is an Essential Part of Abolishing Police and Prisons," Medium, October 7, 2020.

264. Sandy Brady, "Freddie Gray's Life a Study in the Sad Effects of Lead Paint on Poor Blacks," *Washington Post,* April 29, 2015.

265. Lewis, "Disability Justice."

266. "Mass Incarceration: The Whole Pie 2020," Prison Policy Initiative, March 4, 2020, https://www.prisonpolicy.org/reports/pie2020.html.

267. Radley Balko, "Flashbangs Under Fire," *Reason*, February 17, 2010; Jasbir K. Puar, *The Right to Maim: Debility, Capacity, Disability* (Durham, NC: Duke University Press, 2017), https://www.dukeupress.edu/the-right-to-maim.

268. "Militarized Swat Teams under Scrutiny as Toddler Recovers from Grenade," NBC News, July 7, 2014, https://www.nbcnews.com/news/us-news/militarized-swat-teams-under-scrutiny-toddler-recovers-grenade-n150246.

269. Alecia Phonesavanh, "A SWAT Team Blew a Hole in My 2-Year-Old Son," Salon, June 24, 2014.

270. "Family of Baby Injured During Raid Awarded $3.6 Million," Associated Press, March 1, 2016; Kevin Sack, "Door-Busting Drug Raids Leave a Trail of Blood," *New York Times*, March 18, 2017; "Man Awarded $11M after Police Drug Raid Ends in Shooting," Associated Press, February 27, 2020.

271. Jolie A. Doggett, "This Is What Activism Does to Your Body," *Huffington Post,* August 9, 2019.

272. Jessica Caporuscio, "How Are Diabetes and Stress Linked?" Medical News Today, August 30, 2019, https://www.medicalnewstoday.com/articles/326193; "The Genetics of Migraine," American Migraine Foundation, May 18, 2017, ihttps://americanmigrainefoundation.org/resource-library/genetics-of-migraine/.

273. Jennifer Pelts, "Woman Wrote About Police Killings Before Officer Killed Her," Associated Press, October 20, 2016; "NYPD Sergeant Indicted for Murder and Other Charges in Death of Deborah Danner," Office of the District Attorney, Bronx County, press release, May 31, 2017, https://www.bronxda.nyc.gov/downloads/pdf/pr/2017/44-2017%20Sgt.%20Hugh%20Barry%20Indicted.pdf; Danner v. New York (D. NY, filed January 12, 2018); James C. McKinley Jr., "Medic Offers Sharply Different Account of Woman's Death at Hands of Police," *New York Times*, February 1, 2018.

274. Colleen Long and Jennifer Peltz, "As NYPD Trained on Mental Illness, a Call Ended in Shooting," Associated Press, June 2, 2017; McKinley Jr., "Medic Offers Sharply Different Account."

275. "NYT: NYPD Sergeant Charged with Murder in Death of Deborah Danner," New York Association of Psychiatric Rehabilitation Services, June 2, 1017, https://www.nyaprs.org/e-news-bulletins/2017/nyt-nypd-sergeant-charged-w-murder-in-death-of-deborah-danner.

276. LaShawn Harris, "Beyond the Shooting: Eleanor Gray Bumpurs, Identity Erasure, and Family Activism against Police Violence," *Souls* 20, no. 1 (2018): 86–109.

277. Margot Hornblower, "Slaying by NY Police Adds to Racial Tension," *Washington Post*, February 10, 1985.

278. Leonard Bruder, "Police Kill Woman Being Evicted; Officers Say She Wielded a Knife," *New York Times*, October 30, 1984; "Pathologist Accused of False Reports," *New York Times* news service, January 27, 1985, https://www.nytimes.com/1985/01/27/nyregion/chief-medical-examiner-s -reports-in-police-custody-cases-disputed.html; 99 Cong. Rec. 5945 (1985), https://www.govinfo .gov/content/pkg/GPO-CRECB-1985-pt5/pdf/GPO-CRECB-1985-pt5-2.pdf; "A Year Since the Bumpurs Murder," Unity Archive Project, accessed April 2021, https://unityarchiveproject.org /article/a-year-since-the-bumpurs-murder/; Hornblower, "Slaying by NY Police Adds to Racial Tension"; William Murphy, "Reinstatement of Cop in Bumpurs Case Brings Strong Reactions," Associated Press, February 2, 1985.

279. Frank J. Prial, "Judge Acquits Sullivan in Shotgun Slaying of Bumpurs," *New York Times*, February 27, 1987.

280. Bruder, "Police Kill Woman Being Evicted"; Todd S. Purdum, "Questions Swirl Around a Fatal Shooting by Police," *New York Times*, January 5, 1988; Joseph Fried, "Brooklyn Woman, Thirty-Five, Slain after Slashing an Officer," *New York Times*, August 30, 1979, https://www.nytimes.com/1979 /08/30/archives/brooklyn-woman-35-slain-after-slashing-an-officer-death-follows.html.

281. "Annual Report 1984," New York City Police Department, accessed April 2021, https://www.ojp .gov/pdffiles1/Digitization/121490NCJRS.pdf.

282. "A Year Since the Bumpers Murder," Unity Archive Project.

283. "Bumpurs Justice Committee Denounces Sham Trial," Bumpurs Justice Committee press release, January 20, 1987, Richie Pérez Papers, Hunter College Center for Puerto Rican Studies Library and Archives, https://centroca.hunter.cuny.edu/Detail/objects/17979#.

284. "A Year Since the Bumpurs Murder," Unity Archive Project.

285. "New York City Housing Authority 2019 Fact Sheet," New York City Housing Authority, accessed April 2021, https://www1.nyc.gov/assets/nycha/downloads/pdf/NYCHA-Fact-Sheet_2019_08-01 .pdf; Tom Engelhardt, "Nick Turse, the Pentagon as Global Landlord," Tomdispatch.com, July 11, 2017, https://tomdispatch.com/nick-turse-the-pentagon-as-global-landlord/; Alan Cowell, "Bomb at Resort in South Africa Kills Six Whites," *New York Times*, December 24, 1985, https://www .nytimes.com/1985/12/24/world/bomb-at-a-resort-in-south-africa-kills-six-whites.html; Alan Cowell, "School Boycott Is Erasing Dreams in South Africa," *New York Times*, December 1, 1985.

286. Caesar Beats, "Korryn Gaines Traffic Stop," YouTube video, August 2, 2016, https://www .youtube.com/watch?v=WZODTT-r4Gw; Baynard Woods, "Korryn Gaines: Police Killing Highlights Baltimore's Lead Poisoning Crisis," *The Guardian*, August 5, 2016; "Did Korryn Gaines's March Police Arrest Cause Her Miscarriage?" BET.com, August 4, 2016, https://www.bet.com /news/national/2016/08/04/did-korryn-gaines-march-police-arrest-cause-her-miscarriage-.html.

287. Alison Knezevich, "Court Documents Say Police Kicked Open Door at Korryn Gaines' Apartment," *Baltimore Sun*, August 3, 2016; Elizabeth Janney, "Family of Korryn Gaines Wins $38 Million Appeal Against Police: Court," Patch.com, July 1, 2020, https://patch.com/maryland /owingsmills/family-korryn-gaines-wins-38m-appeal-against-police-report.

288. German Lopez, "Eight Cops Allegedly Used an Elite Baltimore Police Team to Plunder the City and Its Residents," Vox.com, February 13, 2018, https://www.vox.com/policy-and-politics/2018 /2/2/16961146/baltimore-gun-trace-task-force-trial; Justin Fenton, "Baltimore Police Officer Charged in BB Gun Planting Incident as Gun Trace Task Force Fallout Continues," *Baltimore Sun*, January 15, 2020.

289. Steve Contorno, "Barack Obama Says the Minimum Wage Was Higher during Ronald Reagan's First State of the Union," Politifact.com, January 29, 2014, https://www.politifact.com/factchecks /2014/jan/29/barack-obama/barack-obama-says-minimum-wage-was-higher-during-r/.

290. Torsten Ove, "Pittsburgh to Pay Paralyzed Motorist Leon Ford $5.5 Million," *Pittsburgh Post-Gazette*, January 17, 2018; Robert Davis, Nicole Henderson, and Christopher Ortiz, *Can Federal Intervention Bring Lasting Improvement in Local Policing?* (New York: Vera Institute of Justice, 2005).

291. Matt Stroud, "A Death in Pittsburgh Shows How Police Tech Can Go Horribly Wrong," The Verge, June 29, 2016, https://www.theverge.com/2016/6/29/12059122/police-tech-violence-taser -bruce-kelly-jr-case; Bob Mayo, "Some Charges Held, Others Dismissed against Bruce Kelley Sr, Father of Man Killed After Killing K-9," Pittsburgh Action News 4, March 3, 2016, https://www

.wtae.com/article/some-charges-held-others-dismissed-against-bruce-kelley-sr-father-of-man-killed-after-killing-k-9-aren/7478228; Karen Kane, "Port Authority K9 Officer Aren Memorialized by Man and Beast," *Pittsburgh Post-Gazette*, February 4, 2016.

292. Dustin Gibson, interview with author, 2020.

293. "What Are We Talking About When We Talk About a Police-Free Future?" MPD150.com, accessed June 2021, https://www.mpd150.com/what-are-we-talking-about-when-we-talk-about-a-police-free-future/.

294. "911 Statistics," NENA.org, accessed June 2021, https://www.nena.org/page/911Statistics#:~:text=An%20estimated%20240%20million%20calls,more%20are%20from%20wireless%20devices.

295. "The Oakland Power Projects," Critical Resistance, accessed April 2021, http://criticalresistance.org/chapters/cr-oakland/the-oakland-power-projects/; "Know Your Options Workshops," Oakland Power Projects website, accessed June 2021, https://oaklandpowerprojects.org/know-your-options-workshops.

296. "Cahoots Media Guide," White Bird Clinic, accessed April 2021, https://whitebirdclinic.org/wp-content/uploads/2020/06/CAHOOTS-Media-Guide-20200626.pdf; "San Francisco's New Street Crisis Response Team Launches Today," San Francisco Mayor's Office press release, November 30, 2020, https://sfmayor.org/article/san-franciscos-new-street-crisis-response-team-launches-today; Alexandra Meeks, "Los Angeles Will Create Unarmed Crisis Response Teams for 911 Calls," CNN News, October 14, 2020, https://www.cnn.com/2020/10/14/us/los-angeles-unarmed-crisis-response-teams-911-calls/index.html.

297. "Watch: Full Details Behind Baltimore Police Shooting and Killing Young Mother Next to Her Son," BET.com, August 2, 2016, https://www.bet.com/news/national/2016/08/02/look--baltimore-police-shoot-and-kill-young-mother-in-her-home.html; Manny Fernandez, "Freddie Gray's Injury and the Police 'Rough Ride,'" *New York Times*, April 30, 2015; Leonard Greene, "Louima's Haunted High Life Ten Years Later," *New York Post*, July 30, 2007; "History of Chicago's Reparations Movement," Chicago Torture Justice Center, accessed April 2021, https://www.chicagotorturejustice.org/history; Flint Taylor, "How Activists Won Reparations for the Survivors of Chicago Police Department Torture," *In These Times*, June 26, 2015.

298. Audre Lorde, *The Cancer Journals* (New York: Penguin Classics, 2020).

299. "What Is Disability Justice?" Sins Invalid.

300. David Wallace-Wells, *The Uninhabitable Earth* (New York: Tim Duggan Books, 2019).

301. Ellora Derenoncourt, "Can You Move to Opportunity? Evidence from the Great Migration," Job Market Paper, January 25, 2019, https://scholar.harvard.edu/elloraderenoncourt/job-market-paper.

302. Wayne Blanchard, "Worst Disasters Lives Lost," FEMA Emergency Management Higher Education Project, July 5, 2006, https://training.fema.gov/hiedu/docs/hazdem/appendix-worst%20disasters%20lives%20lost.doc; John C. Hoyt, *Drought of 1936*, United States Department of the Interior Water Supply Paper 820 (Washington, DC: Government Printing Office, 1938), https://pubs.usgs.gov/wsp/0820/report.pdf; "Heatwave of July 1936," National Weather Service website, accessed June 2021, https://www.weather.gov/arx/heat_jul36; "The July 1936 Heatwave," National Weather Service website, accessed June 2021, https://www.weather.gov/ilx/july1936heat.

303. "Timeline: The Dust Bowl," PBS American Experience, accessed June 2021, https://www.pbs.org/wgbh/americanexperience/features/dust-bowl-surviving-dust-bowl/; Christopher Klein, "Ten Things You May Not Know About the Dust Bowl," History.com, March 21, 2019, https://www.history.com/news/10-things-you-may-not-know-about-the-dust-bowl; Jeff Berardelli, "A Devastating Dust Bowl Heat Wave Is Now More Than Twice as Likely, Study Says," CBS News, May 21, 2020; "1930s Dust Bowl, Deaths Estimated in the Thousands," *Lincoln Journal Star*, June 5, 2017.

304. Cecilia Rasmussen, "LAPD Blocked Dust Bowl Migrants at State Borders," *Los Angeles Times*, March 9, 2003; "Mass Exodus from the Plains," PBS.org, accessed April 2021, https://www.pbs.org/wgbh/americanexperience/features/surviving-the-dust-bowl-mass-exodus-plains/; "Into the Valley: Stories of California Exile," West of West Center, accessed April 2021, westofwestcenter.com/.

305. "Climate Change and Disaster Displacement," Office of United Nations High Commissioner for Refugees, accessed April 2021, https://www.unhcr.org/en-us/climate-change-and-disasters.html.

306. Laura A. Bakkensen and Lala Ma, "Sorting Over Flood Risk and Implications for Policy Reform," *Journal of Environmental Economics and Management* 104 (November 2020); Marshall

Shepherd, "Are Black and Rural Residents in the South More Vulnerable to Tornadoes Due to Radar Gaps?" *Forbes*, March 20, 2021.

307. Junia Howell and James R. Elliott, "As Disaster Costs Rise, So Does Inequality," *Socius: Sociological Research for a Dynamic World* 4 (December 2018): 1–3; "When Disaster Strikes, More Money for Whites, Less for Blacks," LAist, accessed April 2021, https://laist.com/projects/2020/the-big-one/tbo-wealth-gap.html.

308. Kari Marie Norgaard, "Colonization, Fire Suppression, and Indigenous Resurgence in the Face of Climate Change," *YES! Magazine*, October 22, 2019; Susie Cagle, "Fire is Medicine: The Tribes Burning California Forests to Save Them," *The Guardian*, November 21, 2019; Carl Zimmer, "Humans Lived in North America 130,000 Years Ago, Study Claims," *New York Times*, April 26, 2017; Tatiana Schlossberg, "12,000 Years Ago, Humans and Climate Change Made a Deadly Team," *New York Times*, June 17, 2016.

309. Jaime Lowe, "The Incarcerated Women Who Fight California's Wildfires," *New York Times*, August 31, 2017; Amika Mota, "I Saved Lives as an Incarcerated Firefighter," *Guardian*, September 1, 2020; Adam Eaton, "Kamala Harris and Her Connection to Inmate Firefighters," E&E News, August 20, 2019, https://www.eenews.net/stories/1061004553; Alexander Sammon, "How Kamala Harris Fought to Keep Nonviolent Prisoners Locked Up," *American Prospect*, July 30, 2020.

310. Thomas Fuller, "Coronavirus Limits California's Efforts to Fight Fires with Prison Labor," *New York Times*, August 22, 2020.

311. Jennifer L. Irish et al., "Simulations of Hurricane Katrina under Sea Level and Climate Conditions for 1900," *Climatic Change* 122 (2014): 635–649; Andrea Thompson, "Ten Years Later, Was Warming to Blame for Katrina?" Climate Central, August 27, 2015, https://www.climatecentral.org/news/katrina-was-climate-change-to-blame-19377; Richard Campanella, "How Humans Sank New Orleans," *The Atlantic*, February 6, 2018.

312. Mirena Sederis and the Critical Resistance Amnesty Working Group, *Amnesty for Prisoners of Katrina: A Special Report* (New Orleans: Critical Resistance, 2007), http://www2.ohchr.org/english/bodies/cerd/docs/ngos/usa/USHRN20.doc; "Katrina Amnesty Campaign: On the Status of Prisoners and Public Safety in New Orleans," Katrina Reader, accessed April 2021, http://katrinareader.cwsworkshop.org/katrina-amnesty-campaign-status-prisoners-and-public-safety-new-orleans.html.

313. "Radtalks: What Could Be Possible If the Law Really Stood for Black Lives?" Racism.org, accessed June 2021, https://www.racism.org/articles/citizenship-rights/slavery-to-reparations/116-racial-reentrenchment/2668-radtalks-what-could-be?start=2.

314. A year after I'd met Jordan, FTP and organizers in Letcher County, Kentucky, with the Letcher Governance Project won a five-year campaign that defeated what would have been the most expensive federal prison in US history. A $510 million maximum-security prison the BOP was attempting to build directly on top of a mountaintop removal site, downstream from a coal slurry impoundment and a mile and a half away from one of the last untouched patches of old-growth forest in Kentucky. The BOP never even broke ground on the project.

315. A. J. Vicens, "You've Probably Never Heard of America's Worst Police Force," *Mother Jones*, February 27, 2015; Danica Coto, interviewed by Ray Suarez, *All Things Considered*, NPR, December 30, 2017, https://www.npr.org/2017/12/30/574810375/as-puerto-rico-rebuilds-police-protest-working-conditions; Isabel Valentín, "We Have to Believe That We Can Change the World Drastically," Earth Justice, September 4, 2020, https://earthjustice.org/blog/2020-september/we-have-to-believe-that-we-can-change-the-world-drastically.

316. Alex Johnson, Daniel Arkin, Jason Cumming, and Bill Karins, "Hurricane Irma Skirts Puerto Rico, Leaves One Million Without Power," NBC News, September 8, 2017, https://www.nbcnews.com/storyline/hurricane-irma/hurricane-irma-skirts-puerto-rico-lashing-it-powerful-winds-flooding-n799086; Sheri Fink, "Puerto Rico: How Do We Know 3,000 People Died as a Result of Hurricane Maria?" *New York Times*, June 2, 2018; Rebecca Hersher, "Climate Change Was the Engine That Powered Hurricane Maria's Devastating Rains," NPR, April 17, 2019, https://www.npr.org/2019/04/17/714098828/climate-change-was-the-engine-that-powered-hurricane-marias-devastating-rains; Hersher, "Climate Change"; "Quick Facts: Hurricane Maria's Effect on Puerto Rico," Reliefweb.int, January 22, 2018, https://reliefweb.int/report/puerto-rico-united-states

-america/quick-facts-hurricane-marias-effect-puerto-rico; Naomi Klein, *The Battle for Paradise* (Chicago: Haymarket Books, 2018); Associated Press, "Thousands of Puerto Rico Police Owed Overtime Call in Sick," NBC News, December 28, 2017, https://www.nbcnews.com/news/latino /thousands-puerto-rico-police-owed-overtime-call-sick-n833136.

317. Think Progress, archive accessed April 2021l, https://archive.thinkprogress.org/uploads/2018/04 /ex-1-to-dckt-2351.pdf.

318. Think Progress, archive.

319. J. Carlee Purdum, "Disaster Work Is Often Carried Out by Prisoners, for as Little as Fourteen Cents an Hour," Texas A&M Today, September 15, 2020, https://today.tamu.edu/2020/09/15/disaster-work -is-often-carried-out-by-prisoners-for-as-little-as-14-cents-an-hour/#:~:text=In%20addition%2C%20 state%20laws%20across,to%20work%20in%20disaster%20conditions.&text=And%20some%20 states%2C%20including%20Alabama,is%20offset%20through%20federal%20subsidies.

320. "St. Louis History," Soulofamerica.com, accessed June 2021, https://www.soulofamerica.com/us -cities/st-louis/st-louis-history/#:~:text=Attracted%20by%20wartime%20production%20 jobs,to%20segregated%20housing%20and%20schools; Catherine Brahic, "Climate Myths: The Cooling After 1940 Shows CO2 Does Not Cause Warming," *New Scientist*, May 16, 2007; "From a Dimmer Past to a Brighter Future?" EarthObservatory.com, November 5, 2007, https://earthob servatory.nasa.gov/features/GISSTemperature/giss_temperature4.php; Kriangsak Jenwith- eesuk et al., "Construction of Polluted Aerosol in Accumulation that Affects the Incidence of Lung Cancer," *Heliyon* 6, no. 2 (February 2020); Jules Bernstein, "Agricultural Area Residents in Dan- ger of Inhaling Toxic Aerosols," UC Riverside News, February 3, 2020, https://news.ucr.edu /articles/2020/02/03/agricultural-area-residents-danger-inhaling-toxic-aerosols.

321. "St. Louis and the American City," MappingDecline.lib, accessed June 2021, http:// mappingdecline.lib.uiowa.edu/map/; Chris Naffziger, "More Than Forty African-American Churches Were Demolished in Mill Creek Valley," *St. Louis*, September 19, 2019; "Living Near Highways and Air Pollution," American Lung Association, January 5, 2021, https://www.lung.org /clean-air/outdoors/who-is-at-risk/highways; Ryan DeLoach and Jenn DeRose, "Urban Renewal and Mill Creek Valley," Decoding The City, http://www.decodingstl.org/urban-renewal-and-mill -creek-valley/#:~:text=In%201958%2C%20St.,95%25%20of%20whom%20were%20black.

322. Iadicola and Shupe, *Violence, Inequality, and Human Freedom*.

323. "Martin Luther King, Jr., I Have a Dream," AmericanRhetoric.com, accessed June 2021, https:// www.americanrhetoric.com/speeches/mlkihaveadream.htm.

324. George Lipsitz, *A Life in the Struggle: Ivory Perry and the Culture of Opposition* (Philadelphia: Temple University Press, 1988); "Protect Your Family from Sources of Lead," EPA.gov, accessed June 2021, https://www.epa.gov/lead/protect-your-family-sources-lead.

325. World Health Organization Regional Office for Africa, *Lead Exposure in African Children* (Braz- zaville: World Health Organization, 2015); "Lead Poisoning and health," WHO.int, August 23, 2019, https://www.who.int/news-room/fact-sheets/detail/lead-poisoning-and-health; Alex Knapp, "How Lead Caused America's Violent Crime Epidemic," *Forbes*, January 3, 2013; Harriet A. Washington, *A Terrible Thing to Waste* (New York: Little, Brown Spark, 2020).

326. Office of Juvenile Justice and Delinquency Prevention, "Understanding the 'Whys' Behind Juve- nile Crime Trends," November 2012, https://www.ojp.gov/pdffiles1/ojjdp/grants/248954.pdf.

327. Office of Juvenile Justice and Delinquency Prevention, *Understanding the "Whys" Behind Juvenile Crime Trends* (Philadelphia: University of Pennsylvania, 2012).

328. Jamie Lincoln Kitman, "The Secret History of Lead," *The Nation*, March 2, 2000; Washington, "A Ter- rible Thing to Waste," 68–69; David Richards, "New Report Highlights Magnitude of Global Lead Poisoning in Children," National Institute of Environmental Health Sciences, October 2020, https:// www.niehs.nih.gov/research/programs/geh/geh_newsletter/2020/10/articles/new_report_highlights _magnitude_of_global_lead_poisoning_in_children.cfm#:~:text=The%20report%2C%20 %E2%80%9CThe%20Toxic%20Truth,Centers%20for%20Disease%20Control%20and.

329. "Blood Lead Levels in Children Aged 1–5 Years," Centers for Disease Control and Prevention, April 5, 2013, https://www.cdc.gov/mmwr/preview/mmwrhtml/mm6213a3.htm; Robert J. Sampson and Alix S. Winter, "The Racial Ecology of Lead Poisoning," *DuBois Review* 13, no. 2 (2016); "Did Lead Poisoning and Outrage over Police Violence Set the Stage for Korryn Gaines's Death?" *Wash- ington Post*, August 3, 2016; Brady, "Freddie Gray's Life a Study in the Sad Effects of Lead Paint."

330. Paromita Hore et al., "Blood Lead Levels and Potential Risk Factors for Lead Exposures among South Asians in New York City," *Journal of Immigrant and Minority Health* no. 19 (2017); "Health Department Launches Awareness Campaign on Lead Exposure for the South Asian Community," NYC Health, January 30, 2019, https://www1.nyc.gov/site/doh/about/press/pr2019/lead-exposure-for-the-south-asian-community.page; https://www1.nyc.gov/site/doh/about/press/pr2019/lead-exposure-for-the-south-asian-community.page.

331. "Northern Hemisphere Just Had its Hottest Summer on Record," National Oceanic and Atmospheric Administration, September 14, 2020, https://www.noaa.gov/news/northern-hemisphere-just-had-its-hottest-summer-on-record#:~:text=August%202020,-According%20to%20scientists&text=The%20Northern%20Hemisphere%20had%20its%20hottest%20August%20on%20record%20with,five%20warmest%20occurring%20since%202015.

332. Richard Acosta, "Protesters File Lawsuit Following Arrests at Flint Town Hall Held at Church," *Michigan Live*, April 12, 2018; Joshua Barajas, "Police Deploy Water Hoses, Tear Gas Against Standing Rock Protesters," PBS NewsHour, November 21, 2016, https://www.pbs.org/newshour/nation/police-deploy-water-hoses-tear-gas-against-standing-rock-protesters; Devin Leonard, "The Billionaire behind the Dakota Access Pipeline Is a Little Lonely," *Bloomberg Businessweek*, March 27, 2019; Lisa Friedman, "Standing Rock Sioux Tribe Wins a Victory in Dakota Access Pipeline Case," *New York Times*, March 25, 2020.

333. Richard Kent Evans, "Child of Black Activists Bombed by Police: 'My Activism Is My Religion,'" *Truthout*, February 28, 2021.

334. "About MOVE," Philadelphia Assembled website, accessed June 2021, http://phlassembled.net/sovereignty/index/move/.

335. Richard Kent Evans, "Move: Religion, Secularism, and the Politics of Classification" (doctorate dissertation, Temple University, 2018); Jill Sederstrom, "What Is MOVE and How Did Their Years-Long Battle with Philadelphia Police End in Tragedy?" Oxygen.com, December 9, 2020, https://www.oxygen.com/crime-news/what-is-move-and-how-did-their-years-long-battle-with-philadelphia-police-end-in-tragedy.

336. Ed Pilkington, "MOVE 9 Freed After Forty Years in Jail over Philadelphia Police Siege," *The Guardian*, May 25, 2019; Ed Pilkington, "A Siege. A Bomb. Forty-Eight Dogs and the Black Commune That Wouldn't Surrender," *The Guardian*, July 31, 2018.

337. "I'm from Philly. Thirty Years Later, I'm Still Trying to Make Sense of the MOVE Bombing," NPR Code Switch, May 13, 2015, ttps://www.npr.org/sections/codeswitch/2015/05/13/406243272/im-from-philly-30-years-later-im-still-trying-to-make-sense-of-the-move-bombing; Lindsey Gruson, "Philadelphia Chief Says He Wanted Fire to Burn," *New York Times*, October 19, 1985.

338. "This Day in History: Policeman Daniel Faulkner Found Dead," History.com, accessed June 2021, https://www.history.com/this-day-in-history/policeman-daniel-faulkner-found-dead.

339. Chenjerai Kumanyika interviews Ruth Wilson Gilmore, *Intercepted* (podcast), June 10, 2020, https://theintercept.com/2020/06/10/ruth-wilson-gilmore-makes-the-case-for-abolition/.

340. Nick Estes, "A Real Deal," *Jacobin*, August 6, 2019; "What Is New Consensus?" New Consensus blog, accessed June 2021, https://blog.newconsensus.com/about.

341. "James Connolly, We Only Want the Earth," Marxists.org, accessed June 2021, https://www.marxists.org/archive/connolly/1907/xx/wewnerth.htm; "National Climate Impact Call: The Red, Black, & Green New Deal," M4BL, March1, 2021.

342. Bill Hutchinson, "Atatiana Jefferson Had Gun in Her Hand before Being Shot by Cop, Nephew Tells Investigators," ABC News, October 15, 2019, https://abcnews.go.com/US/nephew-atatiana-jefferson-tells-investigators-retrieved-gun-shot/story?id=66286765.

343. "Disproportionate Representation of Native Americans in Foster Care across the United States," Potowami.org, April 16, 2021, https://www.potawatomi.org/blog/2021/04/06/disproportionate-representation-of-native-americans-in-foster-care-across-united-states/.

344. Nicholas Borgel-Burroughs, Ellen Barry, and Will Wright, "Ma'Khia Bryant's Journey through Foster Care Ended with an Officer's Bullet," *New York Times*, May 8, 2021.

345. Robin D. G. Kelley, "'Western Civilization Is Neither': Black Studies' Epistemic Revolution," *The Black Scholar* 50, no. 3 (2020); Erin Miles Cloud, "Toward the Abolition of the Foster System," in *Scholar and Feminist Online* no. 15.3 (2019), https://sfonline.barnard.edu/unraveling-criminalizing-webs-building-police-free-futures/toward-the-abolition-of-the-foster-system/.

346. Burroughs, Barry, and Wright, "Ma'Khia Bryant's Journey."

347. Jorge Rivas, "Trayvon Martin Petition Surpasses One Million Signatures, Supporters Also Sending Skittles to Police Chief," *Colorlines*, March 22, 2021.

348. Elizabeth Davis, Anthony Whyde, and Lynn Langdon, *Contacts between Police and the Public, 2015* (Washington, DC: US Department of Justice, 2018); Asher and Horowitz, "How Do the Police Actually Spend Their Time?"; Kriston Kapps, "Too Many People Are Calling 911. There's a Better Way," Bloomberg, July 20, 2017, https://www.bloomberg.com/news/articles/2017-07-20/memphis-uses-data-and-innovation-to-curb-911-abuse; "Call for Service 2020," Nola.gov, accessed June 2021, https://data.nola.gov/d/hp7u-i9hf/visualization; Elisha Fieldstadt, "Murder Map: Deadliest US Cities," CBS News, April 19, 2021, https://www.cbsnews.com/pictures/murder-map-deadliest-u-s-cities/66/; "Ranking of the Most Dangerous Cities in the World in 2020, by Murder Rate Per 100,000 Inhabitants," Statistica.com, accessed June 2021, https://www.statista.com/statistics/243797/ranking-of-the-most-dangerous-cities-in-the-world-by-murder-rate-per-capita/.

349. Rachel Anspach, "These Black Teens Are Demanding that Chicago Invest in Schools Instead of Police with #NoCopAcademy," April 2, 2018, https://www.mic.com/articles/188687/these-black-teens-are-demanding-that-chicago-invest-in-schools-instead-of-police-with-nocopacademy; Steven Cox, David Massey, and Connie Fitch, *Introduction to Policing* (Thousand Oaks: Sage, 2019).

350. "Ideology," Dream Defenders.org, accessed June 2021, https://dreamdefenders.org/ideology/.

351. Taylor Nicole Rogers, "There Are 614 Billionaires in the United States, and Only 7 of them Are Black," BusinessInsider.com, September 4, 2020, https://www.businessinsider.com/black-billionaires-in-the-united-states-2020-2; Manning Marable, *How Capitalism Underdeveloped Black America* (Chicago: Haymarket Books, 2015).

352. "A Question of Security: Violence against Palestinian Women and Girls," Human Rights Watch, November 6, 2006, https://www.hrw.org/report/2006/11/06/question-security/violence-against-palestinian-women-and-girls; Daniel Weishut, "Sexual Torture of Palestinian Men by Israeli Authorities," *Reproductive Health Matters* 23, no. 46 (2015); "A Question of Security," Human Rights Watch; "Statistics from the Association of Rape Crisis Centers in Israel," Association of Rape Crisis Centers in Israel website, accessed June 2021, https://www.1202.org.il/en/union/info/statistics/arcci-statistics.

353. H.R. 1258, 116th Cong. (2020); "Reps García, Pressley, and Jeffries Introduce Transit Parity Resolution," Office of Congressman Jesus García press release, December 10, 2020, https://chuygarcia.house.gov/media/press-releases/reps-garcia-pressley-and-jeffries-introduce-transit-parity-resolution#:~:text=Currently%2C%20Congress%20uses%20a%2040,been%20allocated%20to%20public%20transit.

354. The Red Nation, *The Red Deal: Indigenous Action to Save Our Earth* (New York: Common Notions Press, 2021).

355. Miriam Zoll and James Boyce, *The New Environmental Activists* (Amherst, MA: Political Science Research Institute, University of Massachusetts, 2003).

356. Dixon and Piepzna-Samarasinha, *Beyond Survival*.

357. George Lipsitz, "Ivory Perry and the Fight Against Lead Poisoning in St. Louis," *Synthesis/Regeneration* no. 41 (2006).

358. "National Book Foundation Medal for Distinguished Contribution to American Letters," video, Ursula K. Le Guin website, accessed June 2021, https://www.ursulakleguin.com/nbf-medal#:~:text=We%20live%20in%20capitalism%2C%20its,art%2C%20the%20art%20of%20words.

359. Jodi Brown and Patrick Lanagan, *Policing and Homicide 1976–98: Justifiable Homicide by Police, Police Officers Murdered by Felons* (Washington, DC: US Department of Justice, 2001); "Fatal Force," *Washington Post*; "FBI Releases 2019 Statistics on Law Enforcement Officers Killed in the Line of Duty," FBI.gov press release, May 4, 2020, https://www.fbi.gov/news/pressrel/press-releases/fbi-releases-2019-statistics-on-law-enforcement-officers-killed-in-the-line-of-duty; "FBI Releases 2018 Statistics on Law Enforcement Officers Killed in the Line of Duty," FBI.gov press release, May 6, 2019, https://www.fbi.gov/news/pressrel/press-releases/fbi-releases-2018-statistics-on-law-enforcement-officers-killed-in-the-line-of-duty; "Law Enforcement Officers Killed and Assaulted: FBI Releases Police Line-of-Duty Death Statistics for 2017," FBI.gov press release, May 10, 2018, https://www.fbi.gov/news/stories/2017-leoka-line-of-duty-death-statistics-released-051018.

ACKNOWLEDGMENTS

It takes a village to write a book.

I have to thank Robin D. G. Kelley first. During a breakfast years ago, I told Robin that I wanted to enter a doctoral program to start making sense of an endless Google doc that I created with notes, questions, fears, and dreams around abolition and violence. He said, "Skip graduate school. Write a book *now*. We are in the middle of a freedom movement." When I experienced doubt about the strength of my arguments, the beauty of my sentences, and the limited time I had to complete this book, Robin's words reminded me that I was writing toward liberation and not perfection. It is impossible to be a student of the Black Radical Tradition without engaging in Robin's work. His book *Freedom Dreams* is a bible. His brilliance is only outmatched by his kindness, and I'm grateful for the love, meals, friendship, and mentorship that I've received from him, his wife LisaGay, and their beautiful child Sekou.

I'm grateful to Darnell Moore for many reasons. For being fly. For helping me brainstorm titles of the book and opening his home to me. His organizing, thinking, and writing around love, activism, and queerness has made me a better thinker, writer, and friend. Darnell also introduced me to Alessandra Bastagli, whose thoughtful editing turned my questions, fears, and dreams into a manuscript. I'm grateful to her and everyone at Astra House for turning that manuscript into a book, and to my publicist Emily Lavelle for putting it in front of you. I am also grateful to my wonderful agent, Alia Hanna Habib, who saw the entire process through, often tripling as a reader and therapist.

While writing the book, Nyle Fort gave me the idea of starting a "pre-book club" so that I could have a community of support during the writing process. I was terrified of asking anyone to read my messy drafts but I am grateful for everyone who did: Rathna Ramamurthi, Rena Karefa-Johnson, Felipe Hernandez, Jen Parker, Meena Jagannath, Michelle Alexander, Ashley Carter, Nyle Fort, and Amna Akbar. They asked me hard questions and told me to make good on my claims. They told me when I needed to share more of myself, or more history, or offer better examples. They celebrated with me when I finished chapters and finalized titles and settled on the book's cover art.

This book would not have been possible without many others who read chapter drafts, worked through challenging concepts with me, and agreed to interviews. Gratitude to Jordan Mazurek, Dustin Gibson, Phil Agnew, Asha Ransby-Sporn, Zelda Holtzman, Dominique Morgan, Naomi Murakawa, Onyinye Alheri, Inez Bordeaux, Kayla Reed, Jamani Montague, Heath Pearson, Manisha Sinha, Walter Johnson, George Lipsitz, Bridget Purcell, John Wessel-McCoy, Hamid Khan, Jasson Perez, Mickey Dean, and Thomas Mariadason. I'm especially grateful to Rachel Herzing.

Thanks to the brilliant Lorenzo Bradford, who provided timely and thorough research and analysis while dealing with my sometimes untimely and complex requests. And to Darren Ankrom for fact-checking. I was also lucky to find Alayna Sibert through my middle school language arts teacher, Ms. Betty Crawford. Alayna's love and passion for the history of Black St. Louis helped me unearth horrific and beautiful details about my old neighborhoods and schools.

Beyond the people who worked directly on the project, there were countless others who inspired it. Thousands of them whose names I will never know. They poured into the streets, made calls, signed petitions, sang, cried, marched, plotted, and chanted toward freedom. Many of them have lost families, faced prison and the grave, and continue to be shackled by the state for daring to fight back. I am grateful I was able to share small pieces of their stories here. Some, I do know by name, including Pete O'Neal, who is living in exile for his political beliefs and commitments to Black liberation. We must free all political prisoners.

I am also grateful to the mentors, organizers, artists, scholars, and political organizations that have shaped my thinking, writing, and activism. There are entirely too many to name. But I would like to acknowledge Critical Resistance, Dream Defenders, Action STL, BYP100, Belinda Hall, Fees Must Fall, Law for Black Lives, the Movement for Black Lives, Keeanga-Yamahtta Taylor, Mariame Kaba, Ruth Wilson Gilmore, Craig Gilmore, Angela Davis, Dylan Rodriguez, Adam Eliott-Cooper, Montague Simmons, Hiram Rivera, Talila Lewis, Amanda Alexander, Tomiko Brown-Nagin, Jamala Rogers, Judith Browne Dianis, Thomas Harvey, Brendan Roediger, Purvi Shah, Barbara Ransby, John Chasnoff, Marbre Stahly-Butts, Justin Hansford, Brad

Brockman, Cornel West, Khiara Bridges, and my editor at *The Guardian,* Amana Fontanella-Khan. It is only because I have been around others more curious than me, and more radical than me, that I have been inspired to build a better world.

My family and friends have been indispensable throughout the learning and writing process. Their love and support helped me finish a book during a global pandemic, economic crisis, and an uprising, and I am especially grateful for the calls, prayers, and check-ins with Porcia Hall, Luisa Batiz, Aja Monet, Mmiri Mbah, Christina Joseph, Jordan Stockdale, Kristin Turner, Grandon Purnell, Stanley Talbert, McKenzie Thomas, Mike Milton, Josie Duffy Rice, Donna Harati, and Titilayo Rasaki.

My sisters—Courtnie, Kayla, and Vickie—are three of the most resilient, kind, and hilarious people I know. While I spent several months locked in a room, they made sure that I ate (when they weren't demanding that I cook), took breaks, held me to my movie night promises with pizza and popcorn, and loved my children with their time and energy. They listened to me obsess over story details and held me tight when they learned about painful parts of my life for the first time. They are the foundation of my village.

I am grateful to Geuce and Garvey, whose patience, kindness, curiosity, and wisdom have made me a better person. Years of them asking questions taught me to explain the horrors of cops, capitalism, and cages to little kids, which has in turn helped me explain abolition and the world we deserve more simply. Nothing has challenged me to practice what I preach more than parenting these precious beings, and I am grateful that God is allowing me to guide them during our time together on this planet.

Robin Kelley introduced me to *Freedom Dreams*, but Nyle Fort made me believe that they can come true. Nyle's commitment to fighting for the life we deserve to live has touched many of my best sentences, ideas, and projects—figuratively and literally. I'm grateful for his spiritual, emotional, and intellectual labor for this book and much more, which he provided while also finishing his dissertation. Thank you for all of the beautiful moments that reminded me why it had to be written.

ABOUT THE AUTHOR

Derecka Purnell is a human rights lawyer, writer, and organizer. She received her JD from Harvard Law School, and works to end police and prison violence by providing legal assistance, research, and training to community-based organizations through an abolitionist framework. Her work and writing has been featured in the *New York Times*, NPR, *The Atlantic*, the *Boston Globe, Harper's Bazaar, Cosmopolitan, The Appeal, Truthout, Slate*, and many other publications. Derecka is currently a columnist at *The Guardian*. She lives in Washington, DC.